H.M. KING EDWARD VII.
COLONEL-IN-CHIEF
OF THE ROYAL REGIMENT OF ARTILLERY

Taken at Woolwich on the occasion of his Inspection in October 1904.

THE HISTORY
OF
THE ROYAL ARTILLERY
FROM THE INDIAN MUTINY TO THE GREAT WAR

DEDICATED BY
HIS MAJESTY'S GRACIOUS PERMISSION TO
KING GEORGE V.
COLONEL-IN-CHIEF OF THE ROYAL ARTILLERY

VOLUME II
(1899–1914)

MAJOR-GENERAL SIR JOHN HEADLAM, K.B.E., C.B., D.S.O.
COLONEL-COMMANDANT, R.A.

The Naval & Military Press Ltd

published in association with

FIREPOWER
The Royal Artillery Museum
Woolwich

Published by
The Naval & Military Press Ltd
Unit 10 Ridgewood Industrial Park,
Uckfield, East Sussex,
TN22 5QE England
Tel: +44 (0) 1825 749494
Fax: +44 (0) 1825 765701
www.naval-military-press.com

in association with

FIREPOWER
The Royal Artillery Museum, Woolwich
www.firepower.org.uk

The Naval & Military Press

MILITARY HISTORY AT YOUR FINGERTIPS

… a unique and expanding series of reference works

Working in collaboration with the foremost regiments and institutions, as well as acknowledged experts in their field, N&MP have assembled a formidable array of titles including technologically advanced CD-ROMs and facsimile reprints of impossible-to-find rarities.

In reprinting in facsimile from the original, any imperfections are inevitably reproduced and the quality may fall short of modern type and cartographic standards.

Printed and bound by Antony Rowe Ltd, Eastbourne

PREFACE.

THE genesis of this portion of Regimental History, and the method followed in its planning, have been described in the preface to the preceding volume, and require no explanation here. But a word must be said as to the changes in the arrangement that have now been made.

In Volume I the activities of the Regiment were grouped under the three departments of Organization, Armament, and Training, with little distinction between the branches—Field, Siege, and Coast. This method was necessitated by the length of the period covered, and by the fact that for the greater part of that period the three departments worked quite independently of each other, while the lines of demarcation between the branches had not become so clear-cut as they became later. In the period covered by this volume the conditions were very different. Its length a dozen years instead of forty, and those years devoted to definite preparation in which the developments in Organization, Armament, and Training were co-ordinated to a common aim. On the other hand, the breach between the branches widened by the separation between mounted and dismounted, and the general trend towards specialization. A different treatment was required, and the method adopted has been to record the developments of each branch in a separate narrative, and to show under each how the three departments worked together in its preparation for war.[1]

It may be thought that undue attention has been devoted to matters which are familiar to the present generation. But regimental history is not written for one

---

[1] In dealing with the field army artillery matters peculiar to horse, mountain or heavy artillery have, as far as possible, been relegated to a separate section at the end of each chapter.

generation only, and the story of how the artillery which took the field in 1914 was prepared for its task may be expected to grow in interest. The pre-War generation are, moreover, entitled to an acknowledgment not only of what they accomplished during those strenuous years, but also of what they planned, even if it only came to fulfilment when war had loosened the purse-strings. The temptation to point the moral by reference to the experiences of the Great War has, however, been sternly resisted. It will be for the historian of the Regiment in that time of trial to tell how the theories of this period of preparation emerged from the ordeal.

During the years chronicled in this volume there passed away the last of the Crimean and Mutiny veterans, as well as many of their successors who were held in high honour in the Regiment. Their names will be found recorded in the chapters of this, and the preceding, volume, which deal with their activities, and it has not, therefore, been considered necessary to add any formal biographical notes. Nor has it been found possible to name all those for whose help in the presentation of this account I am so greatly indebted. But I take this opportunity of expressing my sincere gratitude to the officials, both civil and military, of the War Office, the India Office, the Ordnance and Royal Artillery Committees, and the Royal Artillery and Royal United Service Institutions, as well as to the many brother officers who were prominent during the period recorded, and have been ungrudging in their help towards its presentment here. Mention may, however, be made of three who have died during the writing of this volume, and who, despite their great age, took the liveliest interest in the work—Colonel Charles Chenevix Trench who, when well over 90 had the preceding volume read to him, Generals James Cecil Dalton and Sir Desmond O'Callaghan, and Colonel Julian R. J. Jocelyn, the Historian of the Royal Artillery in the Crimea and the Mutiny. Their hearts were in the Regiment, and in every effort to preserve its history and traditions, and they grudged neither time nor trouble in furthering this effort to recall the events, and to recapture the spirit of that period of preparation.

JOHN HEADLAM.

CRUCK MEOLE HOUSE,
 HANWOOD, SHROPSHIRE.
 April, 1934.

NOTE.

During the period from 1860 to 1914 there were many changes in the nomenclature employed to denote units of artillery. These changes will be found described in Part I, but to have followed them throughout the narrative generally would have been confusing to the reader. The term "brigade" has therefore been used for the lieut.-colonel's command generally, and "company" for the major's command in the garrison artillery. These were the terms in use at the beginning and end of the period.

For the same reason the expression "heavy artillery" is used in the sense it bore up till the Great War, that is as meaning "heavy field", or "position" artillery, corresponding to what is now termed "medium" artillery.

Abbreviations have been avoided as a rule, but to save space the words "Royal Artillery" have been omitted when it appeared that this could be done without risk of misunderstanding, as, for instance, when speaking of "the Mess"—"the Institution"—etc.; and the various publications of the latter have been referred to throughout simply as "the Proceedings". Nor has it been thought necessary to repeat "of the Mounted and Dismounted Branches" whenever mentioning the "Separation".

The term 'gun' has been used generally to include all types of ordnance, except where it has been necessary to differentiate.

The extracts from Regulations and Orders are published with the kind permission of the Controller of H.M. Stationery Office.

CONTENTS.

INTRODUCTION.
THE COLONELS-IN-CHIEF.
THE MASTER-GUNNERS.

PART I.—THE WAR YEARS (1899—1902).

CHAPTER		PAGE
I	The War Office	1
II	The Regiment	20

PART II.—THE FIELD ARMY ARTILLERY.

III	The South African Influence	41
IV	The Re-armament—General	71
V	,, ,, —Technical	88
VI	Re-organization	128
VII	The Manchurian Influence	151
VIII	The French Influence	184
IX	The Final Phase	206

PART III.—THE SIEGE ARTILLERY.

X	The South African Influence	243
XI	The Manchurian Influence	247
XII	"Fortress Warfare"	258

PART IV.—THE COAST ARTILLERY.

XIII	The Armament	267
XIV	The South African Influence	282
XV	The Manchurian Influence	289
XVI	"Fighting the Fixed Armament"	316
XVII	The Land Fronts	337

PART V.—THE AUXILIARY ARTILLERY.

XVIII	The Local Corps, the Militia and the Volunteers	345
XIX	The Special Reserve and the Territorial Force	357

PART VI.—THE REGIMENTAL INSTITUTIONS.

XX	The Department and the Establishment	369
XXI	The Institution and the College	378
XXII	The Repository and the School	389
XXIII	The Mess and the Bands	404

APPENDICES.

		PAGE
A	Army Order 149 of 1899	417
B	Terms of Reference to the Equipment Committee, 1901	419
C	Précis of Conditions for the new Equipments, 1901	420
D	Précis of Conditions for the new Equipments, 1913	423
E	Distribution of Units, 1914 ... Opposite page	424
F	Report of Divisional Artillery Commander, 1914	425

vii

INTRODUCTION.

1860—1899.

THE forty years from 1860 to 1899 recorded in the previous Volume of this History fall into three periods. The first, which covered the 60's and 70's, was marked by that curious lethargy which overtook the Regiment just when the replacement of its smooth-bore armament by rifled guns might have been expected to inspire activity. In the 80's came the "renaissance", when all branches in turn woke up to a realization of the purpose of their existence, and set to work to learn how to shoot. In the last decade of the century this technical phase was succeeded by a tactical revival in which the branches made an earnest endeavour to visualize their various tasks in war, and to prepare for them. But the wars of the last half-century had been for the most part waged against foes practically unprovided with artillery. The Royal Artillery was without war experience, and the army at large was sceptical as to its value in the field. No wonder if, when the call from South Africa came in 1899, it found that the Regiment had been slow to realize the changes that had come over warfare during the last quarter-century.

1899—1914.

In this Volume the story is carried on from the coming of that call to the far more serious one of 1914, and here again the years fall into well-marked divisions. First the "war-years"[1] (1899—1902), then the dozen years from 1902 to 1914 devoted to definite preparation, divisible again into periods in which different influences were predominant. The first of these was naturally that of our own experiences in South Africa, but before these had

---

[1] For the reason given in the preface to Volume I the services of the Regiment in South Africa will be related in a separate volume.

time to become stereotyped Manchuria supervened with its lessons for the Siege and Coast Artillery as well as for that of the Field Army. For the latter there followed next the enthusiasm for everything French which came with the *entente cordiale*. Lastly, for all branches, a final phase in which attention was concentrated on putting the last touches to all that affected their readiness for war. But in spite of this diversity of influences the whole period of preparation was dominated by one general feature. In the words of the Esher Committee, as applicable to the Royal Artillery as to the War Office:—"For the first time in the long history of Reform its intricate problems have been approached from the point of view of war rather than from those of peace. The scheme is based upon the consideration that the preparation for war is the primary object".

The War-Years (1899—1902).

Although the South African War may appear of minor importance to those who have seen, or heard of, the Great War, it was serious enough for the army of the day, and especially perhaps for the Royal Artillery owing to their lack of war experience. At the end of the XIXth century a medal was a rare adornment on a gunner's breast, and to such a generation the vast expansion of the Regiment, and the maintenance in the field of such an unprecedented number of batteries, must in any case have been a severe strain. But circumstances had combined to render it particularly so in 1899, for in that year, only a few months before the outbreak of war, two of the greatest reforms in the history of the Regiment had been effected by the abolition of the office of the Deputy Adjutant-General, R.A., and the separation of the Mounted and Dismounted Branches. In Part I of this Volume it will be told how the new administration took the strain; how new batteries and new units of every kind, were raised; how the schools and colleges and auxiliary forces of the Empire were called upon for officers; how the factories of the

Continent were searched for guns; and how these and other measures taken by the War Office affected the Regiment during the war-years.

The South African Influence (1902—1904).

In South Africa all arms experienced for the first time the sensation of being under artillery fire, and it changed their attitude towards the Royal Artillery amazingly. Instead of being put aside as matters of merely technical interest, artillery questions were henceforward hotly debated at staff conferences and submitted for decision by the highest authorities. "Co-operation" became a word to conjure with.

For the field army artillery such a conception of action as had been exemplified only a month before the war in the "Dress Rehearsal" by the horse and field artillery of the Aldershot Army Corps[1] was unquestionably out of date. A new "doctrine" must be evolved, and must provide for the heavy batteries of the garrison artillery which had established their right to inclusion in the field army artillery. Siege artillery also must learn to adapt its methods to use in the field, so as to be available to supplement the field army artillery. Even the coast artillery felt the influence of South Africa, for the general ill-feeling towards the British Empire, so openly manifested throughout Europe during the war-years, brought home to the country the possibility of our coaling stations and other overseas possessions being attacked. The "blue-water school" had denounced the "heresy of fixed defences" during the controversies of the 80's and 90's, and had scoffed at the idea of the coast artillery ever being called upon to stand to their guns in earnest. But when there seemed a chance of these theories being put to the test public opinion took alarm.

And so, for all branches of the Regiment, the years immediately succeeding the South African War were

---

[1] Vol. I, Chapter XI.

devoted to a thorough overhaul of organization, armament, and training in the light of war experience. The value of its lessons to the Empire, to the Army, and not least to the Artillery, was scarcely realized until they were absorbed in a far greater struggle. But the Empress Frederick had seen it, and expressed it to Queen Victoria in prophetic words :—[1]

> "I look upon this war, dreadful as it is, as of immense use to England in many a way! First, it has shown us where the weak points in our armour are, and we can remedy them; then it has caused the others who envy us and wish us ill, to 'show their hand'. . . . Then it will weld the Empire together : in short . . . in spite of losses and reverses the experience we shall have gained will be a strength and a blessing to us hereafter".

The Manchurian Influence (1904—1910).

If at first there was a tendency to over-emphasize the lessons of the veldt, the lapse of time soon supplied the corrective. For within a couple of years of the signing of the Treaty of Vereeniging war broke out between Japan and Russia, and its lessons were not for one branch alone. The battlefields of Manchuria showed heavy and mountain batteries ranged alongside the horse and field, and the heaviest pieces of the siege train brought into action. Port Arthur provided the siege and coast artillery with the first object lesson since Sevastopol in the attack and defence of a naval base, and confirmed the teaching of history as to the vulnerability of the land fronts of coast fortresses.

No time was lost in profiting by these lessons. While the war was still raging in the East a new quick-firing equipment was put into the hands of the horse and field artillery, the newly formed heavy brigades joined the field army, and the siege artillery found a new range where, in

---
[1] *The Letters of Queen Victoria*—G. E. Buckle.

alternate years, they could learn to adopt their methods to the conditions of field warfare. To the coast artillery the Russo-Japanese War brought still more revolutionary changes. Strategical with the Japanese Alliance and the growth of the German Navy—tactical with the appearance of Dreadnoughts and Super-Dreadnoughts, "Blockers" and "Boomsmashers"—technical in the remarkable development of the range, accuracy, and volume of fire from war-ships.

Re-armament.

The re-armament of the first decade of the century was very different, both in inception and conduct, from the haphazard affairs of the past. Instead of waiting for suggestions from gun-designers, the initiative was taken by the users in the shape of a list of the conditions they required, and the skill of the designers was thus directed into the right channels from the outset. Instead of partial efforts, in which a new equipment had generally become obsolete before it had reached all those for whom it was intended, all the batteries of the field army artillery—horse, field, mountain, and heavy—were re-armed in little more than a decade. And not only those on the Home, Indian and Colonial Establishments: under the inspiration of Imperial Conferences, the Dominions also competed for priority of supply.

On this scale re-armament became an operation of such magnitude as to bring it within the orbit of many unexpected forces. Foreign and domestic politics, financial and industrial interests, made their influence felt, and many difficulties other than technical had to be surmounted before the new weapons reached the batteries so anxiously awaiting them.

Re-organization.

The first step towards basing artillery organization upon tactical requirements was taken during the South African War by the brigading of horse and field batteries.

Mr. Haldane's great measures of re-organization followed, and the outstanding feature of these was the adoption of the division as the unit. It gave at last to the field army artillery an organization and a chain of command based upon war requirements. For the first time senior officers of artillery trained in peace the brigades and batteries they would command in war. For the first time the peculiar problem of artillery mobilization was faced, and the formation of ammunition columns without the sacrifice of batteries provided for.

The recognition of coast defences as commands analogous to the divisions and brigades of the field army, and the placing of the branch schools of gunnery under coast defence commanders, served the same purpose for the coast artillery as the formation of divisional artillery did for the field army artillery. But the organization of this branch was exceptionally difficult owing to the excessive proportion of its strength serving abroad. Its circumstances were investigated by a plethora of committees, but the requirements of overseas garrisons had to be met, and eventually the unpopular measure of localizing companies was adopted.

The French Influence (1910—1912).

With the *entente cordiale* came a lifting of the veil which had shrouded the French Artillery since its re-armament in 1897. English officers were allowed to watch the famous "75's" at practice, as well as at manœuvres, and doubts began to be expressed as to whether the performance of our new quick-firers came up to their promise. Battery organization, equipment, principles of employment, methods of fire, and systems of practice, all came under review. Never before had the mounted branch been subjected to such a fire of criticism. The more conservative element in the Regiment put up a stout fight, but after a year of discussions and trials the French school carried the day, and the Regulations of 1912 were admittedly modelled on the *Réglement* of 1910.

The new manual was subjected to the severest scrutiny, and not by artillery officers only. The interest shown was a striking testimony to the important place that the artillery now held in the army. It was clear that there was much to learn from the French, even if all the methods which suited one nation were not necessarily applicable to the other. In the short period available much was accomplished in assimilating the general principles while modifying some of the details, so that the artillery took the field in 1914 with a well-considered doctrine which commanded general confidence. Far transcending all other results of the French influence, however, was the effect which it had on the hitherto insoluble problem of co-operation. Whatever question there might be as to the possible effect of "tactical practice" on the gunnery—about which many were justifiably perturbed—there was no doubt that it brought about a vast improvement in mutual knowledge. During the last two summers before the War many brigadiers and senior regimental officers of cavalry and infantry had the opportunity of seeing the positive result of their orders to artillery brigades and batteries in actual effect upon the targets: many artillery officers were made to realize more fully than ever before that their choice of positions and targets for their guns would be limited by the dispositions and requirements of the other arms; and, most important of all, all ranks were inveigled into much profitable dispute as to their respective parts in combined operations —the first step towards real co-operation.

The French influence was confined to the field army artillery, but about the same time—the commencement of the second decade of the century—other causes were bringing about almost equally important changes in the other branches.

In the siege artillery special siege manœuvres and staff tours, and the investigation of possible contingencies in the event of war, had shown the necessity for once again including the duties of all arms in fortress warfare in the general military curriculum. *Combined Training* had said not a word on the subject, but a special manual was promised, and although this never materialized, the *Field Service Regulations* which superseded *Combined Training* in 1909, devoted a whole chapter to "Siege Operations". This laid down the general procedure to be observed, and the duties of all arms, while artillery and engineer manuals, which followed, gave the more technical details.

The coast artillery, like the siege, had been promised an official guide in the shape of a *Manual of Coast Fortress Defence*, but as in the case of the siege manual, this promise was never kept. The issue of a confidential manual on *Fighting the Fixed Armament* did much, however, to fill the gap. It definitely established the position of coast defences in the scheme of Imperial Defence: it gave to the coast artillery a gunnery based on the new science of calibration: and although their demand for more powerful weapons met with little response, much was done to improve the means of fighting those they had. The organization of the fortress was taken up, and this meant co-operation all round. With the navy in order to learn what to expect in the shape of attack, and to ensure working together in defence—with the infantry who were entrusted with the protection of the open batteries and posts—with the field army artillery in handling the movable armament in defence of the land fronts. But the great problem of how the companies abroad were to be kept up to strength without detriment to the efficiency of those at home remained unsolved.

Mechanization and Aviation.

The mechanization of heavy and siege artillery had been envisaged ever since the South African War, and fittings for "engine draught" included in their equipment. But as long as steam was the motive power no progress was possible, and the first tractors showed no advantage over horses for gun-teams. In another direction, however, mechanization was of incalculable value to the field army artillery, for its adoption for a portion of the ammunition supply service solved the problem of field artillery mobilization.

In the air the advent of dirigibles made it plain that aviation was becoming a matter of vital interest for the artillery. Experiments in observation from, and shooting at, balloons and kites showed that these presented no serious difficulty, but it was soon seen that the ordinary armament could not deal with air-ships, and when the aeroplane appeared there was a tendency to accept the difficulty of hitting such a target as insoluable. Wiser counsels prevailed, and before the War much preliminary work had been done with experimental anti-aircraft equipments—13-pr., 18-pr., 3″, and 4″—although the only ones which actually reached the service were some pompoms which were hastily modified for the defence of localities. Definite instructions for the co-operation of aircraft with artillery had been issued, but practically nothing had been done towards the solution of the gunnery problems involved.

The Final Phase (1912—1914).

The last years before the War saw increased activity in every branch of the Regiment, and in every detail of its preparation. There were practice mobilizations and ammunition supply exercises for the Expeditionary Force, and the most ambitious army manœuvres ever attempted at home, in which the artillery of that force appeared for the first time complete in commanders, staffs, and units. The possibility of obtaining enhanced effect from the shrapnel fire of the 13-prs. and 18-prs. was investigated, and the defects in these equipments were remedied as far as was feasible. At the same time the necessity for the re-armament of the field artillery in the near future was accepted, and the first step taken towards it by the formulation of the conditions which the new equipment should fulfil.[1]

For the siege artillery the army manœuvres marked a new stage, for in those of 1912 siege batteries made their first appearance in the ranks of the field army. Their position as regards armament was, however, still unsatisfactory. The idea of depending upon the old muzzle-loading "high-angle" guns taken out of coast defences as substitutes for heavy howitzers had been abandoned, but much time had been lost. It was only on the day before that on which war was declared that the experimental equipment, to become so familiar to the army in France as "Mother", could be reported as fit for approval.

In the coast artillery on the contrary it was the *personnel* rather than the *matériel* that was causing anxiety. The rushing of reinforcements to the defended ports on the east coast during the Agadir crisis gave point to the general uneasiness regarding the adequacy of the artillery garrisons. The whole question of the manning requirements of the home ports, and how they were to be met during the trooping season, was under serious consideration to the last. And so, also, was the question of the promotion of the officers of the garrison artillery. In spite of all prognostications to the contrary, the coast artillery had undoubtedly profited by the separation of the mounted and dismounted branches. But the officers had a legitimate grievance in the block in their promotion which had resulted from the South African War. It was only in 1913, after much agitation in the Press and in Parliament, that a tardy and partial measure of relief was afforded by the grant of special facilities for retirement to those most seriously affected.

Straws show the way that streams flow, and it is often the little things that afford the best clue to the actual position. How seriously the situation was regarded may

---

[1] Appendix D. Read in conjunction with the Report in Appendix F, this gives a contemporary picture of great value.

be judged from the fact that the time for the periodical examination of field guns was altered so as to run no risk of the batteries being short during the summer months, while the coast artillery were ordered to keep full-charge plates on the elevation-indicators of their guns, and to alter their sight-covers so as to allow of the gear being continually ready for action.

Perhaps, however, the most convincing representation of the state of the field army artillery at this supreme moment in its history is contained in the Report from which extracts are given in Appendix F. For this was written by one of the divisional artillery commanders of the Expeditionary Force during the "precautionary period", and it was actually signed on the "first day of mobilization".

THE COLONELS-IN-CHIEF.

"The Duke".

In March 1904 there passed away, in his 85th year, the first Colonel-in-Chief of the Royal Artillery. Appointed "Colonel" of the Regiment in 1861, and "Colonel-in-Chief" in 1895, the Duke of Cambridge had been at the head of the Regiment for more than half his long life, and had become almost a traditional figure to generations of artillerymen. The vast majority had derived their earliest impression of military ceremonial from their first "Duke's Day" at the Academy, and had received their commissions at his hands. During their service many had been brought into close contact with His Royal Highness at manœuvres and inspections, at the War Office, or at the Regimental Dinner, at which he so regularly presided. By his kindly disposition, his sympathetic interest in regimental affairs, and the way he identified himself with their interests, the Duke had endeared himself to all, and his death was felt as a personal loss by many who had never had the fortune to exchange a word with him.

Edward VII.

Six weeks after the Duke of Cambridge's death King Edward VII conferred upon the Regiment the signal honour of himself becoming its Colonel-in-Chief. A copy of the General State of the Royal Artillery on that day was forwarded to His Majesty, who thereupon expressed his wish that this should be repeated annually at the first Levée of the season, as is still done.

To show that his assumption of the Colonelcy was no mere formality, His Majesty came down to Woolwich in the following October and inspected on foot-parade the two brigades R.H.A. and three brigades R.F.A. in garrison. After a visit to the Academy the King returned to lunch at the Mess, where he took the chair as President,

The General State of the Royal Regiment of Artillery on the 1st May, 1904

	R.H.A.			R.F.A.			R.G.A.			Officers on Half-pay and Extra Regimental Employment.	Total
	Officers	Warrant Officers	N.C.Os. and Men	Officers	Warrant Officers	N.C.Os. and Men	Officers	Warrant Officers	N.C.Os. and Men		
Home ...	109	6	2,936	555	32	15,121	329	65	9,958	—	29,111
India ...	61	3	1,844	251	9	7,974	195	13	5,018	—	15,368
Colonies ...	13	—	350	90	5	2,553	328	38	7,811	—	11,188
Unposted ...	—	—	—	37	—	—	82	—	—	—	119
	—	—	—	—	—	—	—	—	—	734	734
	183	9	5,130	933	46	25,648	934	116	22,787	734	56,520

NOTE. The above is a copy of the General State of the Regiment presented to King Edward VII on the day on which His Majesty became its Colonel-in-Chief. From this event dates the annual presentation of the State by the Master-Gunner at the first Levée of the Season.

and after luncheon honoured the officers present by being photographed with them. It may be noted that His Majesty wore a *blue* tunic as shown in the photograph taken at Woolwich, reproduced as a frontispiece to this Volume.[1] Not content with seeing the horse and field artillery at Woolwich, His Majesty followed up his visit there by an inspection of the Royal Garrison Artillery at the Clarence Barracks, Portsmouth, in February, 1905. The force on parade consisted of two heavy batteries, one siege company, and three coast defence companies, and was thus representative of all except mountain artillery. At the conclusion of the inspection His Majesty proceeded to the Mess, where he drank to the health and prosperity of the Regiment, and signed the Visitors Book, adding the words "Colonel-in-Chief" after his name. Before leaving he was photographed with the general and field officers.

George V.

On the death of King Edward in May, 1910, His Majesty, King George V was graciously pleased to assume the position thus left vacant, and in 1913 he followed King Edward's example by inspecting the Regiment at Woolwich. On this occasion the parade was a mounted one, and His Majesty rode from the Mess with the Duke of Connaught, followed by the Queen and Princess Mary in a landau, and escorted by the Riding Establishment. The troops on parade consisted of one brigade R.H.A., three brigades R.F.A., a heavy brigade R.G.A., and a field brigade of the Territorial Force. As on the occasion of King Edward's inspection their Majesties visited the Academy at the conclusion of the parade, and then returned to the Mess for lunch, after which they honoured the officers by having their photographs taken with them.

---

[1] The tunic itself is now in the Institution, having been presented by Queen Alexandra.

A gratifying token of His Majesty's appreciation was the receipt, a week later, of a magnificent silver-gilt cup inscribed :—

PRESENTED

TO

THE OFFICERS MESS

OF

THE ROYAL REGIMENT OF ARTILLERY

BY

KING GEORGE V

COLONEL IN CHIEF

APRIL THE 9TH 1913.

THE MASTER-GUNNERS.

The year which saw the creation of the Regiment saw also the abolition of the historic office of "Master-Gunner of England" after an existence of nearly five centuries. His two subordinates, the Master-Gunners of Whitehall and of St. James's Park, survived the disappearance of their chief, but the former soon dropped out, so that by the end of the XVIIIth century there remained only the Master-Gunner of St. James's Park. And in 1796 this office took on its present-day form by the appointment to it of a general officer of the Royal Artillery. But by an oversight the pay remained unaltered.[1]

At the beginning of the period chronicled here it had been held for twenty years by General Sir Robert Gardiner, G.C.B., K.C.H., a veteran whose active service had commenced with the capture of Minorca, and had included the Walcheren Expedition as well as the Peninsula and Waterloo. He was succeeded by the first artillery Field-Marshal, Sir Hew Ross, G.C.B., famous in regimental annals for his twenty years command of the Chestnut Troop. He only held the office for four years, and was followed in succession by General William Wylde, C.B., who had seen much fighting in Spain during the Carlist Wars, and been Equerry to the Prince Consort; by General Poole Vallancey England, who had taken part in the expeditions to the Weser, the Cape, and South America, before serving in the Peninsula; and by Sir John Bloomfield, G.C.B., the last of the Peninsula and Waterloo veterans. Sir John St. George, G.C.B., who followed, was the first from the Crimea, where he had

---

[1] More than a century later, during the inspection of a pay office, it appears to have struck the inspector as curious that the modest emoluments of one of the eighty-three 3rd class Master-Gunners on the strength of the Royal Artillery should be remitted monthly to Messrs. Cox & Co. When next the office fell vacant it became a purely honorary one.

commanded the Siege Train in the final bombardment. His successor, General Sir Collingwood Dickson, v.c., G.C.B., had helped to serve the two field guns which were brought forward into the heart of the Russian position at the Alma, and had commanded the two guns of position which exerted such a decisive influence in the fight at Inkerman. Even more distinguished was the last holder of the office before the Great War, Field-Marshal Earl Roberts.

In conclusion it may be mentioned that the Master-Gunner is selected by the King, personally, from among the Colonels-Commandant. He is not necessarily the senior, but as the Deputy for the Colonel-in-Chief he takes his place as head of all regimental institutions, selects the representative Colonel-Commandant for the year, and recommends officers for appointment to that rank.

PART I.

THE WAR YEARS.

(1899—1902.)

CHAPTER I.

THE WAR OFFICE.

The abolition of the Deputy Adjutant-General—The Separation of the Mounted and Dismounted Branches—The Augmentation of the Horse and Field Artillery—The Provision of Officers—The Promotion of Officers—The Provision of Guns—The Mowatt Committee—The Ehrhardt Guns—The Skoda Howitzers.

IN this introductory chapter an attempt has been made to show the special difficulties which confronted the officers responsible for artillery matters at Headquarters when War was declared in 1899, and how these were surmounted. After nearly half a century of "small wars", in which there had been little demand for guns—beyond a mountain battery or so—they were called upon to despatch overseas a force of artillery larger than had ever before left these shores. And their task was rendered infinitely more formidable by the fact that the crisis supervened so closely upon the great administrative changes about to be described.

Since the creation of the office of Deputy Adjutant-General, Royal Artillery, in 1795, many generations of artillerymen had looked upon its holder as the arbiter of their fate, and had accepted the "Royal Artillery Regimental Orders" which he issued, as their military gospel. The abolition of the office, and the cessation of regimental orders, caused, therefore, no little perturbation; and it was deemed advisable to reassure officers by the issue of a circular letter explaining the new distribution of artillery work between the departments of the War Office. The chief feature of the change was the appointment of two Colonels for Royal Artillery—an Assistant Military Secretary and an Assistant Adjutant-General—and on the 1st April 1899 these appointments were taken up by Colonels J. C. Dalton[1] and E. O. Hay,[1] the former from the Garrison the latter from the Field Artillery. The Assistant Military Secretary dealt with first appoint-

---

[1] Major-General J. C. Dalton, Colonel Commandant, d. 1931.
Major-General E. O. Hay, C.B., Colonel-Commandant.

THE WAR YEARS.

CHAPTER I.

The Abolition of the Deputy Adjutant-General.

ments to the Regiment, with appointments to horse and mountain artillery, with staff and extra regimental appointments generally, and with promotions, retirements, honours, and rewards. The Assistant Adjutant-General dealt with postings, transfers and exchanges within the branches of the Regiment, with appointments to the instructional staff, and with drill and discipline. In the other departments at the War Office no new appointments were necessary, but the departments dealt direct with the artillery as with the cavalry and infantry instead of having to communicate through the Deputy Adjutant-General. Thus the Quarter-Master-General took charge of the roster of batteries for service abroad, their allotment to stations, and their moves, as well as all questions connected with food, forage, and remounts. The Director-General of Ordnance became directly responsible for the supply and inspection of armament and equipment generally.

The Separation of the Mounted and Dismounted Branches.

As told in Volume I, the Regiment had been separated into two "Corps" in June 1899, but a further Army Order[1] had to be issued in the very month in which war was declared in order to settle various subsidiary matters such as the designations of officers and of units, the conditions for exchanges, &c., &c. Appointments to the Horse Artillery, the Hyderabad Contingent,[2] the Honourable Artillery Company, the Norfolk Volunteer Artillery, and Volunteer Position Corps, were reserved for the Mounted Branch, those to the Mountain Artillery, the Militia Artillery, and Volunteer Corps (with the above exceptions), for the Dismounted Branch.

At the time of the separation some sixty officers on the "mounted list" were serving with the garrison artillery, and, owing to the necessity of absorbing them, it was estimated that promotion in the mounted branch would

---

[1] Appendix A.
[2] The Hyderabad Contingent was a force maintained under treaty with the Nizam. It included four field batteries armed with obsolete guns, which were officered from the Royal Artillery in much the same way as Indian Mountain Batteries. They were disbanded in 1903.

THE WAR OFFICE.

for some time be slower than in the dismounted. But the war came, some sixty new batteries of horse and field artillery were raised, and the rate of promotion of majors and captains of the mounted branch forged far ahead of that of their contemporaries in the dismounted one. This naturally led to some dissatisfaction, and the blame was put upon the scheme of separation although the advantage would have been on the other side had it not been for the war. Many thought also that if separation had been delayed until South African experience had caused the revival of heavy artillery, the cleavage would have been between the field army artillery—including mountain, heavy, and possibly siege—and the coast artillery. This, it may be noted, was the line of demarcation adopted in the United States Artillery which was separated at about the same time into "Field" and "Coast".

There were, of course, some difficulties at first. Previous to the separation all artillery units in any station had been under the command of the senior artillery officer, and some of these were slow to realize the change that had been brought about by the separation. It had to be made clear that units of the different branches must now be viewed as entirely independent as regards training, discipline, and interior economy; and that the senior officer of one branch had no more right to assume control of units of the other branch quartered in the proximity than of cavalry or infantry.

Some legal difficulties which resulted from the division into two "corps" may also conveniently be mentioned here, although they did not actually arise until later. For instance the idea of converting heavy batteries in India into field howitzer batteries, and a field brigade at home into a mountain brigade, had both to be given up because they would involve the transfer of the *personnel* from the "corps" of R.H. & R.F.A. to that of R.G.A. and vice versa. Similarly, when the formation of heavy batteries of garrison artillery was being considered at home it was a question whether the attestations of R.G.A.

CHAPTER I.

The Separation of the Mounted and Dismounted Branches.

4 THE WAR YEARS.

CHAPTER I.

The Separation of the Mounted and Dismounted Branches.

recruits would not have to be altered if these became fully horsed units. The difficulty did not arise with mountain batteries, for their status as dismounted units was not affected by the guns being carried on mule back.

There was also the question of the "corps" to which cadets should be commissioned. The old rule had been that the only ones posted to field batteries on first appointment were the senior artillery cadet and the winner of the riding prize. After the separation officers would remain all their regimental life in the branch to which they were first posted, and it was decided that the principle on which cadets obtained commissions in the Royal Engineers according to their place on the passing-out list must be extended to the mounted and dismounted branches of the Royal Artillery.

The Augmentation of the Horse and Field Artillery.

The variety of questions involved in the "Separation", of which only an indication has been given here, would have been sufficient in themselves to tax the skill and energy of the officers entrusted with the administrative duties hitherto carried out in the office of the D.A.G., R.A. Hardly, however, had the new system been established than they were confronted, as we have seen, with the demands of war, and that on an unprecedented scale.

During the 90's the number of horse and field batteries had been increased from 20 and 80, respectively, to 21 and 95,[1] but under the stress of war far larger additions were soon necessary. The requirements in artillery for the three cavalry brigades and two army corps in South Africa were 7 batteries of horse and 30 of field artillery, and these were all either in South Africa or under orders by the end of 1899. In addition to the two army corps there were, however, in South Africa 18 battalions of infantry and some 42,000 Militia, Imperial Yeomanry, Volunteers, and Colonial Forces, with only some 30 guns between them. To provide these 60,000 men with guns at the established proportion of four and a

[1] In some case by the conversion of depôts into service batteries.—Vol. I, pp. 120-1, and 139-40.

quarter per thousand would require 37 batteries, and there was still the 7th Division to be provided for, making the total requirements for South Africa 43 batteries, towards which there were available at home only 24. This was serious enough, but it was the provision of artillery for home defence that was causing the greatest anxiety. For the one army corps and cavalry brigade, 3 horse and 18 field batteries would be required.

It was obvious that a very large number of batteries must be raised at once, and when in February 1900 Lord Lansdowne unfolded the plans of the Government, which included an increase to the artillery of 7 horse and 56 field batteries, there was very general approval. No time was lost, and within twelve months of his declaration in the House of Lords the Army List showed 28 batteries R.H.A. lettered from "A" to "B/B", and 151 batteries R.F.A. numbered from "1" to "151".

The last years of the XIXth century had seen a considerable augmentation of the garrison as well as the field artillery, the number of companies having been increased from 66 to 77,[1] and the establishment of those in the great Mediterranean fortresses raised. But thirteen companies had been sent to South Africa, and the general hostility towards the British Empire indicated the possibility of coaling stations and other overseas possessions being attacked. There was some uneasiness as to the adequacy of the artillery garrisons, and the raising of further companies of coast artillery was seriously considered, only to be eventually deferred as will be told later. The question of officers could not wait, and the steps taken for their provision will now be considered in conjunction with those of the field artillery.

In addition to the very large number of officers required for the new batteries, the war made demands upon the artillery for many purposes in addition to the replacement of casualties—staffs, pompom sections, ammunition

---

[1] To some extent, as in the case of the field artillery, by the conversion of depôts into service companies.

CHAPTER I.

The Provision of Officers.

columns, colonial corps, &c., &c. And the difficulty of meeting these demands was enhanced by the fact that at the outbreak of war there were a large number of vacancies due to previously approved increases in establishment which had not yet been filled. Various expedients had therefore to be resorted to.

The flow from what may be termed the "ordinary" sources was increased by accelerating the courses at the Academy, by offering a larger number of commissions for competition to the Militia, and by accepting some university candidates who had qualified for infantry.[1] To supplement these sources direct commissions without examination were offered to the Militia and Volunteers, and then in succession to the Royal Indian Engineering College, the Royal Military College Canada, the Universities, the Colonies, the Public Schools, and to those nominated by Lord Roberts as Commander-in-Chief in South Africa.

The following table shows the number of officers obtained from these various sources between the 1st January, 1899, and the 30th September, 1901.

	Ordinary Sources			Direct Commissions		
	R.F.A.	R.G.A.	TOTAL	R.F.A.	R.G.A.	TOTAL
Royal Military Academy	139	184	323	—	—	—
Royal Military College, Canada	—	2	2	—	—	—
Royal Indian Engineering College	—	1	1	5	16	21
Militia Artillery	24	46	70	48	72	120
Volunteer Artillery	—	—	—	19	11	30
Royal Marine Artillery	—	—	—	1	—	1
Royal Malta Artillery	—	—	—	—	2	2
Universities & Colleges	2	4	6	107	74	181
Colonies	—	—	—	50	15	65
Lord Roberts' List	—	—	—	9	1	10
Militia Engineers	—	—	—	2	—	2
Militia Infantry	—	—	—	—	2	2
Public Schools	—	—	—	14	2	16
Miscellaneous	—	—	—	3	3	6
	165	237	402	258	198	456

[1] At that time the commissions offered for competition at the universities did not include any in the Royal Artillery.

THE WAR OFFICE. 7

All direct commissions were discontinued after those referred to in the above table had been allotted, and officers were obtained only from the following sources in addition to the Academy—at which the course was restored to two years:—

Royal Military College, Canada—one a year.
Royal Indian Engineering College—six a year for three years.
Militia Artillery—according to vacancies at the time of the half-yearly competitive examinations.

No ordinary combatant commissions were given from the ranks, but owing to the rapid promotion and consequent difficulty of finding experienced officers for armament duties and depôts, authority was obtained to add considerably to the establishment of District Officers. A District Officer was appointed to each depôt, several more to armament duties in the Mediterranean, and advantage was also taken of the opportunity to obtain some much-needed District Officers and Quarter-Masters for the District Staff, School of Gunnery, &c. The number of Quarter-Masters and Riding-Masters was also increased to provide for the new depôts being formed. The total of commissions given from the ranks is shown in the following table:—

	R.F.A.	R.G.A.	R.A.	TOTAL
District Officers	—	—	44	44
Quarter-Masters	8	11	—	19
Riding-Masters	9	—	—	9
	17	11	44	72

The various exigencies of the war which had caused such difficulties in obtaining officers, had naturally caused also a great acceleration in the rate of promotion, especially in the junior ranks. The average service of the seniors in the ranks of captain, lieutenant, and 2nd lieutenant, on the 1st July in the years 1899 and 1901 are given in the following table:—

Chapter I.

The Provision of Officers.

The Promotion of Officers.

CHAPTER I.

The Promotion of Officers.

	R.F.A.		R.G.A.	
	1899	1901	1899	1901
Captains	18·5	15·5	18·5	18·5
Lieutenants	10·5	6·1	10·5	5·8
2nd Lieutenants	3·0	1·2	3·0	1·2

The inevitable result was a relaxation of the rule regarding examinations for promotion. "Provisional" promotion, subject to subsequent qualification, was first introduced, but in February, 1900, officers promoted while on service in South Africa, were given exemption from subsequent examination, and in June 1901, this concession was extended to all officers who might be promoted while on active service.

On the revival of the rank of 2nd lieutenant in 1887, no establishment was fixed but it was arranged that they should serve three years before being promoted. When, however, 2nd lieutenants of cavalry and infantry (who were on an establishment) were being promoted earlier than this, and were thus superseding 2nd lieutenants of artillery, the injustice of the arrangement was recognized, and an establishment of lieutenants and 2nd lieutenants was approved in February 1901 for the Royal Artillery, in the proportion of three lieutenants to two 2nd lieutenants. A proviso was added that in the event of no vacancy occurring before the completion of three years service a 2nd lieutenant should then be promoted under the provisions of Article 29 of the Royal Warrant.

The lesson of the war, as far as the provision of officers was concerned, was the extreme difficulty of keeping up the supply of subalterns with any knowledge of their work.

During the war-years, when new units were being raised, and the necessity for trained officers was greatest, the presence of so many without any military training whatever tended to lower the whole standard, and this was accentuated by the rapid promotion. Similar conditions prevailed as regards appointments to horse and mountain

THE WAR OFFICE.

artillery. In both cases the qualifying service had to be reduced, and the rule restricting appointment as captain to those who had served as subalterns relaxed. The Indian Government were also obliged to relax the language qualifications for Indian mountain batteries.

The various measures taken to obtain officers from other than the normal sources were no doubt necessary, and it will be readily admitted by those whose memories go back so far that the widening of the field of selection brought into the Regiment among the "Persons"[1] many officers who were a real acquisition. On the other hand the acceptance of a certain number of candidates without educational qualification was to prove a serious embarrassment for many years to come. How such officers were to be dealt with in justice to the service and to themselves was one of the most awkward aftermaths of the war.

The finding of the officers for the new batteries had been a difficult task; the provision of the guns was even more of a puzzle, for in matters of equipment there can be no compromise. A man can be made into an officer by a stroke of the pen, a gun cannot be improvised. It was indeed fortunate that in the first month of the war the responsibility for the supply of artillery *matériel* should have been entrusted to one of the ablest of the many able men whose names are inscribed on the roll of the

CHAPTER I.
The Promotion of Officers.

The Provision of Guns.

---

[1] This nickname for officers who had received direct commissions dated from the Crimean period when the following advertisement appeared in the *Times* of the 8th June, 1855 :—

"Early in July next FORTY PERSONS between the ages of "17 and 19 will be appointed to the Senior or Practical Class in "the Academy at Woolwich, and TWENTY other PERSONS "will be provisionally commissioned, and placed under the Director "of Artillery Studies at Woolwich. These appointments will be "made by the Secretary of State for the War Department after a "competing examination by examiners named by him."

·The applicants were to be British-born subjects.

Colonel F. Duncan, the author of the *History of the Royal Regiment of Artillery* was the first "person".

CHAPTER I.

The Provision of Guns.

Royal Artillery.[1] Sir Henry Brackenbury had shown true military insight as a young subaltern, for he had been one of the very few to realize before the Franco-German war the changes which rifled guns would effect in artillery tactics, and he had shown courage and determination in demanding that artillery training should keep pace with these changes. Since those early days he had earned a high reputation in various important offices at home and abroad, and he was now to crown his career by providing the artillery with the armament without which it would have been powerless. His predecessors at the head of the Department which carried on at the War Office the duties previously performed by the Board of Ordnance had rarely seen service beyond the confines of the Regiment; Sir Henry's broader experience gave his mind a wider range, and the qualities of vision and "drive" which he had shown as a subaltern enabled him to devise and carry through projects which went far beyond the bounds of ordinary administrative procedure.

He had made it a condition of accepting the appointment that the manufacturing departments should come under his charge, and no sooner was he installed than he undertook a comprehensive survey of his responsibilities. This soon showed him that in addition to deficiencies of armament there was lacking anything in the shape of a real war reserve. Such reserves as existed were merely a collection of a few items likely to be wanted on emergency, and they were always liable to be depleted—as had indeed been done only shortly before in order to create new batteries. The matter brooked no delay. By the end of the year he had completed his enquiries; and in January 1900, on the very day on which Colenso was being fought,

---

[1] General the Right Honourable Sir Henry Brackenbury, P.C., G.C.B., Colonel Commandant, d. 1914. He was appointed Director-General of Ordnance in October 1899—the historic title of "Master-General" was not revived until the creation of the Army Council a few years later.

GENERAL THE RT. HON. SIR HENRY BRACKENBURY, P.C., G.C.B.
COLONEL-COMMANDANT, ROYAL ARTILLERY.

THE WAR OFFICE.

he presented the result in a series of masterly papers. These dealt in turn with the reserves of guns, mountings, &c., for coast batteries, the replacement of obsolete guns in the movable armament of fortresses, the completion of the siege train, and the reserves of guns, carriages, and ammunition for the field artillery.[1] To cover the whole he asked for a loan of fifteen millions, so that he might place all the orders for delivery within three years. And he insisted that it was useless to create reserves unless authority was given to keep these reserves up to the established standard, replacement following automatically upon issue, as was the case in the navy and in the army in India, but not in the army at home.

There was no attempt to dispute Sir Henry's conclusion that the position was "full of peril to the Empire", or to cavil at the supporting details. So impressed indeed were the Government by the danger revealed that they at once appointed a special Committee composed of civilian administrators of great eminence[2] to examine and report upon the proposals. The list of witnesses examined includes all those alive at the time whose names are prominent in the annals of gunmaking, from the veteran Sir Andrew Noble downwards, and, in addition, many who had held high administrative office in other spheres. The Report of the Committee, rendered with commendable promptitude, became the Magna Charta of those responsible for the armament of the artillery throughout the whole period between the South African War and the Great War. Briefly summarised its recommendations were:—

CHAPTER I.

The Provision of Guns.

The Mowatt Committee.

---

[1] In addition to machine guns and other matters outside the scope of an artillery history.

[2] Sir Francis Mowatt, Permanent Secretary to the Treasury. Mr. George Windham, M.P., Parliamentary Under-Secretary of State for War. Mr. E. Grant Burls, Director-General of Stores at the India Office.

12 THE WAR YEARS.

CHAPTER I.

The Mowatt Committee.

That the reserves of guns, mountings, &c., for coast artillery should be on a basis of one for every ten in the approved armament.[1]

That the question of movable armaments should be referred for the consideration of an expert committee.

That the siege train should be completed, and

That the reserve of guns and carriages for the field artillery should be on a basis of 25%.

More important, however, by far than the fixing of definite reserves was the endorsement by the Committee of the principle so strongly urged by Sir Henry Brackenbury that the authorized proportion for reserve should be included in all orders for equipment, and that any issue from reserve should be automatically replaced.

Another point in connection with the provision of war material on which the Mowatt Committee enunciated an important principle was with regard to the proportion of such orders to be allotted to the "Trade" and to the "Ordnance Factories" respectively. The sudden and unprecedented demand for munitions caused by the outbreak of the South African War had shown that the private firms were not so organized as to be able at once to increase materially their deliveries when a crisis occurred. In this case the pressure had been met by borrowing from the Navy and from India, but such a source could obviously not be depended upon, for, in the prophetic words of the committee's report—"the time might come when the country would find itself simultaneously engaged in a great war by sea and by land, during which India and the Navy so far from being able to lend to the Army, might themselves have to make very heavy demands". In order that the private firms might be so developed as to be capable of expansion, the committee recommended that a definite proportion of all orders, including the more delicate articles, such as fuzes, not hitherto entrusted to the

---

[1] For stations abroad this was calculated on the number of that nature in the station, for stations at home on the number in Great Britain.

THE WAR OFFICE.

trade, should be given to them, and that the Ordnance Factories should have as their primary function the creation of a standard of workmanship, and the demonstration of the true cost of production.[1]

Sir Henry's formidable batch of demands had been submitted in January 1900. In February the Government had appointed the Mowatt Committee to examine them: in March that Committee had reported; and in April Parliament voted ten and a half millions for building up a true war reserve, not only of guns and ammunition but of every conceivable category of war requirements, together with the necessary store-houses, AND EACH YEAR THE ARMY COUNCIL HAD TO CERTIFY PARLIAMENT THAT THE RESERVE WAS INTACT.[2]

Sir Henry was not, however, the man to fold his hands and wait inactive for his far-sighted action to bear fruit in due season. The position was critical, and casting precedent to the winds, he determined to take the unheard-of course of going into the European market, and purchasing what suitable material he could find there. A short digression is therefore necessary regarding the position.

In the last years of the XIXth century it had become certain that the principle of "quick-firing" which had been so successfully applied to naval and fortress armaments, would soon be extended to field guns, although in their case the problem was a far more difficult one. In a fort or a ship there was no limit to the weight of the mounting, which could moreover be made a part of the whole structure, and immobility of the mounting was therefore easily obtained. To ensure the carriage of a field gun remaining stationary on the ground when the

CHAPTER I.

The Mowatt Committee.

The "Ehrhardt" Guns.

---

[1] This is perhaps scarcely Regimental History, but the adoption of this rule touched the interests of artillery armament so closely, and so continuously, during the years that followed, and it has been so generally misunderstood, that this short notice appeared advisable here.

[2] It may be mentioned that the Mowatt reserve of guns for the Expeditionary Force had been landed in France before the last day of mobilization.

gun was fired was a very different matter; and yet this was the essential quality which differentiated the true quick-firer from all others. Gunmaking firms were continually claiming to have found the solution: and many designs showing great ingenuity were placed upon the market, and occasionally sold to minor powers—the guns bought by the Transvaal just before the war are a good example. But these, although fully entitled to the titles "rapid-firing", "tir-accéleré", or any of the other similar designations rife at the time, were not true "quick-firers" in that they were lacking in the essential quality of immobility in action.

It is to the French that the honour of being the first to solve the problem unquestionably belongs. They had re-armed their artillery in 1896-7, and it soon began to be whispered that their new guns were something far in advance of anything known elsewhere. They claimed indeed to be able to get a rate of fire of from twenty to thirty rounds a minute, and showed their faith in the justice of their claim by reducing all their batteries from six guns to four, and by radically modifying the tactical rôle of their artillery. The manœuvres of 1900 saw the debut of the famous "75's", and the batteries—guarded by the police against too close examination—were the cynosure of all eyes. But it was to be some years yet before they were to be seen at practice, and still more before their secret was to be disclosed. Their design and manufacture, and the success with which their secret was kept[1], form perhaps the most remarkable achievement in the history of artillery armament.

In England efforts to improve the horse and field guns had culminated in six experimental batteries of new and converted 12-pr. and 15-pr. B.L. equipments, and these were under trial in September 1899. Their chief feature was the addition of a spade suspended from the axle, but while it saved time and toil in running up, this spade

---

[1] It was not known even whether the buffer was hydraulic or hydro-pneumatic.

accentuated the jump, thus necessitating relaying for every round. It did, however, undoubtedly admit of a very considerable increase in the rate of fire, and when war broke out it was, therefore, decided to fit these axle spades to all guns sent from home to South Africa. To meet requirements for the new batteries being raised further improvements of mechanisms and other minor modifications were introduced which eventually resulted in the 12-pr. Mk. IV on Mk. II carriage and the 15-pr. Mk. IV on Mk. IV carriage.

To return now to Sir Henry Brackenbury's resolution to tide over the critical period by purchasing guns abroad. Among the establishments visited by his emissaries was an engineering firm at Dusseldorf, the "Rheinische Metallwaaren und Machinenfabrik" hitherto unknown as gunmakers. Here an extremely clever engineer, Herr Ehrhardt, exhibited to Major Turner[1] a 15-pr. equipment in which the whole of the recoil was taken up by a top-carriage so that the carriage itself remained absolutely steady when the gun was fired. Major Turner reported that a coin placed upon the tyre of the wheel had not been shaken off, and our Military Attachés at Berlin—two gunners in succession[2]—corroborated it. Here was proof positive that the tales told of the French "75's" were not the fables that many had thought—the true Q.F. field gun for which everyone had been searching had been found at last. An order was given to the firm for the whole equipment of the field artillery of an army corps, with three batteries for reserve, proof, etc., eighteen batteries in all, with their ammunition and other wagons, spare parts and stores, and five hundred rounds a gun.

The whole transaction had, however, to be carried through with the utmost secrecy, for in the then state of feeling in Europe, and especially in Germany, public opinion

---

[1] Colonel A. H. P. Turner, R.A., d. 1929.

[2] Lieut.-General Sir J. Grierson, K.C.B., Colonel-Commandant, d. 1914, and Brigadier-General W. H. H. Waters, C.M.G., C.V.O.

would never have tolerated the idea of providing Great Britain with such an accession to her strength. The inspection[1] of the material was carried out at the factories, and each battery was despatched, as soon as completed, to Hamburg for shipment. Sixteen ships were chartered for the service, the material was all packed in cases, especially marked and numbered, and consigned as "Machinery and Explosives". It was arranged with the Customs that cases so marked should be delivered on inward sufferance without examination—their contents known only to the representative of the consignees, and to the heads of departments, civil and military, most closely concerned, not more than half-a-dozen in all.[2]

During the autumn of 1900 this great mass of packing cases accumulated in the Arsenal. They contained:—

Guns—mounted on their carriages ...	108
Limbers	275
Ammunition Wagons	162
Forge, Store, etc. Wagons	54
Ammunition—complete rounds ...	54,000

It was not until the last case had arrived that the secret was revealed, and then no concealment was made.[3] The effect was instantaneous and profound. The artillery of what was then termed "The Aldershot Army Corps" was once more fit to take the field, and with an armament

---

[1] The fuzes were a new departure in our service in that they were carried in the shell. For their safety a certificate was accepted from a foreign artillery officer who guaranteed that they had been so carried in the service to which he belonged for 14 years without accident.

[2] One day an excited foreman rushed into the office of the Royal Gun Factory to say that "one of those packing cases on the quay had broken open and there is a gun inside". The Superintendent, equally in the dark, made speed to the War Office to tell of the discovery and ask what it meant.

[3] Herr Ehrhardt asked if he might exhibit a gun in the Earls Court Exhibition of 1901, and the War Office had "no objection". The particulars appeared in List of Changes, § 10726 of November, 1901.

markedly in advance of that of any Great Power except France. There might be defects in detail, especially as regards interchangeability, and there were many differences from what was customary in English equipments, which were an annoyance to English users; but it was obvious to all who saw the guns at practice—as all were free to do—that they were real quick-firers. Not the least of the benefits derived from their purchase was the object-lesson they afforded to artillery officers, especially those about to be entrusted with the business of re-armament, as to what they might fairly demand of the designers. They saw in the Ehrhardts for the first time what "long-recoil" really meant.[1]

It was not only the field artillery whose armament was deficient when the War broke out. The siege artillery had only 6″ howitzers, and it was known that Pretoria had been defended by modern forts armed with powerful guns. For the attack of these such weapons had neither the requisite range nor power, and again the Director-General of Ordnance looked abroad. He had armed the artillery on which we relied for home defence with guns from Germany: for howitzers of sufficient power to deal with the Transvaal fortifications he went to Austria. Here in outline is the story of how he obtained them.

In November 1899 it had come to his knowledge that the firm of Skoda of Pilsen had in stock four 24cm howitzers on mobile mountings, and that a German agent was negotiating with the firm with a view to purchase. Their ultimate destination would in that case presumably be the Transvaal, and so Sir Henry stepped in. By the end of February 1900 he had effected a deal. Officers were despatched to Pilsen to learn the working of the howitzers; a company was placed under readiness to embark, its orders stating that it would be equipped with four howitzers of large calibre, and should therefore be drilled and re-

---

[1] There were many amusing stories of the surprise shown by those who saw them fired for the first time. "Their guts are all coming out" was the first impression, sometimes more idiomatically expressed.

ceive as much practical instruction as possible with the available weapons of that description at its station. It was made up to war establishment with observers (specialists) from the two siege companies left at home, and with reservists selected as far as possible from those having some knowledge of siege work. A provisional handbook of the "9·45" (as it was named) was got out, and copies sent to the company—"not to be opened until after the ship had left Gibraltar".

Meanwhile a steamer had been acquired, and on the 25th March she sailed from Trieste "direct to Shanghai". But she put into Gibraltar, and there discharged her cargo on to the New Mole, thence to be reloaded into a freight ship which arrived from England on the 6th April. The labour employed was military working parties, and there was some delay, although they worked night and day. The soldiers were unaccustomed to the work and to sailors' methods, and the cases were large and difficult to handle. There were complaints by both sides, but all these delays were of little account compared with the unfortunate blunder of the Harbour-Master who posted the ship as carrying "stores for Government from Trieste" instead of "general cargo and in for coal" as had been arranged. The inevitable results followed. There were paragraphs in the Austrian newspapers, and Trieste became suspicious about cargoes for Shanghai. Another steamer had to be found to bring the balance of the thousand rounds a gun contracted for, but in this case the cargo was transhipped at Gibraltar without being landed, and thanks to this precaution there was no hitch in the proceedings. This account may be appropriately closed with a few words from a private letter :—

"I don't think we shall have any trouble, for we were able to keep a promise we made on the last occasion to procure decorations from the —— Government for two of the head officials who helped us".

As will be told in the Volume giving the account of the South African War, the howitzers reached their destination without further adventures, and were handed over to the company sent out to man them. But their services were not required, and so when trouble started in China they were sent on to their original destination after firing, it is believed, only one round.[1] Here again they were disappointed, for Peking, like Pretoria, had been captured without their aid, and they found their way back to England without having had the opportunity to prove their worth.

---

[1] Sir Stanley von Donop was on his way with some mounted infantry to withdraw a picquet on a hill just outside Pretoria which had been attacked. The officer commanding the 9·45″ howitzers, who had been waiting for weeks for the chance of a shot, spotted the object of the mounted infantry and promptly supported them by firing a round over their heads which fell just where the picquet had been, and scared away the Boers.

CHAPTER II.

THE REGIMENT.

The Regiment at Home—The Army Corps Scheme—The Brigading of Horse and Field Batteries—Battery Titles and Precedence—The School of Gunnery—The Regiment in India—The War Memorial.

CHAPTER II.

The Regiment at Home.

IN the last chapter an account was given of the more important measures carried out by the officers responsible for artillery matters at the War Office during the South African War.[1] In this chapter the effect of these, and of other war measures, upon the Regiment at large will be traced.

In May 1900 there remained at Home only two horse and twelve field batteries. Of the latter only half were even nominally serviceable, and in these none of the subalterns had more than six months service. During the year new batteries were rapidly raised, but these were batteries only by courtesy. Their section commanders were all young and inexperienced, and many of them had not passed through the Academy, or indeed received any military training, while the immaturity of the men is shown by the constant complaints regarding their poor physique—a matter of importance now that "running up by hand" was becoming a fashionable method of occupying a position.[1] In many cases batteries did no practice as units, but sent "details" which were formed into composite batteries at the practice camp, and drilled under the gunnery instructor.[2] On the other side of the picture,

---

[1] There were in consequence trials of different methods of running up with dragropes, &c., &c.

[2] It may be of interest to put on record the composition of these details at Okehampton in 1900:—

1st	Details from	V. W, X, Y Batteries.	
2nd	,,	,, 97, 98, 99	,,
3rd	,,	,, 113, 114, 115	,,
4th	,,	,, ⎱ 116, 117, 118	,,
5th		⎰	
6th	,,	,, 119, 120 121	,,

THE REGIMENT.

however, a new generation of battery commanders was coming on, bred up in modern methods of gunnery, stimulated by war experience, eager for further progress.

How garrison companies were sent out to South Africa, either with 4·7″ or 5″ guns on travelling carriages, or to take over from the Navy the guns which they had taken into the field on improvised mountings, has been told in the last chapter. It was plain that in future the Royal Horse and Royal Field Artillery could no longer enjoy a monopoly of the Field Army Artillery—the Royal Garrison Artillery had earned its right to a share. But to rely on being able to take companies from coast artillery at a time of what might well be a national emergency was obviously to court disaster, and various proposals for the provision of such batteries in combination with siege artillery were considered. They all fell through, however, and during the war-years nothing was done beyond the insertion of a paragraph in *Field Artillery Training* to the effect that three companies of garrison artillery, formed as a brigade, would be included in the corps artillery.

Only two of the four "Siege Train" companies had been sent out to South Africa, and only one of these had been expanded to two batteries in accordance with the scheme.[1] Even so the siege companies left at home had been reduced to a parlous condition, and the idea of forming a "Siege and Fortress" branch of the garrison artillery, on a similar footing to mountain artillery, was revived. Five years earlier it had been suggested that such a branch might well be constituted out of the siege companies at home and in India, together with the heavy batteries in the latter country, and there had been desultory discussion with India. But the proposed conversion of the Indian heavy batteries into field howitzer batteries put them out of court, and a proposal to form the new branch of the siege companies alone had to be dropped for financial reasons owing to its involving the formation of a fourth siege com-

CHAPTER II.
The Regiment at Home.

---

[1] Vol. I, Chapter XIV.

22   THE WAR YEARS.

CHAPTER II.
The Regiment at Home.

pany in India. Nothing daunted, the advocates of a separate branch now proposed that the siege companies should be combined with the heavy batteries which were to be formed at home to constitute a "Siege and Position" branch. The somewhat unusual step of calling upon the senior officers of the Regiment for their views was taken, and as opinions were about equally divided it was decided not to proceed with the scheme. Thus when the war-years closed the siege companies were still left with reversion to coast defence awaiting them as soon as they had attained proficiency in their work as siege artillerymen.

In coast defence these years had brought a great revival of interest as a result of the ill-feeling towards the British Empire previously alluded to, and under the auspices of the Institution Mr. Jane[1] drove home the lesson in lectures at Woolwich and the great coast fortresses. These lectures, and the discussions which followed them, in which many of the leaders of opinion, naval and military, took part, did much to counteract the unfortunate impression that coast artillerymen would never be called upon to fight their guns in earnest. There were joint naval and military trials at Plymouth in 1900 to test the attack by torpedo-craft and the defence by quick-firing guns, and manœuvres in the Mediterranean in which the coast defences of the great fortresses stood on guard against naval attack by day and night. Revised instructions for the preparation of defence schemes were issued, and the responsibility of the coast artillery in the "Regulation of Traffic in Defended Ports in Time of War" was extended.[2] Most important of all, the adequacy of the artillery garrisons for fighting the armament was seriously tackled for the first time. It had not been unknown for changes in armament to be made without any reference to those responsible for providing the men, but in 1901, as a result of the combined naval and military exercises in that and the preceding year, a com-

---

[1] Mr. F. T. Jane, author of *Jane's Fighting Ships*.
[2] First recognized in *Garrison Artillery Training, 1899*.

THE REGIMENT. 23

mittee under Colonel Bally[1] was appointed to consider the question. It is to that committee that the coast artillery owe the adoption of definite principles for the calculation of the number of men required to man their guns, which resulted in the introduction of "Manning Tables" in 1903.

CHAPTER II.

The Regiment at Home.

An important change was also made in the position of the "specialists". These had been added when the scientific progress in the XIXth century had caused the *matériel* to forge ahead of the *personnel* owing to the low general standard of education. The theory was that with a district establishment of skilled men to carry out such duties as laying, range-taking, &c., the actual working of the guns could be left to less highly trained men in the companies.[2] The result was that each elaboration of equipment had come to mean the creation of a new brand of specialist until the coast artillery was eaten up with them. There were many difficulties in connection with the existence of this considerable body outside the company organization, and in 1901 the layers and a proportion of the range-takers and telephonists were transferred to companies, but with the position-finders and machinery gunners a considerable number were still left in the district establishments.

Another step authorized during the war-years, with the object of setting free more men in the companies for military duties, was the replacement of those employed on semi-military work by reservists and discharged soldiers.

Much was also done during the war-years to render service in the coast artillery more attractive. The concentration of the companies in comfortable central barracks where the amenities of garrison life could be enjoyed, was undoubtedly to the taste of the majority of all ranks, although there were some who deplored the separation of the men from their guns.

---

[1] Major-General J. F. Bally, c.v.o., d. 1913.
[2] The famous Royal Commission of 1859 had gone still further, for they had considered it unnecessary to take into account at all the number of gunners required to man the vast armament they recommended, on the ground that these could be obtained so easily from the civil population.

CHAPTER II.

The Army Corps Scheme.

Ever since the Franco-German War the basis of army organization had been in theory the Army Corps, but in practice, except for the "Army Aldershot Corps", there had been little trace of this organization. A few months before the end of the South African War, however, Mr. Broderick, the Secretary of State for War, launched upon a somewhat astonished country the grandiose "Army Corps Scheme" associated with his name.[1] The whole of the troops in the United Kingdom were divided into six "Commands", each of which was to provide an army corps and a cavalry brigade on mobilization, although in three out of the six a considerable proportion of the troops, and especially the artillery, were to be furnished "from auxiliary sources". Impractical and short-lived as the scheme proved, it is notable regimentally as having introduced several important reforms in artillery command and organization. It may, indeed, be claimed for it that it was the first attempt to deal with the thorny subject of artillery command on any definite principle. Thus in each of the first three commands—Aldershot, Salisbury, Ireland —a Major-General was appointed to command the whole of the artillery of the army corps, and a Colonel to command the corps artillery. There was some attempt also in these commands to collect the corps artillery and constitute it as a real unit, and to allot the divisional artillery to its divisions. And further, a matter of great importance to the coast artillery, the scheme recognized "Fortresses and Defended Ports" as separate military organizations outside the Field Army, although it still included them in the "Commands".

The war was just drawing to a close, and it was assumed that with the return of the army from South Africa the distribution of the field batteries would be :—

Home	... ...	105 ⎫
India	... ...	42 ⎪
South Africa ...	... ...	3 ⎬ 151
Egypt	... ...	1 ⎭

[1] By a "Special" Army Order of March, 1902. The army corps organization is more fully discussed in Chapter VI.

This would provide the full complement of field artillery for five out of the six army corps, and the sixth might well depend upon "auxiliary sources" for its guns as for so much else. The transfer in 1903 of a howitzer brigade to the Indian establishment was the first blow, but it was anticipated that a new brigade would be raised to replace it;[1] the real obstacle to the realization of the scheme as far as the artillery was concerned was the want of accommodation at home. The utmost for which barracks could be found in the United Kingdom was 90 batteries, and 26 of these were in stations pronounced unsuitable for artillery occupation.[2] The only solution was to defer the return of batteries from South Africa, and, regrettable as such a course was, it had to be accepted. Instead, therefore, of the distribution shown above, the actual distribution in 1903/4 was:—

Home	...	...	...	90
India	...	...	...	45
South Africa	...	...	...	15
Egypt	...	...	...	1

Total: 151

Funds were allotted liberally enough for the building and reconditioning of barracks, but it must be years before these were available for occupation, and meanwhile the bringing home of the six batteries surplus to the latest decision as regards the garrison of South Africa was a matter of urgency. So came into being Borden "Camp".

The most casual perusal of Vol. I of this History will have shown that the successive reorganizations which

---

[1] This was delayed for want of accommodation, and then dropped out.

[2] Birmingham, Bradford, Bristol, Coventry, Leeds, Sheffield, Trowbridge, Weedon, Athlone, Ballinrobe, Belturbet, Clogheen, Cork, Fermoy, Fethard, Limerick, Longford, Waterford. The great majority were single battery stations, and many were long-abandoned cavalry barracks built in or near industrial towns during the Chartist troubles. They had, for the most part, no ground for battery training beyond the barrack squares, and were so scattered that brigade training was out of the question. Those, who were fortunate enough to serve in them will, however, recall their social and sporting attractions.

26 THE WAR YEARS.

CHAPTER II.

The Brigading of Horse and Field Batteries.

formed so large a part of regimental history during the latter half of the XIXth century had one characteristic in common. Administrative convenience in peace rather than tactical efficiency in war was ever the ruling factor. A suggestion that there might be some connection between military organization and tactical requirements had indeed been made by Lord Harris's Committee of 1888, but had been dismissed as "based principally upon tactical requirements", and therefore beyond their purview. General Marshall's Committee of 1898 faced the issue, with the following definite declaration:—

"The problem is complicated by many considera-
"ations; of these the Committee attribute the greatest
"importance to tactical efficiency, and therefore consider
"that any reorganization of horse and field artillery
"must be based upon the recognition of the tactical unit
"now called the brigade-division, and that all other
"matters should give way to the full development of
"the Lieut.-Colonel's command".

Their hand had been greatly strengthened by an incident which had occurred in the previous year. The first muttering of the coming storm in South Africa had caused the despatch of a field artillery brigade to Natal. But under the system then in force the batteries to compose it had to be those at the top of the roster for foreign service. And so the batteries were assembled from three different stations, the lieut.-colonel and adjutant from two more.[1] Two years later, when the storm had almost burst, and a brigade had to be hurried out from India, a similar procedure was followed[2]—and this in spite of the definite adoption of the brigade as the tactical unit, and the attention paid to its training which had formed such a marked

---

[1] The lieut.-colonel from Aldershot, the adjutant from Hilsea, the batteries from Dorchester, Woolwich, and Weedon.

[2] The batteries were sent from Secunderabad, Ahmednagar, and Deesa; the lieut.-colonel from Lucknow; and the adjutant from Rawalpindi.

THE REGIMENT.

feature of Sir Evelyn Wood's command at Aldershot. A more striking commentary on the divorce between training and administration could scarcely be imagined.

It was not as if experience were lacking. The despatch of oversea expeditions was no novelty in our history. Sir Augustus Frazer, who commanded the horse artillery at Waterloo, had exposed the consequences of similar action at that time in words which might well have been applied at Home or in India eighty years later:—

CHAPTER II.

The Brigading of Horse and Field Batteries.

"On its being intended to send out an expedition "from England . . . . the companies are generally—"indeed it might be said always—at different stations, "usually belong to different Battalions of Artillery, "and, as may be supposed, are frequently in different "states of readiness and efficiency. . . . . In this "situation it becomes the duty of the Senior Artillery "Officer . . . . to determine how an organized body "shall be formed out of the component parts which "successively arrive from different stations at the point "of debarkation. Let it be supposed that the com-"ponent parts are all separately good, that the officers "and men are well equipped and well instructed, ... "the horses strong and well trained. Yet, even on this "supposition, these parts must be unknown to each "other; there must be a want of unity of system".

The same thing had happened when it was decided to form field batteries for the Crimea. The eight companies first for service were assembled at Woolwich, and men and horses were transferred to them from all over the country.

The lesson had, however, been learnt at last. The war had been but two months in progress when the possibility of giving permanence to the brigades in South Africa was being considered at the War Office, and in 1900 it was decided:—

(i) To make the three batteries which had long been held to be the tactical unit of field artillery required in

28 THE WAR YEARS.

Chapter II.

The Brigading of Horse and Field Batteries.

modern European warfare, the permanent administrative unit in peace time.

(ii) To group the whole of the field batteries in threes in the roster for foreign service.[1]

(iii) To proceed at once with the appointment of a full staff for each brigade in South Africa and at Home.

Before the end of the year the system had been extended to the horse artillery, but with two batteries only in the brigade, so as to fit in with the organization of the corps artillery.

Battery Titles and Precedence.

In 1889 the batteries of horse artillery had been "lettered" and the field batteries numbered according to their seniority, and in 1901 this simple method was extended to the garrison companies, and the cumbrous geographical designations, meaningless to the Royal Artillery, disappeared. Instead, however, of following the natural order of seniority, as in the field artillery, the garrison companies were unfortunately numbered according to their place on the roster for foreign service, and the same thing was done with the horse and field artillery brigades. There was widespread resentment, for the senior units of all branches found themselves deprived of their pride of place. Thus the Chestnut Troop lost the "right of the line" by being put into the Vth Brigade, the 1st Field Battery, the senior of all, found itself in the XLIIIrd Brigade, and the garrison companies were similarly displaced.[2] Those who objected were put off with the mysteries of rosters and reliefs, and were told that sentiment must be subordinated to such practical matters. But the grievance was brought to the notice of the King when

---

[1] There was one battery over, and the 56th in Egypt therefore remained unbrigaded for some years. The field batteries were first shown in brigades in the Army List for January, 1901, the horse batteries in March.

[2] It was under consideration in 1913-14 to renumber the garrison companies according to seniority as explained in Chapter XIV.

THE REGIMENT.

he visited Woolwich in 1904, and this was followed up by a letter from Sir Arthur Bigge in which he expressed His Majesty's hope that "when the question of the reorganization of the artillery is finally settled it will be found practicable to restore the old Chestnut Troop to its position: the King can see no reason why this should not be done". Such a communication could not be disregarded, and in 1906 the brigades of horse and field artillery were renumbered to correct such anomalies—to the expressed satisfaction of the Colonel-in-Chief.

The honours being won by batteries in the field in South Africa directed attention to the loss which the Regiment had sustained by the disappearance of many batteries which had rendered distinguished service. The raising of so many new batteries offered an opportunity, and it was therefore decided that in order to perpetuate the distinguished services of old units of Horse, Field, and Garrison Artillery which had at various times been reduced, certain batteries and companies should be considered as reformed from the reduced units, and should carry on their traditions. This decision was promulgated in Army Order 112 of 1901, which contained lists showing the batteries and companies, and the reduced units from which they were respectively to be considered as reformed.[1]

Another manifestation of the same desire to perpetuate former honours may be found in the claims which were made during the war-years by various batteries to have such titles as "The Eagle Troop", "The Rocket Troop", etc., officially recognized. The Commander-in-Chief (Lord Roberts) and the Secretary of State decided, however, in April 1902 that titles should not be granted to artillery units except in the case of "The Chestnut Troop", by which

---

[1] It was slightly amended in January 1902 owing to changes in the designation of Bengal Troops brought to notice by Major-General F. W. Stubbs, the historian of the Bengal Artillery. One of the troops whose traditions it had been proposed to carry on was a native troop which had mutinied and taken a leading part in the defence of Delhi.

30   THE WAR YEARS.

CHAPTER II.

The School of Gunnery.

designation "A" Battery R.H.A. had been known since the Peninsular War.

An event of far-reaching importance in the History of the Regiment was the acquisition of Salisbury Plain in 1899. Only one brigade practised there in that year, but its value was at once apparent, and the representative of the Regiment at Headquarters was quick to seize the opportunity for a long-needed move of the School of Gunnery for Horse and Field Artillery.

Even at the time of the creation of this school in 1891 it had been obvious that Shoeburyness was anything but a suitable headquarters. It is true that the Commandant became *ex officio* Commandant at Okehampton in the summer, and was then able to carry out practice under more or less service conditions. But even in the summer there was a certain amount of instructional work at Shoeburyness, and throughout the winter the whole of the staff were occupied there with courses and gunnery problems, such as trials of systems of ranging and so forth. It is unnecessary to labour the unsuitability of the sand ranges for such work, or the inconvenience of the move from Shoeburyness to Okehampton and back again every year; but there was no alternative, for none of the practice camps then in use were possible as winter quarters. With the acquisition of Salisbury Plain the opportunity came. In January 1900 Colonel Hay, the Assistant Adjutant-General for Royal Artillery, pressed for the move to ground where work could be carried out over country similar to much to be found on the Continent, and where gunnery need no longer be divorced from tactics. This last serious bar to efficiency had been the point on which General Williams had based his attack on the school when first formed; and Sir Evelyn Wood, now Adjutant-General, pressed the point, citing the experience of the war then in progress "where every day indicates the importance of raising the tactical and fire efficiency of our artillery". The Secretary of State approved of "this much needed

THE REGIMENT. 31

change", and in June 1900 a Board recommended that Netheravon should be handed over.

Alas, the school failed to realize its good fortune. Difficulties were raised as to the accommodation of all sorts, more especially as to the suitability of Netheravon and Syrencote for conversion into quarters for the staff, their distances from the ranges, and so forth. The matter dragged on for two or three years more, and was eventually shelved on account of the opposition of the school, in spite of Colonel Hay's repeated attempts. A dozen years were to pass before the chance came again, and during those years the development of Salisbury Plain as the artillery practice camp *par excellence* was to be in other hands. It is perhaps the only blemish on the school's escutcheon.

Within a month of this attempt to get the Horse and Field School of Gunnery moved from Shoeburyness a committee on Garrison Artillery Instruction and Training under Lieut.-General J. F. Owen[1] presented its report, and this contained very important recommendations affecting the work of the School of Gunnery in connection with both Siege and Coast Artillery. As regards the latter the dominating idea was that all instruction should be under the officer commanding the Royal Artillery in the fortress, who should be given sufficient staff for the purpose, and, as a corollary, that the branches of the School of Gunnery at Portsmouth, Plymouth, etc. (the establishment of which had been such a feature of the revival of coast artillery training in the 90's) should be localized. The school of Gunnery at Shoeburyness would then be retained as the centre of garrison artillery instruction, charged with the training of the officers and non-commissioned officers of the instructional staff, and for this purpose it was recommended that the Long Course should be extended to twelve months, and become a "Gunnery Staff Course". The result of these recommendations

CHAPTER II.

The School of Gunnery.

---

[1] General Sir John F. Owen, K.C.B., Colonel-Commandant, d. 1924

CHAPTER II.

The School of Gunnery.

will appear when considering the history of the Coast Artillery in the following years, but the proposals to move the Horse and Field School from Shoeburyness, and to localize the Coast Artillery Branch Schools, both made in the early months of 1900, are mentioned here as important repercussions of the War affecting the School of Gunnery.

The "Owen" Committee had also recommended that, in view of the probability that the extended use of guns of position in South Africa would obtain in future wars, all garrison companies should be given some training in their use, for which purpose the school at Lydd should be further developed. In consequence of this recommendation, as will be told later, the Royal Military Repository at Woolwich was closed as a school of instruction in May 1900, and the remainder of the staff transferred to Lydd where, for the past ten years, the Superintendent of the Repository had acted as Commandant during the practice season. Thus Lydd became the Siege Artillery Branch of the School of Gunnery, charged also at first with instruction in the use of guns of position.

It was, however, far from being an ideal site for such a purpose. Selected originally for the "Lydd Experiments" of the 80's on account of the absence of inhabitants, it had gradually drifted into being a summer practice camp and a place for Ordnance Committee experiments. In the very year that saw its establishment as the Siege Artillery School its best range was appropriated for musketry, and this although the remaining area only allowed of practice up to some four thousand yards, and all South African experience pointed to the necessity for long-range fire. Nor was the inadequacy of range its only defect. An absolutely level plain of shingle covered with scrub it offered no possibility of practice by the siege artillery in the use of their observation of fire instruments except from artificial observing stations constructed for the purpose. For guns of position it was equally unsuitable, for the mirage upset their direct laying—then the normal method —and the deep shingle made movement almost impossible.

THE REGIMENT. 33

Year after year there were inquiries, and the conclusion arrived at with greater confidence on each occasion was that the ranges were quite unsuited for their purpose as regards both their extent and nature, and that the School should be moved to a locality where ground suited to the requirements of modern siege and heavy artillery training was available.

If, like the Horse and Field, the Siege Branch of the School of Gunnery was condemned to unsuitable ground for some years longer it was through no fault of its own. A movement was commencing which, gathering strength from year to year, was to effect a fundamental change in siege artillery training. For the experience of the large number of garrison companies which, in addition to the siege companies, had been working in the field in South Africa, had shown the necessity of relaxing the rigid siege artillery methods for such work. The chief point of interest in the practice of 1901 was the inclusion of some series for 6″ howitzers fired off the ground without platforms. Such a proceeding was quite outside anything contemplated in *Siege Artillery Drill 1900*, which had indeed shown little advance on its predecessor of 1896 except in legislating for breech-loading instead of muzzle-loading howitzers.

The requirements of India in artillery in all its varied aspects were exhaustively discussed during the war-years, from the broad question of the proportion of guns to bayonets in the field army to the rival merits of guns and howitzers for heavy batteries.

The mobilization of the horse, field, and mountain artillery had been considered by a committee at Simla in 1898, and the report of this committee, with the views of the Indian authorities on the subject were sent home during the autumn of 1899. The state of affairs was indeed sadly in need of examination. Like all other British troops in India the artillery had no reserves to fall back upon, but, unlike the cavalry and infantry, artillery units were not maintained in peace at an estab-

CHAPTER II.

The School of Gunnery.

The Regiment in India.

lishment sufficient to enable them to mobilize without assistance. While the peace establishments of regiments and battalions allowed of their proceeding at war strength after discarding their "unfits", the peace and war establishments of batteries were practically the same. Since then there must always be some "unfits" who must be left behind, the mobilization of the artillery meant a general post of men and horses in which every battery had to take part. Such a scheme obviously transgressed every principle of war organization, and it was now proposed to apply the same principle to the artillery of the field army as was in force in the other arms, and to make up for the increased establishment of these batteries by reducing that of the remainder. Thus came into being the two Indian establishments—"higher" and "lower".

It did not, however, escape the notice of critics that the proportion of artillery allotted to the field army was far below that considered necessary in Europe. At home efforts were being made to bring the proportion of guns up to five or six per thousand; India seemed contented with three—and a considerable proportion of these only mountain guns. The locking up of more than half the mobile artillery in "obligatory garrisons" while the field army was so inadequately gunned appeared absurd to the critics at home until they learnt that the garrisons were of districts not of places, and that mobility was the very essence of their power to deal with local risings.

To return to the field army. The real crux of all artillery mobilization—the provision of ammunition columns —was accentuated in a country in which there were no European reservists, and no suitable horses in civil life which could be drawn upon. The only reserve was the batteries of the Hyderabad Contingent,[1] and there was no getting away from the necessity of adding the nuclei at any rate of ammunition columns to the peace establishment of the artillery in India. Before the war was over the

---
[1] See p. 2.

THE REGIMENT. 35

horses were ready in the depôts, and in 1902/3 the nuclei of five horse and seven field artillery columns were in existence.

The brigade organization for the horse and field artillery, when first communicated to India, had met with strenuous opposition on both economical and political grounds, but the War Office were firm. The Government of India were informed in June 1900 that the system had been definitely decided upon for the Imperial Service, and that it therefore became absolutely necessary that it should be recognised in India and adopted as soon as possible. There was no further hesitation and, although it was not proposed to extend the system in its entirety to the mountain artillery, steps were taken, as will appear later, to bring batteries to camp together under lieut.-colonels in view of the fact that on service they would probably have to work in brigade.

It was not only in number of guns that the field army artillery in India was deficient; it suffered also from the want of any field howitzers, and South African experience was showing their value daily. The first idea was to convert the heavy batteries, but the value of such batteries was being manifested even more strikingly than that of the field howitzers, so that such a step would be a flouting of war experience. Conversion was also hedged about with legal difficulties as already mentioned, while to reduce companies of garrison artillery and raise batteries of field artillery in their place, would throw the delicate machinery of drafts and reliefs out of gear. It was eventually decided to add a field howitzer brigade to the strength of the artillery in India, and the IVth Brigade was earmarked for India as soon as it could be spared from South Africa.

In mountain artillery the war years saw the raising of a new Indian mountain battery—the "Abbottabad"—and the formation of the "Frontier Garrison Artillery" out of the Punjab Garrison Battery. This corps was composed of Indian soldiers from both British and Indian mountain

CHAPTER II.
The Regiment in India.

batteries who had lost some of the activity required for work on the hill-side, but who were quite capable of garrison duty in the forts along the Frontier. The mountain batteries were thus relieved of the duty of finding sections for such employment—the worst use to which they could be put. But perhaps the greatest boon which these years brought to the mountain artillery was the issue of 10-pr. B.L. guns in place of the 2·5″ R.M.L. The batteries in India were no longer made a laughing-stock by such anachronisms as the black powder charges with their clouds of smoke, which gave away the positions of the British mountain batteries in South Africa so disastrously.

In this, and the preceding chapter mention has been made of the more important measures which affected the Regiment during the South African war. But no account of these "war-years" would be complete without reference to the steps taken by the Regiment to commemorate the memory of their comrades who had fallen in action, or died of wounds or disease during the campaign.

The Treaty of Vereeniging was signed on the 31st May 1902, and in the following January a Regimental Meeting, presided over by Lord Roberts, decided on the erection of a monument in London. To carry out the arrangements a working committee under Major-General Sir George Marshall was appointed.

It was hoped at first that the monument might be erected in Waterloo Place between the United Service and Athenæum Clubs, and a design and model for this site were prepared by Mr. W. R. Colton, A.R.A., to whom the task had been entrusted. Unfortunately this project had to be abandoned, and eventually the present site in the Mall received the approval of His Majesty. The alteration naturally involved a change of design, and considerable delay and expense, so that the monument was not ready until 1910. Even then much disapproval was expressed at the position of the names on the floor of the platform, where in wet weather they got covered with mud, and a further sum was required for their removal to the bronze

THE REGIMENT.

panels in the wall, bringing the total cost up to over eight thousand pounds.

The unveiling ceremony took place on the 20th July 1910, in combination with a Memorial Service in St. Paul's Cathedral.

The great space under the Dome was filled with a congregation representing all ranks of the Regiment, in which Cadets from the Royal Military Academy were faced by Pensioners from the Royal Hospital. On the steps a Guard of Honour was mounted by the Royal Garrison Artillery, Shoeburyness, with the R.G.A. Band from Portsmouth. At the West Door the Duke of Connaught was received by Lord Roberts, the Master-Gunner, and Sir Robert Biddulph, the senior Colonel-Commandant. In the Procession up the Nave the Chaplain-General and the aged Dean—supported by the Duke—were preceded by the Choir of the Cathedral and the Regimental Band (intermingled), and were followed by the General Officers of the Regiment.

During the service His Royal Highness, by pressing a button in the Cathedral, caused the covering to fall away from the Memorial in the Mall. Here a square had been formed in front of the shrouded monument, with a battery of the Royal Horse Artillery on the right, of the Royal Field Artillery on the left, and a Firing Party of the Royal Garrison Artillery from Sheerness in front. As the covering fell the firing party presented arms, the Last Post was sounded, the three volleys were followed by the Reveillé, and the ceremony closed with the National Anthem and the Regimental Slow March played by the Mounted Band. Shortly afterwards the Duke of Connaught arrived, together with many of those who had attended the service in St. Paul's, and the proceedings ended with a March Past of the troops.

PART II.
THE FIELD ARMY ARTILLERY.

CHAPTER III.

THE SOUTH AFRICAN INFLUENCE.

(1902—1904.)

The Manual of 1902—Concealment—Dispersion—Reconnaissance—Observation of Fire—The Practice Camps—Competitive Practice—Brigade Practice—Divisional Practice—Personal Equipment—Mechanization—India—The Manual of 1904.

Field Howitzers—Mountain Artillery—Heavy Artillery.

DURING the first few years after the South African War the experiences of the veldt were naturally paramount. Their influence had indeed made itself felt long before the war ended, for on the conclusion of its first phase, there had come home with Lord Roberts many senior artillery officers who had rendered conspicuous services, but for whom there was no scope in the guerilla warfare which was coming on. Prominent among them were Major-General Sir George Marshall,[1] who returned from the command of the Royal Artillery in South Africa to that at Aldershot; Major-General Sir William Knox,[2] who had held with skill and determination a section of the Ladysmith defences, and now went to the command of the artillery in Ireland; Colonel F. W. Eustace[3] who had been right-hand man to Sir John French with the horse artillery of the cavalry division, and was appointed Commandant of the School of Gunnery, Horse and Field; and

[1] Major-General Sir George H. Marshall, K.C.B., d. 1909.
[2] Major-General Sir William G. Knox, K.C.B., Colonel-Commandant, d. 1916.
[3] Major-General Sir Francis J. W. Eustace, K.C.B., Colonel-Commandant, d. 1925.

42   THE FIELD ARMY ARTILLERY.

Chapter III.
The Manual of 1902.

Colonel L. Parsons[1] who had gained a great reputation for his handling of the artillery in Natal, and now became Colonel-on-the-Staff II Army Corps and Commandant of the practice camp on Salisbury Plain.

These officers were thus placed in the positions in which their services could be of the greatest value in bringing the lessons of the war to bear upon the training of the field army artillery, and the first-fruits of their efforts appeared with commendable promptitude in the shape of *Field Artillery Training 1902*. For a full explanation of the "doctrine" with which the artillery had taken the field in South Africa, reference must be made to the previous volume of this history, but, to put it very briefly, it consisted in first silencing the enemy's artillery and then "preparing" the advance of the infantry by turning the guns on to the part of the enemy's position selected for attack. In order to carry out this programme it was considered necessary to bring into action from the earliest possible moment a number of guns superior to that of the enemy. But the war had not been long in progress before gunners began asking themselves what was to be done if the only result of bringing into action this imposing array of artillery was the arrival among them of shells from invisible guns, or bullets from equally invisible rifles? And when so-called pursuing columns were halted in South Africa at the fall of the first hostile shell, while the artillery were forced to waste invaluable time in attempting that quite impossible task "silencing the enemy's guns", they remembered how, many years before the war, General Sir W. J. Williams[2] had written: "Artillery are not taken into the field to fight artillery, perhaps our artillery duel is a phantom. There may be an artillery duel if a general has no plan. If a general knows how to strike, and sees where to strike, he will not wait for an artillery duel".

---

[1] Lieut.-General Sir Lawrence W. Parsons, K.C.B., Colonel-Commandant, d. 1923.

[2] See Vol. I.

THE SOUTH AFRICAN INFLUENCE. 43

Similarly, it was soon evident that the power of concealment given by long range and smokeless powder rendered the turning of the guns on to the point selected for attack prior to the infantry advance quite useless, while it warned the enemy of the intention. Many artillery officers shared the view of a foreign observer who summed the matter up:—"Many times it happened that ammunition and still more valuable energy were wasted on a fruitless bombardment without any profit accruing thereby to the infantry. When it came to the turn of the latter to advance everything still remained to be done; with what discouragement cannot be told, nor with what loss, for if discouragement is injurious in any state of life as a cause of helplessness, in war it is the first and surest factor of defeat".

It was borne in upon the more progressive thinkers in the Regiment that battles were no longer such straightforward affairs as had been inferred from the pre-war manual, that it was not always wise to put all your cards on the table, that the enemy would probably have the range to all likely positions, and that in consequence the mass methods and exposure in the open derived from the German practice of 1870 were out of date. It seemed that our tactics had not moved with the times; that our imagination had failed to visualize the effects of smokeless powder; and of the increase in the range, accuracy, and rapidity of fire of both guns and rifles. It was admitted that the effect of these changes had been accentuated by circumstances peculiar to the South African War—the large scale of the natural features of the country, and the clearness of the atmosphere, combined with the "unorthodox" methods of the enemy—but what the Boers had been able to do with a comparatively insignificant number of modern guns, used with cunning, had made a deep impression upon all who had fought against them.

There was at first a natural tendency towards an indiscriminate imitation of Boer methods, but this received little official encouragement. *Field Artillery Training 1902*

CHAPTER III.

The Manual of 1902.

44   THE FIELD ARMY ARTILLERY.

<small>CHAPTER III.</small> introduced no revolutionary changes in the principles governing the employment of artillery in the field, but it
<small>The Manual of 1902.</small> struck a fresh note from its opening page. The rigid adherence to regulation methods which had found expression in the phrase "Show it me in the book" might have been justifiable when the whole idea of fire tactics and fire discipline was not only new but unwelcome, and old adhesions had to be broken down however painful the process, but it was certainly out of date. The new manual took the line that what was required was not the jettisoning of established principles, but more flexibility in their application. Its preface roundly declared that a training manual could at best be but a guide for normal conditions: to meet the ever-varying circumstances of active service, officers must depend upon their powers of initiative, self-confidence, and resource. These were no longer to be checked by the enforcement of a rigid adherence to the very letter of the law, officers were to trust to their common-sense rather than to their memory. But it was recognized that if the leading-rein was to be cast off more attention must be given to the attainment and development of intelligence and self-reliance by military study. And there must be no slackening in the technical training. Freedom of tactical handling demanded gunnery of a high order—first and foremost the ability to shoot with accuracy from covered positions.

<small>Concealment.</small> It was the inability to shoot—and hit—from under cover that had been responsible for the discouragement given to the occupation of such positions in the last century. The batteries realized that with the appliances then available they were incapable from covered positions of giving their comrades of the other arms the support that they needed, and rather than fail in this their first duty, they were prepared to face the enemy in the open. It was magnificent but it was not war, at any rate as it could be waged with a European power armed with quick-firing guns. However much the gallantry of the batteries who fought it out in the open in South Africa might be admired,

THE SOUTH AFRICAN INFLUENCE. 45

it had to be admitted that only the want of methodical ranging and concentration on the part of the enemy saved them from annihilation.

The pre-war manual (F.A.D. 1896) had given, as the first requisite of a position for guns, a clear view of the targets over the sights and, after detailing other desirable attributes, had completed the list with "Lastly cover". Nothing could have been more definite. The post-war manual (F.A.T. 1902) took a very different line. After stating that the choice of the actual position depended mainly on tactical considerations, it continued "it may often be behind cover". The first task of the post-war artillery was, therefore, to face and solve the problem of practice from such positions, and the howitzer brigades showed the way.

Their first efforts at finding a method were elementary to a degree—almost childish in their simplicity. In 1901 the lines of fire were marked with aiming posts laid out by means of "laying cords" with which the layers measured off equal distances from the aiming posts planted by the battery commander. Such a system was obviously only applicable to the open undulations of our practice ranges, and what was wanted for war was a system which would enable batteries to take advantage of any description of cover or means of concealment available. For this they must have some means of getting the line of fire by observation and calculation from any point from which a view of the target could be obtained, and next year saw various appliances for doing so under trial—a "Director" on the lines of the German "Lining Plane", and for use in conjunction with it a "Field Plotter" devised by Lt.-Colonel H. G. Smith and Serjeant-Major O. Rooney of the School of Gunnery.[1] The next winter saw the "short field" courses at Shoeburyness trying out various methods of using these adjuncts, and before the practice season

CHAPTER III.

Concealment

---
[1] Major-General Sir Herbert Guthrie Smith, K.C.B., Colonel-Commandant, d 1930: and Captain Owen Rooney, d. 1934.

46   THE FIELD ARMY ARTILLERY.

CHAPTER III.

Concealment.

of 1903 a workable system had been promulgated, and the necessary "Indirect laying stores"[1] approved for the service. The "fishing-tackle" soon disappeared.

The system was, of course, dependent on accurate range-finding. The mekometer had superseded the telemeter[2] in the last century on account of being quicker and less conspicuous in working, and with the clearly defined targets then in use at practice, and expected in war, the fact that its accuracy depended upon two observers bringing their instruments to bear upon exactly the same point presented no great difficulty. But when the Boers showed that such targets were no longer to be counted upon in war, and targets at practice changed their character accordingly, the inaccuracy that resulted led to the re-introduction of the telemeter for howitzer batteries, and to some suggestion of its extension to gun batteries.

There still remained the difficulty of communication between the observing station and the battery. Megaphones were found too limited in range, a chain of orderlies repeating messages proved quite unreliable, and signallers had been abolished for horse and field artillery in 1899. Naturally enough battery commanders were reluctant to quit their guns for the observing station for fear of losing touch. So the Regiment took the matter into its own hands: amateur signallers sprang up as if by magic: their official recognition followed;[3] the semaphore proved admirably adapted to the requirements; and the "double chain" solved the problem until displaced by the telephone, which in 1903 was still "under consideration".

Dispersion.

Closely allied with the question of covered positions was that of the control of the fire of dispersed batteries. Napoleon, who never forgot that he was an artillery officer, was the first to inculcate the concentration of gun fire on the

---

[1] See Chapter V.

[2] The Telemeter had been introduced for "artillery in the field" in 1891, superseding the "Watkin Field Large" range-finder.

[3] Army Orders August 1903. The adjutant and at least one other officer per brigade were required to qualify at the School of Signalling, and the adjutant to act invariably as instructor to the brigade.

THE SOUTH AFRICAN INFLUENCE. 47

point of attack. "When once the combat has grown hot", he wrote, "the general who has the skill to unite an imposing mass of artillery suddenly, and without his adversary's knowledge, in front of some point of the hostile position may be sure of success". This was the accepted doctrine up to the South African War, but the Boers, untroubled by doctrinal theories, used their guns singly in well-placed and well-masked shelters, and the effect of their fire led to a great call for similar dispersion on our part. It was not realized that this effect existed chiefly in the minds of those who had seen much service without ever before experiencing the sensation of being the object of artillery fire; and that the scattered guns could never obtain any decisive result owing to their inability to concentrate their fire. "Extended order" became the cry of the day, and so far did the reaction extend that shortly after Sir Redvers Buller resumed the Aldershot Command he issued a memorandum on the training of artillery in which the independent action of single guns was inculcated. This was going too far, and the memorandum was cancelled before it had done any harm. It remained for Sir Evelyn Wood to point out that it depended upon the ground whether the great tactical principle of superiority of fire could best be attained by massing guns or dispersing them—"the handling of artillery so as to obtain concentrated fire required skill in the use of ground and in fire control, and to assert that concealment can rarely be obtained for guns unless used singly or in sections was to confess incapacity".

CHAPTER III.
Dispersion.

It was clear that the concealment in movement and in action now insisted upon could only be obtained by a far closer study of the ground than had obtained in the past. And there was the enemy to be thought of also. Failure to reconnoitre ground sufficiently thoroughly, and to ascertain that it was clear of hostile riflemen, had led to disaster in South Africa. There was general unanimity of opinion as to the necessity of every battery being able to do its own patrolling—a task which had not previously been considered

Reconnaissance.

CHAPTER III.

Reconnaissance.

as a part of the duty of the artillery. "It is better to have signallers of your own than to have to borrow them of the infantry, and scouts of your own than trust to the cavalry" was one of the lessons of the war. And since in the wide open spaces of a modern battlefield a battery commander intent on correcting the fire of his guns might well fail to notice some unexpected movement of friend or enemy, there came the recognition of "look-out" men as well as of patrols.

The reconnaissance of brigade and battery commanders ceased to be the hasty and almost perfunctory procedure of pre-war days, and became a real search in which judgment had to be exercised in reconciling the often conflicting claims of tactical and technical advantages. All this required time, so commanders had to get well ahead of their batteries,[1] and thus there came into being the "battery leader", and the study of the art of leading. To conform to the movements of the battery commander, to set a suitable pace, and to choose ground which would take the least out of the teams, and bring the battery on to the right spot without giving away its approach to the enemy, was no simple task. Then as the equipments became more complicated and delicate, section commanders and Nos. 1 were in turn pushed out to the front to avoid rough going and choose good platforms in action. What a different picture the advance of artillery into action in 1903 presented from that pictured by General Williams only a dozen years before.

To obtain the intelligent co-operation of all these links in the chain—patrols, ground-scouts, battery-leader, lookout men—battery commanders must train them to use their wits and their eyes. Many found it hard to get out of the old groove of teaching a soldier his trade as a parrot

---

[1] "I found on service that there was nothing battery commanders were so slow to learn as the importance of riding sufficiently ahead of their batteries to facilitate orders from the C.R.A. reaching them from the front and to get time to select the best route before their batteries were chock-a-block on top of them". (*General Parsons*).

THE SOUTH AFRICAN INFLUENCE. 49

is taught to talk. But the movement was greatly assisted by the appearance in the *Proceedings* of February, 1902, of a remarkable article by Colonel Parsons on *Training the Intelligence and Powers of Observation of Officers, Non-commissioned Officers, and Men*. It at once attracted widespread attention in all arms of the service, and went through many editions in pamphlet form.[1] The regular instruction of non-commissioned officers in map-reading and finding their way about a strange country, which had been enjoined by a Regimental Order as long before as 1889, but had never been seriously practised, became a regular part of the training,[2] and was encouraged by the issue of a dozen pairs of binoculars to each battery in 1903, and by the loan of mounted infantry cobs to those on the lower establishment.

Closely allied to this study of ground was the observation of fire. With the longer ranges and more difficult targets being introduced at practice camps, the weakness of many battery commanders in this respect became very apparent. Commandants spoke out strongly—"Bad observation is a fatal defect in an artillery officer"—"An officer who cannot range his battery properly is useless"— and they did not hesitate to recommend the removal of officers whose powers of observation did not seem likely to improve. Confidential reports by camp commandants on the capacity of each battery commander for fighting his battery were introduced, but it was recognized that opportunities for acquiring the faculty must be given, and for that purpose majors and captains were encouraged to attend the camps as spectators. At the same time it was realized that it was foolish to wait until an officer was

CHAPTER III.

Reconnaissance.

Observation of Fire.

---

[1] It was republished during the Great War, and again, by special request, during the writing of this volume.

[2] Before the manœuvres in 1903 the Royal Artillery of the II Army Corps trained over a hundred non-commissioned officers and men, (three despatch-riders and nine signallers from each brigade) to look after themselves and their horses, and find their way about the country.

50   THE FIELD ARMY ARTILLERY.

CHAPTER III.
Observation of Fire.

actually in command of a battery before giving him any practice in ranging, and it was arranged that each battery officer should fire a series during battery practice—shortly extended to include adjutants.

The attention thus paid to location of targets and observation of fire brought the question of telescopes and field glasses to the fore. There were lectures at the Institution and disquisitions on optics in the *Proceedings*, in which the advantages and disadvantages of the stereoscopic glasses just put on the market by Zeiss, as compared with the service "Galileans" were a fruitful subject of debate. But all were agreed that a good telescope was an essential part of the equipment of every brigade and battery in the field, instead of being only allowed to siege batteries as was then the regulation. In 1902 the "special signalling" telescope became the "Telescope Field Artillery Mk. II", and next year was fitted with sighting vanes and a saddle so that it could be used on the same stand as the newly introduced "director".

The Practice Camps.

With these developments in fire tactics and fire discipline there came a corresponding extension of the work of the practice camps, greatly stimulated by the addition of Salisbury Plain[1] to their number in 1901. At last the field artillery were in possession of a range on which the usual "practice camp conditions" were conspicuous by their absence, for the space was ample, and the ground, without being featureless, allowed of movement in all directions. Here, for the first time, brigade commanders could be given a free hand in the application of the accepted principles for the employment of artillery to an actual problem on the ground; here battery commanders could select their positions in accordance with their task unfettered by considerations of safety; here battery leaders could devote their attention to the use of the ground in

---

[1] The headquarters of the practice camp were at first at Bulford, where also huts were erected for the batteries practising. In 1904 headquarters moved to Larkhill.

THE SOUTH AFRICAN INFLUENCE. 51

accordance with the tactical requirements unhampered by the necessity of finding a practicable route between bogs and boulders; and here, finally, it was possible to demonstrate that fire discipline in a battery involved not only the accurate discharge of their technical duties by all ranks, but also the exercise of their intelligence and powers of observation.

No man could have been better fitted to make the most of the opportunities afforded by the new range than its first commandant, Colonel Parsons. Gifted with a bright and arresting way[1] of bringing out the lessons of the war, he was just the man to widen the scope of the training. Fortunately too, Sir Evelyn Wood[2] came to the command of the II Army Corps in 1901, and gave all possible support to the efforts of a man after his own heart, one who, as he wrote at the time, "is one of the best, if not the best, instructor I have met in the army".

The necessity for intimate combination between gun and rifle had been forced upon all by their experience in South Africa. Colonel Parsons, who had given such a lesson in this co-operation in Natal, made great efforts to obtain the actual presence of the other arms, so as to give reality to the training of the artillery on Salisbury Plain. Thanks to his efforts something was occasionally done in the way of attaching cavalry or yeomanry for reconnaissance, but the conflicting claims of regimental training were generally overpowering.[3] The want was especially

CHAPTER III.

The Practice Camps.

---

[1] When officers were lacking in initiative, and urged in excuse "It is not in the book", he used to turn on them with "Is there anything in the book to say you are not to do it?"

[2] A reform which is owed directly to Sir Evelyn Wood, is the periodical relief of depôt batteries at practice camps. As commander of an Army Corps he insisted upon carrying it out in spite of the School of Gunnery, and once tried it was taken up generally.

[3] The only artillery which habitually enjoyed the co-operation of infantry during their practice were the two horse batteries of the Honourable Artillery Company. Under the command of their Colonel, the Earl of Denbigh, who had served many years in the Royal Artillery, the infantry and artillery trained together on Salisbury Plain, to their mutual advantage.

CHAPTER III.

The Practice Camps.

felt as regards working with an escort, and the training of artillery patrols was made very difficult by the absence of any troops to represent the enemy.

Okehampton was still the summer headquarters of the School of Gunnery for Horse and Field Artillery. In spite of its obvious disadvantages when compared with Salisbury Plain, Dartmoor possessed certain characteristics of considerable value, and by an admirable arrangement the artillery of the I and II Army Corps used these ranges in alternate years, thus obtaining the advantages of both while avoiding too great familiarity with either.

For the IV Army Corps a new range was found at Trawsfynydd, where a regular practice camp was first formed in 1903. From that date the local ranges which had been used from time to time by the brigades quartered in the north of England dropped out—to the great benefit of their training. Next year the ground at Trawsfynydd was largely increased, but for some years no shelter of any kind was afforded for horse or man, and practice there often meant real hardship.

In Ireland, Glen Imaal, which had been acquired just before the war, proved a great improvement on the old range at Glenbeigh. Like Trawsfynydd the area first purchased was inadequate as anything but a shooting gallery, but it was enlarged in 1904, and it had one great advantage over all the other ranges in the possession of natural features—woods, banks, hedgerows—which were lacking elsewhere.

Among the most prominent lessons of the war was the comparative invisibility of the enemy. The camps vied with each other in devising targets which should more nearly represent what might be expected in war. Guns firing smokeless powder, the location of which had proved such a puzzle on the veldt, were a difficult problem, and it cannot be claimed that any real success was attained during this period. Better fortune attended the efforts to improve the representation of infantry advances for which a series of "surprise" targets pulled up in succession was adopted

THE SOUTH AFRICAN INFLUENCE. 53

in 1901—the familiar "jumpers" of many years to come. They proved invaluable in making batteries alert, in quickening ranging, and in accustoming battery commanders to distribute their fire in both depth and width. Deep "S" shaped Boer trenches filled with standing dummies tried the accuracy of ranging for elevation, fuze, and line. To represent the attacks of cavalry a new moving target on curved sheets of corrugated iron took the place of the old "barrel" targets.

Ranges, which had averaged only 2,000 yards in 1899, crept up steadily, reaching 2,300 in 1900, 2,600 in 1901, 3,200 in 1902, 3,600 in 1903, and (on Salisbury Plain) 4,000 in 1904.

This extension of range, combined with the reduction in the visibility of targets, introduced a new problem. "Pointing out the target" became an art in itself, and proved a great stumbling block to the majority of battery commanders until the introduction of the "clock code" system.

The scale of ammunition for practice was 400 rounds for battery practice with another 200 for brigade practice, but this last was only allowed to batteries at certain camps. In 1901 Okehampton was the only one so favoured: next year Salisbury Plain was promoted to the higher scale; and in 1904 Glen Imaal. At Trawsfynydd no battery got more than 400, and in the first year (1903) some got only 100—on the plea that they had only recently returned from active service.

All through the last decade of the XIXth century the conduct of competitive practice had been the subject of lively discussion. It had been made more and more practical until, in the last years, it had been extended to include the whole of the battery practice. But with the widening of the scope of the training after the war, there arose a very general feeling that instruction was still being too much subordinated to competition. The rules governing the competition denied to brigade commanders any opportunity for completing the training of their batteries

CHAPTER III.

The Practice Camps.

Competitive Practice.

CHAPTER III.

Competitive Practice.

Brigade Practice.

during their practice, and made it impossible for camp commandants to vary their schemes, rearrange their targets, or introduce special problems to suit the functions of particular equipments. It was therefore decided in 1901 to confine the competition within the brigade, and the field artillery dropped out of the contest for the Centenary Cup[1]. But even thus modified the spirit of competition still reacted unfavourably upon instruction, and so after 1904 batteries were "classified" throughout their battery practice, and wore the badge they had qualified for, irrespective of what others had done.

The South African War established the brigade as a permanent unit, and in spite of the exigencies of accommodation more than half the brigades had been brought together within three years (1900-1903). In a good many more brigades two out of the three batteries were concentrated, and all moved together under their lieut.-colonel in changes of station. In 1903 a further step was taken by the abolition of that mouthful of a title "Brigade-Division".[2] But the old tradition of non-intervention in battery training died hard, and there were still lieut.-colonels who stayed at home with their adjutants when their batteries went to practice. It must however be said in mitigation that the position of the brigade commander at practice was somewhat anomalous.

Sir Evelyn Wood, to whom the artillery owed already such an immense debt for his work at Aldershot in the

---

[1] Chapter XV.

[2] Previous to 1881, when two batteries were brought together for drill or manœuvre they were termed a *brigade*, although that term was also used with an entirely different meaning for an administrative organization. In 1881 a Regimental Order laid down that batteries in the same station were to be grouped in *divisions*, but in 1885 this title was changed to *brigade-division*, which, if clumsy, possessed at least the virtue of distinctiveness. The reversion to *brigade* had the serious defect that it gave to the lieut.-colonel's command the title which in the other arms had from time immemorial denoted that of a general officer. There would have been many advantages in adopting either the cavalry or the infantry name for the lieut.-colonel's command, but there were objections to both "regiment" and "battalion".

THE SOUTH AFRICAN INFLUENCE. 55

90's, and whose command at Salisbury now included both the great practice camps of Okehampton and Larkhill, detected the weak spot with his usual acumen, and set himself to find a remedy. He saw at his visits to these camps how the brigade commander was apt to find himself ignored,[1] how he had to stand aside when his batteries were carrying out the most important part of their training. While making handsome acknowledgments of all the good work of the school of gunnery, he drew attention to the danger of experts usurping the functions of commanding officers.

CHAPTER III.

Brigade Practice.

The commandants of the practice camps were directed to discuss the matter at their annual conference, but, as was perhaps but natural, they insisted upon the necessity for keeping the instruction in their own hands. Their two main arguments in favour of the system to which Sir Evelyn Wood had objected were, firstly, that since the primary object of sending batteries to practice camp was to test the training they had received, the man responsible for that training was scarcely the right man to do it; and secondly, that four camp commandants were more likely to secure uniformity of training than forty brigade commanders, some of whom were sure to have ideas of their own to ventilate. But next year (1904) some steps were taken to bring the brigade commanders more into the picture by entrusting them with the whole conduct of the first day's practice, and in some camps giving them charge of the tactical part during battery practice.

The Field-Marshal had undoubtedly been right in upholding the principle that brigades should be trained by those who would command them in war. But the commandants had reason on their side when they maintained that someone of higher rank than the lieut.-colonel was required to conduct the practice, although they had not yet realized that the practice should not be regarded as a

---

[1] As a writer at the time put it:—"It is the culminating point in the training and yet the lieut.-colonel has less voice in it than the camp serjeant-major".

56   THE FIELD ARMY ARTILLERY.

CHAPTER III.
Brigade Practice.

test, but as a stage in the training. The true solution had escaped both—namely that there should be senior artillery officers who would actually command and train in peace the artillery they would command in war.

Divisional Practice.

In 1903 Sir William Knox arranged for the concentration of the batteries in Ireland—so many of which were in single-battery stations—at training centres at which entrenching, bridging, and such like, could be practised as well as more technical artillery work. So successful did this bringing together of batteries prove that next year he carried it a step further by arranging for two brigades to go to practice at the same time. Batteries were enabled to practice with their full complement of wagons, patrols, mounted signallers, etc.; officers were given a double opportunity of perfecting themselves in observation by watching the fire of others; and brigade and battery commanders had the off days to rub in the lessons learnt at the previous day's performance. Similar arrangements had been in force for some years in India and South Africa, to the great advantage of the training, but it was hard to get the authorities in England to take the matter up. It was not until 1906 that two brigades were tentatively brought into practice camp together on Salisbury Plain. Once tried, however, there could be no doubt as to the increased facilities for instruction which it gave, and next year the *Instructions for Practice* recommended that one day's "divisional" should be the rule at all camps.

Personal Equipment.

The South African War revived a very old controversy regarding the provision of a personal weapon for horse and field artillerymen. The non-commissioned officers and gunners of the horse artillery had always been armed with the light cavalry sword, and when field batteries were recognized as mobile units their mounted non-commissioned officers were similarly armed. The gunners of field batteries retained, however, the sword-bayonet of the garrison artillery, and the drivers of both horse and field were en-

THE SOUTH AFRICAN INFLUENCE. 57

tirely unarmed.[1] The only fire-arms in a battery were a dozen carbines on the limbers, and this was in accordance with the generally accepted theory that the weapon of the gunner was his gun, and that in action he was better without anything to distract his attention from it. But the Germans had found out in 1870 that "here and there, on the march or in quarters, artillery might have to guard their skins",[2] and as the space between the various echelons on the battlefield lengthened, the defenceless position of wagon lines and ammunition columns could not be gainsaid. In spite of much facetious comment on the danger involved, the drivers were all provided with revolvers before the South African War broke out. That war soon showed, however, that what was really required by all ranks was the rifle. In consequence of the many occasions on which their value both in action and on the march had been demonstrated, and of the practical inconvenience caused by the helplessness of artillery in camp and during movements by rail, Lord Roberts increased the number of carbines carried by batteries from 12 to 48, and Lord Kitchener followed this up with a recommendation that the carbine (or light rifle) should be recognized as the personal weapon of all artillerymen, and that the cavalry sword, sword bayonet, and revolver should no longer form part of their equipment. After some discussion with India—who wanted a double-barrelled pistol—the proposal was approved, and 48 M.LE. rifles were issued to each battery, to be carried, 6 by mounted patrols in rifle-buckets, 12 slung by baggage guards, and the remainder in spring clips on the limbers. It was ordered that every man was to be trained in their use, and to wear a

CHAPTER III.

Personal Equipment.

---

[1] In spite of the fact that a committee appointed by the Duke of Wellington had expressed themselves as "decidedly of opinion that some defensive weapon is necessary for the artillery drivers, whose situation in action is arduous, and often much exposed to attack".

[2] Prince Kraft. In the 2nd Afghan War the drivers had to be served out with whatever arms could be found, including even captured Enfields, for the protection of the horse lines. In the Zulu War revolvers were issued to mounted men, and all gunners except working numbers carried slung carbines.

CHAPTER III.
Personal Equipment.

bandolier with 50 rounds—thus accentuating the position of the rifle as the weapon of all, and ensuring an ample supply of ammunition being always available whenever required.

But it was a shock to many when, on the occasion of King Edward's visit to Woolwich to inspect the Regiment as Colonel-in-Chief, the R.H.A. Guard of Honour were seen presenting arms instead of carrying swords.

Mechanization.

The use of traction engines in South Africa to move guns such as the 6″ Q.F., weighing with its field carriage over twelve tons, or more than double the limit for animal draught, opened the eyes of artillerymen to the possibility of "engine traction" for guns. It is true that on the one occasion when an engine was employed to take a gun into action it failed to complete its task, and it was necessary to fall back upon the despised ox-teams, although this had been glossed over in the published accounts. It was impossible to imagine a fussy, noisy, smoky, monstrosity like the engines in South Africa being generally used to bring guns into action, but it was recognized that mechanical transport was still in its infancy, and that the day might come when a more practical form of tractor for the purpose would be evolved. When the formation of heavy batteries was first under discussion in 1901 it was suggested that they might need sheds for traction engines rather than stables for horses; Lt.-Colonel H. C. L. Holden[1], the Superintendent of the Royal Gun Factory, was leading the way in the consideration of the possible adaptation of the "automobile" for the purpose; the Mechanical Transport Committee arranged in 1903 for a competitive trial of engines and tractors for heavy draught; and patterns of engine draught connectors were got out for 4·7″ and 5″ guns and 6″ howitzers. Even if it proved impossible to obtain a tractor which could be relied upon to take heavy guns across all natures of ground, and place them in position with rapidity and certainty, there was always the

[1] Brigadier-General Sir H. Capel L. Holden, K.C.B., F.R.S.

THE SOUTH AFRICAN INFLUENCE. 59

possibility of adopting mechanical traction for ammunition columns, and this was frequently proposed. The objections which were urged at the time were that in South Africa it had only proved successful when working continually in fine weather between two points, and that since ammunition cannot be improvised or obtained locally, and troops cannot "do without" even temporarily, it would be a great risk to introduce it for ammunition columns before it had been proved suitable for general transport work. Such in outline was the position of mechanization for artillery purposes during the period immediately following the South African War.

During this period the Inspector-General of Artillery in India was Major-General T. B. Tyler.[1] He had gone out from the commandantship of the School of Gunnery, Horse and Field, and he had at once set himself to establish a close touch between India and the gunnery staff at home. When the war came he spared no pains to see that the lessons of South Africa were not missed by the artillery in India, and with the arrival of Lord Kitchener as Commander-in-Chief this was assured for all arms. It was in India, indeed, that were held the first manœuvres in which the lessons of the South African War were exemplified on a large scale. About Christmas 1902 forty thousand men met on the historic field of Panipat—now seamed with "Boer" trenches—and it was generally agreed by the continental critics that the tactics showed a sounder appreciation of the experiences of the war than anything seen in Europe.

In 1903 General Tyler was succeeded by General Parsons from Salisbury Plain, and his first care was with the practice camps. At home the number of these camps had been reduced to four, which were well equipped, and commanded by specially selected officers, assisted by a staff of instructors from the school of gunnery and experienced range and recording officers. In India there

CHAPTER III.
Mechanization.

India.

---

[1] Major-General T. B. Tyler, C.S.I., Colonel-Commandant, d. 1923.

was no school of gunnery to supply instructors, and owing to the large number of camps many were left without expert supervision and comparatively devoid of appliances for training. General Parsons arranged for the best qualified officers being appointed gunnery and range officers in each command for the whole practice season. And if the camps were comparatively poorly equipped as regards appliances, the almost limitless extent of the ground generally available gave a freedom in choice of position, and a consequent reality to reconnaissance, which were in marked contrast to the cramped conditions at home.

Delay in the supply of plotters and directors made it difficult to keep pace with the strides that were being made at home in the development of indirect fire, although much ingenuity was displayed in improvising makeshifts. Similarly the control of the fire of dispersed batteries was dependent upon the reappearance of signallers, which had been abolished as at home for horse and field artillery. Here again batteries set themselves to fill the gap, and thanks to the generous assistance of regiments and battalions in lending instructors and instruments, much progress was made before official action could take effect. By 1904 all had been properly equipped, and sanction had been obtained for an increase of six men and four horses in the peace establishment of batteries belonging to the field army.

The extension of the brigade system to India, and the assembling of outlying batteries for brigade training before practice, also did much to ensure progress on the right lines. The great bar to such progress was the inadequate allowance of ammunition—only 480 rounds. Continued efforts to get it increased to the home figure of 600 met with an annual rebuff when the estimates came up for approval. It was still one of the "Important questions under discussion" in 1913.

The re-issue in 1904 of *Field Artillery Training 1902* in an "amended" edition marked the progress made since the war. The chapters on fire discipline and fire tactics

THE SOUTH AFRICAN INFLUENCE. 61

were entirely re-written to meet the requirements of cover and dispersion, and now contained workable systems for directing the fire of a battery from a covered position, and for controlling that of a brigade when its batteries were scattered. The two technical problems which had confronted the artillery when called upon to put into force the tactical lessons of the war had thus been solved—in theory at any rate. But the handling of all the strange appliances made ranging a terribly deliberate process, and this reacted upon the rest of the gunnery, and slowed everything down. Immersed in complicated technical problems, battery commanders were apt to lose sight of tactical considerations, and to forget that time might be almost as important when occupying a position under cover as when galloping into action in the open.

As regards the general principles governing the employment of artillery in the field the manual showed, however, considerable reluctance to abandon old faiths. Contrary to the views held by the more advanced school of thought in the Regiment, the "artillery duel" and the "preparation" of the infantry attack still found a place. But if the "doctrine" disappointed many, it had to be acknowledged that otherwise the new manual showed throughout an appreciation of the lessons of the war. It could hardly have been otherwise for the pages of the *Proceedings* for the last two years had shown unmistakably with what zeal and assiduity their impressions of the war and its lessons were being threshed out by artillery officers. South Africa had been the first experience of active service for the great majority, and every aspect of its inspiration was reflected in their contributions. "Artillery notes from the veldt" told of marching and fighting, and the side-issues of campaigning found a place as well—from "the care of horses on board-ship" to "the mounting of guns on railway trucks". There were, of course, many fantastic suggestions, but, taking them all in all, the value of the lessons learnt on the veldt was unquestionable. And not the least important was that

62 THE FIELD ARMY ARTILLERY.

CHAPTER III.

The Manual of 1904.

henceforth training, armament, and organization must all be based upon war requirements. New wars and new weapons might bring new theories, but these could safely be built up on so sure a foundation.

The manual of 1904 marked the high-water mark of South African inspiration—it marked too the turning of the tide. Reports from Manchuria were soon challenging the conclusions formed on South African experience. And while the war was still raging in the East, the new quick-firing equipment, so laboriously evolved, was put into the hands of the horse and field batteries, and heavy batteries were taking their place alongside them. The R.G.A. had joined the R.H.A. and the R.F.A. to form the Field Army Artillery, and the formation of the Expeditionary Force was to provide it at last with an organization and system of command capable of developing its powers. In the next three chapters some account of this Re-armament and Reorganizaion will be given before passing on to the consideration of the influence which the Russo-Japanese War exerted upon the Training.

FIELD HOWITZERS, MOUNTAIN AND HEAVY ARTILLERY.

Field Howitzers.

As related in Volume I, field howitzers, which had dropped out of the service on the adoption of rifled guns in 1860, were reintroduced during the last decade of the XIXth century. Their tactical rôle was not definitely formulated, however, until 1897, and although the first battery (37/R.F.A.) had been employed with conspicuous success in strict accordance with this rôle at Omdurman in 1898, there had not been time for the army, or even the artillery at large, to grasp the correct principles before the

THE SOUTH AFRICAN INFLUENCE. 63

South African War broke out.[1] In consequence the field howitzer batteries were used in that war to a great extent for purposes for which they were not intended or equipped. They were frequently called upon to move as ordinary field artillery, with disastrous results for their subsequent mobility: their lyddite shell were frittered away on the most unsuitable targets, and consequently failed to fulfill the exaggerated expectations which had been entertained on their introduction. There were, however, notable exceptions, where their value was clearly shown, and the Krupp howitzers in the hands of the Boers earned a great reputation among those who were subjected to their fire. In consequence a field howitzer brigade was included in the corps artillery, and an important share assigned to them in the most critical task of the field artillery—the close support of the infantry attack.[2] They were thus brought into much closer touch with the gun batteries, instead of being regarded as a race apart, and their procedure became a matter of general interest, especially when the necessity of firing from covered positions was forced upon all. Indirect fire had from the first been the normal method of the howitzer batteries, and they were better equipped for the purpose, so that their presence at practice camps was of real value to the gun batteries in affording an object lesson in this novel requirement.

The danger was indeed that the howitzer batteries might be led to assimilate their practice too much to that of the guns. The absurdly exaggerated ideas[3] regarding

CHAPTER III.

Field Howitzers.

---

[1] A paper on technical considerations and fire tactics was written in January 1900 by Majors Paterson and Hickman, instructors respectively in field and siege artillery, for the use of howitzer brigades going out to South Africa.

[2] Not only for their power of searching deep trenches as stated in F.A.T. 1902, but of maintaining fire on them until the assaulting infantry had got much closer than was possible with flat trajectory guns.

[3] The distinctive yellow fumes which too often accompanied the burst were generally hailed as proof positive of their effect, while in reality they indicated failure to detonate.

64   THE FIELD ARMY ARTILLERY.

CHAPTER III.

Field Howitzers.

the capabilities of lyddite had failed to materialize, and the Boer howitzers had used shrapnel with considerable effect, so there arose a demand for shrapnel for our howitzers, and some had even been sent to South Africa. In 1902 trials were carried out at howitzer practice on Salisbury Plain, and it was reported to compare very favourably with that of the 15-pr. against targets representing troops in the open; while against those in trenches or behind natural cover its effect should be much greater. Further trials in 1903, both at home and in India, increased this good opinion, and the howitzer batteries began to show a tendency to employ shrapnel with full charges on all occasions. The Commandant[1] of the School of Gunnery (Horse and Field) protested against the futility of field howitzers playing at being guns, pointing out that the small number of rounds they carried made it necessary to confine their use to purposes for which the guns would not be effective. Their primary value was for putting shell into places which neither a gun shell nor a rifle bullet could reach, and for this a steep angle of descent was necessary. The securing of such an angle of descent must therefore be the first consideration in the mind of the commander of a howitzer battery when choosing his position and charge.

Mountain Artillery.

The first effect of the South African War was disastrous for the mountain artillery. The batteries in South Africa had been put almost out of court by the fact that their guns still fired black powder, and heavy batteries had become all the fashion. *Personnel* must be found for these latter, and there was an unfortunate dictum by Lord Roberts that "there is nothing in mountain artillery work which an ordinary gunner could not learn in a week"— forgetting the highly trained native establishment which in India took charge of the mules. Be this as it may, the decision was that the new heavy batteries should be formed

---

[1] Colonel (now Major-General) W. E. Blewitt, C.B., C.M.G., C.B.E.

THE SOUTH AFRICAN INFLUENCE. 65

from siege companies, and that to compensate the siege artillery Nos. 4 and 10 mountain batteries on their return from Egypt and South Africa respectively should be converted into Nos. 106 and 107 siege companies.[1] And, to make a clean sweep of mountain artillery on the home and colonial establishment, the mountain artillery depôt at Newport was abolished, and the keeping up of the mountain batteries in India divided among the garrison artillery depôts.

CHAPTER III.

Mountain Artillery.

In India things were very different. The brigade system was adopted for the British batteries at Rawalpindi, Ambala, and Quetta, and though it was found impossible to extend it to the Indian batteries, these were collected at mountain artillery practice camps[2] where they learnt to work in brigade. On coming out as Inspector-General in 1903 General Parsons carried their training a step further by insisting on mountain artillery occasionally joining their comrades of the field artillery in the plains so as to learn something of their rôle as part of the divisional artillery.

It was becoming yearly more evident that Indian mountain batteries should be major's commands like all other batteries and companies of artillery. They mustered nearly 300 men, and it was urged that this required a field officer, especially in view of the isolated stations of many of the batteries. In 1904 definite proposals for this, and other measures calculated to increase the attractions[3] of service in the mountain artillery, were put forward, but it was not until 1908 that the change from a captain and

---

[1] No. 10 was converted into No. 107 in 1903, but the return of No. 4 was unexpectedly delayed, and when it got home in 1905 it was broken up, and No. 106 was never formed.

[2] In one respect these mountain artillery camps were ahead of all owing to the presence of infantry, who worked regularly with the guns, being in some cases attached to batteries as escorts right through the practice.

[3] The popularity of the mountain artillery was seriously affected by its separation from the mounted branch, and by the rival openings for active service which the heavy artillery appeared likely to offer.

CHAPTER III.

Mountain Artillery.

Heavy Artillery.[1]

four subalterns, to major, captain, and three subalterns, began to come into effect.

It should be noted that in 1901 all the Indian batteries were given titles and had their numbers taken away—only to be restored two years later with the addition of a "20", so that No. 1 became 21, and so on.

The most striking experience of the South African War—as far at least as the artillery were concerned—was the use the Boers made of heavy guns. The way they brought them into action, and got them away again, however difficult the ground, and the use they made of their long range,[2] came as a revelation to the British army—and not to the British alone. Although heavy batteries had dropped out of the service at home since the Crimea, it was guns of "position" which had saved the day at Inkerman, and the "Bail Batteries" were still the most picturesque feature of the artillery in India. But the value of all these had lain in their *power*, whereas the Boers demonstrated the value of *range*. It is true that the actual effect of their long-range fire was generally insignificant, but the sense of being outranged was certainly humiliating, if not demoralizing, and in some cases it had caused premature deployments with unfortunate results. The Germans were quick to grasp the significance of the new development, and as early as 1901 raised ten new companies of Foot Artillery, thus laying the foundation of that powerful heavy artillery which was to play such a prominent part in the Great War.

Coast defence companies had been converted into heavy batteries in South Africa, but this was merely a temporary expedient. The question of putting the use of

---

[1] This term is used in the sense which it bore up till after the Great War, that is as meaning "Heavy Field" or "Position" Artillery corresponding to what is now termed "Medium".

[2] The guns were not only of much greater calibre than ever before used in the field, but the Boers had no hesitation in lengthening their range by such expedients as increasing the charge and digging a hole for the trail. The muzzles sticking up in the air were a familiar feature fo the earlier battle-fields.

THE SOUTH AFRICAN INFLUENCE. 67

heavy guns in the field on a permanent footing must be faced; and in due course it was decided to form a brigade of heavy artillery by the conversion of three siege companies.[1] After courses of instruction at Lydd, in the spring of 1903, the brigade went into camp at Aldershot, each battery having four 4·7″ guns, 15 cobs, and 60 hired draught horses with civilian drivers. They had many difficulties to contend with. The 4·7″ equipment was quite unsuitable for work in the field, the horses were mostly foreign, and although of a heavy type were not to be compared with those used by the Volunteer position batteries, and the harness was old field artillery pattern which required much fitting. There were none of the usual artificers of a mounted unit—saddlers, shoeing-smiths, etc.—but the horse and field artillery gave every assistance, and such infantile troubles were got over. The most serious question was the system of draught. In South Africa, though oxen had been generally used with both 5″ and 4·7″ guns, some 5″ on 40-pr. R.M.L. carriages were horsed, four horses abreast with outriggers, and this was the method now adopted. Even if the civilian drivers had been accustomed to leading on foot—of which they had had no experience—it would have been impossible for them to control the two inner horses,[2] and eventually it settled down to the Volunteer system of horses in pairs led by their drivers on the near side, assisted by a gunner walking on the off side. But it was considered wiser not to venture on marching past, and on ceremonial parades the brigade was entrusted with the firing of the salute, and did so at the inspection of the 1st Army Corps by the King and President Loubet in 1903—its official début.

CHAPTER III.
Heavy Artillery.

---

[1] Nos. 26, 31, and 35.

[2] "No finer sight has ever been seen at Aldershot than when one fine fresh Monday morning a 4·7″ limber, with four heavy horses attached to it, bolted in the Long Valley, charged through and through a brigade of cavalry, and in order not to be partial to one portion of the mounted arm, satisfactorily accounted for a battalion of mounted infantry before it was finally captured". Lecture by Colonel H. C. D. Simpson, *Proceedings*, Vol. XXXI.

68 THE FIELD ARMY ARTILLERY.

CHAPTER III.

Heavy Artillery.

The brigade took its share, however, in the army manœuvres, and these were followed by practice at Rhayader in September, so that the batteries did not start on the homeward journey to their winter quarters at Portsmouth and Plymouth until the beginning of October, having been five months under canvas.

The range at Rhayader in Wales, which had been hired particularly for the heavy artillery, was somewhat lacking in amenities, and the thousand-foot climb from the camp to the gun-park was a trying preliminary to the strenuous work of handling heavy guns on a particularly boggy moor. The commandant and staff from Lydd conducted the practice, and the one remaining siege company sent a hundred men to make what preparations were possible on the ranges. The brigade itself was new to the work, and officers and men had been fully occupied all the summer with other cares, so there is no need to dwell on their first year's practice. The next year it was very different. The guns were still the 4·7″'s, but they had been greatly improved by the addition of a sole-plate to prevent the trail digging into the ground : field artillery indirect laying stores were used with success; and trial of various methods of draught showed that mounting the drivers as in field artillery was much the most satisfactory system.

Meanwhile the 2nd Heavy Brigade had been formed of Nos. 24, 48, and 108 Companies R.G.A., and it also practised at Rhayader, taking over for the purpose the horses and equipment of the 1st Brigade.

Thus the Heavy Artillery had been successfully launched on its existence at home, and the two brigades, formed in 1903 and 1904 respectively, remained unaltered in their composition until the Great War.

In India the heavy batteries had been deprived of their elephants in 1900, as told in Volume I, and left with only their "bails". At Lord Curzon's great Durbar at Delhi in 1903 two of these batteries were horsed as an experiment, and next year the horsing of the guns and first-line wagons of all four batteries was approved. At the same

THE SOUTH AFRICAN INFLUENCE.

time two more batteries were formed by the conversion of one of the three siege companies and a garrison company, and these were equipped with 5″ B.L. guns on converted 40-pr. carriages, with bullock-draught on South African lines. In 1904 the heavy artillery in India therefore consisted of :—

- 2 batteries with 30-pr. B.L. guns and horse-draught (8-horse teams and native drivers).
- 2 batteries with 5·4″ B.L. howitzers[1] and horse-draught as above.
- 2 batteries with 5″ B.L. guns and bullock-draught.

Field Artillery Training 1902 contained a bald announcement—already quoted—of the inclusion of a heavy brigade in the corps artillery, but it was silent as to how it should be employed. With the formation of the 1st Heavy Brigade a manual was obviously necessary, and accordingly a "Provisional" *Heavy Artillery Training* appeared in May 1903. It was naturally based almost entirely on South African practice, and, after the first year's training at Aldershot and Rhayader, a committee was assembled to consider the whole question. The real point at issue was whether the training should be on the lines of siege or of field artillery, and, since the decision affected the whole future of the heavy artillery, a brief summary of the arguments will be put on record here.

The advocates of field artillery methods pointed out that the heavy batteries now formed part of the field army, and that their training should therefore be assimilated to that of the field batteries with which they must co-operate—to associate them with the siege artillery in their training could not fail to render them less adaptable to the rapidly changing conditions of the battlefield.

On the other side it was urged that the batteries belonged to the Royal Garrison Artillery, and according to the scheme under which they were formed they were to

---

[1] Replaced later by 4″ B.L. guns.

CHAPTER III.

Heavy Artillery.

be interchangeable with the siege companies.[1] In any case they must revert to coast artillery when their turn for foreign service came round. If the methods of heavy artillery were assimilated to those of the siege they would be able to supplement the latter in the attack of fortresses, and vice versa. The heavy artillery must not be allowed to succumb to the glamour of the mounted branch.

Such, briefly, were the rival arguments. Those of the field artillery carried the day, and the new edition of *Heavy Artillery Training* which came out in 1904 showed unmistakably the trend towards field artillery methods. Drill for the occupation and change of positions found a place for the first time, and so also did the field artillery methods of engaging moving targets and of switching fire from one target to another. The effect of practice on the rough Welsh ranges was shown by the space devoted to the difficulties due to the disappearance of ranging rounds in bogs and hollows, and the complications of the angle of sight—difficulties which had never made their influence felt at Lydd. The use of "observation of fire instruments" whenever time and conditions of ground admitted was no longer insisted on, but was only advocated as an assistance in ranging. The battery took the place of the section as the normal unit for fire discipline, and its commander, instead of being absolutely tied to his guns, and obliged to rely upon the reports of observers, was encouraged to observe for himself so long as he could communicate his orders by megaphone or by orderlies. In the following year the process was continued by the issue of "corrigenda" which substituted the director and plotter method of finding the line of fire for the elaborate siege system.

---

[1] The heavy batteries were supposed to devote their winters to siege work, and to change places with the siege companies every three years.

CHAPTER IV.

The Re-armament (General).

The Reason for Re-armament—The Equipment Committee—A Startling Suggestion—Financial Difficulties—Legal Difficulties—Technical Difficulties—The Order of Issue—Field Howitzers—Heavy Guns—Mountain Guns—Pom-poms—The Technical Committees—Conclusion.

WITH the growth of armies, the increase in the proportion of guns to rifles, and the greater cost of modern equipments, artillery re-armament had become a far more formidable undertaking in the XXth century than it had been in the XIXth. And yet the advances made in the application of the quick-firing principle to field guns found all nations faced with the necessity of shouldering this heavy burden; and the re-armament of the Royal Artillery that ensued will ever be memorable for having given to the Regiment the weapons with which it went to war in 1914. It has, moreover, claims other than technical to notice here if history is to serve as any guide in the future. For it was not only the most complete, but also the most methodically conducted of all the operations of this nature recorded in Regimental History, besides being rich in examples of the effect of those extraneous influences which are so apt to be forgotten or ignored by soldiers. Therefore, before touching on more technical considerations in the next chapter, it seems desirable to indicate here, in outline at least, the procedure adopted, and the part played by political, financial, and industrial interests. It will be seen

72 THE FIELD ARMY ARTILLERY.

CHAPTER IV.
The Reason for Re-armament.

how the Foreign Office, the India Office, and the Home Office, as well as the Treasury, found themselves involved, how Railway and Shipping Companies were drawn into the affair; how Party Politics played their part; and how the power of Public Opinion ultimately carried the day.

It is necessary now to return to the purchase of the Ehrhardt guns by Sir Henry Brackenbury in 1900, as recorded in Chapter I. Their performance proved beyond doubt that the French claims for their "75's" were justified, and that the problem of applying the quick-firing principle to a field gun had indeed been solved. The Cabinet at once accepted the necessity for re-arming the horse and field artillery; and so urgent was the matter considered that, although hostilities were still in progress in South Africa, Lord Roberts was directed to send home commanders of artillery brigades and batteries "selected for their eminence and experience" to form an Equipment Committee under the presidency of Sir George Marshall, to which might be entrusted the task of recommending a quick-firing equipment for the service.

The Equipment Committee.

Preliminary steps had already been taken to facilitate their work. A very careful examination of the development of field artillery equipment from the Napoleonic period had been prepared at the War Office with the results of experiments since the decision to re-arm with breech-loaders in 1880, tables of foreign service equipments, and translations of the views of foreign authorities on the subject. A questionnaire regarding the behaviour of the various equipments in the field had been sent to a large number of officers in South Africa; and within a week of the occupation of Pretoria a committee had been assembled "to consider and report on the organization of the horse, field, and heavy batteries, to note any defects which came to light during the campaign, and to suggest how they might be remedied". There had also been ordered from English, Continental, and American firms specimen guns of their most recent designs, and a considerable amount

THE RE-ARMAMENT (GENERAL).

of information had been accumulated by the Ordnance Committee during the trials they had carried out in 1898/9. All this material was at the disposal of the Equipment Committee, and the Ordnance Committee relieved them of all investigations into the strength and ballistics of the guns, and all details of the ammunition.

Sir George Marshall reached England in December 1900, and in January 1901 the Equipment Committee was officially constituted.[1] Their first action was to formulate the conditions[2] which the new equipments should fulfil, and to ask gun-making firms to submit designs to meet these conditions. They thus appealed to the inventive genius of the country, and by taking the designers into their confidence as to what the soldiers wanted, directed their energies into the right direction. It was a startling innovation on established custom at the time, but has served as a commonplace of procedure since.

From the designs submitted in accordance with these conditions the most promising were selected,[3] and orders were given for the manufacture of single guns of each design. These "specimen" guns were tried in 1902, and it was found—as will always be the case—that although none were suitable for the service as they stood they were genuine quick-firers, and all contained features of great merit. The problem was how to combine into a composite design the features in which any of the specimens showed a marked superiority over the others. Here again the committee made a departure from precedent to which the success eventually attained was greatly due. The representatives of the Firms were called into conference, and were persuaded to agree to the possibility of a composite

CHAPTER IV.

The Equipment Committee.

---

[1] The terms of references are given in Appendix B.

[2] The Conditions are given in Appendix C, but they were considerably modified as the trials went on and showed what was feasible. Their chief interest lies in the revelation of what was thought to be required and attainable by the most experienced officers at the time.

[3] Horse artillery—2 Ordnance Factories, 2 Armstrong, 1 Vickers.
Field artillery—1　　　,,　　　　　,,　　1　　,,　　1　　,,

74 THE FIELD ARMY ARTILLERY.

CHAPTER IV.

The Equipment Committee.

design, embodying—as its broadest features—an Armstrong gun, with Vickers recoil arrangements, and Ordnance Factories sighting and elevating gear and system of carrying ammunition. The working out of such a design presented many difficulties and took time, but eventually four complete batteries of this equipment were ready for trial in 1903. The trials were successful, and, after conferences in which it was decided to adopt the Vickers mechanism with the Armstrong guns, and to assimilate the 18-pr. carriage in all respects to the 13-pr., the Equipment Committee were about to bring their labours to a conclusion with a unanimous recommendation of these equipments—a 13-pr. for horse artillery, a 18-pr. for field artillery.

A Startling Suggestion.

The stage was indeed set for such a conclusion when a bomb-shell was thrown into the midst by the suggestion of one of the members that the superiority of the 18-pr. over the 13-pr. was not sufficiently marked to warrant its introduction into the service.

In the previous year Brigadier-General Sir James Wolfe-Murray[1] had contributed a paper to the *Proceedings* under the arresting title of "Do we require Field Artillery?" which had aroused wide-spread interest. Taking as his text the aphorism "the demands of peace are always for mobility, those of war for power," he asked whether there was any real necessity for the maintenance of an intermediate class between horse artillery and "heavy" or "position" artillery; and suggested that we had not got sufficient fast-moving, i.e., horse artillery, for our wants having regard to the probability that in the future we should make a much more extended use of mounted troops; nor sufficient heavy artillery for our field troops, i.e. guns possessing the maximum of shell power consistent with a sufficient modicum of mobility to keep up with dismounted men. In view of these considerations he suggested that there was no place for an intermediate class

---

[1] Lieut.-General Sir James Wolfe-Murray, K.C.B., Colonel-Commandant. d. 1919.

THE RE-ARMAMENT (GENERAL).

of artillery, which—to use a hackneyed phrase—was neither fish, flesh, fowl, nor good red herring.

The suggestion now made raised the same question although in a different form. It was based on the fact that, contrary to all expectations, trials had shown the 13-pr. to be a better shooting gun than the 18-pr. even up to extreme ranges; and it proposed to take advantage of this quality to secure the undoubted advantage of one gun for both horse and field artillery without crippling the horse as had been the result of giving them the field gun in the 80's. The proposal had, no doubt, many attractive features, especially under the conditions of the British Empire, where field artillery might be called upon to work over all sorts of country, and probably often with mounted troops, and it was decided to carry out comparative trials. For these the 13-pr. and 18-pr. fired, in addition to their own shell, some of $14\frac{1}{2}$ lb. and of 20 lb., and the results showed that neither the 13-pr. nor the 18-pr. was as accurate as the 14-pr., while the 18-pr. owing to its concentration of weight on the gun wheels was very difficult to manhandle. On these results Colonel Blewitt[1] definitely recommended the adoption of the 13-pr., but with a $14\frac{1}{2}$ lb. shell, for both horse and field artillery, pointing out that, except when the rate of fire was the maximum possible, which would rarely be the case, the lighter gun could equalize the greater number of bullets in the heavier shell by the employment of a slightly increased rate of fire, and that the bullets would then be better distributed.[2]

It is not necessary to pursue the arguments further, but it has been thought advisable to devote some space to the question because of the great interest taken in the discussion at the time, and of the immense importance of the decision. The Equipment Committee stated that they

CHAPTER IV.

A Startling Suggestion

---

[1] Major-General W. E. Blewitt, C.B., C.M.G., C.B.E.

[2] It must be remembered that the only projectile in use, or contemplated, was shrapnel.

76 THE FIELD ARMY ARTILLERY.

CHAPTER IV.

A Startling Suggestion.

saw no reason to depart from their original recommendation of the 13-pr. and 18-pr., but the Secretary of State was not satisfied, and called upon various distinguished personages within and without the War Office for their individual views—much, it was whispered, to their embarrassment. Such diverse authorities as Lord Roberts and Mr. Arnold-Foster expressed their opinions, and the question was finally referred to the Prime Minister for decision. Mr. Balfour sided with the Committee, and in 1904 the 13-pr. and 18-pr. Q.F. were approved for the re-armament of the Royal Horse and Royal Field Artillery respectively.

It is awe-inspiring to speculate on what would have been the result if Mr. Balfour's casting vote had been given the other way, and we had gone into the War with only the 13-pr. for field as well as horse artillery, although of course with a $14\frac{1}{2}$-lb. shell.

This is not the place for a discussion of the merits or defects of the new equipments. As will be seen in subsequent chapters they did not escape criticism. But in justice to those responsible it may be pointed out that *at the time of their adoption* the 13-pr. stood in a class by itself both for mobility and shooting qualities, while the 18-pr. with a mobility equal to the other field guns of the day was far their superior in shell power. So much indeed was this the case that the particulars of the new equipments, when published in 1904, were received with a very general incredulity both in Europe and America. As a writer in the *Revue Militaire* put it—"England hopes to turn out a Q.F. gun more powerful than that of any other nation, and which is at the same time only to weigh 37 cwts. when limbered up. These figures are not unnaturally received with a certain amount of scepticism. Experience alone will show the degree of stability possessed by the English gun when firing".

Financial Difficulties.

With the acceptance of the Committee's recommendation by the Military Authorities, and the Prime Minister's approval, it might well be thought that difficulties and delays were at an end, and that the placing of the contracts

By permission of Punch.

OUR GUNLESS ARMY.

MR. BULL: "WHERE ARE THESE QUICK FIRING GUNS I WAS PROMISED AGES AGO? I CAN'T GET ON WITHOUT 'EM."

PRESIDENT OF THE COMMITTEE OF NATIONAL DEFENCE: "QUITE SO. QUITE SO. BUT OUR FIRST CONSIDERATION IS THE BUDGET."

[In spite of the undertaking given by Mr. Arnold-Foster, as to the re-arming of the artillery with quick-firing guns of the new pattern, only about one-twentieth of this equipment has at present been supplied. See recent articles in the *St. James's Gazette*.]

would follow automatically. Far from it. During the years of experiment politicians had been ready enough to assure Parliament and the public that they were fully alive to the urgency of the need, and only too anxious to order the guns if the gunners would make up their mind as to what they wanted. But there was a very different tale to tell when the recommendation had been made, and ordering the guns meant finding the money to pay for them. Fortunately for the country the great force of Public Opinion had been wakened to the danger of delay. Articles urging the necessity for action began to appear in responsible newspapers of all shades in politics: there was a cartoon in *Punch*; and finally, on the 15th December, 1904, *The Times* came out with one of those special articles which cannot be ignored. On Christmas Eve the orders were given.

The right method would have been to place contracts for the whole of the requirements at once. This course would have greatly expedited manufacture, and allowed of a definite programme of issue, and it was strongly pressed by the military authorities, but, alas, to no avail. Year by year progress was hindered by uncertainty as to the money that would be forthcoming, and the re-armament of the artillery in India before that at Home was even contemplated, so as to postpone the evil day. It is unnecessary to dilate on the certain result of sending all this novel material out to a country in which none of the batteries had any experience with it, and where there were none of the experts who had designed and manufactured it to be called in if anything went wrong—as was inevitable if such complicated equipment were placed in inexperienced hands. When the proposal was announced in Parliament there were fortunately members who were not slow to detect and to denounce this "shabby and mean" attempt to relieve the home finances at the expense of the Indian taxpayer.

Later on, when the ammunition began to come in from the factories, legal difficulties cropped up. Up to this time ammunition had always been packed by com-

CHAPTER IV.

Financial Difficulties.

Legal Difficulties

CHAPTER IV.

Legal Difficulties.

ponents, i.e. shells, fuzes, cartridges, tubes, in separate cases.[1] The system was the despair of regimental officers, but convenience for storage and inspection in peace had long been allowed to over-ride the requirements of war. In South Africa, however, there had been many instances of components going astray owing to their separate packing, thus rendering the whole consignment useless; and when it was discovered that the Boers were actually issuing the ammunition for the guns captured from us in boxes containing complete rounds, the *non possumus* attitude had to be abandoned. The principle that the ammunition for the new guns should be issued and stored in complete rounds was accepted, and it was only when the deliveries began that it was realized that the combination of shell, cartridge, fuze, and primer in one package transgressed the by-laws for the carriage and store of explosives made by the Railway Companies under the Explosives Act. Somewhat protracted negotiations with the Home Office and the Railway Clearing House ensued before a way could be found out of this impasse.

Technical Difficulties.

No sooner were these authorities placated than technical delays and difficulties arose. Before the ordnance works could commence the manufacture of the new material they had to be provided not only with hundreds of working drawings but also with innumerable "jigs and gauges", taking months to make and costing thousands of pounds. Then, with mass production, weaknesses cropped up which had not shown in the hand-made specimen equipments, and which the trial batteries had not revealed. The first of these was only brought to notice through the action of the King. The steps taken for the re-armament of the Regiment had been watched with interest by its Colonel-in-Chief, and in accordance with His Majesty's wish two of the first batteries to receive the new equip-

---

[1] And, to make matters worse, with a different number of each component in its package. For instance shells were packed six in a box, cartridges a hundred in a case, friction tubes twenty, and so forth.

THE RE-ARMAMENT (GENERAL). 79

ment marched from Woolwich on the 13th May, 1905, for inspection in the garden of Buckingham Palace. On their return it was found—to the consternation of all concerned—that half the tubes in which the rounds were carried in the limbers and wagons had given way. The incident seemed inexplicable after the trials undergone, for two complete batteries of each nature (13-pr. and 18-pr.) had been subjected to the most exhaustive tests imaginable. They had each fired a couple of thousand rounds, they had been knocked about over the bogs and boulders of Dartmoor, and they had been put through a special travelling trial of many hundreds of miles, all at the hands of four service batteries.[1] Eventually the cause was found—the trot over the granite "setts" of the Old Kent Road had set up a vibration in the metal of which the tubes were made, and plaited Indian cane was substituted for metal in the tubes. It was a test which it had never occurred to anyone to simulate, and which might never have been made, had it not been for the King's summons, until the *pavé* of the road to Mons found the flaw.

What appeared at first sight to be a much more serious failure occurred with the fuzes. It had been decided to adopt the German rather than the French type of fuze, and in their manufacture none could approach the great firm of Krupp. Eventually his design and "trade secret" were acquired, and nothing could have been better than the performance of those used during the trials—probably 20,000 at least. But when ordinary supply had been ordered, and those made in England began to come in, disquieting reports of their failure at proof were received. This difficulty also was eventually overcome, but not without some delay and considerable anxiety.

There was a still more alarming shock in store. When the batteries began to take their new guns to practice it was found that a certain number were definitely bent.

CHAPTER IV.

Technical Difficulties.

---

[1] "W" and "Y" R.H.A., 26th and 92nd R.F.A.

80 THE FIELD ARMY ARTILLERY.

CHAPTER IV.

Technical Difficulties.

There was a natural outcry on the part of battery commanders at being asked to shoot with "damned crooked guns". The matter engaged the very serious attention of the Ordnance Committee for some time before the cause was found to lie in the composite equipment which required the fitting of guns designed by one firm to cradles designed by another. This had involved the moving of the ribs from the centre line of the guns, which caused an unequal contraction on cooling, in some cases of sufficient intensity to cause a warping of the gun. Fortunately it occurred to Sir Desmond O'Callaghan, the President of the Ordnance Committee, that a long shell passing through the bore at a comparatively high velocity must cause a considerable straightening moment, and practice confirmed this theory, for range and accuracy trials carried out from two of the straightest and two of the most crooked guns obtainable showed nothing to choose between them. There was considerable relief when the result was announced at a conference at Okehampton, but the design was modified for future manufacture.

The Order of Issue.

Such technical difficulties must be accepted as incidental to the introduction of an entirely novel equipment; the more important only have been touched on here, simply as examples of what is to be expected. When all these difficulties had been surmounted and production was assured, there remained the question of the order in which the re-armament should proceed. This touched strategical and political interests of the first importance, and brought into the discussion the Foreign Office as well as the General Staff.

The chance of war during the process of re-armament had always to be borne in mind, and just when the new equipments were coming along, there came the Moroccan crisis, followed by the Algeciras Conference of 1906. The only safe course was to make the Division the unit of re-armament, including in it not only its ammunition columns but also all the ammunition and spare parts stored for it in ordnance depôts. But it was hard to make

THE RE-ARMAMENT (GENERAL). 81

even artillery officers realize this. Every command was clamouring for the new guns and every form of pressure was put upon the Master-General of the Ordnance by interested parties in order to obtain at least a battery.

Some risks were run, but by the midsummer of 1906 the cavalry division and six divisions at home had been completed, and good progress had been made with India. The replacement of the guns in South Africa, which were very much worn, could be taken in hand.

In order to avoid overloading the narrative, no reference has, so far, been made to field howitzers. The re-armament of the howitzer batteries was, however, part of the task entrusted to the Equipment Committee, and their efforts to find a successor to the 5″ B.L. howitzer were carried on *pari passu* with those which resulted in the adoption of the 13-pr. and 18-pr. Broadly speaking the procedure was the same, and it need not therefore be followed in any detail. There were, however, certain special features which are worthy of record here.

In laying down the conditions to be fulfilled the Committee were guided, as in the case of the guns, by their experience in South Africa, where the Krupp field howitzers in the hands of the Boers had made a great impression upon those who had been subjected to their fire. Progress was slow, however, for none of the first models proved satisfactory. In particular they failed conspicuously in accuracy when compared with one of the captured Krupp 12 cm howitzers which had been sent home for comparison. Experiments were carried out with many designs of projectiles and rifling, including reproductions of the Krupp, and there were visits to Essen to discuss the possibility of purchase. This all took time, and it was not until 1905 that the Committee were sufficiently satisfied in the matter of design to recommend the manufacture of further trial equipments. Four[1] of these were tried in the

CHAPTER IV.

The Order of Issue.

Field Howitzers.

---

[1] Ordnance Factories, Armstrong, Vickers, and the Coventry Ordnance Works. This last was a combination of engineering firms who, on the strength of the re-armament, were able to build large works at Coventry.

82   THE FIELD ARMY ARTILLERY.

CHAPTER IV.

Field Howitzers.

following year, and of these the Coventry design proved so satisfactory that a whole battery was ordered from that firm. The trials with this battery followed the usual course, but progress was slow, and it was not until the end of 1908 that the 4·5" Q.F. could be recommended for adoption, and then to the regret of many, with its length reduced.

Heavy Guns

The determination to add heavy batteries to the field army artillery, and the steps taken to form such batteries have been told in Chapter III. They were temporarily armed with 4·7" guns, but there was no desire to perpetuate these for their defects for use in the field were well known to gunners although the name "four-point-seven" had taken the public fancy.[1] Directly after the occupation of Prètoria Lord Roberts had been called upon for his opinion on the subject, and had given the conditions to be fulfilled as "Range 10,000 yards, weight behind team not more than 4 tons, shell of as large a capacity as possible". With this to guide them the Ordnance Committee were called upon to take up the question, and experimental guns were ordered. The procedure followed in the case of the Horse and Field Artillery was then repeated by the appointment in October, 1902, of a Heavy Battery Committee similarly constituted of officers who had had experience in South Africa, the majority with both horse-drawn and ox-drawn guns, under the presidency of Colonel Perrott,[2] who had commanded the Siege Train.

In their first report, rendered in April, 1903, the Committee dismissed the 4·7" and the 30-pr.[3] from further consideration on account of the poor striking energy and effect of their shell in comparison with the 60-lb. shell of the experimental guns, especially when viewed from the

---

[1] See Chapter XVIII.

[2] Major-General Sir T. Perrott, K.C.B. d. 1919.

[3] The gun with which some of the Indian heavy batteries were armed.

target end of the range. As regards the three experimental equipments under trial, they accepted the Armstrong gun, but found none of the carriages suitable for use in the field. They therefore recommended that new designs of carriages should be called for, which could be more easily worked by the detachments. The new equipments which resulted were subjected to long and continuous trials throughout 1904, including firing trials at Shoeburyness and Rhayader; rough usage trials at Woolwich, and over a specially made rough-usage course at Shoeburyness; travelling trials on the 200 mile march to Rhayader and during practice there; and stability trials with both horse-draught (shaft and pole) and mechanical traction. This exhaustive test showed the necessity for extensive modifications, and it was not until 1905 that final approval was given to the 60-pr. B.L. equipment for heavy batteries. The weight was unfortunately half-a-ton over the maximum aimed at.

India did not then adopt the 60-pr. A specimen was sent out for trial, but the Indian authorities were convinced that it was too heavy for service in the generally broken and difficult country across the Frontier, so the War Office bought it back again—at what price history does not relate. There was, however, no doubt that the 30-pr., 4″[1] and 5″ B.L. guns in the Indian heavy batteries had to be replaced by more modern weapons—the question was: should these be guns or howitzers? Eventually, in view of the fact that the only howitzers still in the service in India were those of the one brigade of field howitzers and the two siege companies, it was decided that the heavy batteries should be re-armed with medium howitzers. Some attempts were made to utilize the old 5·4″ previously in the Indian service, but without success, and a new design had just been got out, and recommended for adoption when the War came.

---

[1] These 4″ B.L. guns had replaced the 5·4″ howitzers in the two heavy batteries armed with the latter.

84 THE FIELD ARMY ARTILLERY.

CHAPTER IV.

Mountain Guns.

There remained only the mountain artillery, but this proved a most difficult problem. The South African War had found the mountain batteries, both British and Indian, still armed with the 2·5″ R.M.L., the famous "screwguns" of the Afghan War and many a frontier expedition. But muzzle-loaders firing black powder were an anachronism in the XXth century, and the plight of the two batteries in South Africa was indeed a pitiable one. Moreover the guns were wearing out fast, and something must be done to avoid the necessity of ordering more of such out-of-date weapons. A 10-pr. was accordingly somewhat hastily approved in 1901, but it was a makeshift, and in 1905 conditions were formulated for a "long-recoil" carriage. Following the precedent of the field artillery a special committee was formed under Colonel Cleeve[1], and India sent selected mountain artillery officers to serve on it. Specimen equipments were ordered for trial; and from these trials there emerged in 1908 the possibility of using the 10-pr. gun on the new carriage. It took some years to get over all the difficulties of this conversion, but eventually the combination was approved under the title of "2·75″ B.L."[2]

For many years, however, India had been demanding a mountain howitzer as well as a mountain gun, and the mountain artillery committee issued conditions for such an equipment, and obtained some specimens for trial. But none of these proved satisfactory, and meanwhile every year brought to light new devices for securing stability. Unless the equipment was to be out-of-date before it was approved a fresh start was necessary. New conditions were accordingly approved in 1912, and specimen howitzers ordered. These were under trial when the War was declared, and eventually resulted in the 3·7″ Q.F.

Pom-poms.

One of the surprises of the South African War had been the appearance on the Boer side of 37 ᵐ/ₘ Vickers-

---

[1] Major-General W. F. Cleeve, C.B. d. 1922.
[2] Not to be confused with the 2·95″ Q.F. referred to in Chapter V.

THE RE-ARMAMENT (GENERAL). 85

Maxim guns—soon to be known all the world over as "pom-poms". If their one-pound shells did little actual damage, the rapid arrival of a belt-full was undoubtedly alarming, and no time was lost in providing the British army in South Africa with similar weapons.[1] As regards their future use, a "Pom-pom Committee" recommended in 1901 that they should be retained as part of the equipment of the field army, and that if the artillery would not take them they should be given to the mounted infantry. The Equipment Committee held that their moral effect, which was at first admittedly great, would soon wear off when it was realized that their actual effect was inappreciable, and that the introduction into the service of a weapon, having only possible or probable moral effect as a reason for its existence, would be a retrograde step. As for the argument, commonly advanced, that they were good range-finders, the employment for such a purpose of a vehicle requiring six horses seemed scarcely a practical proposition. In spite of the unwillingness of the artillery they were allotted as an extra section to horse batteries, until the issue of their new quickfirers. The pom-poms were then transferred to the cavalry,[2] and so drop out of our regimental history.

As will have been gathered from the above, the re-armament had involved the formation of a considerable number of special committees—the Horse and Field Artillery Equipment Committee in 1901, followed by the Field Howitzer Committee; the Heavy Battery Committee in 1902; the Mountain Artillery Committee in 1905. With all the above the Ordnance Committee[3] had been associated,

CHAPTER IV.
Pom-poms.

The Technical Committees.

---

[1] In deference to popular clamour, fifty guns and a million and half rounds were ordered. A comparatively small proportion of the ammunition was ever fired, and many thousands of rounds had eventually to be broken down and scrapped.

[2] In 1904-5-6 the pompom sections of many cavalry regiments carried out their annual practice at Larkhill.

[3] Some account of the formation of the Ordnance Committee and of its fore-runner the Ordnance Select Committee will be found in Volume I of this History.

H

86 THE FIELD ARMY ARTILLERY.

CHAPTER IV.

The Technical Committees.

and each successive stage of the work had been divided into two parts in which the Ordnance Committee undertook the investigation into the construction of the guns, strength ballistics, etc., and all details of the ammunition. But this multiplication of special committees was not a convenient method of doing business, and it was therefore decided in 1907 to make a re-arrangement. Under this the Ordnance Committee and the Ordnance Research Board[1] were amalgamated under the title of "Ordnance Board", and a new body was formed to consider matters of artillery equipment from the point of view of the users, under the title of the "Royal Artillery Committee".

The Ordnance Select Committee of 1860 had consisted almost entirely of officers of the Regiment: the reconstituted Ordnance Committee of 1881 had been given a wider membership. A further expansion was now agreed upon between the War Office and the Admiralty, and at the same time a system of direct communication between the Admiralty and the Board was inaugurated. The constitution of the Board and the Committee when they came into being on the 1st January, 1908, were as follows:—

ORDNANCE BOARD.

A naval and military officer, alternately, as President and Vice-President.
Two naval officers.
Two military officers.
The ordnance consulting officer for India.
The superintendent of research,
    with consulting engineers, chemists, etc.

ROYAL ARTILLERY COMMITTEE.

The President or Vice-President of the Ordnance Board.
The two military members of the Ordnance Board.
The ordnance consulting officer for India.

---

[1] Formed in 1906 from the Explosives Committee which had been formed in 1900 under Lord Rayleigh.

Two regimental officers of the horse and field artillery. Two regimental officers of the garrison artillery, with associate members representing field howitzers, mountain artillery, the Royal Engineer Committee, etc.

Chapter IV. The Technical Committees.

In the preceding pages no attempt has been made to give anything approaching a complete account of the business of re-armament even on its non-technical side. All that has been attempted is to place on record the more salient features of an operation of which the right timing and conduct must always be of vital importance to any nation. It is not to be undertaken inadvisedly, for it is so costly that even by the richest it can only be repeated at comparatively long intervals. The estimate for the horse and field artillery only at Home was well over four millions—it would be far more now. We were fortunate in the time, for we were able to re-arm with true quick-firers just when our old guns were wearing out. If the Government had yielded to the pressure of a vociferous party, and re-armed before the South African War, we should have got an equipment little better in principle than those in the service, though no doubt with many improvements in detail. It would not have been a true quick-firer, and it would have been a hard task to persuade any Government to re-arm again before 1914.

Conclusion.

The operation once decided upon, it must be pushed through without unnecessary delay. The period of experiment will certainly be long and tedious, and uneducated opinion will grow impatient, as it will, to a greater extent, at the inevitable delay between the placing of the orders and the first deliveries. But neither process can be hurried with impunity. When, however, the stage of production has been reached, it must be carried through as rapidly as possible, for the transition period will be fraught with peril.

In all these matters artillery officers can do much to guide public opinion towards the formation of a sound judgment, regardless of popular clamour.

CHAPTER V.

The Re-armament—Technical.

Introduction.

Care of Equipment—Tests for Experimental Equipments—Uniformity of Pattern—Modification of New Equipments—Conversion of Old Equipments.

Guns and Carriages.

Long Recoil—Independent Line of Sight—Oscillating Sights—Dial Sights — Clinometers — Breech Mechanisms — Elevating Gear — Wheels—Axletree Seats—Shields—Field Howizters—Heavy Guns —Mountain Guns.

Instruments.

Indirect Laying Stores—Telescopes and Binoculars—Range-Finders— Scales and Bubbles—Tests and Adjustments.

Ammunition.

Cartridges—Case Shot—Common Shell—High-explosive Shell—Shrapnel Shell—Combined Shell—Star Shell—Percussion Fuzes—Time and Percussion Fuzes—Mechanical Fuzes—Fuzes for Star Shell— Fuze-Setters—Fuze-Indicators—Practice Projectiles—Drill Ammunition.

Harness and Vehicles.

Breast Harness—Technical Vehicles—Material for Repair.

Introduction.

Chapter V.
Introduction.

This is not a technical treatise, and any attempt to include in it a complete account of the re-armament from a technical point of view would be out of place. It would, on the other hand, be incomplete as regimental history if it did not record the more important technical developments, for at no period since the introduction of rifled guns in the

THE RE-ARMAMENT (TECHNICAL)

middle of the XIXth century had general interest in matters of equipment been so keen. The virtues and defects of the new guns were the subject of constant discussion, and of comparison with those of continental armies, and with the latest productions of the great gun-making firms at home and abroad.[1]

In the following pages, therefore, mention will be made of all the more important features which distinguished the new equipments, those which were common to the majority being first described. Some account will also be given of various matters connected with the progress of the re-armament generally which seemed of rather too technical a nature to be included in the general account given in the last chapter.

Of the many services indirectly rendered by the purchase of the Ehrhardt guns an important one was the education they gave in the need for care in the treatment of quick-firing equipments, for their uneven shooting and frequent break-downs when not carefully tended were object-lessons which none could deny. The demand for greater power, and at the same time for greater rapidity of fire, could only be met by more complicated construction. This meant additional weight which could only be compensated for by lightening of material and consequent loss of strength. Carriages of weaker construction, containing moreover delicate mechanism, could not stand the jolts and jars of rapid movement as had done those of previous patterns with their simpler design and stronger construction. The old days of galloping into action heedless of obstacles were gone. Nos. 1 had to learn really to lead their guns, picking ground which could be driven over without damage, and to choose good platforms on which to bring them into action, without which full advantage could not be obtained from their special powers.

CHAPTER V.
Introduction.

Care of Equipment.

---

[1] These were described year by year in the *Proceedings* by Captain (now Major-General) L. R. Kenyon, C.B., and Colonel (now Brigadier-General) H. A. Bethell, C.M.G.

90   THE FIELD ARMY ARTILLERY.

CHAPTER V.

Care of Equipment.

The first rifled guns—the "Armstrongs" of the 60's—had required special attention in comparison with their predecessors the smooth-bores, and an extra artificer had been allowed to each battery to look after them. A reversion to this system was the substitution in 1904 of a carriage-smith for one of the two battery wheelers. In the following year this was followed up by the attachment of an armament artificer belonging to the Army Ordnance Corps to each brigade.[1] At the same time the appointment of wheelers was stopped so that they might die out gradually and be replaced by fitters—their *raison d'être* had vanished with the elimination of wood from the equipment except for the actual spokes and felloes. The importance of section commanders acquiring a proper knowledge of the equipment was not lost sight of, and a month at the Ordnance College[2] was added to the course for "young officers" of the field artillery.

Outside the ordinary questions connected with the care of equipment in the field, various matters had come to notice in South Africa on which guidance was lacking. The investigation of these and the insertion of the necessary instructions in the manual was one of the by-products of that war.

There had been many instances of the cartridges of batteries in action being exploded by the enemy's rifle fire, and there had been one case of the vehicles of a section being involved in a conflagration. Trials were therefore carried out to ascertain the effect of rifle fire, of gun fire, and of conflagration, on ammunition in ammunition and general service wagons, and the results were published by means of a paragraph in *Field Artillery Training 1906* describing the nature of the risk and the action to be taken.

---

[1] And to horse batteries with cavalry brigades. It was extended to India in 1911.

[2] See Chapter XXI.

THE RE-ARMAMENT (TECHNICAL)

Instructions were also inserted in this manual as to the best methods of disabling or destroying guns of modern type, and as to the responsibility for performing this duty in the case of guns captured from the enemy when they could not be carried off. The latter was a matter of some importance to the Regiment, for their traditional privilege in this respect had been challenged in South Africa. It was now laid down definitely that "the Royal Artillery will perform this duty".

CHAPTER V.

Care of Equipment.

The various tests to which the new equipments had been subjected had been evolved as the trials proceeded, but experience showed that this was not a satisfactory method. After consultation with representative officers, and a careful consideration of such practical difficulties as the finding of suitable roads and the interruption to battery training, the following definite series of tests was laid down. These had to be undergone when loaded with an extra 10%, and throughout only such care as could be given by battery artificers with the tools available on service was allowed.

Tests for Experimental Equipments.

(i). Twenty miles a day for five consecutive days over the Arsenal course. This was a track of granite setts and cobblestones with various obstacles to be surmounted.[1]

(ii). Exposure in the open for a month.

(iii). A repetition of (i).

(iv). Two hundred miles a day for five consecutive days.

Another point on which there had been no established custom was the adoption of the same patterns of equipment in the Imperial and Indian services. The general idea at the amalgamation was no doubt that this would

Uniformity of Pattern.

---

[1] Later on it was proposed to adopt a "travelling machine" as in use abroad. This consisted of a pair of 9-ft. drums on which the vehicles were placed. The drums could be revolved at any speed desired to simulate walk trot or gallop, and rough ground could be represented by slats upon them. This would be a great relief to batteries, but not so good a representation as the Arsenal course.

92 THE FIELD ARMY ARTILLERY.

Uniformity of Pattern.

be done, as shown by the well-known case of the adoption of shaft-draught in 1859, but India had broken away in adopting a lighter pattern of siege howitzer and a heavier pattern of field howitzer. Many disparities in perfectly immaterial details had also crept in, as for instance in the patterns of axletree arms the difference in which only came to notice when supplies of the 13 and 18-pr. equipments for India were due from the trade. No one knew the reason for the difference, but it was obviously undesirable, and so after a trial at home the Indian pattern was approved for the Imperial Service.

Modification of New Equipments.

The general issue of the new equipments naturally brought a sheaf of suggestions for improvements. For the most part these did not merit very serious consideraation since the authors could not have experience at all comparable with that of the officers of the committee who had recommended the designs, or of the batteries which had carried out the trials. Later on, when all ranks had gained familiarity with the equipments the position was different. Experience under all the varying conditions even of peace service, and progress in gun design, showed the necessity of some modifications, and it will probably be convenient to anticipate events and notice in this chapter, when describing the various equipments, the alterations and additions that it was found practical to make before the War.

There were also, of course, various alterations to all the equipments due to cutting the weights too fine—taking up of "play", strengthening of parts which had shown weakness and so forth, and a stronger wheel—C.45—was found necessary.

Unfortunately the cumulative effect of these alterations, small though most of them were individually, was to increase the total weight behind the team to a somewhat alarming extent. By 1909 this had gone up:—

13-pr. from 30cwt. 0qr. 12lb. to 32cwt. 3qrs. 24lb.
18-pr. from 38cwt. 2qrs. 6lb. to 40cwt. 0qr. 16lb.

THE RE-ARMAMENT (TECHNICAL) 93

Mention must also be made of those modifications in design which, for financial or technical reasons could not be applied to the existing equipments, but which had been decided upon for incorporation in any new equipment when the time for another re-armament should come. These will be considered in Chapter IX.

CHAPTER V.
Modification of New Equipments.

A discussion of the modifications that were made during the Great War would be beyond the scope of this history. In many cases these were due to causes which could hardly have been anticipated, such as the right material not being available, or the extension of manufacture from the great armament firms to factories which had no experience of munitions work. It must at the same time be admitted that the strain to which the equipments were to be subjected had never been provided for. Prolonged and rapid firing beyond all previous conception—especially with only partially trained detachments—was a test far beyond anything that had been suggested in the trials.

With the re-armament of the Field Army Artillery there came the question of bringing the older equipments up to date. The Ehrhardt guns, which had been brought into the service as "15-pr. Q.F.", were given cordite charges in place of ballistite,[1] and on issue to the horse artillery of the Territorial Force had their axletree seats removed and shields added. A system of conversion for the 15-pr. B.L.[2] submitted by General Mondragon of the Mexican Artillery was considered, but was found to be prohibitive in cost. Eventually it was decided simply to fit the carriage for long recoil, which would greatly increase

Conversion of Old Equipments.

---

[1] This did not improve their shooting, but was necessitated by the fact that ballistite would not stand the extremes of climate incidental to the British service.

[2] The 15-pr. B.L. was originally the 12-pr. of 7 cwt. introduced for both horse and field artillery in 1883. In 1895 it was superseded by the 12-pr. of 6 cwt. for horse artillery, and converted to a 15-pr. for field. In 1899 it was again modified by the substitution of single-motion breech mechanism for the old three-motion, and the addition of an axle-spade. There were many marks with slight variations.

CHAPTER V.

Conversion of Old Equipments.

the rapidity of fire and permit the addition of a shield. After trials in 1907-8 a design was approved, and the 15-pr. B.L. became the 15-pr. B.L.C. It was issued to the field artillery of the Territorial Force in time for practice in 1909.

With the 5″ field howitzer no such extensive alteration was considered practicable, but its most serious shortcoming, that of range—only 4,800 yards—was ameliorated by the introduction of 40-lb. shells, with which a range of 6,000 yards could be obtained. Shrapnel shell were also approved, and although not included in the equipment of batteries, some were allowed for annual practice.

Directly after the South African War prolonged trials were carried out with a view to perfecting the mounting and sighting of the pom-poms. In view, however, of the decline in their popularity, and the improbability of any more being required, it was decided in 1904 to take no further action.

GUNS AND CARRIAGES.

Long Recoil.

In describing the purchase of the Ehrhardt guns in Chapter I it was explained how a carriage which would remain stationary on the gun being fired was the essential feature of the new equipments. In order to obtain a non-recoiling carriage the gun must be allowed to recoil freely on the carriage, and to provide for this it was placed in a cradle through which it could slide, checked by a hydraulic buffer and returned to the firing position by springs. There were arrangements, differing in detail in the individual equipments for equalizing the resistance during recoil, and so avoiding any tendency of the carriage to lift, also for bringing the gun to rest gradually on return to the firing position. The length of recoil varied from 41″ in the 13 and 18-prs. to 60″ in the 60-pr., the recuperator springs being double-banked to avoid excessive length. The position of the buffer and springs

THE RE-ARMAMENT (TECHNICAL) 95

relatively to the gun was also different in the different natures, but the general principle was the same.

In order to allow some traverse without disturbing the trail spade when anchored, a "carriage body" or "top carriage" was interposed between the cradle and the trail, its front end pivoted about the axle, its rear sliding across the trail, and giving some 4 degrees to each side.

The advantages of the non-recoiling carriage may be summed up as giving a great gain in rapidity, accuracy, and protection over the recoiling type. By attaching the sights and elevating gear to the non-recoiling portion the layers could follow the target continuously, and all could sit close to their work so that the whole service of the gun was accelerated. It allowed also of a shield being employed to advantage, which was not the case when the numbers had to "step clear" before firing.

The difference between the new equipments and those of the earlier ones in which there had also been a cradle with buffer and springs was in the length of the recoil allowed to the gun. When first applied this movement was short, the object being merely to communicate the shock of the gun's recoil to the carriage gradually, not to reduce the recoil of the latter.

The "rocking-bar" or "bar and drum" sights adopted with the new equipments were a great improvement on the old tangent and fore sights, and the bar formed a convenient support for a telescope so that the system lent itself to the combination of telescopic and open sights, the adjustments for elevation and deflection being common to both—a much more convenient arrangement than the telescopic sight on the trunnion introduced with the first B.L. guns in the 80's. But the great development in sighting which followed from the adoption of the non-recoiling carriage was the system known as the "Independent Line of Sight". Under the old system the elevation due to the range had first to be put on the tangent sight, and the sights then aligned on the target, any alterations of range requiring resetting of the sight

CHAPTER V.

Long Recoil.

The Independent Line of Sight.

Chapter V.

The Independent Line of Sight.

and relaying of the gun. Under the new system the two operations of aligning the line of sight on the target, and giving the necessary elevation for the range, were separated and performed independently by different numbers, and the layer could keep his sight on the target, undisturbed by changes in elevation. The system had the further advantage of being equally applicable to indirect laying by the use of a simple clinometer attached to the rocking-bar sight on which the angle of sight was set. On the other hand owing to the difficulty of combining the reciprocating principle with rocking-bar sights any difference in level of wheels had to be allowed for by deflection. Since also the elevation of the gun was quite independent of the amount the sight was raised or lowered, the old rule for this could not be employed. Various devices for indicating the difference in level were tried in 1911-12-13, but no decision was reached.

Oscillating Sights.

With heavy equipments such as the 60-pr., with which there must often be considerable and varying differences of level of wheels, and with which accuracy of line was often of great importance when engaging narrow targets, such as shielded guns at long ranges, it was important to avoid the necessity for constantly measuring the distance and calculating the required correction. The 60pr., therefore, was provided with an ordinary tangent sight and fore sight on one side, instead of a rocking-bar sight, and a special "oscillating" sight on the other. By cross levelling this latter any difference in level of wheels was automatically allowed for, thus avoiding the necessity of giving a calculated deflection.

Dial Sights.

In its original form the dial—or, as it was first called, the "lining-plane" or "goniometric" sight—was a very simple article, consisting only of a sighting bar pivoted in the centre of a circular dial graduated in degrees, which was mounted on the shield, or on a pillar in unshieded guns. Even so it was a great improvement on the "gun-arcs" which had been improvised in South Africa; but it had two serious blemishes. In the first place, in order to view

THE RE-ARMAMENT (TECHNICAL)

an aiming point not in the line of fire, the layer had to change his position thus probably losing the protection of the shield: in the second place, being on the shield, it did not move with the gun when the traversing gear was used. All the new equipments were, however, provided with sights on this principle, although with successive improvement in detail, and these were numbered 1 to 6 according to the particular equipment with which they were used. In the meanwhile the "Panorama" sight had appeared, and after careful trials with various patterns in 1907-8-9 the "Goerz" was adopted for the service under the title of "Dial Sight, No. 7". It consisted of a vertical telescope with a horizontal eye-piece and a top prism which could be turned so as to give a view in any direction without moving the eye-piece. The layer, therefore, need not move from his seat, and with a carrier giving elevation and deflection the dial sight could be used for direct as well as indirect laying. Like the original sights, the carriers were numbered to show the equipment with which they were to be used, but No. 7 sight could be used with all.

Satisfactory as the No. 7 Dial Sight was, its carriage presented considerable difficulties, and all through 1912 and 1913 trials of various arrangements were going on. It was not until 1914 that a pattern of leather case to carry the sight and carrier on the shield was approved.

In spite of the addition of clinometers to the rocking-bar sights it was thought advisable to provide the new equipments with separate clinometers for miscellaneous purposes. The old "Watkin" pattern was slow to set, and difficult to read, so it was replaced by a foreign pattern consisting of a simple segmental frame, with a degree scale on the arc, at the centre of which a radial arm carrying a spirit level was pivoted.

All the experimental 13 and 18-pr. guns had single-motion breech mechanisms, some of the swinging-block and some of the sliding-wedge type. The committee finally decided to recommend the Vicker's mechanism,

CHAPTER V.

Dial Sights.

Clinometers.

Breech Mechanisms.

98 THE FIELD ARMY ARTILLERY.

Chapter V.
Breech Mechanisms.

thus adhering to the swinging-block type which had been in use with all the later British B.L. and Q.F. guns. It was in a new[1] form, however, in that the breech-screw was tapered with its largest diameter towards the front, thus forming a wedge secure against the possibility of being blown out. Noticeable also was the simplicity of the mechanism which could be dismantled by the removal of only three hinge-pins. The firing mechanism was a simple "trip-action" in which the layer released the percussion striker by means of a conveniently placed firing lever.

In the 4·5" howitzer, however, the sliding-wedge type of breech-mechanism, previously only used in 3-pr. and 6-pr. Q.F. guns, was reintroduced. Quite irrespective of the type of breech-mechanism the firing arrangements of a howitzer could not be so convenient as those of a gun, owing to the wide range of elevation. At first a lanyard was employed which had to be hooked in, and this naturally caused much complaint by those who had to use such a clumsy method. Eventually it was found possible to substitute a short toggle, and abolish the objectionable lanyard.

With mountain and heavy guns we get back to bare charges, and the consequent necessity for including an obturator in the breech-mechanism. It was hoped that an automatic tube supply would get over this disadvantage in the case of mountain guns, and various designs, becoming ever more complicated, were tried from 1911 onwards, but with disappointing results. Some breech-mechanisms so fitted were under trial in India in 1914.

With the 60-pr. it was considered advisable to have a cylindrical breech-screw, and in order to get "single-motion" with this, special means were necessary to seat and unseat the obturator, and to obtain the necessary clearance for swinging the screw clear. For this a sliding

---

[1] This was its introduction to the Imperial service but it had been in use in the Vickers 2·95" Q.F. in Colonial Service since 1897.

THE RE-ARMAMENT (TECHNICAL) 99

hinge-bolt was introduced. The firing arrangement included a safety shutter and tube extractor, and admitted the insertion of a new tube without opening the breech in the event of a missfire.

The elevating gear of all the new equipments embodied the principle of the "Independent Line of Sight" already explained, but the method of application varied. In the field guns it consisted of a double-ended screw the upper portion of which moved the gun relatively to the line of sight, and so gave the elevation due to the range, while the lower portion moved the line of sight and gun together relatively to the horizontal. These gears were worked by hand wheels on the right and left of the carriage, with on the right a range-dial, on the left the rocking-bar sight.

With the 4·5″ howitzer, since leading at high angles of elevation is not practicable, and time would be lost in depressing and elevating again, means were provided for disconnecting the howitzer from the elevating gear and lifting the breech by hand into the loading position, and then replacing it at the original angle of elevation.

From time immemorial the Royal Artillery had pinned their faith on their tall five-foot wheels and had scoffed at those of smaller diameter favoured on the continent as synonymous with a lower standard of mobility. But experience with the 4′ 6″ wheels of the Ehrhardts showed that there might be something to be said on the other side, and after a careful examination of the question the Committee decided on 4′ 8″ for the new field equipments, retaining 5′ wheels only for the heavy batteries.

Another new feature was the addition of a dust-cap and the consequent disappearance of the old linch-pin with its leather tie. The dust-cap on the outer end, and an "L" leather inside, excluded dust and grit from the pipe-box and at the same time prevented the lubricant working out.

For the brakes, the "swinging-arm" type was adopted. In this the brake-blocks were carried on arms pivoted to the trail, and connected by actuating rods and ball-crank levers. By turning a handle on these, either in front or

CHAPTER V.

Breech Mechanisms.

Elevating Gear.

Wheels.

100   THE FIELD ARMY ARTILLERY.

CHAPTER V.

Wheels.

behind the shield, the blocks could be jammed against the tyres or withdrawn. A quick-release was also provided for use when making short changes of position without limbering up. Disc springs gave resilience to the system, and prevented the wheels being locked when travelling.

Axletree Seats.

In the effort to get the "power" which war experience had demanded in the new field gun without exceeding the limit laid down for the total weight behind the team, the designers had been obliged to increase the weight on the gun wheels far beyond that on the limber wheels. In order to reduce this it was decided to remove the axletree seats, thus reversing the decision of 1871 which had done so much to extend the tactical rôle of the field artillery. The acceptance of the fact that a quick-firing gun must always be accompanied by its wagon made this possible without restricting the mobility. The 13 and 18-pr. equipments thus became precisely similar, differing only in dimensions.

Shields.

An important feature of all the new equipments except the 60-pr.[1] were the gun shields, and the use of bullet-proof steel for the limber and wagon boxes also, thus removing the last vestige of wood from the equipment. Both these and the gun shields had a lower portion hinged so that it could be turned up for travelling and lowered in action, and the howitzer shield had a top portion on the same principle.

Many incidents in the South African War had shown what value shields would have been, but when their adoption was first proposed there were not wanting objectors who feared that the gunners would take cover behind them instead of "standing up and working their guns".[2]

---

[1] The 60-pr. had bullet-proof covering over the spring cases.
[2] Similarly when the guns were painted khaki before the great cavalry manœuvres in India in 1891 the Press deplored this attempt at "hiding" the guns as out of tune with the traditions of the R.H.A., and certain to have a bad effect on the *moral* of the men.

THE RE-ARMAMENT (TECHNICAL)

CHAPTER V.

Shields.

In Manchuria neither side possessed shielded guns, but both Russians and Japanese frequently improvised them, and there were well authenticated instances of batteries so protected sustaining both artillery and infantry fire for prolonged periods with comparatively trifling loss. There was no question but that shields would be a feature of all new field artillery equipments, for guns at any rate. As regards field howitzers there was considerable doubt as to their necessity, and with the experience of the 5″ howitzers in South Africa there was great reluctance to any increase of weight. Eventually, after much discussion, it was decided in 1908 that the 4·5″ howitzer equipment should include shields, but for heavy guns the decision at the same time was to the opposite effect. The conditions were, of course, very different. To obtain good protection a large, and consequently heavy, shield would be necessary, and even so the detachment would lose its protection every time the gun was fired owing to the necessity for standing clear of the recoil.

The general adoption of shields for field guns led to some change of opinion regarding the power of artillery to withstand attack. It had been contended by infantrymen before the end of the last century that guns in action were at the mercy of riflemen if they could creep up to within a thousand yards, and South Africa had shown the justice of their contention. But what could such marksmen do against shielded guns, each gun and its attendant wagon forming a bullet-proof fort? As Von Lobell's annual report on military matters in 1907 said—"Infantry will have to renounce its favourite practice of attempting to silence guns in action: they had better leave this to the artillery". A different complexion was, however, put upon the matter by improvements in bullets. Our shields were tested with the service rifle at 400 yards, but the French "D" and the German "S" bullets considerably reduced the range up to which shields were proof against rifle fire. There were trials in 1912 of steel of superior quality, and, with the adoption in 1913 of the dial

I

102 THE FIELD ARMY ARTILLERY.

Chapter V.

Shields.

sight as the normal method of laying, the provision of a hinged flap to cover the rocking-bar aperture as in the 4·5″ was taken up for the 13 and 18-prs. The trial was in progress in July 1914.

In the foregoing paragraphs attention has been drawn to the more important innovations which were incorporated in the new equipments of the horse, field, field howitzer, mountain, and heavy artillery. In addition to these the following features, special to particular natures, deserve notice.

Field Howitzers.

A peculiar difficulty in designing a field howitzer carriage is the large range of elevation demanded in it. All field army artillery weapons must be capable of point-blank fire, and in the case of the howitzer from that up to 45° is required. This complicates the control of the recoil; the trail must have a wide opening to admit the breech of the howitzer when elevated, and the trunnions must be high or the breech will strike the ground in recoil, while if they are unduly high the stability will be affected. The system adopted in the 4·5″ equipment was one by which the recoil varied automatically with the elevation,[1] being greatest at low elevations where the tendency to jump and run back was greatest, while at the higher elevations it was short thus reducing the clearance required. The method of control was by means of a rotating valve actuated by gearing attached to the cradle. The axletree was cranked in order to keep the weight low, the howitzer itself being above the cradle.

Heavy Guns.

The 60-pr. brought many innovations. Owing to the weight of the gun and carriage a "travelling position" for the gun had to be provided so as to equalize the weight on the gun and limber wheels. For this purpose it was mounted on a saddle which could be moved along the trail. In order that the balance of the pole might not be affected it was arranged that the pressure

---

[1] From 40″ when horizontal to 20″ at 45°.

THE RE-ARMAMENT (TECHNICAL) 103

on the limber should come on a point directly above the axletree, and this in turn involved the provision of a special device to separate the two ordinary functions of a limber-hook and trail eye—viz. the support of the trail and the draught of the carriage. This device consisted of a "coupling block" into which the trail-eye fitted, and it rested upon a curved surface to compensate for the varying inclination of the pole due to changes of gradient. The limber was fitted for horse, bullock, and engine draught.

Practical experience showed the necessity of considerable modifications. An altered spade allowed of the abolition of firing shoes. The substitution of tackle for running back gear further reduced the total weight, but on the other hand some parts which were not sufficiently rigid had to be strengthened. In order to reduce the excessive recoil at high angles a new design of control cylinders, tank, and plunger was approved in 1912.

The 10-pr. B.L. was a breech-loader and fired cordite, and its 10-lb. shell[1] and 6,000 yards range were a great improvement on the 7-lb. shell and 4,000 yards range of its predecessor. But its gas sealing arrangements were not at first so satisfactory, and its carriage was of the same simple recoiling type. The mountain artillery could scarcely be expected to remain content with a rigid carriage when long recoil was the order of the day. The new carriage eventually decided upon was on the same general lines as that of the 13 and 18-prs. modified to meet the limitations imposed by its division for pack transport. It was provided with a shield, and a special feature was the cranked axletree by turning which the height of the gun axis could be raised from 32 to 43 inches, thus allowing of the increase of elevation from 15 to 22 degrees, or reduced in order to get better cover. For use on this carriage the 10-pr. gun was converted by the removal of the trunnions, the

CHAPTER V.

Heavy Guns

Mountain Guns.

---

[1] Its common shell proved of great value in breaching the walls of "Tongs" in the Tibet expedition of 1904.

weight of shell was increased to 12½lbs., and the whole equipment was given the name of "2·75″ B.L." It was approved for the service in 1911.

While on the subject of mountain artillery some mention must be made of another equipment which had been in use before the end of the XIXth century by the Egyptian Army. There was a Vickers 75 mm gun—really a howitzer—firing a 12½-lb. shell and an 18-lb. double shell. Under the quaint title of "The Millimetre Gun" it had gained much popularity with the West African Frontier Force owing to its power of dealing with stockades and such contingencies of jungle fighting. But in range, accuracy, and shrapnel effect it was inferior to the 10-pr., and the equipment was quite unsuited for mountain work. It was, however, brought into the service under the title of the "2·95″ Q.F." for the movable armament of some coaling stations for which it was excellently adapted. It was the first pack equipment to be fitted with a buffer, but, like those in many field equipments previous to the re-armament, this buffer was only to ease the strain on the carriage, not to eliminate its recoil.

Before leaving the subject of mountain equipments mention must be made of a change of considerable importance which was generally adopted with the introduction of the new equipments, viz: the fitting of these for draught. To the mountain artilleryman of the straitest sect the idea of putting his mules into draught was anathema. But study of the experience of foreign nations which maintained large forces of mountain artillery, and especially perhaps of Russian "horse mountain" batteries in Asia, showed the value of this method of relieving the mules of the weight on their back when circumstances rendered it practicable. The issue of mountain guns to movable armaments at many of the coaling stations clinched the argument, for the full scale of mules required for pack was out of the question. All the new equipments were therefore provided with fittings on the trail for shafts,

THE RE-ARMAMENT (TECHNICAL)

the pack saddlery was adapted to take these, and the necessary modifications were made to the wheels.

CHAPTER V.

Mountain Guns.

INSTRUMENTS.

The manual of 1906 was the first to give any description of the appliances which were coming into use in order to facilitate shooting from covered positions. They consisted of clinometers, aiming posts, field plotters, directors (with stand and telescope), and gun-arcs.[1] But before indirect laying could become a really practical system it was necessary that the gun should be fitted with a dial sight, clinometer, and range-indicator. These were provided with the new equipments, so nothing more need be said here of the gun arcs.

Indirect Laying Stores.

The *aiming posts* require little description, they remained practically unaltered, although improved by painting, by varying the shape of the heads of those of alternate guns, and by the provision of a special pair for the battery commander. The latter, of a less cumbersome pattern, with a saddle bucket, were only introduced in 1914.

The *field plotter* was designed to solve mechanically the triangle TOB, which was the first requirement if fire was to be directed from an observing station at some distance from the guns. It obviated the use of a slide-rule and any calculations. A simple instrument, it only required one small modification during the whole period. Marks III and IV were similar, but designed for heavy and siege artillery respectively. The *director*, with which the plotter was used, consisted of a simple boxwood rule with sighting vanes, revolving on a circular graduated base-plate mounted on a tripod stand. In 1910 a new pattern, "No. 3", was approved, designed to give greater accuracy in the

---

[1] These were boards about a yard long, graduated in half degrees, with, at each graduation, a hole for the reception of an acorn-shaped foresight.

CHAPTER V.
Indirect Laying Stores.

measurement of horizontal angles and angles of sight. A novel feature was the addition of a compass so as to enable lines of fire to be laid out when the battery director could not be seen from the observing station, or when the latter's director was in such a position that there was difficulty in laying it on the battery. In enclosed country this might well be the only way of getting the line of fire, and the addition of a similar compass to No. 1 Director was under trial in 1914.

The *stand* consisted of a carrier with spirit level, pivot, base-plate (graduated to 180% each way), and legs.

The carriage of the director and its stand on a horse presented some difficulty if good protection was to be combined with ease of withdrawal. There were prolonged trials of various patterns of cases, and approval was only given in the last years—that for the stand in 1913 and for the director itself in 1914.

Angle of Sight Instrument.—With the increased use of covered positions the correct ascertaining of the angle of sight had become one of the chief problems of a battery commander, and naturally many ingenious devices were put forward to assist him in finding it with reasonable accuracy from positions to which it was not convenient to carry an instrument on a stand such as a No. 2 or No. 3 director. Eventually an instrument was approved under the above title, to be shortly followed by an improved pattern which was provided with a gunmetal slide so that it could be used on the director stand if required. It consisted of a brass box forming a prismatic telescope and containing the necessary spirit level, etc.

An "electric level" which could be fitted to a pair of binoculars, so as to give a zero, was also proposed, but the pair ordered for trial were only received in July, 1914.

Telescopes and Binoculars

The telescope introduced in 1903 was that previously known as the "special signalling", which changed its name to "Telescope Field Artillery Mark II", and was fitted with sighting vanes and a saddle so that it could be used on the same stand as the director. No expense had been

THE RE-ARMAMENT (TECHNICAL) 107

spared in providing batteries with which was considered the best available instrument, but unfortunately the experience of the clear atmosphere of South Africa had resulted in an obsession for high power, and the year in which the telescopes were tried at home was also abnormally dry. No sooner had the telescopes been procured than the climate returned to normal, and their high power only magnified the mist. The Royal Artillery had to be equipped for fighting in any climate and the only solution was variable power. Accordingly, after trials in 1906 and 1907 the Telescope Variable Power was approved—No. 1 for siege artillery, No. 2 for heavy.

The *binoculars* of which a dozen pair were issued to batteries in 1903, were all of the Galilean pattern, but there was soon a demand for prismatic glasses which had made their name in the South African War. The most generally used patterns of these, chiefly by Zeiss and Ross, were brought into the service, and numbered for distinction, while a large number of miscellaneous makes were simply divided into classes. As a result of the experience with time shrapnel ranging in 1910, the question of fitting graticules came to the front. These were really indispensable both for time shrapnel ranging and for obtaining parallelism of lines of fire, but the engraving of the graticules delayed matters, and it was not until 1913 that a "No. 3" pattern was adopted, fitted with a glass diaphragm. It was nearly as good as No. 2 (the siege artillery pattern) but smaller and cheaper.

With the extension of the use of covered positions and distant observing stations the importance of accurate range-taking became evident. There was a tendency to reconsider the claims of the telemeter, which was still used by howitzer batteries, and was undoubtedly more accurate than the mekometer,[1] and its improvement was

CHAPTER V.

Telescopes and Binoculars.

Rangefinders.

[1] In the *Proceedings* for 1906 (Vol. XXXIII) there is a very interesting paper by Bombardier Ansell of the 2nd Field Battery, giving the results of eleven years experience as range-taker in India, South Africa, and England, with the three service instruments—The Watkin Field Range-finder, the Telemeter, and the Mekometer.

CHAPTER V.

Range-finders.

taken up. The tripods were made to fold up, the instrument was graduated to 10,000 yards, and in 1911 Mark IV was introduced for heavy artillery, provided with a prismatic telescope, capable of taking ranges up to 20,000 yards.

But there was no getting away from the fact that the three pickets with their flags were still very conspicuous, and that the range-taker had two operations to perform— the fixing of the right angle and the measuring of the base —before he could apply himself to the range-taking proper. To do so he had to go from end to end of a base, which was certainly 50 and might be 125 yards. What was wanted was an accurate one-man instrument. The Marindin had been introduced for the infantry in 1909, and the artillery clamoured for something of the same sort, with its advantages of a single observer, rapidity of action, and possibility of taking ranges of a moving object, even if these advantages necessitated increased weight, size, and delicacy of the instrument. In 1908 the Royal Artillery Committee took up the matter, and formulated the conditions to be fulfilled, and in 1909 seven different instruments were tried on Salisbury Plain. For field artillery the Zeiss was preferred, and a dozen were obtained and tried during the next two years with satisfactory results. There were obvious objections to being dependent on a foreign country for the supply, and possible repair, of such an essential part of our artillery equipment, and a specification was got out in the hope that some English firm might be able to meet the requirements. Eventually, in 1913, a Barr and Stroud pattern was approved as "Range-finder Artillery No. 1". It was of the coincidence type, with a metre base, and read to 10,000 yards. Mark II was generally similar but the size of the inverted field was reduced. A Zeiss instrument for heavy artillery, embodying some extra features for taking the range of aircraft was tried in 1913, and in 1914 one of a still improved pattern was ordered for trial. It was not delivered.

It was desired to have one stand suitable for use with

THE RE-ARMAMENT (TECHNICAL) 109

either the Zeiss (of which another 40 had been obtained) or the Barr and Stroud, and trials in 1913 resulted in the introduction of Mark I, followed shortly by Mark II which differed in material and details.[1] Adjusting laths suitable for both patterns took a similar course. Cases for carrying the equipment by a mounted man required much adding of felt pads, steadying girths, etc., before they could be considered satisfactory.

Chapter V. Rangefinders.

A side-light on the interest taken in sighting and similar instruments during these years is given by the changes made in the marking of graduations to facilitate reading. The first step was to agree on some principle which should be applicable to all such instruments, and the arrangement adopted was that "Right" and "Depression" graduations should be in red, "Left" and "Elevation" in black. In 1909 the right side was to be silvered, figures in black, the left side black with white figures. In 1911 this was superseded by white on a black ground for right, black on brass for the left.

Scales and Bubbles.

The spirit bubbles also came in for attention; and at practice in 1912 a coloured bubble, known as the "cats-eye" was tried, approved, and made the service pattern for all instruments having spirit-levels.

The importance attached to the accurate adjustment of the various instruments, with which the field army artillery was so amply dowered during this period, is shown also by the yearly elaboration of the regulations for their testing and adjustment.

Tests and Adjustments.

AMMUNITION.

For the new field guns the Equipment Committee insisted upon "fixed" ammunition as affording the greatest rapidity of loading and firing, while minimising the

Cartridges.

---

[1] A "hanger" was provided for use when taking ranges without the stand. It consisted of a leather breastplate and shoulder straps, with a pair of iron wire supports for the instrument

110 THE FIELD ARMY ARTILLERY.

CHAPTER V.
Cartridges.

number of men with the gun. The combination of the whole round in one piece also obviated all chance of the omission of any component in supply. For howitzers, fixed ammunition was impossible owing to the different charges used, and "case" ammunition was adopted as the nearest substitute. For mountain and heavy guns there were reasons for retaining "bare" charges. With both natures the saving of weight was of consequence, while the loss of rapidity of fire was not important for heavy artillery, and in the case of mountain was discounted by the chance of a dinted case causing difficulty in loading.

Although in cordite an almost absolutely smokeless powder had been found there were still difficulties about the charges. Gunpowder priming gave an appreciable amount of smoke, sufficient in some cases to give away the position, and guncotton and other smokeless primings tried had grave objections, due either to liability to hangfires, want of stability or tendency to affect the ballistics. Gunpowder had none of these objections, and was used abroad, so in 1906 it was accepted for the igniters of all service charges.

No sooner was this question settled than the keeping qualities of cordite began to cause anxiety. There were explosions—or rather conflagrations—in India and elsewhere, but when it was found that the temperature in the limber boxes had been as high as 140 degrees, it was decided that all that was necessary was some protection from the sun.

The cases also began to give trouble. At one time a good many jams occurred in rapid fire, and a key had to be provided to which a drag-rope could be hooked for their extraction. A change in the drill got over this trouble, but it recurred in a more serious form in 1913 owing to insufficient hardening of the brass, for which a manufacturing test had to be introduced. Splitting was more alarming, but after careful trials as regards danger to the detachments, it was decided that all that was re-

THE RE-ARMAMENT (TECHNICAL) 111

quired to avoid damage to the mechanisms was a gas escape hole in the carrier ring.

Finally there were complaints of missfires. These were found to be due to the powder shaking out of the primers when travelling, so a Mark II primer was introduced and Mark I declared obsolete.

The most serious matter connected with the ammunition, and one that was never satisfactorily overcome, was the case of "blank". An endeavour to find a reliable smokeless blank cartridge had followed immediately on the introduction of smokeless powder in the last century, but had met with no success. In 1902 a present of a dozen rounds of their smokeless blank by the German Government gave hopes of a solution, but failed again. That issued for manœuvres in 1904 was described as resulting in "a squib-like action giving little or no sound and considerable smoke". The discovery of "sonite" promised well, and it was adopted for all field guns in 1906, but the manœuvres of 1913 were the first in which nothing but smokeless was used.

In the old smooth-bore days case-shot had been the favourite projectile of the horse and field artillery, especially of the former. With the introduction of rifled guns much of the old rapidity of fire was lost, and it was suspected that the rifling by imparting some rotation seriously diminished the effect of the shot. But right up to the end of the XIXth century the final episode of the practice at Okehampton was the advance of a brigade at the gallop to expend its allowance of case at the dummies in flight. South Africa gave the death-blow to that. Colenso had shown the power of the rifle to make impossible the approach of guns to case—or double case—range, and although at Diamond Hill it had been used with effect by one section in defence, further experience had pointed to its want of stopping power. In the later stages of the South African War, when columns were engaged in rounding up cattle, some battery commanders carried out trials which showed that shrapnel set at 0 were

CHAPTER V.
Cartridges.

Case Shot.

THE FIELD ARMY ARTILLERY.

Case Shot. far more effective, and this conclusion was confirmed by official experiments during the re-armament. It was, therefore, decided not to provide any case for the new equipments,[1] but to insist upon T & P fuzes being so made that, when set at 0, they would burst the shrapnel within 50 yards from the muzzle.

Common Shell. The old powder-filled common shell had been given up for field guns with the introduction of the 15-pr. B.L. and only lingered on in the equipment of mountain artillery, in which also the "double" shell for the destruction of the enemy's strongholds had been a tradition since the days of the little 7-pr., the nose of whose double shell when rammed home still "peeped coyly from the muzzle".

High-explosive Shell. With the abolition of common shell[2] for field guns had come the introduction of the field howitzer, with lyddite as its sole projectile. Trials at the time seemed to show that this was about the smallest calibre with which satisfactory results with high-explosive could be expected, and this opinion was confirmed by the very general failure of the 5″ howitzer lyddite to detonate in South Africa—a failure which was for some time obscured by the belief of the army that the yellow smoke, which too often accompanied their explosion, denoted detonation. There was no question, however, but that high-explosive shell must be provided for the 4·5″ howitzers and 60-prs., the question was whether a satisfactory high-explosive shell could be obtained for the 13 and 18-prs. Trials were carried out when the latter equipments were in the experimental stage, and again a few years later as a result of the Manchurian War, but without much success. At the same time it was proved by experiment that shrapnel might be trusted to do all that was necessary to put a

---

[1] Except for mountain guns.

[2] Vol. I, pp. 252-3. Common shell were, however, used largely at practice to represent both shrapnel and lyddite. They were cheap but very unpopular.

THE RE-ARMAMENT (TECHNICAL)

shielded gun out of action, and also to penetrate the wall of any ordinary farm house and burst in the room behind. There were reports of many Japanese guns put out of action by prematures with their high-explosive shell, and nervousness as to the possibility of explosions in the limbers in fast movement. The general opinion was that any gain in effect to be hoped for with such shell with field guns was not worth the risk inseparable from their transport and firing.[1] The best solution appeared to lie in the recognition of the distinction between the functions of gun and howitzer, and the leaving of high-explosive shell to the latter, and this was confirmed by the very successful trials on Salisbury Plain with the 4·5″ howitzer lyddite against Rushall Down Farm placed in a state of defence, and against the bomb-proofs of a field work. In 1914 the only field army artillery to carry lyddite shell were the field howitzer and heavy batteries and those mountain batteries armed with 2·75″ guns. The soundness of this course was generally accepted both by the authorities and by regimental opinion, in consideration of the addition of a howitzer brigade to each division, which provided for the shrapnel fire of the guns being supplemented by the high-explosive shell of the howitzers.

Before leaving the subject of high-explosive shell mention must be made of the difficulty of designing these so as to range the same as shrapnel. With both the 4·5″ howitzer and the 60-pr. it was of importance that they should do so in order that ranging might be carried out with lyddite when the observation of percussion shrapnel was difficult, and also so as to allow of changing from one to the other at any moment, as when the proximity of our own infantry in the final stage of an attack, made accuracy of fire of supreme importance. This necessitated

---

[1] The final views of the authorities on this vexed question will be found in the conditions laid down in 1913 for a new field gun.—Appendix D.

114 THE FIELD ARMY ARTILLERY.

Chapter V.
High-explosive Shell.
Shrapnel Shell.

the lyddite being made of the same weight and external dimensions as the shrapnel, in spite of the appreciable reduction in the bursting charge, and consequently in the effect of the burst which this entailed.

One of the most important lessons of the South African War had been the utter inefficiency as a man-killing projectile of common shell when fired from guns, even against defined and located targets, and the efficiency of good time shrapnel under similar circumstances. With the disappearance of case-shot, and the general disinclination to consider the introduction of high-explosive shell for field guns, shrapnel reached the peak of its popularity. "One shell and one fuze" appealed to the great majority, and every effort was made to increase the effectiveness of the shrapnel.

Since the bullets were the only "useful" part of the shell the first object was to reduce the proportion of weight devoted to other parts so long as sufficient strength was retained to prevent setting up in the bore or breaking up in flight. By using the best material and methods it was found possible in the 18-pr. to devote practically half the total weight to the bullets.

The next question was the right size and material for the bullets. In order to get as many as possible into the shell they must be small, but to be effective they must have a striking energy of 60 ft.-pounds. They must therefore be made of the heaviest material. Lead was too soft, so a small amount of antimony was added. Trials showed that for field guns the best size of these "mixed metal bullets" was 41 to the pound, for field howitzers and heavy guns a little heavier to compensate for the low velocity of the former, and to allow of a large bullet area with the latter. The result was the following:—

13-pr. — — 236 bullets at 41 to the pound.
18-pr. — — 374 ,, ,, ,, ,, ,, ,,
4·5″ — — 492 ,, ,, 35 ,, ,, ,,
60-pr. — — 990 ,, ,, ,, ,, ,, ,,

THE RE-ARMAMENT (TECHNICAL) 115

Another point had however to be taken into consideration now that common shell had disappeared, viz. that shrapnel when burst on graze should give sufficient smoke for observation during ranging. Year after year as ranges increased battery commanders pleaded more and more strenuously for an increase in the smoke. There were also suggestions that special "smoke" shrapnel, possibly with coloured smoke, might be useful for indicating points for concentration of fire and for blinding portions of the enemy's position. Experiments with various substances—ranging from amorphous phosphorous to chalk—as a substitute for the resin between the bullets always ended in disappointment. Some gave prematures in action, some were thought to be liable to spontaneous ignition in store, some might poison a wound and were inadmissible on humanitarian grounds. There were grave objections to the introduction of another nature of shell, and eventually it was decided that with the means of communication available the use of smoke shell for indicating a point for concentration of fire was unnecessary, and that the idea of using them for blinding the enemy was a "cuttle-fish policy, too fanciful for our consideration"—even though it had found some favour on the continent. The final result of the whole discussion was that 13 and 18-pr. shrapnel were provided with powder pellets in the central channel in addition to the ordinary bursting charge. These pellets were intended also to increase the angle of opening, for South African experience had demanded a wider spread of the bullets than that of the 15-pr. shrapnel which were designed for forward effect. In practice, however, the pellets were found to cause an excessive "scatter", and they were accordingly withdrawn. This resulted in the bursts—especially in the case of the 13-pr.—being too small for observation. The attempt to find some smoke-producing composition had, therefore, to be resumed, and was proceeding in 1914.

It was not only the interior of the shell that came up for consideration. Trials showed that the form of fuze

CHAPTER V.

Shrapnel Shell.

116 THE FIELD ARMY ARTILLERY.

CHAPTER V.

Shrapnel Shell.

and head combined was one cause of the good shooting of the Ehrhardts, and that an increase in the radius of the ogive did also materially increase the range.[1] A Mark II shrapnel was, therefore, introduced for the 13 and 18-prs. in which the head was struck with a 2-calibre radius (instead of $1\frac{1}{2}$), and for the 4·5″ howitzer with 3-calibre radius. It was also decided that in future the shape of the fuze should conform to that of the head.

Combined Shell.

Ever since the introduction of shielded guns experiments had been going on abroad with various designs of a combined shrapnel and high-explosive shell for their attack; and in England there was a call for a shell which would give a better destructive effect when burst on graze than shrapnel. It was not until 1913, however, that trials with "universal" shell were authorized, and these were still in progress when war was declared.

Star Shell.

Star shell had proved their value on many occasions in the Indian frontier fighting, as they had in Afghanistan, and the war in Manchuria had shown the value of artillery fire at night. It was therefore decided to provide the new field guns with star shell, and also to take up the improvement of the pattern of those in the equipment of the mountain guns and field howitzers, which had always retained them. The problem proved a difficult one and many new designs followed each other between 1907 and 1914. The star shell were never issued as part of the equipment of the 13 and 18-prs. but a small stock was held for issue if required.

Percussion Fuzes.

The introduction of lyddite shell for mountain and heavy guns, as well as for field howitzers, demanded a percussion fuze which was sufficiently sensitive to act on graze with guns, and at the same time so quick in action that howitzer shell should not have time to bury before bursting. Still another problem was the securing

---

[1] This subject is further discussed in chapter XV under the head of "Calibration".

THE RE-ARMAMENT (TECHNICAL) 117

of complete detonation without the use of methods which would contravene our safety regulations.

The "Direct Action" principle was safe and instantaneous, but it could not be depended upon for graze action: a "graze" fuze on the other hand, depending upon the forward movement of a pellet, which necessarily left a gap, could not be so quick, and required special arrangements to guard against prematures in handling, in the bore, and in flight. Graze Fuze, No. 4, introduced in 1900 and sent to South Africa, had to be almost immediately withdrawn on account of prematures, and the number of blinds with the direct-action fuzes Nos. 1 and 13 led to the discontinuance of all practice with lyddite in the years after the South African war. Eventually the "Fuze, Percussion, D.A. with Cap, No. 17, Mark I" was approved in 1909 for use with lyddite shell for all field, heavy, and siege guns and howitzers, although the rarity of complete detonation with it was a general complaint at practice. It was not until 1913 that the Ordnance Committee were able to recommend No. 44 to take its place as combining the mutually contradictory qualities of being a true detonating fuze and of being quite safe for keeping in the shell, in store or in batteries. But, alas, it projected from the shell ¾ of an inch more than No. 17, and so would not fit into any of the boxes. It was a question whether the fuze should be redesigned to suit the equipments, or vice versa, with the possibility that a redesigned fuze might affect the ranging of the shell, and so undo all the trouble that had been taken to make the lyddite and shrapnel range the same. After much discussion it was decided to modify the receptacles, and No. 44 was the approved fuze for 4·5″ howitzers and 60-pr. guns in 1914.

With shrapnel the only projectile for field guns, the principal projectile for mountain and heavy guns, and coming into use with howitzers, the provision of the best possible time fuze was a matter of the utmost importance. For years the conditions had been growing increasingly difficult: the lengthening of ranges necessitated longer

CHAPTER V.
Percussion Fuzes.

Time and Percussion Fuzes.

K

118   THE FIELD ARMY ARTILLERY.

CHAPTER V.

Time and Percussion Fuzes.

burning[1]: the higher velocities demanded greater regularity: the adoption of quick-firing called for the abolition of safety pins and "clamping", and the carrying of shell fuzed.

There were two entirely different types to choose from —"ring" fuzes such as had been in use in the British service ever since the first "time and concussion" had proved its worth in the Afghan War, and those in which the composition was contained in a tube which was punched or bored like the French. The latter had the great advantage of being absolutely waterproof, of allowing wider graduations, and of facilitating the use of an automatic fuze-setter. On the other hand once punched they could only be used at that range, or at a shorter one, while ring fuzes could always be re-set. Whether this fear of "wasting a round"—a purely peace consideration—carried weight with the Committee, bred up in the tradition of economy of ammunition at practice, is not known, but rightly or wrongly they decided to adhere to the "ring" type.

Of this type there was no question but that those made by Krupp were the best. They had been used by the Egyptian Artillery in the Sudan, by the United States in the Philippines, and by the Argentine troops in the Andes, and they had shown consistent reliability under these varied conditions—high altitude, the dry heat of the desert, the damp heat of the tropics. Through Messrs. Vickers they were obtained for the trials of the 13 and 18-prs., and gave such excellent results that they were recommended for adoption. So came into the Service the "80" series.[2]

---

[1] The so-called "blue fuzes" (No. 57) sent out to South Africa in 1900 increased the shrapnel range of the horse and field guns by 1800 yards.

[2] The fuzes in the service at the end of the XIXth century were numbered in a "50" series: those which superseded them in the early years of the XXth were in a "60" series.

THE RE-ARMAMENT (TECHNICAL) 119

Adoption for the service naturally implied manufacture in England, and hence arose the difficulty referred to in the last chapter. Financial and other questions connected with the acquisition of design, "trade secrets", etc., had been satisfactorily dealt with, but as the fuzes made in England began to come in there were serious failures at proof. When so regulated as to "arm" and give bursts on graze at low elevations, they could not pass the ordeal of the jolting and rough usage trials, and vice versa. It was only after a long series of trials that the cause of the trouble was ascertained to lie in the change from metric to English standards of measurement which affected the mechanical fit of the very small parts on which the action depended. The necessary modifications were made, and there was no further trouble from this cause.

CHAPTER V.

Time and Percussion Fuzes.

In principle No. 80 fuze differed little from the 60 series already in the service, but it was very different in appearance, being made of aluminium, and so shaped as to continue the ogive of the shell. Perhaps the most startling innovation was the adoption of a 2-inch fuze-hole gauge, in place of the old "General Service", adherence to which had come to be regarded almost as an article of faith, any departure from which savoured of heresy. The change had the great advantage of allowing greater space in the interior of the body for the mechanism, but what ensured the immediate popularity of the fuze with all ranks was the absence of safety pins and clamping nuts.

This had been one of the conditions on which the Equipment Committee had been most insistent, but there were many efforts to get these objectionable features restored, especially in connection with the other condition to which the committee attached almost equal weight, viz.: that the shell should always be carried fuzed. The legal difficulties caused by this decision have been alluded to in the last chapter, and no sooner had these been surmounted than objections were advanced from the point of view of inspection. And when reports came in of explosions in the limbers during travelling trials in India they were made the excuse for further efforts to get the safety pins restored.[1] In the case of the longer burning fuzes of the 80 series—Nos. 81, 82, and 83—these were successful, but the absurdity of providing a quick-firing equipment for the field artillery, and then handicapping its essential quality—rapidity of fire—was too obvious to be gainsaid. Another proposal to add a safety shutter was also negatived, but the claims of "safety first" were partially satisfied by the addition in the Mark IV fuze-covers of a device which held the setting stud in the "safety" position.

Fuze-covers were a necessary concomitant of the decision to carry the shell fuzed, but it proved hard to find a satisfactory pattern, and there was nothing to protect the fuze after the cover had been uncapped. Orders were issued to limit as far as possible the number of fuzes uncapped, and a Mark III fuze was introduced in which spaces between the different parts were waterproofed with a special composition, which greatly improved the regularity of the burning. But advantage was taken of these circumstances by those who were opposed to the carrying of shell fuzed, and for a time their views prevailed, to the extent that the practice was given up during peace, and the old plan of issuing the fuzes in tin cylinders reverted to. There were, however, grave objections to this arrangement, not only in the batteries but in the ammunition columns, and in 1912 a Mark IV fuze was approved in which the cover was a component of the fuze, fixed to it before it was screwed into the shell. Once again it was ordered that all 13 and 18-pr. ammunition should be issued fuzed from Woolwich, and that a considerable portion of those in store should also be so kept. The re-

---

[1] There was some doubt whether the fuze or the primer was to blame, but examination of fuzes showed that many had shifted from the "safety" position, and elaborate experiments were made as to tensioning, and careful records kept of prematures at all practice at home and in India.

THE RE-ARMAMENT (TECHNICAL)

quirements of war had prevailed over the convenience of peace, but the struggle had been tough.

In spite of the various set-backs which have been recounted, which were only to be expected in view of the striking departures from precedent which accompanied the introduction of No. 80, the field artillery had no doubt found in it a fuze which was far superior to any previously in the service. The search for a longer-burning fuze of the same type for field howitzers and heavy guns proved more difficult. It was not until 1910 that No. 82 was approved for the former, and even then the reports of its behaviour at practice were very unsatisfactory. Being a howitzer fuze it depended upon centrifugal force to arm, and it was credited with both blinds and prematures. A Mark II was brought out in 1912 in which certain alterations were made in the percussion portion and a safety pin added. For the 60-pr. it was at first intended to use No. 81, a fuze which had been adopted by the Navy for long range shrapnel fire with heavy guns, but eventually it was decided to introduce No. 83. It was an improvement on No. 80 in that the lighting pellet was not central, and there was therefore no risk of its being driven on to the needle by a blow on the head of the fuze, but like No. 82 it had a safety pin.

At the same time that the various fuzes of the new type were being introduced, as described above, steps were being taken to bring up to date the fuzes of the old G.S. gauge. As early as 1903 trials had shown that No. 60, the fuze used with B.L. field and mountain guns, could be converted to "initial friction", and thus become a "quick-setting" fuze. Various other modifications were made, and these fuzes took their place in the service for B.L. field, mountain, and heavy guns and howitzers as Nos. 62, 63, 64, and 65.

With so much attention being given to the subject of time fuzes it is not to be wondered at that many minds were turning towards the possibility of substituting some mechanical arrangement for what was, after all, neither

CHAPTER V.

Time and Percussion Fuzes.

Mechanical Fuzes.

CHAPTER V.

Mechanical Fuzes.

more nor less than a firework. This was no new idea, and at the time of the re-armament two designs of mechanical fuze were under consideration, and that of Mr. Thompson, which had been under trial since 1885, had advanced to the stage when its performance could be compared with that of No. 80. Its advantages were substantial—it was not affected by variations in muzzle velocity, nor by atmospheric changes, and it was comparatively immune from deterioration in store. Moreover each individual fuze could be tested periodically for accuracy of time-keeping. But if made in brass its weight was prohibitive, and in aluminium it never gave such good results. Eventually, after trials in the 13 and 18-prs. and the 60-pr., in which the results did not come up to expectation, it was decided in 1909 to abandon the attempt to obtain a mechanical fuze for the new equipments.

Fuzes for Star Shell.

Mention has been made of the increased importance attached to the use of star shell, and this involved the provision of a satisfactory fuze. Owing to the feeble shock of discharge the ordinary fuze would not "arm", so a special pattern had to be introduced—the only "Time" as distinguished from "Time and Percussion" in the land service. The fuze adopted, No. 25, was introduced for the 10-pr. mountain gun in 1905, and after the Manchurian War extended to all guns and howitzers firing star shell. Marks II and III followed in due course, the latter having the system of waterproofing introduced for the No. 80 Mark III.

Fuze-Setters.

The trials in 1899 with the improved 12 and 15-pr. B.L. equipments had shown that even with them—and they were not true quick-firers—a rate of fire could be attained which was in excess of the rate at which the fuzes could be set. It was believed that the French got over this difficulty by the use of a "débouchoir" by which fuzes could be set mechanically, and the provision of something on the same lines for the 13 and 18-prs. was early in the minds of the Equipment Committee. The first pattern—approved in 1906—was not a success, and "con-

THE RE-ARMAMENT (TECHNICAL)

ditions" were, therefore, drawn up and designs called for. The trials of some instruments made to these designs brought out the fact that the graduations on the No. 80 fuze were too small, and that no fuze-setter would be reliable unless the ammunition were gauged within very close limits. For the next four years there were constant experiments with various designs of automatic and hand setters,[1] and the necessity of reducing the limits of dimensions and making some slight modifications in the designs of the fuzes was agreed to. There was much reason to believe that a satisfactory automatic fuze-setter could only be designed to work with the French type of fuze, but in the hope of avoiding such a drastic change it was decided to simplify the problem by abandoning the principle of the "proportional corrector". In accordance with this decision the conditions for a fuze-setter were modified, and re-issued in February, 1914, and new designs were coming in during the last months before the War.

The 13 and 18-pr. equipments as originally issued had a fuze-dial with which the right corrector had to be found at each range. In 1907 a new pattern dial was tried with which, once the proper corrector setting had been found at one range, the dial readings would be correct—or very nearly so—at all ranges under like conditions. This proved an enormous advantage when firing at moving targets, changing target, or ranging with time shrapnel, and was accordingly adopted under the title of "proportional corrector".

In spite, however, of its obvious advantages, the principle did not prove popular. It was said that in practice the length of corrector found at one range did not work out right for other ranges, and that the simplest correction involved calculation. Moreover the difficulty of designing an automatic fuze-setter was undoubtedly increased by the yard and fuze scales being graduated in

---

[1] The hand setters proved very unpopular and were soon given up.

CHAPTER V.

Fuze-Indicators.

such a way that an alteration of corrector made a proportional correction at various ranges and not an equal correction throughout. And everyone was clamouring for a fuze-setter. So when, after the practice season of 1913, brigade and battery commanders were asked their views as to the comparative merits of the two systems—proportional and non-proportional—an overwhelming majority were in favour of the latter.

Meanwhile—quite unconnected with the principle of proportional corrector—the form of fuze-dial had been found inconvenient in use, and the "bar-indicator" was approved in 1911 to take its place. This had the great advantages of having large divisions, and being easily set and checked, and was generally popular, with the result that its use was soon extended to all mobile equipments firing shrapnel.

The provision of a suitable fuze-indicator for howitzers was complicated by the number of different charges. The first pattern, with a separate scale for each charge, was universally condemned, and various devices employing only one scale were under trial until 1914 in connection with the system of ranging howitzers in yards described in chapter VII.

Practice Projectiles.

The expense of modern service projectiles led to a demand for a cheaper pattern for use at practice. When issued, however, objections were raised on the score that their bursts did not really give the same effect as the service shell, and that they were, therefore, bad for training. Various improvements were made, and by the end of the period under consideration all field and siege howitzers and heavy guns used a proportion of cast-iron common or old lyddite shells, with different bursting charges to represent service shrapnel and lyddite. Field guns alone fired nothing but their service shrapnel.

Drill Ammunition.

In order to make the most of the quick-firing qualities of the new equipments great attention was paid to the loading drill, and this naturally led to a demand for drill ammunition. That first provided for the 13 and 18-prs.

THE RE-ARMAMENT (TECHNICAL) 125

consisted of empty cartridge cases and shell with burnt out fuzes. Dummy wooden breech-blocks were also provided to enable loading to be carried out without damage to the mechanisms. For instruction in working the extractors each battery was also allowed six empty cartridge cases with rims not turned down, and for drill purposes generally six cases plugged with wood and with drill percussion primers. The 4·5″ howitzers had similar drill cartridges, and also dummy cartridges in which the components of the charge were made up to represent the service charges. With the greater attention paid to rapidity in the service of the guns under the French influence, there were complaints of awkwardness in the handling of service ammunition at practice, and the whole question of drill ammunition and the possible use of loading machines was taken up again in 1913, and trials were going on in 1914.

For the 60-pr. the problem was different. Owing to the great weight of the shell and the small clearance with the seating of the obturator, the drill shell required a driving band, and at the same time this must not jam in the bore, but must be capable of easy extraction. Here also trials were going on in 1914.

CHAPTER V.

Drill Ammunition.

HARNESS AND VEHICLES.

The re-armament was made the opportunity for a thorough overhauling of the equipment in all its branches, and not only in its more technical aspects, and some of the more important changes made will here be referred to. They were for the most part the direct result of South African experience, for many a hard practical lesson apart from gunnery and tactics was learnt by the batteries during their endless treks over the veldt.

Pole-draught had superseded shafts in 1895, but the neck-collar was still retained in spite of persistent efforts on the part of the Commander-in-Chief (Lord Wolseley) to get breast-harness adopted. The present generation of regimental officers can little realize the time and trouble

Breast Harness.

126 THE FIELD ARMY ARTILLERY.

Breast Harness.

devoted by all ranks to the eternal "collar-fitting"—well might artillery saddlers bear the title of "collar-maker". Different theories of how a collar *ought* to be fitted were hotly debated, and then with the least change in condition all the labour of fitting was lost. And in war there was not only change of condition but casualties to be reckoned with, and the necessity of making the best of remounts of all sorts and sizes. It was no wonder that before the war was over batteries who had had practical experience of mule breast-harness were calling out for the abolition of neck-collars—the wonder was why this had not been done a century before.[1] The committee took the matter up, there were trials with various patterns in 1903, and in the following year "Harness, Breast, Pole Draught, R.A." was officially adopted. It had many subsidiary advantages, of which perhaps the most important was that the harness was quite independent of the saddle, and there was no longer any necessity for retaining the old special pattern brass-bound artillery drivers saddle,[2] while the question of saddles on the off horses could be treated on its merits. An interesting side-light on the adaptability of the breast-harness was given by the fact that it was found equally suitable for the heavy horses of heavy batteries.

Technical Vehicles.

As in their harness, so in many of their vehicles, the veldt found out the unpractical nature of much of the equipment of the army, and not least that of the artillery. "Technical" vehicles abounded, and the third line of batteries showed a quaint assortment of wagons—"Artillery", "Ammunition and Store", "Forge", and "Store", not to mention the "Captain's Cart". Ex-

---

[1] For the expedition to Egypt in 1801, a number of horses were purchased at Constantinople and sent to Marmorice. "Such poor undersized animals as they were rendered it necessary . . . . to lay aside all the heavy parts, such as neck-collars . . . . and replace them with light leather breast-collars . . . .". General Lawson's report, quoted in the *History of the Royal Regiment of Artillery*, Captain Francis Duncan, Vol. II, p. 113.

[2] No doubt a relic of the old postilion saddle. Its cantle was handsomely bound with brass, and many felt a sentimental regret at its disappearance.

THE RE-ARMAMENT (TECHNICAL) 127

perience soon showed that the true principle was to confine the use of technical vehicles to services for which they were absolutely indispensable, and to use the general service vehicles for all other transport.

It was not only the vehicles that required overhauling: this was equally necessary with their contents. And here the artillery were probably the worst offenders. Batteries had gradually been loaded up with masses of stores, and especially with so-called "Material for repair". Under cross-examination quarter-master-serjeants, farriers, wheelers, and collar-makers, had reluctantly to confess that in three years campaigning in South Africa they had never encroached upon this useless load. The greater part was in consequence relegated to ammunition columns or even to ordnance depôts.[1]

CHAPTER V.
Technical Vehicles.
Material for Repair.

NOTE.

For further comparison between the equipments used by the Royal Artillery during the South African war of 1899—1902 and the Great War of 1914—1918, see a paper on "Artillery Equipments used in the Field during the last 25 years" by Major-General Sir Stanley von Donop, which appeared in the Jubilee Number of the Journal.

---

[1] A spare axletree was for instance, carried for years, until it was discovered that it could only be fitted in a workshop. Another good example was the provision for spare horse-shoes. Heavy and inconvenient shoe-pockets, a fruitful source of galls, were carried by every horse. After a thorough trial by the whole of the artillery of the Aldershot Army-Corps in 1903, they were abolished in favour of a valise on each vehicle with assorted shoes for use in replacing any lost by the team on the march. For "shoeing up", a supply of complete sets of assorted sizes, calculated at 40% of the number of horses, was carried in the baggage wagons.

CHAPTER VI.

RE-ORGANIZATION.

The Esher Committee—The Expeditionary Force—Artillery Organization—Artillery Command—The Divisional Artillery—The Ammunition Columns—Artillery Mobilization—The Training Brigades—The Depôts—India.

CHAPTER VI.

The Esher Committee.

FOLLOWING closely upon the re-armament of the field army artillery described in the last two chapters, came the re-organization of the military forces generally from which there emerged the Expeditionary Force. This re-organization, the most complete in the history of the British Army, affected every arm and service, regular and auxiliary, and none more closely than the Royal Artillery. It therefore demands more than passing notice in regimental history, and perhaps a deviation from chronological sequence may be permitted here in order to bring together in one chapter the whole series of measures which came into force during the first decade of the century.

The Report of the Royal Commission on the conduct of the South African War had shocked public opinion, and in November, 1903, the Prime Minister (Mr. Balfour) appointed a Committee, consisting of Lord Esher, Sir John Fisher, and Sir George Clarke,[1] to advise as to a remedy for the state of affairs disclosed. Their scheme for the re-constitution of the War Office, submitted in January, 1904, and at once accepted, affected the Regiment in several particulars. All questions connected with artillery *personnel* were placed under the Director of Personal Services in the Adjutant-General's Department, and thus came into being "A.G.6". All the technical work of the artillery and engineers was brought under one head by the abolition of the office of Inspector-General of Fortifi-

---

[1] Viscount Esher, Admiral of the Fleet Lord Fisher, and Lord Sydenham of Combe.

RE-ORGANIZATION. 129

cations, and the revival of the great historic office of Master-General of the Ordnance, with Directors of Artillery and of Fortification under him. At the same time the dual control over the Ordnance Factories of the Financial Secretary was abolished, and undivided responsibility placed upon the Master-General. There was also brought into being an Inspectorate of the Forces, under the Duke of Connaught as Inspector-General, in which Major-General Sir A. N. Rochfort[1] was appointed Inspector of Royal Horse and Royal Field Artillery.

The most vital achievement of the Esher Committee was, however, the creation of the General Staff. For the first time in the history of the British Army there came into being a branch of the staff which, untrammelled by the daily cares of administration, could devote its energies to preparation for war in its widest sense. But its full development took some years. In 1904 it was only established in the War Office; it was not until 1906 that it was extended to Commands, and then only at Home, for Lord Kitchener (as we shall see later) would not accept some of the conditions for India. It was further considered by the Imperial Conference of 1907, and after some modification established as an Imperial General Staff in 1909, and as such adopted in India in 1910.

In the following chapters the work of the General Staff in the training of the artillery will be frequently referred to, but mention must be made here of the large proportion of artillery officers who were to be found serving upon it from the very first. Both at Headquarters and in Commands, the names of many well-known gunners are to be found throughout the whole period between its establishment in 1904 and the War. At home Major-General Sir J. M. Grierson was the first Director of Military Operations: in India both the Directors of the General Staff at Army Head Quarters were gunners. This was a very different tale from that told in the last

---

[1] Major-General Sir Alexander Rochfort, K.C.B., C.M.G. d. 1916.

130   THE FIELD ARMY ARTILLERY.

CHAPTER VI.
The Expeditionary Force.[2]

volume of this History, when the army staff was practically closed to the Regiment.[1] The Esher Committee did not enter upon questions of army organization, beyond stating that their recommendations were independent of the form which any re-organization of the army might assume. They did, however, indicate clearly enough their opinion of the grandiose scheme of 1902 with its phantom corps. This was, however, already doomed, and in January, 1905, a new scheme appeared with the extravagancies of its predecessor severely pruned. The only army corps which remained in being was that at Aldershot—"The Army Corps" as it was termed—and the number of divisions was reduced to eight all told.

The scheme was never received very seriously, for the Government was tottering to its fall, and in the following year Mr. Campbell Bannerman assumed office, and appointed Mr. Haldane Secretary of State for War. It was indeed fortunate that at this critical moment the country found an administrator of such energy and ability, for it was becoming ever clearer that our military plans must be based upon the possibility of having to take part in a continental war. Within a month of his taking office an inquiry from France as to what form our help might be expected to assume in the event of an unprovoked German attack showed that we had not a single division that was a reality, and that although the field artillery consisted for peace purposes of 99 batteries, only 42 could be put into the field. Such a situation was intolerable to the mind of one who had the courage to face the purpose for which the army existed.

The army corps as a unit had never existed in more than name, although it had theoretically formed the basis

---

[1] In 1905, owing to the large number of artillery officers who qualified high on the list at the competitive examination for the Staff College, a small increase was made in the number of vacancies allotted to the Regiment.

[2] First termed "The Striking Force".

RE-ORGANIZATION

of our war organization since the Franco-German War had brought everything Prussian into fashion. In the Peninsula and the Crimea the army had fought in Divisions,[1] and Mr. Haldane determined to build up the army in self-contained divisions. The existing divisions had a strength of only two infantry and two field artillery brigades: a review of the available units showed that these might be made to furnish six divisions of three infantry brigades each, with the necessary army troops and troops for the line of communication. In July, 1907, Mr. Haldane announced his plan in the House, in December, 1907, the "Expeditionary Force" came into being.

CHAPTER VI.

The Expeditionary Force.

The artillery consisted of:—

The Cavalry Division	2 brigades R.H.A.
Mounted Brigades	1 do. do.
Each Infantry Division	3 gun brigades, R.F.A.
	1 how. do. do.
	1 heavy battery, R.G.A.
	1 divisional ammunition column R.F.A.

Field army tables and war establishments were promulgated in due course, and peace establishments and terms of service arranged so as to produce the necessary drafts for India in peace and the war strengths on mobilization. Of the 99 field batteries in the home establishment the gun brigades took 54, the howitzer brigades 12, or a total of 66.

The one gap in the artillery organization was that there were only sufficient howitzer batteries to provide 2-battery brigades. How this gap was filled, and how the 33 batteries not included in this Expeditionary Force were utilized, will be explained later when describing the mobilization arrangements.

---

[1] There was, however, a corps organization in the Waterloo campaign.

THE FIELD ARMY ARTILLERY.

CHAPTER VI.

Artillery Organization.

After the above brief sketch of the changes in army organization which brought into being the "Expeditionary Force", the changes which they entailed in artillery organization may be examined in greater detail. In the Peninsula the artillery of the field army had consisted of but one battery per division: in the Crimea of only two. The Franco-German War of 1870 had, however, brought realization of the great part which might be played by artillery in modern war, and all nations had increased the proportion of guns to bayonets. In the British army the growth had been continuous, sometimes in the shape of additions to the corps artillery, sometimes to the divisional. The following table, in which the army corps of three divisions has been taken as the unit, shows this progress at a glance. No mention has been made in it of the horse artillery allotted to the cavalry brigades or divisions since this remained throughout at the proportion of one battery per cavalry brigade.

Date	An Army Corps or three Divisions.	Horse	Field	Howitzer	Heavy	Total
In 1871	Corps Artillery	3	3	—	—	6
	Divisional Artillery	—	6	—	—	6
						12
In 1874	Corps Artillery	3	2	—	—	5
	Divisional Artillery	—	9	—	—	9
						14
In 1886	Corps Artillery	2	3	—	—	5
	Divisional Artillery	—	9	—	—	9
						14
In 1895	Corps Artillery	2	6	—	—	8
	Divisional Artillery	—	9	—	—	9
						17
In 1901	Corps Artillery	2	—	3	3	8
	Divisional Artillery	—	18	—	—	18
						26
In 1907 [1]	Divisional Artillery	—	27	6	3	36
In 1909 [1]	Divisional Artillery	—	27	9	3	39

[1] The Expeditionary Force.

RE-ORGANIZATION.

Experience in South Africa showed the value of artillery units being accustomed to work directly under general officers commanding formations of all arms. The post of G.O.C., R.A., was abolished by Lord Kitchener on his succeeding to the chief command, and on Lord Roberts' return to England the handing over of cavalry brigade batteries and divisional artillery to general officers commanding brigades and divisions was seriously discussed. But the time was not yet ripe, and the army corps scheme of 1902 provided major-generals to command the whole of the artillery of the army corps[1] as well as colonels to command the corps artillery. Under the scheme of 1905, however, the command of all field troops was entrusted to divisional (and cavalry brigade) commanders, the G.O.C's., R.A. disappeared, and colonels were appointed to command and train the "horse and field artillery units not allotted to divisions or brigades". There thus remained no senior officer of artillery commanding in peace the units which he would command in war, for even the one major-general, R.A., left—at Aldershot—no longer commanded the artillery. His position had, indeed, become a very invidious one, and this was brought prominently to notice on the occasion of a ceremonial parade, when he, and the major-general R.E., were ordered to take up their position for the march past *opposite* the saluting post. So indignant was Major-General Sir Elliot Wood, R.E., that he resigned his appointment in protest, and the incident led to the substitution of a "staff officer for artillery", with a place among the general staff of the command, for the major-general R.A.

Turning now to the divisional artillery, the allotment of a second brigade in 1901 naturally assumed the appointment of a commander, but this was refused as "not required in war or peace". The divisional practice instituted at Glen Imaal in 1904 brought the subject to the front again, only to be negatived once more, but on this

CHAPTER VI.

Artillery Command.

The Divisional Artillery.

---

[1] For the first three Army Corps only—Aldershot, Salisbury, and Ireland—the only ones which had any pretence to reality.

L

CHAPTER VI.
The Divisional Artillery.

occasion as likely to lead to interference with artillery brigade commanders and to reducing the responsibility of general officers commanding divisions. With the re-armament in 1905 and 1906 the need of a divisional artillery commander became still more urgent, for it was obvious that the handling of quick-firing guns so as to obtain full value from their power would be no easy task. To expect its efficient discharge by an officer only appointed on mobilization, without giving him any opportunity for practice in peace, could only lead to disappointment in war. But such arguments made no impression until the adoption of the "big divisions" in the Expeditionary Force settled the question. No one had the temerity to maintain that a force of artillery of the size and complexity of the new divisional artillery could be left without a commander even in peace. At first indeed it was proposed that he should be only a colonel, with an adjutant for staff; but the strength of the divisional artillery nearly approached that of an infantry brigade in men, and surpassed that of a cavalry brigade in horses; the position of its commander was analogous to that of their brigadiers, and in common fairness he must be given the same rank. The new brigadier-generals accordingly took up their duties at the end of the training season of 1907.

There was still, however, some conflict of opinion as to whether they should be actual *commanders*, or primarily advisers, with functions more nearly approximating to those of staff officers, and it was directed that this point should be studied and reported on after the training of 1908. There was nervousness also as to how their appointment would affect the gunnery training, and it was proposed that the rank of the Commandant School of Gunnery for Horse and Field Artillery should be raised, and that he should be employed in visiting and reporting on the practice of divisional artilleries on much the same lines as were unfortunately adopted in coast artillery.[1] It is curious how long it took to realize fully the implications

---
[1] Chapter XV.

of the appointment of a divisional artillery commander. The need for such a commander was obvious to artillerymen as soon as a second brigade was added to the divisional artillery, but it took seven years to get this admitted by the authorities, and when eventually the appointment was approved it was entirely on the score of the commander requiring experience in the work he would have to do in war, and not at all on account of his value for training, as to which, there was indeed, as we have seen, some apprehension. The necessity for a divisional artillery commander in order so to train its units as to ensure their combined action in accordance with the special powers and characteristics of each nature, as well as the co-operation of the divisional artillery as a whole with the rest of the division, does not seem to have been recognized. This was perhaps not surprising, for the fundamental principle that troops should be trained in peace by those who would lead them in war was quite new to the artillery. But as soon as the opportunity came it was quickly grasped, and not only by the artillery. Now that the practice of their artillery was conducted by one of their own subordinates, instead of by some "Camp Commandant" over whom they had no control, general officers commanding divisions began to take the same interest in its training as in that of the other arms. Their presence on the ranges acted as a stimulant to the technical work as well as giving guidance in the tactical; and afforded them with their staffs an opportunity of studying artillery employment.

A serious handicap to the work of divisional artillery commanders was the inadequacy of their staffs. Cavalry and infantry brigades had their brigade-majors in peace as in war, but for some unexplained reason the artillery were only allowed staff-captains who were not staff college officers, and were not allowed to wear staff badges. Year after year field operations brought out the fact that the staff work of the divisional artillery required an equal, if not a greater, staff knowledge and acquaintance with the

136 THE FIELD ARMY ARTILLERY.

Chapter VI.

The Divisional Artillery.

other arms than that of the infantry: year by year the injustice to individuals and the loss to the higher education of the artillery was stressed; but to no avail.

With the establishment of the Divisional Artillery as a definite organization it was proposed that the title of "Brigade" should be transferred to it. There were obvious objections to the use for a lieut.-colonel's command in the artillery of the title that belonged to a brigadier-general's command in the other arms. The divisional artillery, on the other hand, was approximately the same size as a cavalry or infantry brigade, and the title of "artillery brigade" would, therefore, be in every way appropriate for it. Moreover the lieut.-colonel's command might then be called a "regiment" or a "battalion" thus again falling into line with the other arms. But there were objections to having "regiments" within a "Regiment", and "battalion" found no favour in the mounted branch. So, after much discussion, it was decided to make no change.

The Ammunition Columns.

The only war in recent years in which ammunition columns had been utilized to any extent by the British army was that in South Africa. This had familiarized all arms with their existence and duties, and the accounts from Manchuria of battles lasting for days instead of hours accentuated their value. The adoption of quick-firing guns by the artillery brought their requirements in ammunition still more prominently to the front. The question of how they were to be supplied was a difficult one, but a decision was forced upon the War Office by the imminent arrival of the new equipments from the manufacturers. Three ammunition wagons per gun had been ordered, and how these were to be divided between batteries and ammunition columns affected barrack accommodation, that bugbear of military reformers.

In 1905, therefore, the whole subject of ammunition supply in the field was thoroughly investigated in the light of historical examples, ranging from the Franco-German War to that still raging in Manchuria, and of the changes in organization being adopted by foreign armies.

RE-ORGANIZATION.

The most important point to be settled was whether ammunition supply in the field should remain the duty of the artillery as had been the invariable rule in the past. During the South African War this question had been much discussed, and the conclusion then arrived at was that the advantages were all in favour of the continuance of this practice. This conclusion was now confirmed, and in view of the importance of this decision, the main arguments on which it was based will be summarized here.

In the first place ammunition was in quite a different category to anything else. While the requirements of the supply services were continuous, and could be foretold with reasonable certainty, the replenishment of ammunition was intermittent, and neither the quantities, nor the times when they would be wanted, could be even approximately foreseen. Unlike food or clothing, ammunition could never be obtained locally, nor could troops be put on half rations without serious consequences. Further, under certain circumstances, as had occurred in South Africa, and as would be the case in any hostilities on the Indian Frontier, our ammunition might be of incalculable value to the enemy. But experience showed that officers of the administrative services, overwhelmed as they were with a mass of general issues, could not differentiate in their treatment of ammunition. For these reasons, and in view of the fact that the movements of ammunition columns were essentially tactical, the replenishment of ammunition beyond the advanced depôts must be a function of the fighting troops. This being so (and the artillery necessarily looking after their own supply) the addition of small-arm ammunition, with its comparatively small bulk and simplicity of packing, would be a matter of no difficulty as regards either handling or carriage. For the above reasons it was decided that the supply of ammunition for all arms should be entrusted to the artillery as heretofore.

At the same time the continuance of the use of ammunition columns as a reserve of men and horses for the batteries was questioned. Opinion was changing

THE FIELD ARMY ARTILLERY.

Chapter VI.

The Ammunition Columns.

towards replacing such casualties in the artillery under normal circumstances in the same way as those of the other arms. It was, however, recognized that there was a very real difference in this respect: casualties in cavalry or infantry meant so many men less in the ranks, but the regiment or battalion was still in being, while casualties in a battery might mean that the guns could not be kept in action. For this reason, when the old rule was done away with, it was allowed that deficiencies in the batteries might be temporarily filled from the columns, so long as the men and horses so lent were returned when the reinforcements arrived. As regards *matériel* the tendency was rather in the other direction, to extend the use of the ammunition columns as the normal reserves, by relegating to them the greater part of the "material for repair", "spares", etc., previously carried by the batteries and thus reduce the transport required by the latter.

There remained still to be decided the number of rounds to be carried in the field, and how these were to be distributed between the batteries and the ammunition columns. So great was the importance attached to the subject that the Chief of the General Staff (Sir Nevill Lyttleton) decided to consult personally the leading military personages of the day—Lords Roberts, Kitchener, and Methuen, Sir Redvers Buller and Sir Henry Brackenbury. After consideration of their replies it was decided that the following should be the allotment per gun and howitzer[1]:—

		Per Gun	Per Howitzer
In Batteries ...	Gun limber	24	12
	Two ammunition wagons	152	96
		176	108
In Columns ...	One ammunition wagon	76	48
	General service wagon	248	44
		500	300

[1] For the final allotment for all natures in the field army artillery see Chapter IX,

RE-ORGANIZATION.

The army corps organization provided an ammunition column as an integral part of each artillery brigade, and, an "ammunition park" as a third line for each army corps, commanded by a lieut.-colonel directly under the general officer commanding the artillery of the army corps. This unwieldy unit had never taken the field in South Africa as a whole, and the title of "park" was objected to as inapplicable to a field unit. With the reorganization of 1905 divisional and corps troops ammunition columns were therefore substituted for the ammunition park, and this was the arrangement when the expeditionary force was formed. It remained in force, but advantage was taken of the development of mechanical transport, with the high mobility and wide radius of action it conferred, to reduce the amount of ammunition carried by the divisional ammunition columns by a half, and to hand this over to a mechanized unit under the Inspector-General of Communications, to be called the "divisional ammunition park". The amount of ammunition under the orders of the divisional commander was thus considerably reduced, but on the other hand the mobility of the division was increased, and the smaller divisional ammunition column could march close up to the second line transport instead of the day's march in rear as previously ordered.[1]

The new system was worked out in detail, and then tested in a staff tour in 1910 and in the manœuvres which followed, in which the 2nd Division was brought up to war establishment. It proved sound and workable, and the organization and rules for its working accordingly found their place in the manual of 1912.

The scheme for the Expeditionary Force not only gave the artillery an organization which provided for training in peace and command in war, it also faced for the first time the peculiar difficulties of artillery mobilization. At

CHAPTER VI.

The Ammunition Columns.

Artillery Mobilization.

---

[1] At the same time all G.S. wagons carrying ammunition were transferred from brigade to divisional ammunition columns, thus increasing the mobility of the former and reducing the congestion of the roads in the immediate vicinity of an action.

140   THE FIELD ARMY ARTILLERY.

the prospect of war, regiments and battalions gathered in many officers temporarily employed outside their ranks; the artillery, on the contrary, had to find officers for various regimental duties, only required on mobilization, and, above all, had to create entirely new combatant units in the shape of the ammunition columns we have been considering.

As long ago as the Russian scare of 1878 the question had been brought to notice by the inability of the Ordnance Department to find even a cadre to take over the ammunition column equipment which they had ready and were prepared to issue. For the Egyptian Expedition of 1882 the force of artillery fell considerably short of the full complement for an army corps, so there was no difficulty in providing an ammunition column by the simple process of converting a field battery into one. When a field artillery brigade had to be hurriedly despatched to South Africa in 1897, it was necessary to deplete other batteries of 189 men and 272 horses, thus reducing them to skeletons. In 1899 and 1900 mobilization was fortunately in stages. It meant in practice robbing batteries which it was thought would not be required, and then, when the tide of mobilization flowed on, and these batteries had to be sent on service, they had in turn to be filled up, and were not as efficient as they would have been if they had not been subjected to this destructive process. As for the ammunition columns, we may turn to a contemporary description—"an ammunition column when mobilized consisted of reservists from all over the country, officers taken from batteries and depôts when they could least be spared, horses from anywhere, wagons, harness and equipment out of store where they had been lying for years".

Short service—3 years colour and 9 years reserve—had been introduced in 1903, in order to build up a reserve, but it had broken down as regards the production of drafts for India, besides being intensely unpopular from the training point of view, especially in its effect of reducing the standard of driving. It looked as if the reservists would have to be used as substitutes for serving soldiers instead of supplementing them. So in 1906 there was a return to 6 years with the colours and 6 years in the reserve, and the Secretary of State put forward his scheme for supplementing the regular *personnel* of the Expeditionary Force by men on a non-regular basis. Under this scheme combatant units which might go into action at the outset of a campaign, such as batteries and brigade ammunition columns, were to be made up to strength on mobilization by regular reservists only, but units which would not be immediately brought into action, such as divisional ammunition columns, would receive the non-regular *personnel*. These latter would also be counted on to make good wastage since they would be subjected to intensive training from the moment of mobilization.

The R.H.A. and the R.G.A. required no assistance in mobilization, for their own regular reservists were sufficient for all purposes. They were therefore not concerned with the scheme, but the R.F.A. would require:—

For divisional ammunition columns ...	5,034
For six months wastage	8,945
	13,979
Towards this there might be expected from serving soldiers and regular reservists (immature and unfit) left behind—say	3,729
Leaving to be provided on a non-regular basis	10,250

The source from which it was proposed to obtain these ten thousand field artillerymen was the artillery militia, which (except for two corps required for coast defence) it was proposed to convert into "Royal Field Reserve Artillery".

CHAPTER VI.

Artillery Mobilization.

There were grave doubts in many quarters as regards the efficiency, either as regards discipline or training, of units as large as divisional ammunition columns composed almost entirely of men obtained on a militia basis. The suitability of such men for replacing casualties in brigades had also to be considered.[1] The quesiton was referred to a committee of artillery officers under the presidency of Major-General Parsons, and after some modifications had been made in the scheme so as to provide a sufficient proportion of regular reservists in the divisional ammunition columns for replacing casualties, the suitability of militiamen was accepted.

Experience confirmed these misgivings. The militia were all garrison artillery, the *personnel* generally drawn from men living on the coast, and unfitted by calling and occupation for a mounted service. The non-commissioned officers were unable to ride and too old to learn, and had little authority. The original intention of organizing the Royal Field Reserve Artillery in self-contained units, formed by the conversion of militia corps without other change, had to be abandoned. At the end of 1908 it was decided that the units of Royal Field Reserve Artillery should be disbanded, and the "special reservists" (as the *personnel* were now entitled) allotted to the training brigades. This, however, is anticipating events: it is necessary to return to the introduction of the scheme in 1906, for serious opposition had arisen from another quarter.

The Training Brigades.

An essential feature of Mr. Haldane's scheme was the abolition of all units not required in the Expeditionary Force, and the utilization of the resources thus saved for

---

[1] In the course of the Army Debates, Mr. Belloc, the member for Salford, speaking as one who had had practical experience of driving guns in the French army, bore witness to the high reputation which English artillery drivers bore abroad, and the magnificent professional tradition behind it. He did not believe that men worthy and able to take the place of the trained drivers we should lose at the beginning of a great war could be obtained on a militia basis.

RE-ORGANIZATION. 143

the filling up of gaps in it. But when it was realized that among the redundant units were thirty-three batteries of the Royal Field Artillery something like consternation was caused, and not in regimental, or even military circles alone. Intense indignation was expressed at the idea of disbanding such a number of efficient batteries—it was a catastrophe to be avoided if in any way possible, and the artillery officers at the War Office devoted themselves to thinking out some plan by which they might be saved. The solution of the problem was due to Colonel May,[1] who proposed that they should be made into "training brigades", which, while preserving their status as regulars, could be used for the training not only of regular recruits but also of militia, and if necessary of volunteers. They would thus dovetail into the Secretary of State's idea of utilizing the militia to supplement the regulars in the Expeditionary Force, and possibly to assist in the training of the artillery of the Territorial Force, which so far had only been foreshadowed.[2] The suggestion was accepted, and eleven training brigades were added to the organization of the Expeditionary Force.

To these training brigades were affiliated the corps of Militia Artillery which were to be converted into units of Royal Field Reserve Artillery. But, as we have seen, it was soon found that the preservation of these units was impossible, and their disbandment, and the posting of the special reservists directly to training brigades, allowed of important improvements in the organization of the expeditionary force. The number of training brigades was reduced from eleven to six, to correspond with the number of divisions, and one training brigade was allotted to each, with the definite duty of forming the divisional ammunition column.

This reduction in the number of training brigades from eleven to six left five brigades available for other purposes.

CHAPTER VI.

The Training Brigades.

---

[1] Major-General Sir Edward S. May, K.C.B., C.M.G. d. 1935.
[2] An account of the Artillery Militia and Volunteers and of the Territorial Artillery will be found in Part V.

144   THE FIELD ARMY ARTILLERY.

CHAPTER VI.

The Training Brigades.

Two of these brigades were devoted to bringing the six howitzer brigades of the expeditionary force up to their proper strength of three batteries instead of two, thus completing the artillery organization of the expeditionary force. There were three field artillery brigades still available and in view of the prevailing uncertainty as to the ultimate value of territorial field artillery it was decided to set these aside for home defence.

Lord Haldane always deeply resented the accusation—frequently made—of having reduced the horse and field artillery. He claimed that in 1906 he found under 39,000 artillerymen available and left over 54,000 six years later; and that he bequeathed 81 instead of 42 batteries to the expeditionary force, besides providing the territorial army with a backing of 15 regular batteries.[1]

The increase in the number of batteries in the expeditionary force upset the calculations regarding the number of regular reservists required for the mobilization of the field artillery, and it was found necessary to re-introduce a certain proportion of short-service men in order to increase the reserve. Elaborate arrangements were made covering the proportion of 3-year and 6-year men in each brigade; the extension of service by 3-year men was only allowed by exchange with 6-year men; special reservists were not allowed to transfer to the regulars, and so forth —all with the object of ensuring that men of the different categories should be available in the right numbers when required for drafts or for mobilization. The aim of these measures was that the Royal Field Artillery should eventually consist of :—

Regulars—six-year men	9,600
do. —three-year men	5,000
Special Reservists	6,000

The above important decisions, and various less important ones, with which it is unnecessary to burden this

---

[1] Six horse batteries in addition to the three field brigades.

RE-ORGANIZATION.

account, were put in force by a special army order of the 16th March, 1909, giving the "Scheme for the addition of two howitzer brigades to the Field Army, for the formation of Divisional Ammunition Columns, and the changes in the organization of the Royal Field Reserve Artillery consequent thereto".

At the time of the mobilization for the South African War comparatively complete mobilization regulations were in force, but these were based upon the requirements of the cavalry and infantry, and it seems to have been taken for granted that they would prove equally applicable to the artillery. In consequence, the artillery depôts—one horse, and one field, both at Woolwich—were called upon to perform the same work as a regimental depôt, but for vastly greater numbers, and with a much smaller staff. In especial the depôts were called upon to carry out the training of recruits at the same time as the mobilization of units. The same staff cannot, however, do both, for the time of mobilization is the time when the war fever is at its height, and the recruits come flocking in. After the South African War the number of field artillery depôts had been increased to seven and then reduced to four. The scheme contemplated their eventual amalgamation with the Training Brigades when barrack accommodation would permit, hence they were to continue to train regular recruits while the Training Brigades became schools for the Special Reservists. There were long discussions as to the application of the "Cardwell" system to the artillery by linking brigades at home with those abroad, and this was in force until the reduction of the establishment of the depôts in 1907, when the affiliation of brigades to depôts was advisedly broken in order to facilitate the provision of drafts.

The thorny subject of field artillery mobilization was carried a step further by Major-General D. Haig's Committee in 1909, which dealt with the work to be done after the mobilization of the field army. Instead of the existing arrangement, under which the depôts dealt with regulars

CHAPTER VI.

The Training Brigades.

The Depôts.

146   THE FIELD ARMY ARTILLERY.

CHAPTER VI.
The Depôts.

and the training brigades with special reservists, they proposed that the depôts should receive, clothe, and equip all recruits—regular and special reserve—and pass them on to the training brigades, who would train them, as well as all men left behind by batteries or returned from the field. In order to carry this out the number of depôts was increased in 1909 from four to six to correspond with that of the training brigades, and it was decided that they should be located at the same stations as the latter, and be under the same command, as soon as barrack accommodation could be provided.

India

During the early years of the XXth century the system of command and inspection established by Lord Roberts for the artillery in India remained in force. Under that system there was an inspector-general at army headquarters, with an assistant adjutant-general to look after the administrative work, and a brigade-major as personal staff officer. In each of the four commands there was a colonel-on-the-staff in command of the artillery, with a deputy assistant adjutant-general. When, however, two "armies" replaced the four "commands" it was decided to abolish the office of inspector-general, and to replace the four colonels-on-the-staff by two inspectors—one for each army—and an inspector of coast defences at army headquarters. An assistant adjutant-general still attended to administrative matters there, assisted by the brigade-major who had survived the extinction of his chief.

The new arrangement was not a practical one and never worked well. The inspectors were not responsible to, or in touch with, the general officers commanding divisions; and these took little interest in their artillery since the responsibility for the training of the batteries rested upon the inspectors. It was not unusual for the artillery of a division to be away at practice during the period of divisional training, for the dates of practice camps had to be arranged to suit the inspectors. The training of the artillery was being divorced from that of

RE-ORGANIZATION.

the other arms, and tending to become purely technical—a sad falling off from the days when the artillery camps inaugurated by Lord Roberts and Sir Charles Nairne were a feature not only of regimental but of army training, and the I.G.A. was a conspicuous figure at all large gatherings of troops.

The inclusion of the Indian Army in the Imperial General Staff system in 1910, in bringing the whole of the training[1] under the Chief of the General Staff led, however, to a consideration of the position regarding the artillery. The remedy was obvious—the extension to India of the system of artillery command which had proved so successful at Home, and in 1911 the Government of India submitted their proposals, which were at once sanctioned, for the appointment of divisional artillery commanders. In view of the financial situation, they only asked for those for the six divisions which were of the first importance, instead of for the full nine, and without staff[2]. Even so it was probably the most important step taken during the period we are considering towards bringing the training of the army in India up to modern standards. Until this step was taken there was in India a large force of artillery which was not being properly trained in peace, and could not be effectively employed in war owing to the want of officers to command it.

The appointment of divisional artillery commanders made it no longer necessary to retain the two inspectors. On the other hand it became very necessary for the commander-in-chief to have on his staff a senior artillery officer who could ensure that the methods of training in the various divisions made for uniformity, a matter of particular importance in India owing to the absence of any School of Gunnery. The proposals therefore included the abolition of the appointments of inspectors of artillery in

---

[1] Previous to the formation of the General Staff the Adjutant-General had dealt with regimental training, the Chief of the Staff only with combined training.

[2] An orderly officer was allowed during the training season.

CHAPTER VI.
India.

armies, and the revival of that of Inspector-General under the title, as at home, of Inspector of Horse and Field Artillery.[1] He was given the rank of brigadier-general, and to mark his seniority over the divisional artillery commanders, his rank was made "temporary" while theirs was only "local". By a happy selection the first holder of the post was Colonel Mercer,[2] who, as Brigade-Major to Sir Charles Nairne, had been almost as well known throughout the artillery in India as his chief.

Before leaving the subject of artillery command mention should perhaps be made of one difficulty peculiar to India. Horse artillery batteries were definitely allotted to cavalry brigades as at home, but at several stations such batteries were quartered alongside field artillery brigades, and used the same regimental institutions, although quite independent of the lieut-colonel commanding the brigade. There were obvious objections to such a situation, and it was decided that in such cases the field artillery lieut.-colonel should be the regimental commanding officer of the horse battery as well as of his own brigade, but that where there was a cavalry brigadier the lieut.-colonel should exercise command in direct subordination to him—with, as a corollary, the horse artillery major, if the senior, commanding the field artillery brigade whenever the lieut.-colonel was absent.

In matters of armament the horse and field artillery in India were behindhand. None of the batteries sent from India to South Africa in 1899 had been fitted with the axle-spade, and the horse battery had still the old 12-pr. of 7 cwt. Some years were to elapse before the horse artillery received the 12-pr. of 6 cwt., and both horse and field had their guns fitted with axle-spades—improvements which had been carried into effect at home before the turn of the century.

---

[1] At the same time the Inspector of Coast Defences became Inspector of Garrison Artillery.—Chapter XV.
[2] Major-General Sir Frederic Mercer, K.C.M.G., C.B., Colonel-Commandant.

"J" BATTERY, R.H.A.—RAWALPINDI, 1907.
To show Indian Establishment for first Q.F. Batteries.

RE-ORGANIZATION.

As soon, however, as the re-armament of the horse and field artillery had been decided upon at home, there was no delay in placing orders for the *matériel* for India— indeed, as mentioned in Chapter IV, there was at one time the prospect of batteries in India being re-armed before those at home. Lord Kitchener had already taken steps to ensure the batteries having a strength of both men and horses which would enable them to carry an adequate amount of ammunition for quick-firing guns. The new establishment, approved in 1904, provided for three ammunition wagons per gun, those of the "firing battery" with British drivers, the other twelve with Indian drivers. But this made a battery a very different thing to anything previously experienced—in the horse artillery close upon three hundred horses. It was delightful to be able to send the captain with the first and second lines to represent the enemy's cavalry and guns at battery drills, and to have an unlimited supply of horses available for any purpose; but the sections and sub-sections proved too large for the subalterns and Nos. 1 to have that intimate knowledge of men and horses which was the tradition in the Regiment; and the inclusion of fifty Indian soldiers was rather an embarrassment to those not accustomed to dealing with the fighting classes. After much discussion with the War Office it was agreed in 1908 to reduce the number of battery wagons to twelve, all with British drivers, and to hand over the remaining wagons, with their Indian drivers, to ammunition columns. It is interesting to note that this decision entailed increasing the home establishment in order to provide the additional drafts required.

In the past the only link between the battery ammunition wagons and the ordnance field parks consisted of certain so-called "units", which were looked after by the horse battery or field brigade to which they were attached. With a quick-firing armament the provision of something better in the way of ammunition columns could no longer be delayed, and on the arrival of the first of the new

CHAPTER VI.

India.

equipments in 1906 the formation of cavalry brigade and divisional ammunition columns was authorized. The former consisted of two sections—horse artillery and small-arm—the latter of three sections—field artillery, mountain artillery, and small-arm. But the only portions of these columns which were maintained in peace were the horse and field artillery sections. The *personnel* for the mountain artillery and small-arm sections was to be detailed from the batteries, regiments, and battalions concerned on mobilization, and to join the artillery sections at the base where their transport would be provided, and the column formed under the officer commanding the horse or field artillery section.

These latter sections had a small establishment of British non-commissioned officers and gunners, and a considerable number of Indian drivers and horses. Great efforts were made to improve the status of the drivers, and bring them up to the standard of cavalry "sowars", but the officers were only appointed for a couple of years—too short for dealing with natives and there were no Indian officers to assist them. It was not every British officer that had the temperament or the skill in languages required to make a success of such a command: to those who had, it offered a congenial opportunity.

In the last few years the organization of these sections was further improved until the establishment of the artillery in India included nine cavalry brigade ammunition columns and twelve field artillery brigade ammunition columns.

CHAPTER VII.

The Manchurian Influence.

(1904—1911.)

The Rival Artilleries—The New Manuals—The New Doctrine—Covered Positions—Dispersed Batteries—Application of Fire—Rapidity of Fire—The Practice Camps—Ranges and Targets—Night Operations—Aviation—Co-operation—The Forward Observing Officer—Close support—Manœuvres and Field Firing.

Horse Artillery—Field Howitzers—Mountain Artillery—Heavy Artillery.

If allowed to stand alone the lessons of the South African War might have crystallized into a doctrine as unsuited for European warfare as that based upon the Franco-German War had proved for fighting the Boers. Fortunately for the British Army there broke out, just when needed to correct this tendency, the first war of the twentieth century between two great armies organized and trained according to modern ideas. Their armament, it is true, was scarcely up to date. The Russian gun, though immeasurably superior to the Japanese, was still not a true quick-firer, and since it was only issued as troops were leaving for the front, all ranks were ignorant of its capabilities. The Japanese were handicapped by a gun which was in no sense a quick-firer, and which was moreover deficient in shell power, while the mobility which should have resulted from its light weight was discounted by inferior horse-flesh. The Russians had an advantage in shrapnel fire, for their time-fuzes could be set to 6,000 yards, the Japanese only to 5,300. But the latter had high-explosive shell—of which the Russians had none—and could use this up to the extreme range for which their guns were sighted, viz. 6,200 yards.

These facts had to be borne in mind when deducing

152 THE FIELD ARMY ARTILLERY.

<small>CHAPTER VII.
The Rival Artilleries.</small>

lessons for the rôle of quick-firing artillery from the Manchurian War, but even so there was much to be learnt from the experience of the rival artilleries, and a new manual was obviously due.

<small>The New Manuals.</small>

Field Artillery Training 1906 was the first-fruits of the formation of the General Staff, and it marked a real advance in training methods. Progressive training throughout the year, working up through battery, brigade, and divisional artillery training to exercises of all arms, was substituted for the old 70 hours "Annual Course of Military Training". The difficulties of shorter service were recognized by the elimination of non-essentials. A "look-round" in stables took the place of the elaborate ritual of successive mounted inspections in the gun-park, and the reduction in the number of drill movements, which had accompanied each issue of the manual for the last half-century, was carried a step further.

But there had been scarcely time before its publication to realize the potentialities of the new quick-firing equipments, just coming into the service, or to digest the mass of material from Manchuria. Ostensibly written for quick-firing guns, the new manual scarcely caught the "quick-firing spirit". And as further information became available from our representatives at the seat of war—among whom the Regiment was worthily represented—doubts began to creep in as to whether its lessons had been read aright. Already in 1907 different commands were issuing "instructions" as to the application of the principles enunciated in the manual of the previous year. Such variety in teaching did not appeal to artillery officers, and there was a general demand for authoritative guidance. A new edition of *Field Artillery Training* was accordingly brought out in 1908, and it is to this edition we must look to find the full effect of the Manchurian influence.

<small>The New Doctrine.</small>

The "Artillery Duel" as a distinct phase of the battle, reserved for that arm alone, was popularly supposed to be dear to the artillery. But, as pointed out in Chapter III, it was not at the suggestion of artillerymen that in South

THE MANCHURIAN INFLUENCE. 153

Africa invaluable time was so often wasted in attempts to silence hostile guns whose position could rarely be located. The extensive use of covered positions in Manchuria confirmed the impression that this silencing of guns was no longer a practical proposition, and the increased tenacity of life conferred by the adoption of shields appeared to put the matter beyond question. It seemed that shielded and concealed guns might pound at each other all day without doing each other any real harm.[1]

The same considerations applied to the artillery "preparation" of the infantry attack. Here again how many hundreds and thousands of rounds had been wasted in fruitless bombardments without any profit to the infantry. When it came to the turn of the latter to advance they had to do so against an enemy not only unharmed, but warned. Accounts from Manchuria told the same story of the futility of such premature cannonading.

At the same time there could be no doubt that the infantry would require even more than ever the "support" of the artillery. But this support, to be effective, must be combined with the movement of the infantry; and must be directed upon the enemy's guns or infantry according to which was developing the most destructive fire against the advance.

Such a conception of the artillery action affected not only the selection of its targets, but also the manner of its deployment. Manchuria had shown that, futile as might be attempts to silence guns in action, the movement of batteries might be rendered impossible once their position was discovered. But it had shown also that with rapid-firing guns it was no longer necessary to pile gun upon

CHAPTER VII.

The New Doctrine.

---

[1] Allusion may here be made to a marked departure from precedent on the part of the Japanese. Full of sentiment in its highest form, they were at the same time realists, and so, recognizing that material damage to the guns from hostile fire was now so rare as to be negligible, they decided that the only sensible course when a battery was getting the worst of it was to withdraw the gunners.

154   THE FIELD ARMY ARTILLERY.

CHAPTER VII.

The New Doctrine.

gun in order to obtain intensity of fire. Instead of deploying his batteries "in the greatest strength available from the earliest possible moment" as the manual of 1904 had still enjoined, the prudent commander would "push his guns gradually into action, like pawns in the game, wherever resistance is felt to the advance, using only what is required for the preliminary work, and keeping in hand, as in the great wars of a century ago, those required for the close support of the decisive infantry attack".[1]

Such, briefly put, were the salient characteristics of the new doctrine for the employment of artillery in the field, and attention may now be turned to the effect of its acceptance on the training of the artillery. To play its part efficiently in war the artillery must devote its energies in peace to perfecting its technical equipment and methods, and to discovering a means of absolutely merging its action with that of the infantry. The efforts made by the field army artillery to master these tasks during the years which followed the Manchurian War will be considered in this chapter.

Technically they involved :—

 i. The direction of fire from covered positions.
 ii. The control of fire of dispersed batteries.
 iii. The application of fire to service targets.
 iv. The development of rapidity of fire.

Tactically they could all be summed up in the one word "co-operation".

Covered Positions.

The first battle in Manchuria provided an object-lesson in the value of indirect fire, and throughout the war covered positions were extensively used by both artilleries. The manual of 1906 accordingly showed a marked advance in its attitude to such positions. A new section was devoted to the subject of "concealment", in which the advantages

---

[1] Either unlimbered "in observation", or limbered up "in readiness".

THE MANCHURIAN INFLUENCE. 155

and disadvantages of the different natures of covered positions were fully discussed, and the drill for occupying such positions was systematized.[1] In this year also the new 13 and 18-pr. equipments, with their goniometric sights, sight-clinometers, and range-indicators, came into general use and greatly simplified the procedure. But unexpected difficulties cropped up. Clinometer laying, which had leaped into popularity with the new armament, was found to have pitfalls for the unwary in the changes of the angle of sight, especially when engaging moving targets on undulating ground. Then the question of direction, which had been so simple in the days of direct laying, began to assume importance: "finding the line" was added to the requirements of ranging: "parallelism" and "displacement" became words of dread to battery commanders; and all these were further complicated by the attention now being given to "opening-out" and "closing-in" the lines of fire according to the width of the ground to be covered, and to rapid "switches" to deal with fleeting opportunities.

The plotter and director, even in their rudimentary state, had paved the way, but much remained to be done before the appliances were so perfected, and officers so familiarized with their use, as to be able to deal with all the gunnery problems involved without losing sight of tactical considerations. Even with the aid of the "mental picture", evolved about this time, the whole business was apt to be terribly deliberate, and the tactical value of the time element ignored. There were moral considerations also. Further information seemed to show that the Japanese, at any rate, were not so enamoured of covered positions as had been the first impression from their use of them in the war. This had been forced upon them by the inferiority of their armament, but they were very doubtful of the effect which the habitual use

CHAPTER VII.

Covered Positions

---

[1] The year 1906 is memorable for the first official reference to "T.O.B.".

Chapter VII.

Covered Positions.

of such positions might have upon the spirit of the arm. And there were the other arms to be thought of. The stress that was being laid on indirect fire[1] at the practice camps was giving spectators the impression that the artillery were coming to look upon "cover" rather than "effect" as the preponderating consideration. There were complaints of excessive caution having characterized the action of the artillery at manœuvres, and of their consequent failure to afford the infantry the requisite support. A reaction was beginning: artillery officers were warned against the tendency to look upon such matters as the selection of ideal positions for their guns as of more importance than the fulfilment of the duty assigned to them; and reminded that in real warfare artillery ideals have invariably to be subordinated to other considerations.

And so the controversy raged. On the one side those who could not realize that the delays and difficulties which then accompanied indirect fire were only due to deficiencies in the appliances, and that improvements in technical equipment were bound to keep pace with tactical requirements. On the other side those who had the imagination to see all the tactical advantages of concealment, but lacked the wisdom to hasten slowly.

---

[1] Before leaving the subject of indirect fire it may be interesting to record an account of the successful use of this method of fire nearly four centuries ago as reproduced in the *Revue d'Artillerie* of March 1908. As the unknown author relates in the *Livre de Canonerie*, printed in 1561, the artillerists of Therouenne when besieged by the Burgundians in 1534, observed that the enemy often made use of a valley which was completely screened from the guns of the town. By the aid of poles, the direction from one of the batteries over the crest of the hill was plotted out; the poles were then removed and the required line of direction for the guns was marked by bushes specially planted along the crest. At the same time the duty was allotted to flank observers placed on the hill, of communicating to the battery not only the approach of the enemy to the appointed place, but also on the opening of fire, the necessary correction by the aid of signals previously decided on. The concealed fire planned in this way was crowned with success. When the Burgundian infantry columns moving along the valley had approached the direction plotted, the artillery opened fire. On the second discharge a whole rank of the Burgundians lay stretched on the ground and the enemy hastily abandoned the fateful valley.

THE MANCHURIAN INFLUENCE. 157

The first reports from Manchuria had appeared to encourage the advocates of the extreme dispersion of guns related in Chapter III, but further information showed that this was in great measure due to want of a sense of proportion. While there were no examples of such great gun masses as in the Franco-German War, there were few instances of such dispersion as had been seen at our practice camps in the first years after the South African War. The new manual recognized the normal situation as being for the batteries of a brigade to be to some extent dispersed in order to ensure concealment, and contained a new sub-section on allotting the objective and ranging a number of batteries so dispersed. Great attention was given to the various methods of indicating objectives and controlling the fire; panoramic sketches became all the fashion; and the means of communication within a brigade assumed increased importance. While there could be little doubt that for communication between a battery and its observing station the telephone would be an unmixed blessing, there was considerable hesitation as to whether such a link between brigade and battery commanders would not tend to tie the latter to their observing stations and hinder their efforts to watch the tactical situation. The increased attention paid to brigade practice proved conclusively, however, the necessity for providing the brigade commander with the means of communicating with his batteries, and in 1908 cable carts were provided for field artillery brigades and heavy batteries, to be succeeded by limbered telephone wagons which made their first appearance at the manœuvres of 1909. They were a great improvement on the carts, but their weight was excessive for the pair of horses allowed.[1]

Equal in importance to the accurate direction and effective control of the fire was its correct application to the changed conditions of the battlefield. Infantry could no longer be expected to appear in masses, guns were sure

CHAPTER VII.

Dispersed Batteries.

Application of Fire.

---

[1] After the army manœuvres of 1913 the addition of a second pair was agreed to, and included in estimates 1914-15.

158 THE FIELD ARMY ARTILLERY.

CHAPTER VII.

Application of Fire.

to be shielded, and the artillery must be prepared to deal with such targets.

Taking first the infantry. The great extension of formations, and the attention paid to cover, would often make it impossible to locate their exact position. It would then be necessary to spread the fire over an area of ground, and the chapter on shrapnel fire in the new manual had subsections on "Distribution in Depth" and "Lateral Distribution" for use on such occasions. A special form of this distribution was the method known as "searching and sweeping", derived from an incident in the Franco-German War,[1] and developed with the power of quick-firing guns to cover greater front and depth than had been possible at that date. To practise dealing with such problems, targets were arranged to simulate troops appearing and disappearing over a considerable area (many actually moving), and battery commanders who did not distribute their fire over the whole were penalized. It was an astounding commentary on the heresy hunt of 1895.

Turning now to the artillery. The artillery duel had been discarded, but artillery would still be called upon to attack guns—how was this to be done if they were shielded? There was much discussion in the military press of all nations, and much ingenuity in devising special weapons for the purpose. In Germany Generals von Rohne and von Reichenau[2] carried on a controversy in the *Militär Wochenblatt* which attracted much attention: in England definite experiments commenced in 1904 and were continued for the next three years. The first question was whether a direct hit from a percussion shrapnel would put the detachment out of action or whether a high-explosive shell was required. The trials showed that shrapnel could be trusted to do all that was required—to the great relief of the very general nervousness regarding the safety of

---

[1] Prince Kraft's *Letters on Artillery*, chapter IV.

[2] von Reichenau advocated a small-bore gun of very high velocity and flat trajectory, which at first found favour on the continent, but eventually failed in some extensive trials in Switzerland

THE MANCHURIAN INFLUENCE. 159

high-explosive shell in field artillery vehicles. The next question was what was the chance of obtaining such a direct hit. Here the experience of practice seemed to show that, at ranges over 3,000[1] yards, it was too remote to justify the large expenditure of ammunition entailed by the effort. The only alternative was time-shrapnel, and the possibility of penetrating the shields with their bullets was investigated. Various alloys and sizes were tried, and some success was obtained with bullets of tungsten steel. But even these failed at anything over 2,000 yards when the shell burst more than 50 yards short, and they were very expensive. The frontal attack of time shrapnel seemed as little likely to be effective as that of percussion shell. Oblique fire with time shrapnel seemed the only solution, or failing that the bursting of time shrapnel in the intervals so as to get the oblique effect of the outside bullets of the cone. The plunging fire of shrapnel from mortars had, however, been used with success against covered batteries in the American Civil War, and the manual of 1908 alluded to the possibility of using howitzer shrapnel for the attack of shielded guns, although non-committal as to its value. Trials with the 4˙5″ howitzer, later in the year proved most successful.

The special attribute of quick-firing guns is rapidity of fire,[2] and it was obviously the first duty of the artillery to develop this quality of their new guns to the utmost. Rapidity of fire was no new thing in the Royal Artillery. With their smooth-bores the gunners of the Peninsula period had been accustomed to maintain a rate of fire far beyond anything which their successors of the second half of the XIXth century could emulate.[3] It was a point

CHAPTER VII.

Application of Fire.

Rapidity of Fire.

---

[1] In a paper in the "Proceedings" for 1908 Captain H. W. Hill, after a thorough examination of the probabilities, put the limit at 3,500 without undue expenditure.

[2] "La rapidité du tir, qui est la propriété essentielle du canon de campagne". (Réglement de Manœuvre de l'Artillerie de Campagne).

[3] In Colonel Burne's *History of the Mess* an instance is given of 23 rounds being fired in a minute "sponging each time". This was at an inspection by George III in 1770.

160 THE FIELD ARMY ARTILLERY.

Chapter VII.

Rapidity of Fire.

on which the opponents of rifled guns had laid great stress during the controversy before their introduction; and after the change it had to be admitted that, even if artillery did catch cavalry or infantry in close formation, these could always deploy before the guns had done them serious damage. The quick-firer changed all that.[1] Even in Manchuria, although the guns were not true quick-firers, there were instances of troops caught in such a way suffering severely before they could extricate themselves. This power of being able to seize "fleeting opportunities" was a very valuable one. The French had laid great stress from the first on the moral as well as the material effect of such a sudden burst of intense fire, but it was a lesson which the Royal Artillery of the XXth century, brought up in the faith of deliberate, accurate, fire, and economy of ammunition, were slow to learn, There still lingered in the fire discipline checks to rapidity of fire, and indications of a failure to realize the power of the guns to deliver at any moment, without unsettling departures from normal procedure, a fire of the utmost intensity. It was not until the issue of the manual of 1908 that the acquisition of the "quick-firing spirit" could be said to be in a fair way to accomplishment.

The first result was a tendency to go to rapid fire before completing the ranging, and this was encouraged by the issue in 1906 of a new form of practice report in which the record of individual rounds was eliminated. There was no reason why all ranging rounds should not be recorded, but there was no doubt that much of the value of quick-firing guns would be lost without a quickening up of the ranging. Various methods were tried with the Ehrhardts, and the adoption of the "ranging section" reduced the average time from "first gun" to "first time

---

[1] During their first year's experience with the Ehrhardt guns average batteries learned to maintain fire at twelve rounds a minute instead of the six which was all that could be managed with the breech-loaders. And for a burst the Ehrhardts could put in 28 rounds a minute without special procedure to the 14 of the breech-loaders at "magazine fire".

shrapnel"—the defenceless period for a battery—from seven minutes to less than four. With the 13 and 18-prs. further progress was possible, and in 1906 and 1907 "time-shrapnel ranging" was thoroughly tested at all practice camps with varying degrees of success. It was naturally found to be neither a panacea for all ills, as some of its advocates had claimed, nor the unattainable ideal that some of its adversaries had affirmed. No doubt the fact that all practice was conducted with new fuzes was in its favour, and also that on Salisbury Plain the general level nature of the range tended to obscure the difficulties connected with the angle of sight, and the "splash" of the bullets on the chalk could generally be detected. The issue in 1908 of a new fuze-dial with an increased scope of corrector helped, and so did graticuled glasses, but the steep slopes of the mountain ranges always proved a difficulty. The manual of 1906 had permitted considerable latitude in the use of different methods of ranging, that of 1908 simplified matters by laying down only one "method", but one in which either time or percussion shrapnel could be used according to circumstances. There was much discussion on the subject, and for some years the annual training memoranda contained "tips" to help battery commanders, just as had the school of gunnery reports of twenty years earlier, when the "bracket system" was being forced upon a reluctant generation.

All this quickening up of the fire pre-supposed ample ammunition being always at hand in the battery itself. From time immemorial batteries had consisted of six guns and six wagons, and until after the Franco-German War guns and wagons had been inseparable. The demand for greater mobility which followed that war led to the dropping back of the wagons from the guns on reaching the zone of manœuvre, and the sending up of only three to the position when the battery came into action. For more rapid-firing guns this supply was inadequate, and even before the re-armament the number of battery wagons was increased to nine so as to allow of one being sent up to

CHAPTER VII.

Rapidity of Fire.

CHAPTER VII.

Rapidity of Fire.

each gun in action while still keeping three in reserve. Finally with the adoption of a quick-firing equipment twelve wagons were provided, six forming with the guns the "firing battery", of which each wagon accompanied its gun in all cases, while the other six constituted a reserve, to which the inappropriate name of "first line" was given. The movement of this large number of vehicles was not a simple matter, and arrangements were made at all practice camps to give batteries an opportunity of working with twelve wagons. There was much discussion regarding the positions for the firing battery wagons in action; the bringing up of the first line wagons to replace them; and the procedure to be adopted in an advance or withdrawal. As time went on some relaxations were permitted in the rigidity of the rules. In cases when it was of first importance to open fire without a moment's delay, or when rapid changes of position were likely to be necessary, it was permitted to unlimber the wagons instead of unhooking the teams; and the use of limber supply without unhooking was allowed for horse artillery in a cavalry action, and even for field artillery when liable to be charged by cavalry. The heavy losses inevitable in an attempt to bring the first line wagons up to the guns if the position were under fire, led to trials of sleighs pulled up with a tackle for replenishing ammunition, but they proved unpractical. Eventually a loose canvas jacket carrying four rounds was approved, much on the same lines as the portable magazines which formed part of the equipment when the wagons were placed behind the guns instead of alongside them.

The Practice Camps.

The working out of the technical problems we have been considering was the duty of the practice camps, and they set themselves resolutely to the task. In this they were greatly assisted by the change from "Competitive" to "Classification" in 1905, for this loosened the bonds which had hitherto tied the hands of commandants, and resulted in a great widening of the scope of the practice.

THE MANCHURIAN INFLUENCE. 163

The "application of fire to tactical situations" was introduced: the camp staffs vied with each other in the construction of ingenious targets and the elaboration of schemes, so as to represent as closely as possible the tasks which, judging from Manchurian experience, might be expected to confront the artillery in the future.

CHAPTER VII.

The Practice Camps.

The policy of giving the captains and subalterns of batteries the experience of taking a series was extended to include artillery staff officers, adjutants, and in some cases battery serjeant-majors. There followed, as a natural corollary to the practice of subalterns in battery command, that of serjeants in section command. The batteries had reached a very high standard in fire discipline, but, with the more elaborate nature of the targets and schemes, the battery commanders were becoming the weak spot. The prompt and correct application of fire against unexpected targets was a matter in which much training was required, and one in which they could not train themselves. It took brigade commanders long to realize that this was essentially their responsibility.

The necessity for giving more practice in brigade, which would be the rule on service, was at last admitted, and at some camps all orders, even at battery practice, were sent through the brigade commander. More important still was the recognition by the War Office of the necessity of ground for such practice, and sanction by the Treasury of the purchase of additional land for the purpose at Trawsfynydd and Glen Imaal.

Brigade practice was, however, but a stepping stone. It was the adoption of the division as the unit in war and the school of training in peace, with the appointment of divisional artillery commanders, that completed the scheme of artillery training. Heretofore batteries and brigades had gone to practice camps to be "tested" by "camp commandants" who had no responsibility for their efficiency. Henceforth they went to camp so that they might be "trained" by the officers who would command them in war. Practice took its proper place as a stage in

164   THE FIELD ARMY ARTILLERY.

Chapter VII.

The Practice Camps.

the training instead of being a thing apart. Moreover the bringing of two brigades into camp at a time gave the divisional artillery commander and his staff the opportunity for gaining experience in the exercise of executive command under the orders of the general officer commanding the division. The chain of command and training was at last complete.

Ranges and Targets.

On the subject of length of range, reports from Manchuria were conflicting. In many cases the distances at which the artillery opened fire were prodigious, but these might be ascribed to differences of armament, and towards the end of the war there was certainly a tendency to shorten. Every year, however, batteries were called upon to practice at longer ranges and more difficult targets, and the problem of the location of targets was still much to the fore.

For the representation of guns firing smokeless powder an "apparatus firing puffs" was introduced in 1907, and considerably developed in the following years. In conjunction with surprise targets it gave valuable practice in the location of guns whose position was indicated by flashes. This was difficult enough, but what was to be done when not even the flashes could be seen? The value of observation from the air in such cases had not yet been realized, but there seemed to be a possibility of arriving at some idea of the position of the guns if the time of flight of their shell could be ascertained. Captain Rainsford-Hannay[1] took up the subject, and suggested three methods of doing this :—

   (i).   By the graduation of the time fuze.
   (ii). By the difference in time between the report of the gun and the arrival of the shell.
   (iii). By the length of time during which the shell was heard in flight.

The great advance in military aviation after the end of the first decade, and the progress made in locating hidden

---

[1] Colonel F. Rainsford-Hannay, C.M.G., D.S.O.

THE MANCHURIAN INFLUENCE. 165

targets and observing fire from aeroplanes, diverted attention for the time from these proposals. They are nevertheless worthy of record as the first step towards the system of "sound-ranging" which came to prominence in the War.

CHAPTER VII.
Ranges and Targets

A matter in which Manchuria brought about a complete *volte-face* was in the general attitude towards night operations. The Japanese, although strongly prejudiced against anything of the sort, were forced to undertake night operations more and more frequently, and on a larger and larger scale, and the artillery were naturally drawn into them. The withdrawal of artillery from the front line after dark, recommended in the manual of 1902, found no place in that of 1904, while that of 1906 suggested moving the guns into positions by night so as to ensure their being occupied without detection. The possibility of effective fire by night was also taken up at practice camps. There were experiments to ascertain the value of search-lights as an aid, and also to discover their vulnerability to artillery fire; and these were followed up by extensive trials with field guns and howitzers in which considerable success was obtained both in continuing fire by night on a target which had been ranged on by day, and in ranging on a target by night, provided in the latter case that an observer could be established in a forward position. Night firing had been made possible by the attention paid to fire from covered positions: without the appliances provided for indirect fire it would not have been feasible.

Night Operations.

Manchuria also brought to the front again the value of entrenching and this had generally to be done by night. In 1905 a new departure was made by giving each battery at practice a free hand to entrench itself, and a couple of hours to do it in. As in the story of "Duffers Drift" this resulted at first in much misapplied energy, but attention once directed to the subject improvement was rapid, and by 1908 brigades were digging themselves in during the

CHAPTER VII.

Night Operations.

night, and opening fire from their entrenchments at dawn.[1]

All this night work showed the necessity for lights in the battery, just as had been the case in coast artillery ten years earlier. The only lanterns a field battery carried were the two provided for the use of the stable picquet, but by 1910 all wagons and wagon limbers of horse, field, and heavy artillery in the field army were fitted to carry two of the candle lamps approved for the siege artillery for night firing.

Aviation.

There had been instances in the South African War of the use of a balloon for observation, and in the following years there were spasmodic trials at practice camps to ascertain their real value for this purpose, and also how best they might be attacked. After the Manchurian War these experiments were taken up in earnest at both the field and siege camps, and a method of fire was worked out and embodied in the manual. But great changes in aircraft were at hand. In 1908 the "dirigible" made its appearance, in 1909 M. Blériot flew the Channel in a heavier-than-air machine. It was plain that the aeroplane could no longer be neglected, and that, with its speed of 70 to 80 miles an hour, its attack would be a very different proposition from that of a captive balloon or kite.

At the Exhibition at Frankfort in 1909, Krupp and Ehrhardt exhibited a large selection of guns designed for use against dirigibles, and expected to be effective against aeroplanes also. The heavier natures were mounted on platforms drawn by lorries, the lighter on swift motor cars on which the guns might chase and shoot down their quarry. There were tracer shell and sensitive fuzes, but the methods of hitting such elusive objects had not yet been investigated, although the provision of an aerial target was being discussed by the Aeronautical Society.

In spite of the advantage they possessed in their com-

---

[1] A significant step was the moving of the pick-axe and shovel from the limber to the carriage so as to be always at hand.

parative invulnerability there were, however, grave doubts as to the suitability of either the dirigible or the aeroplane for observation of fire owing to their susceptibility to weather and the difficulty of communicating results. The captive balloon, or its rough-weather substitute the kite, could always be depended on, and their direct telephonic communication with the ground was invaluable.

Chapter VII. Aviation.

In the above review of the progress made in the more important branches of technical training, it has been shown that the artillery spared no pains to fit itself for the new demands made upon its technical skill. Its tactical task of finding the means of ensuring complete co-operation with the infantry was more difficult.

Co-operation

It is impossible to peruse again the military literature of this period without being impressed by the emphasis laid upon co-operation, and the reason is not far to seek. Of old infantry and artillery had fought side by side, within the reach of human vision and human voice: the requirements of the moment were obvious to both, and no scheme for ensuing co-operation was needed. But as ranges grew longer and extensions wider, the arms ceased to see or hear what was happening to each other, and co-operation ceased to be spontaneous. Then came the crowning obstacle, smokeless powder. South Africa showed the need, Manchuria more than confirmed it. British officers attached to both Russian and Japanese armies saw how important this question of co-operation had become, and realized also from their intercourse with their colleagues of other nations that there was no army in which this branch of military training was so neglected as their own. As one of them wrote at the time: "We each of us look upon the other arms with mild toleration: we dine with them, play polo with them, and affect a polite interest in each other: but as for combining to practise our joint work—it is not the custom of the army".

Such an attitude could no longer be tolerated, and at last steps were taken in earnest to improve matters. The system of attaching regimental officers to other arms was

CHAPTER VII.

Co-operation.

extended, and there was much discussion as to the best season for attachment and the most profitable employment for the attached officers: the question of expense was for years a stumbling block.[1] An important development was the affiliation of artillery brigades to infantry brigades. Inaugurated on Salisbury Plain in 1907, it soon became general, with the best results in fostering mutual friendship and comprehension in all ranks. But even this, useful as it was, would have availed little but for the adoption of the division as the basis of the field army organization. Consequent upon it came the quartering together, or at any rate the bringing together annually for training, of the units which would have to fight together. This gave life and reality to attachments and affiliations, and to the courses for other arms at practice camps, where only could officers learn to appreciate fully the powers of quick-firing guns. All were agreed that they must get to know and to understand each other better. It was when it came to considering the practical measures necessary to secure co-operation on the battlefield that difficulties began to crop up.

The manual of 1906 still trusted to proximity, insisting that guns must be moved forward until they reached positions from which close co-operation was possible. But one of the lessons of Manchuria had been that on the modern battlefield all movements of artillery by daylight would be impossible, and to delay matters until the advance could be carried out under cover of darkness, as suggested in the manual, might upset the whole plan of operations. The artillery sought for a better way.

The Forward Observing Officer.

Towards the end of the war Japanese artillery officers were sometimes sent forward with telephones, to keep as far as possible with the advancing infantry, and send back their observations to the guns. It was now proposed to adopt this plan, and there arose at once a storm of opposition from both artillery and infantry. Such direct com-

[1] It was not until 1912 that it was made a charge against the Training Grant.

THE MANCHURIAN INFLUENCE. 169

munication between a battery commander and the firing line might, it was admitted, occasionally facilitate piecemeal co-operation between individual units, but in a division or other formation it must sooner or later bring the general plan of action into confusion. To a battalion or company commander in the firing line it might well seem of the utmost importance that his command should be assisted by artillery fire to repel a local counter-attack, or to gain another few yards of ground, but to the general who saw his main attack fail because a subordinate had called off the supporting guns, such decentralization could scarcely appeal.

To this it was replied that no system of communication designed primarily for purposes of command would suffice for the special purpose in view. If news of some sudden emergency, or opportunity, had to filter through the ordinary channel from the battalion commander to the infantry brigadier, from him to the divisional commander, from him, through the divisional artillery commander, to the artillery brigade or battery concerned, what chance was there of action being as prompt as the situation demanded? On the one hand was the Scylla of confusion, on the other the Charybdis of delay.

There was, it was suggested, a middle way. An artillery officer sent forward to observe the fire would be in touch with the infantry, and it would be a great help towards getting the fire directed where it was most required if he sent back information as to the local progress of the fight. And if action upon such messages were left to the discretion of the officer directing the fire in accordance with the orders he had received, they might on occasions be of great assistance in obtaining the close and timely support of the artillery. After much discussion, in which many distinguished officers of both arms took part, the sending forward of such an officer was authorized by the manual of 1908, but an amendment in the following year made it quite clear that he was to be an *observing* officer only.

CHAPTER VII.

The Forward Observing Officer.

170 THE FIELD ARMY ARTILLERY.

Chapter VII.

Close Supports.

The practice of 1909 saw the first appearance of the "Forward Observing Officer", but there were still doubts as to whether his reports would be sufficient to ensure the artillery fire being rightly directed when it came to the crisis of the assault, when the difficulties of the infantry were greatest, and when the support of the artillery should therefore be closest. To many minds "close support" still meant batteries galloping up into the firing line. A more modern school argued that such action was out of date, that it was chiefly derived from peace manœuvres, where the infantry saw nothing of the fire effect; that in war the men in the firing line would see the shells bursting in front of them, and would recognize the support that was being rendered by the guns without caring where they were. In short that what the infantryman wanted was the shells and not the guns. Their opponents maintained that such a conclusion was not borne out by actual experience, that what the infantry required was just that solid support which only the actual presence of the guns could give, and quoted in support of their contention many a glowing page from history. When it was objected that these all referred to a time when the full power of modern fire had not been developed, some striking instances from Manchuria were produced. Such episodes had inspired the pen and pencil of poets and painters, and stirred the blood of generations of artillerymen, and it could never be admitted that they were no longer within the bounds of possibility. That this was the view of both armies in Manchuria was clearly shown by their post-war manuals; and the new *Field Service Regulations* sounded no uncertain note, for it repeated from *Combined Training* the old artillery maxim "the greater the difficulties of the infantry the closer should be the support of the artillery".

Another aspect of the problem of close support was presented by the question of how long artillery fire should be continued over the heads of the infantry. Here again opinion was sharply divided, and here again the question was one of enormous importance to every artillery officer who might be directing the fire of a battery.

THE MANCHURIAN INFLUENCE. 171

There could be no doubt that the culminating moment in an attack was the assault, and that it should therefore also be the culminating moment of the artillery fire. Classic instances of such support in the British Army were to be found in the storming of St. Sebastian in the Peninsular War, and in the assault on the Redan in the Crimea. In South Africa there had been similar cases of fire being continued with great success until the last possible moment. Windham in the Redan had sent back word for the batteries to keep up their fire whether they hit the infantry or not: a battalion commander at Pieter's Hill had borne witness to the value of the artillery support even though several of his men had been hit by the shell. The evidence from Manchuria was generally to the same effect. But the official Regulations were not so explicit. *Combined Training, 1905,* directed the artillery to continue their fire against the position "until the attacking infantry is close to it", and then not to stop, but to direct the fire over the position during the assault. *Field Artillery Training, 1906,* was more concerned with theoretical limits outside which infantry should be "sufficiently safe". This was of little practical value, for it was rare for an attack to be made over dead level ground, and the further instruction that when the fire was "masked" it should be turned elsewhere was no better. The manual of 1908 went into the matter a little further, but still shirked the real issue. What the artillery wanted to know was whether they were to go on firing *even at the risk of causing casualties to their own infantry,* and as to this definite guidance was lacking. A paper[1] which appeared in the *Proceedings* early in 1908 shed, however, considerable light on the infantry point of view. In the opinion of the author, the infantry would accept the risk if they had been given education as to the value of the assistance the artillery

CHAPTER VII.

Close Support

---

[1] "Artillery and Infantry in the Final Stages of the Attack—An Infantry View—by Captain Hon. H. Dawnay, D.S.O., Rifle Brigade—With Remarks by Colonel L. E. Kiggell, after consideration at the Staff College".

fire would be to them, and the extent of the danger. Without such education it was probable that when shell from their own artillery began falling dangerously near they would come to the conclusion that they were being fired on in mistake for the enemy; and if once the infantry waited for the guns to stop firing before they went on, the assault was bound to fail.

It was decided that both arms must be trained for mutual action. The artillery were instructed to arrange schemes at their practice camps which would give practice in this "supremely important" part of their duty in supporting an assault—their infantry being represented by moving or disappearing targets, and the batteries required to direct their fire so as to afford the infantry the fullest support without exposing them to unnecessary casualties.

Infantrymen were provided with brightly coloured flags at manœuvres, by the waving of which they might indicate their progress to the supporting artillery.[1] The advisability of actual trials with the guns firing over the infantry at field firing was discussed at home, and carried out in India on several occasions with marked success. The manual of 1908 devoted considerably more attention to the question than had the previous issue, but while pointing out that the success or failure of the attack might frequently depend upon the continuance of the artillery fire, and definitely fixing the responsibility for ceasing fire upon the artillery, it gave no hint as to the amount of risk the infantry were prepared to take. Fortunately next year saw the issue of *Field Service Regulations,* and here, at last, was definite guidance. "Artillery fire will be continued until it is impossible for the artillery to distinguish between its own and the enemy's infantry. The danger from shells bursting short is more than compensated for by the support afforded if the fire is maintained to the last moment; but in order to reduce this danger it is the duty of artillery commanders

---

[1] This idea, derived from Japanese practice, was given up, after extensive trials at home and in India.

THE MANCHURIAN INFLUENCE. 173

to keep themselves informed as to the progress of the infantry, and to discontinue fire against the objective of the assault when the infantry is getting to close quarters, if such fire cannot be readily observed and controlled" The danger to the infantry was faced, the duty of the artillery commander was defined.

Chapter VII.
Close Support.

In conclusion it may safely be said that the attention devoted to the subject of co-operation had done much to bridge the gulf between the arms. During the discussions many subsidiary questions connected with the action of artillery and infantry had been raised in which an understanding of both points of view was invaluable. Such, for instance, was the distrust of the infantry for "indirect" fire. It had to be explained that indirect laying was more regular, and therefore much safer for them, than direct, and that direct fire entailed positions where the guns would probably be destroyed, and where replenishment of ammunition would certainly be out of the question. The best methods of fire for the artillery to use when supporting an infantry advance, and the safest formations for infantry when passing through artillery fire, were subjects concerning which each arm could learn much from the other. The subject selected by the Committee of the Institution for the prize essay in 1908 was "The means to ensure co-operation between the artillery and infantry of the field army", and the general officer commanding the 4th Division[1] consented to act as one of the judges. There were conferences and lectures—by infantry officers[2] at Woolwich, by gunners in the commands—at which there was much airing of opinions to the mutual advantage.

Co-operation was not, however, a matter which concerned only the different arms composing the field army. In the British service it was almost as essential between the land and sea services, and one effect of the Manchurian

Manœuvres and Field Firing.

---

[1] Major-General (now Lieut.-General Sir Herbert) Belfield, K.C.B., K.C.M.G., D.S.O.
[2] Notably Brigadier-General (now General Sir Richard) Haking, G.B.E., K.C.B., K.C.M.G.

174   THE FIELD ARMY ARTILLERY.

CHAPTER VII.

Manœuvres and Field Firing.

War was to direct attention to the value of careful preparation, as shown by the comparison between the perfect arrangements for the Japanese disembarkation at Chemulpo in 1904, and the absence of all requisites when the United States carried out a similar operation in Cuba in 1898. In order to give some practice in such co-operation joint naval and military manœuvres were instituted for the first time in 1904. In these a force of all arms representing an army corps[1] was transported by sea from Southampton to the coast of Essex, and there landed on an open beach. Unfortunately—as far as the gaining of experience by the artillery was concerned—it was possible to run the horse and gun floats against the beach, and ride the horses and drag the guns ashore. In the re-embarkation some remarkably quick work was done by the artillery.

There were army manœuvres at home in 1909 and 1910 to which considerable regimental interest was given by the appearance of the new divisional artillery at its full strength. Much attention was devoted to the combined action of the different natures of artillery now included, and the way in which batteries were worked forward by covered approaches in the final stage of the attack in order to render the infantry the closest possible support was admired. The difficulties of artillery umpiring were brought much to the fore owing to the increased attention devoted to the question of artillery support. But, as will be shown in the next chapter, the most important manœuvres of 1910 for the Royal Artillery were those which were drawing all eyes to Picardy.

In India in 1906 Sir Horace Smith-Dorrien, commanding the Quetta Division, organized field firing on a scale never prevously attempted. A position over a mile in length was entrenched on the lines of those in Manchuria, and against this the division carried out a systematic attack lasting three days, and culminating in an assault at dawn.

---

[1] It was not until 1911 that confidential instructions for combined operations were issued.

THE MANCHURIAN INFLUENCE. 175

Shot and shell, hand-grenades and trench-mortars, nothing had been neglected which could contribute to the realism of the operations. Similar exercises, including actual firing by the artillery over the heads of the infantry, took place in other divisions and brigades, notably in the Peshawur Division in 1910, and the Indian Training Memorandum definitely stated that the "combined field-firing of a division is the highest point in the training of the troops". Opinion at home was dubious, but a trial with a brigade of infantry and a brigade of artillery on Salisbury Plain in 1909 led to the conclusion that such exercises were valuable for forces of that size, and the expenditure of 15% of artillery practice ammunition was authorized—much to the annoyance of artillerymen generally.

CHAPTER VII.

Manœuvres and Field Firing.

HORSE, ARTILLERY, FIELD HOWITZERS, MOUNTAIN AND HEAVY ARTILLERY.

In the previous volume of this History reference was made to the revival of interest in cavalry during the last decade of the XIXth century, and all through the period chronicled in this volume military opinion continued to ascribe great importance to the independent action of that arm, and to predict a great cavalry battle for the curtain-raiser in the next war. In the British Army especially the experience of South Africa had accentuated the value of mounted troops, and in spite of the fact that the war in Manchuria had provided no example of such combats between masses of cavalry, somewhat exaggerated views as to the possibilities of their employment were frequently expressed. Mounted Infantry, Yeomanry, and Colonial Mounted Rifles, were counted on to reinforce the regular Cavalry, and the possibility of field artillery as well as horse being called upon to act with such mounted troops was envisaged by the reappearance of "Field Calls" in Field Artillery Training.

Horse Artillery.

CHAPTER VII.

Horse Artillery.

Unfortunately the early years of the XXth century had seen some decline in the high reputation for rapidity of movement and accuracy of fire previously enjoyed by the Royal Horse Artillery. From cavalry manœuvres came complaints of tactical hesitation when co-operation, instinctive and instant, was imperative. From practice camps came reports of horse batteries, in spite of their manifold advantages, ranking low in the classification. Attention was drawn to the special qualifications called for in officers, the necessity for strict discrimination in their selection, and the importance of retaining only those who continued to display the necessary qualities. It was but a passing phase, as had been the decline in the efficiency of the garrison artillery described in the last volume, but Regimental History would be incomplete and untrue if reference to such periods were omitted.

With the re-armament the improvement was rapid. In the 13-pr. the horse artillery were given an equipment considerably lighter than that of any other Great Power, so that they might be able to respond to whatever calls might be made upon them by the cavalry. The reorganization of 1905 had placed the batteries belonging to cavalry brigades definitely under the brigadiers, and they were reported upon with the regiments of the brigade, but the batteries belonging to the corps artillery were still separate. The formation of the Expeditionary Force in 1907 showed the whole of the horse artillery as "attached" to cavalry brigades, and "allotted" to cavalry divisions and *Cavalry Training* of that year emphasized the fact that "the guns and cavalry are one organization". The inclusion of a Cavalry Division in the Expeditionary Force had greatly improved matters for it permitted of the organization of the horse artillery previously allotted by batteries to cavalry brigades on a divisional basis under a full colonel, and the assembly of this division for training in 1909 showed marked progress in the co-operation of the two arms. In this year also a special practice camp for horse artillery was instituted at West Down under the

THE MANCHURIAN INFLUENCE. 177

Staff Officer for Artillery at Aldershot, who was earmarked for the command of the horse artillery of the Cavalry Division on mobilization.

Up till this time the practice of the horse artillery had been conducted at the ordinary practice camps, and much on the same lines as that of the field artillery. It was certainly laid down that some series should be arranged to exemplify the special tasks likely to be required of the horse artillery in the course of a cavalry action, but this was difficult to manage at the ordinary camps, at most of which the ground was unsuitable for the rapid movement of either guns or targets. The formation of a special camp on suitable ground ensured attention being primarily directed to the special requirements of the horse artillery; the pom-pom and machine-gun sections of cavalry regiments took part; the officers of the Cavalry School frequently attended; in 1911 there was a special series of trials at which the cavalry brigadiers were present. Thus a school of horse artillery was gradually formed, and a doctrine evolved, which showed its effect in the combination of speed and dash with order and accuracy to which the Inspector of Cavalry bore witness.

Many improvements were also effected in the more technical details. The normal position of the detachment was changed from "left" to "right rear", and of wagons from "rear" to "left rear" thus giving much greater freedom of movement. In action the wagons were always brought up so as to ensure an ample supply of ammunition, but were unlimbered instead of unhooked, which quickened things up considerably.

As regards equipment, the mobility of the 13-pr. and its power of delivering an overwhelming volume of fire, showed it to be in these respects an ideal weapon for horse artillery, but on the other hand certain features inherent in a quick-firer were found to militate against its efficiency. The trail spade, which conferred the power of rapid fire, prevented that free movement of the trail which might be required to keep under fire such a target as cavalry moving

CHAPTER VII.

Horse Artillery.

178   THE FIELD ARMY ARTILLERY.

CHAPTER VII.

Horse Artillery.

rapidly across the front, for the traverse on the carriage was soon exhausted. Its light shell was found to be ineffective against entrenchments or buildings, a matter the importance of which had been brought to light during Mischenko's cavalry raid in Manchuria. There was a demand for some weapon capable of firing a powerful projectile, and yet sufficiently mobile to accompany cavalry. It was recalled that in the first active service of the Royal Horse Artillery—the Expedition to the Helder in 1799—the Chestnut Troop had included two "Royal Howitzers" in its armament, and that many of the troops at Waterloo had been similarly equipped; and it was proposed to add a section of howitzers to each cavalry brigade ammunition column, to be manned when required by detachments from the batteries. But there were many objections to burdening the cavalry division with such a permanent addition, and the 4·5″ field howitzers coming into the service were considerably more mobile than the 5″. It was decided to trust to the howitzer batteries to supply the want should circumstances render it necessary, but it is worthy of record that during the discussion Colonel Paget[1] suggested the use of "something on the lines of the howitzer for mountain batteries for which designs have been called for". This was the 3·7″ and his suggestion is being adopted a quarter of a century after it was made.

Field Howitzers.

The Manchurian War more than confirmed the verdict of South Africa as to the value of field howitzers. There was a call for their transfer from the corps artillery to that of divisions, on the ground that guns and howitzers were complementary, and that the correct use of one would afford the other its opportunity, a co-operation which was unattainable while they belonged to separate formations. The organization of the Expeditionary Force in large divisions allowed of effect being given to this demand by the inclusion of a howitzer brigade in the divisional artil-

[1] Brigadier-General W. L. H. Paget, C.B., C.M.G., M.V.O., d. 1918. *Proceedings,* XXXV.

THE MANCHURIAN INFLUENCE. 179

lery, and the importance attached to their employment was evinced by its being the first purely artillery subject to be set down for discussion at the annual general staff conference. On this occasion Colonel Hamilton Gordon,[1] who had commanded a howitzer battery with marked success throughout the fighting in Natal, explained the tactical value of howitzer fire, and its technical difficulties, stressing the importance of a correct understanding of the principles of employment lest the powers of the howitzers should be frittered away in tasks which the guns could accomplish.

The finding of a satisfactory successor to the 5″ B.L. howitzer proved a tedious business, as has been seen, and it was not until 1910 that the 4·5″ Q.F. howitzer found its way into the howitzer batteries. Much attention had, however, to be paid to the drill, and various mechanical improvements made, before the title of "Q.F." was justified. The retention of safety pins in the fuzes slowed down the shrapnel fire, and the necessity of ranging in degrees instead of yards was a serious handicap. Various ingenious devices to allow of the use of a yard scale were tried, but it was not until the last years before the Great War that the difficulty was got over by the graduation of the sights with a yard scale for the 4th charge, and the issue of a "range rule" to allow of the use of this scale with all charges. It was only then that the ordinary rules[2] for ranging could be made applicable to howitzers.

As explained in Chapter III the South African War brought mountain artillery into disrepute owing to the obsolete nature of their equipment, and so led to the abolition of all representation of that branch on the home and colonial establishment. Manchuria more than restored its reputation, for the Japanese mountain batteries, taking advantage of their power of moving dispersed without attracting attention, and of using approaches impossible to field artillery, had established for themselves a new rôle

CHAPTER VII.

Field Howitzers.

Mountain Artillery.

---
[1] Lieut.-General Sir Alexander Hamilton Gordon, K.C.B., Colonel-Commandant.
[2] With the exception of "collective".

180   THE FIELD ARMY ARTILLERY.

CHAPTER VII.

Mountain Artillery.

as the only form of artillery which could accompany an infantry advance by day. Mountain artillerymen were not slow to drive home the lesson,[1] and an amendment to *Combined Training* admitted the claim. It was even proposed to change the name from "mountain" to "pack" so as to make it clear that its use was not restricted to hill fighting, but the idea had to be abandoned in deference to Indian susceptibilities.

Strained relations with Turkey in 1906 brought another rôle to the fore, for investigation showed that all beaches suitable for landing abutted on bluffs or cliffs which could not be negotiated by wheeled artillery. To carry out the traditional strategy of a descent by sea the army would require mountain batteries, and there were no longer any on the Imperial establishment. The unfortunate result of their abolition was brought into further prominence when it was proposed to organize a 7th Division based on Egypt. Exhaustive enquiries as to the possibility of wheeled artillery operating in any of the theatres of war in the Near East pointed to the advisability of including in such a division at least a brigade of mountain artillery, and many plans for its provision were considered, including the conversion of the unallotted batteries of horse artillery. Eventually it was decided to substitute a mountain battery for the garrison company in Egypt, and one was sent from India to Cairo in 1911, and another raised to replace it in India.

Meanwhile the Imperial Defence Conference of 1909 had established the principle that the Imperial Regulations and Training Manuals should be adopted throughout the Empire as the basis of the organization, administration, and training of the troops. The new *Field Service Regulations* accordingly contained a section on "mountain warfare", and an appendix[2] was added to *Field Artillery*

---

[1] Notably Major (now Brigadier-General) K. K. Knapp, C.B., C.M.G., in the *Journal of the Royal United Service Institution*, 1906.

[2] The appendix was incorporated in subsequent editions (1912 and 1914) with such small amendments as were necessary to complete the assimilation of the methods and the terminology of the mountain artillery to those of the rest of the field army artillery.

THE MANCHURIAN INFLUENCE. 181

Training 1908 giving the information required to make the manual applicable to mountain as well as field artillery. With its issue *Field Artillery Training* covered all branches of the Field Army Artillery.

In 1905 the two heavy brigades made their first appearance at a field artillery practice camp. Both brigades went to Okehampton because the large craters of the shell were held liable to render Salisbury Plain unfit for manœuvre by mounted troops, and Sir Evelyn Wood, who had taken the Plain under his wing from its acquisition, was resolute in his refusal to have it spoilt either by the Howitzers or the Heavies.

The method of practice was quite new to the brigades, and they found conditions very difficult. But in 1906 a new edition of *Field Artillery Training* included a section on the "Employment of Heavy Artillery in the Field", which provided them with the necessary guidance; they received their new 60-pr. equipment; and with a change in the command at Salisbury it was decided that the amenities of the Plain must give way to the advantage of its longer ranges for heavy artillery. By the following year the heavy brigades had shaken off the weight of their title and made a definite advance in entering into the spirit and feeling of the field army.[1] By their success in engaging moving targets they demonstrated the power of the 60-pr. to cause masses of infantry to deploy, and to crush hostile batteries coming into action from positions beyond the effective range of field guns. But Manchuria had shown that to keep them back, as enjoined in *Combined Training*, was to throw away the real advantage of their long range. To utilize this power for searching into the enemy's position, and enfilading his front, the batteries must be pushed well forward.

After the return of the two heavy brigades to their

CHAPTER VII.

Mountain Artillery.

Heavy Artillery.

---

[1] The substitution of limbered ammunition wagons for the old store wagons for the carriage of their ammunition was a great encouragement to mobility.

CHAPTER VII.
Heavy Artillery.

stations at the conclusion of their five months training with the field army the question of the interchange of batteries between heavy and siege artillery, as originally contemplated, came up for further consideration. The theory was that the batteries should train with horses as "heavy field" in the summer, and with steam tractors as "light siege" in the winter. But experience had now shown that the batteries could not be efficient as heavy batteries until they could train all the year round as such, and that the proposed change of rôles must be in every way detrimental to their efficiency in either. It was accordingly decided that they were to be permanent as heavy batteries, and to be quartered :—

> 1st Brigade—in the summer Aldershot, winter Portsmouth.
>
> 2nd Brigade—in the summer Bulford, winter Plymouth and Newport.

Their position was thus regularized, but their situation was still uncomfortable. In the 1st Brigade the batteries had sufficient horses for riding drill; they could each turn out a section horsed; and they were quartered sufficiently near each other to allow of pooling resources so that each battery could turn out in turn complete with guns and wagons. The 2nd Brigade had only 12 horses per battery, and the batteries were scattered, so that their winter training suffered greatly.

The mounting of Nos. 1 was still refused although it was obvious that they could not perform their duties in manœuvre or on the line of march on foot. A rough-rider was, however, allowed to each brigade in 1909. The system of hiring the draught horses for the summer could not be avoided because of the impossibility of stabling them in the winter.

Some consolation might be found for the harsh treatment the heavy brigades received in regard to horses by the advantage they enjoyed regarding drafts—the bane of the rest of the garrison artillery. The annual change of non-commissioned officers and men was not more than 20%, but unfortunately the change of officers went up to nearly 50% in 1910 owing to a decision to limit their service in heavy artillery to three years.

Chapter VII.

Heavy Artillery.

CHAPTER VIII.

THE FRENCH INFLUENCE.

(1910—1912.)

The *Entente Cordiale*—The Picardy Manœuvres—The General Staff Conference—The *Camp de Mailly*—The trials on Salisbury Plain—The Controversies of 1911—The Regulations of 1912—The Practice of 1912—The Doctrine.

CHAPTER VIII.

The Entente Cordiale.

FAMILIARITY with the new equipments of the horse and field artillery led inevitably to some waning of the admiration with which they had at first been regarded. As the years went by doubts crept in as to whether their performance quite came up to their promise, and as to whether they were being used in the way best suited to their powers. These criticisms came especially from those who had been watching artillery progress in France. The "75's" had been the first quick-firers in the field, and although great secrecy had been observed regarding all details of their equipment, and spectators were rigidly excluded from the ranges, training manuals told their tale. The *Réglement de Manœuvre de l'Artillerie de Campagne* of 1903,[1] and the comments of French and German writers, showed plainly that the French had gone much further than we had in modifying their methods in order to exploit to the full the special powers of their guns. This conclusion was confirmed when, with the growing *entente*, the veil was lifted, and representatives of the

---
[1] Carefully analysed in the Journal, Vol. XXX.

THE FRENCH INFLUENCE.

School of Gunnery were permitted to see the French artillery at practice.

The French were not content, however, with revising their technical methods to suit their armament, they subjected their tactical procedure to the same logical scrutiny. The result was seen in 1910 at some notable manœuvres in Picardy, where, as in those of 1900, the French Artillery was the cynosure of all eyes. These manœuvres were planned by General Percin, the Inspector-General of Artillery, to illustrate the methods which he had worked out for securing the co-operation of the artillery and infantry in the battlefield. To his great disappointment they took the form of a contest between two army corps instead of being confined to simple exercises in the employment of their artillery as he had proposed, but the chief interest remained in the action of the artillery. Briefly stated, General Percin's theory was to the following effect :—

(i). The troops employed in carrying out any military operation must be under one command. For any definite "task" the superior commander must, therefore, form a "combat group" of infantry and artillery under the command of the senior infantry officer—*"liaison par le haut"*.

(ii). The artillery of such a group must be divided into "counter-batteries" and "infantry-batteries", and the latter allotted to the support of the individual infantry units. The commanders of these infantry-batteries must establish and maintain communication with the commanders of the infantry units which they are to support—*"liaison par le bas"*.

(iii). The artillery allotted to a "combat group" must return to the control of the higher artillery commander as soon as the task of the group is accomplished, so as to ensure the maintenance of a floating reserve of artillery, ready for any fresh task which may be required.

It is not to be supposed that such a doctrine was accepted without cavil. It was bitterly attacked, especially by artillery officers who objected to being subordinated to

CHAPTER VIII.

The Picardy Manœuvres.

186   THE FIELD ARMY ARTILLERY.

the infantry,[1] and as soon as General Percin's tenure of the Inspectorship had expired a new *Réglement* controverted his ideas in many respects. This was particularly the case as regards placing the artillery co-operating in a combined operation under the orders of the infantry commander. The *Réglement* of 1910 stated that it was only in exceptional circumstances that the formation of the combat-groups advocated by General Percin was to be allowed : in principle the artillery was to remain under the orders of the higher artillery commanders. Even so the *Réglement* subordinated the action of the artillery within narrow limits to that of the infantry. General Percin had insisted that the artillery must strive after tactical rather than technical success—"it is not enough to make a noise, nor even to hit the enemy : the targets must be such as it is tactically important to destroy. . . . it is not sufficient that series should be effective, they must also be opportune"—and this part of his teaching was given full force in the new Regulations, as will be further shown when considering our own manual of 1912, avowedly based upon them.

So great was the importance attached to these developments of artillery training in France that they were made the subject of a full-dress debate at the annual general staff conference in January, 1911. To this were bidden the Inspector of Horse and Field Artillery, the Chief Instructor of the School of Gunnery for Horse and Field Artillery, and the six Divisional Artillery Commanders.[2] Broadly speaking the subject to be considered was whether full advantage was being derived from the quick-firing armament of the horse and field artillery, and the discussion ranged over a wide field in which organization, equipment, methods of fire, principles of employment, and system of training all came under review. The point on which

---

[1] It is interesting to recall the names of the most prominent of these—Foch, Nivelle, Fayolle, Dumezil, Buat.
[2] Brigadier-General W. F. L. Lindsay, Colonel S. C. U. Smith, Brigadier-Generals N. D. Findlay, H. K. Jackson, J. P. DuCane, E. J. Phipps-Hornby, E. A. Fanshawe, and W. L. H. Paget.

THE FRENCH INFLUENCE. 187

criticism was chiefly directed was the conduct of practice. The targets were said to be too difficult, the ranges too long, the ranging too slow, and, above all, tactical training deficient. Arraigned at the Bar of the General Staff, the field artillery branch of the School of Gunnery put up a stout defence, as it had done against the attacks which followed its establishment in 1891. It could not be denied, however, that there were some grounds for suspicion that technical skill was being developed at the expense of tactical efficiency, and this conclusion received the official imprimatur in a circular letter on the conduct of practice which was issued shortly after the Conference. In this it was definitely laid down that it was inadvisable to attach excessive importance to the development of accurate fire on difficult targets at long ranges: the primary efforts should be directed towards making the artillery highly efficient in the support of the infantry during the decisive phases of an action.

At the same time it was decided that the French system should be thoroughly investigated. Lt.-Colonel the Hon. F. R. Bingham[1], Chief Instructor designate of the School of Gunnery for Horse and Field Artillery, was selected for this duty, and by the courtesy of the French authorities he was permitted to attend the senior officers practical course at the Camp de Mailly in the spring of 1911. He found that the *Réglement* of 1910 had materially modified French methods in their gunnery, as in their tactics. No longer did they pin their faith on the *tir progressif*, which had so captured the imagination of indiscriminate admirers in England, nor did they confine themselves to short ranges and positions in the open. It might almost be said that the two artilleries were moving towards the same goal, although from opposite sides. While in England there was a reaction against the excessive use of covered positions, and against the concentration of effort at practice on tricky targets at extreme ranges, in France it

---

[1] Major-General the Hon. Sir Francis Bingham, K.C.B., K.C.M.G., Colonel-Commandant, d. 1935.

CHAPTER VIII.

The "Camp de Mailly".

was being realized that such difficult tasks might sometimes have to be undertaken in war, and that they should therefore be studied in peace.

In the Camp de Mailly[1] the French possessed, in close proximity to the great military centre at Chalons-sur-Marne, a practice ground far superior to any of ours, in extent, in tactical features, and in goodness of "going"; and they made the most of these advantages. But dominated as they were—at practice as in all other parts of their training—by the overwhelming importance of preparation for war, there could be no place for the element of competition, or for range-parties. The instructor was thus free at any time to repeat a series for the enforcement of some gunnery lesson, or to direct a change of target in order to illustrate a change in the tactical situation, without having to think how such alterations in the programme might affect the classification of batteries, or endanger the safety of a range-party. This freedom had immense advantages from a teaching point of view, but the fact that the efficiency of the fire was only judged from the firing point considerably discounted the value of the criticism.

For generations the Royal Artillery had accepted wholeheartedly Prince Kraft's famous maxim "To Hit" : they believed that in war they would be judged exclusively by the effect of their fire : they had seen the results of occupying positions in the open under modern fire, and had learnt by experience the advantages of concealment. In consequence their practice camp system aimed at teaching accuracy of fire from covered positions. To check the laying, and the observation of fire, range-parties were necessary, and consideration for the safety of such parties undoubtedly restricted tactical training. Hitherto this had been accepted as unavoidable, and there had grown up a tendency to consider skill in the solution of complicated

---

[1] Curiously enough it was in the same year (1901) in which our School of Gunnery had the chance of moving to Salisbury Plain, and failed to seize it, that the corresponding establishment in France made their move from Poitiers to Mailly.

THE FRENCH INFLUENCE. 189

gunnery problems as the matter of chief importance, which had shown its effect in a comparative neglect of tactical requirements at manœuvres. In methods of teaching the application of gunnery to tactical situations there was undoubtedly much to learn from the French.

Meanwhile a committee was appointed to carry out on Salisbury Plain a series of trials to ascertain definitely whether the fire power of our horse and field artillery could be increased by any improvements in our methods of fire, and especially of ranging, and if so whether this could be done without any drastic change in the existing equipment and organization of batteries, or whether changes in these were essential to the improvement of our methods.

The president was Lt.-General Parsons, and the list of members, and of officers officially "attending", included the names of all those most familiar as leaders of military thought at the time. Six batteries were placed at their disposal, but unfortunately, owing to various causes, these batteries had little time in which to make themselves conversant with the methods of fire they were to test, and the weather conditions were bad throughout. Consequently the committee found it a matter of considerable difficulty to discriminate between defects inherent in the methods and shortcomings due to their imperfect application. The results were, therefore, not as conclusive as had been hoped, but, even so, the trials shed much light on a very difficult question, and the report of the committee was of great value in the subsequent deliberations. In particular they brought out very clearly the intimate connection which must always exist—and especially in the artillery—between technical and tactical considerations, for they showed how the difference in the weight and design of the shell fired by the "75" and the 18-pr. affected both the battery organization and the gunnery methods of the two artilleries.

The discussion at the staff conference, Colonel Bingham's visit to France, and the experimental practice on Salisbury Plain, were but the most prominent features in a year of debate, which bid fair to reduce to insignifi-

CHAPTER VIII.

The "Camp de Mailly"

The Trials on Salisbury Plain.

The Controversies of 1911.

CHAPTER VIII.
The Controversies of 1911.

cance those controversies which had marked the first stirrings of the spirit of progress in the 90's. General Percin's report—*L'Artillerie aux Manœuvres de Picardie en 1910*—was translated, and issued to all artillery messes; there were articles in the *Army Review*—just started under the aegis of the Army Council—as well as in the *Proceedings*. Foreign artillery regulations were freely quoted —only to be controverted by reports of what the batteries actually did at foreign manœuvres—and examples from Manchuria were cited to prove the truth of every contention. There were, of course, extremists on both sides. On the one hand a "radical school of gunners progressive if somewhat over-gallicized" to whom *rafale* and *tir progressif*[1] were words to conjure with. On the other side the reactionaries, who were convinced that all was for the best in the best of all possible artilleries, and scorned the idea of the Royal Artillery being beholden to any foreigner for instruction. But between these extremes there was a great mass of moderate opinion in the Regiment which, without joining in the rage for French fashions, had an uneasy feeling that the problem of co-operation had not yet been seriously tackled, that our batteries were slow in getting to fire effect, and that the ever increasing complexity of our methods was tending to surpass the capacity of the average battery commander.

Space does not permit of giving here anything like a complete account of the controversies, but in the following précis an attempt has been made to indicate the chief arguments used by the rival parties. They shed as clear a light on the state of artillery training at the time as any account could do, and show the genesis of the remarkable changes which were made in the last years before the War.

Taking the equipment first—since that was the dominating factor—it had to be admitted that the French gun was superior to the British in stability, ease of service, and

---

[1] Eight rounds per gun, each pair with a hundred metres more elevation, the whole fired as rapidly as possible without further orders.

constancy of laying from round to round, and that in consequence it was capable of firing five laid rounds to our three. But the price paid for these advantages had also to be taken into account. The smoothness of the recoil, and the fixing of the carriage to the ground, which rendered relaying unnecessary, involved the use of compressed air in place of springs in the recuperator, and this was held to be unsuitable for the world-wide requirements of the British Empire, owing to the difficulty of keeping the valves in order in tropical countries.[1] The system of *abatage*, or anchoring, which meant that the trail once anchored could not be moved without repeating the operation of *abatage*, was also a serious drawback, especially for horse artillery. The differences in the weight and design of the shell had also to be taken into account. The cry after every war had been for power, and during the war in South Africa there had been no doubt whatever as to the general desire of the army for the heaviest possible shell. In his covering letter to the report of the artillery committee assembled at Pretoria immediately after the occupation General Marshall had advocated a considerable increase in the shell power of the field artillery: from India had come a demand for 30-prs. for field batteries; at home there had been a serious proposal to abolish field artillery altogether and keep nothing but horse and heavy batteries. It was not only in its weight that the English shell differed from the French, and here again the difference was directly due to war experience. The French shell was designed to give a deep longitudinal bullet zone, as had been those of the 15-prs. used in South Africa, but as the result of that war the policy had been reversed, and in those of the 18-prs. a wide dispersion of the bullets had been aimed at.[2] It could justly be claimed

---

[1] There was justification for this in our experience with the hydro-pneumatic mountings of some of our coast defence guns.

[2] "Among the disadvantages of the (British) shrapnel was the very small effective spread of the bullets on bursting—such a projectile was quite ineffective against the deep rifle-pits of the Boers". *Captain Balck, German attaché.*

192 THE FIELD ARMY ARTILLERY.

CHAPTER VIII.

The Controversies of 1911.

for the British equipment that it was the direct result of war experience.

Where the French equipment was undoubtedly superior was in its sighting and fuze-setting arrangements. A panoramic sight was, indeed, about to be introduced for the 13 and 18-prs. which would compare very favourably with the *collimateur* of the 75's; but every attempt to design an automatic fuze-setter to match their *débouchoir* had failed. Year after year every battery commander included in his practice report a passionate demand for such an instrument, so that the corrector once found the rapidity of fire should not be checked by the setting of each fuze by hand. But its design for the English type of fuze presented peculiar difficulties which were never overcome.

As regards battery organization the French had shown their faith in the 4-gun unit by making no increase in the number of batteries when they reduced the number of guns in each. Even when, in 1905, the Germans converted their 1896 equipment into a quick-firing one, they preferred to accept an inferiority of 120 to 144 guns in an army corps rather than return to the 6-gun organization.

The committee which conducted the Salisbury Plain trials, while impressed with the difficulty of controlling the fire of six quick-firers, considered that the trials had not demonstrated sufficient superiority in the 4-gun unit to justify them in recommending such a drastic change. There were many, however, even among the moderate party, who held the view that it was beyond the power of the average officer to do full justice to a battery of six quick-firers, even if they did not go so far as those who maintained that the retention of the 6-gun battery showed a complete misconception of the potentialities of quick-firing guns. None, however, were prepared to face the sacrifice in number of guns which the French had made.

To turn now to methods of fire. The advocates of French methods pointed out that they aimed at rapidity in opening effective fire at short and medium ranges, and expected to paralyze the offensive power of an opponent by subjecting the area in which he was situated to a hail of shrapnel bullets, which, if it did not destroy him, would pin him to the ground. For this they depended upon the rapidity of their ranging, the violence of their *rafales*, and the far-reaching bullet zone of their shrapnel. They preferred positions at medium ranges[1] in which the battery commander could both observe his fire and command his battery by his voice, and spent no time on training rangetakers and signallers. To this it was replied that the uselessness of such plastering of the ground had been amply demonstrated both in South Africa and Manchuria, in both of which it had also been shown that guns were likely to be called upon to fire at longer ranges than ever. Even if these experiences were to be ruled out as "exceptional", and the main artillery positions were within medium range, concentration of fire and enfilade would still demand much longer ranges from some batteries. As regards positions, those advocated by the French would not give complete concealment, and exposure would mean annihilation. True concealment, it was admitted, would frequently entail the separation of the observing station from the guns to such an extent that signal or telephonic communications would be required, and the use of range-finders, directors, etc., would be necessary. And since any battery might be called upon for fire under the drawbacks of long range and distant observing station, a large proportion of the training should rightly be devoted to these difficult conditions: a battery which could shoot well under such disadvantages could be trusted to deal suitably with simple conditions. The French system might be suitable for searching an area at medium ranges, but was not likely to be effective against a target necessitating accurate fire at long range; it might be suitable for a light shell with a deep bullet zone, but not for a comparatively heavy shell with a wide angle of opening;

Chapter VIII.

The Controversies of 1911.

---

[1] Of the 28 examples of artillery action with hostile troops given in the *Réglement* only 5 dealt with ranges of 3,000 yards or more, while out of the 16 examples in *Field Artillery Training* 10 dealt with ranges of 4,000 and over.

it might be right for a four-gun battery but in a six-gun unit would involve a prohibitive expenditure of ammunition. Gunnery, armament, and organization were interdependent.

The controversy raged all through 1911, and there were experiments with French methods at some of the practice camps in addition to the official trials on Salisbury Plain. An ample store of facts and theories had been accumulated, the Regiment was impatient for official guidance. It had not long to wait. With the opening of the new year there appeared a new edition of *Field Artillery Training*, followed in due course by the annual *Instructions for Practice*, and it was at once evident that the pendulum had swung right across the Channel. Defects in equipment could not be remedied by a stroke of the pen, and the reduction of batteries from six guns to four had been found to involve an increase of cost, or a reduction in strength, neither of which could be faced. But changes in gunnery and tactics cost nothing, and those now made were radical in their character, and far-reaching in their effect. Although modified in some important particulars during the intervening period, they formed the basis of the doctrine with which the field army artillery took the field two years later, and therefore demand more than passing notice here.

Quite irrespective of the French influence, the new manual included various subjects of great importance on active service—or "War" as it was now boldly called—which had dropped out altogether, or been only dealt with in relation to such peace requirements as changes of station. Among these may be mentioned the chapter on Movements and Quarterings, which included such practical matters as march discipline, billets and bivouacs, transport by rail, embarkations and disembarkations. More important still was the space devoted to the change of organization which had brought into being the divisional artillery. Instead of vague generalities regarding the responsibilities of "superior artillery officers" there were now precise instructions as to the duties of the divisional artillery commander, both in the training of his command in peace and its command in war. As a subordinate commander he would give orders for the deployment and occupation of positions by his batteries, allot and rearrange tasks and zones, and direct changes of position to meet the development of the battle. It was for him to arrange for the scientific combination of the three natures of artillery comprised in his command, and to utilize each to the best advantage of its special attribute.

CHAPTER VIII.
The Regulations of 1912.

In gunnery the question at issue had been whether British batteries could attain the rapidity of fire of the French by changes of gunnery methods, without change of equipment and battery organization, and without sacrifice of accuracy. In the attempt to do so the new manual gave great latitude to battery commanders. Ranging might be either "collective",[1] "single-gun", "section" or "all-guns", and "time" or "percussion" shrapnel might be used at discretion; but "collective" (a direct imitation of the French) was to be the "normal" method, and it was definitely stated that as a rule no special ranging for fuze should be necessary. At the same time the examples of ranging, to which exception had been taken as tending to make battery commanders trust to the book rather than to their judgment, were reduced from twenty-two to six.

The space devoted to the application of fire was on the other hand greatly extended. There were to be found the appropriate procedure for firing on a village, or a machine-gun, a general's staff or a battery observing station, as well as for the attack of balloons, airships, and aeroplanes. The method of "mastering" the fire of the enemy's

---

[1] Collective ranging was by the alternate fire of half-batteries, and this was objected to by many as a transgression of the section organization, on which great store was set. But it was the only way of applying the method devised for the French 4-gun batteries to our 6-gun. Its adoption led to a revival of the proposals for the extension of the use of half-batteries to manœuvre as well as fire when circumstances rendered the 6-gun unit inconveniently large.

THE FIELD ARMY ARTILLERY.

Chapter VIII.

The Regulations of 1912.

artillery, and of "neutralizing"[1] any further attempts to intervene, were laid down. The object of artillery fire on the enemy's infantry was defined as being either to facilitate the advance of friend, or to prevent that of foe; and it was stated that this object was not likely to be fulfilled unless the fire was sufficiently accurate to cause loss, but that this accuracy should only be looked upon as a means to the end. From this there followed the "registration of zones" which became the great feature of the next year's practice.

The vexed question of choice of position was similarly placed on a more common-sense basis by the division of all positions into the three categories of "open", "semi-covered", and "covered", followed by a general survey of the technical and tactical advantages and disadvantages of each. Attention was drawn to the element of surprise, the retention of mobility, and the immunity from loss, conferred by concealment; with, as a set off against the advantages, the limited power of dealing effectively from covered positions with rapid movement, and unexpected developments.

The most novel feature was the formal recognition of the "semi-covered" position, although there was nothing new about it except its name. It had the attraction of getting over some of the difficulties of covered positions without sacrificing all the advantages of concealment; but the chief reason for the prominence now given to it was that it enabled the battery commander to exercise command by voice—a condition on which the French set great store.

A long new section was also devoted to the methods of occupying positions. The "deliberate" was renamed the "special",[2] and its use further restricted: rules were laid

---

[1] *Field Artillery Training 1912* recognized that it might be advisable to order batteries when exposed to accurate and destructive fire to cease fire temporarily.

[2] During the early years of the century the two methods had borne the titles of "Direct" and "Deliberate": In 1909 the "Direct" became the "Ordinary": now the "Deliberate" became the "Special".

THE FRENCH INFLUENCE. 197

down for the first time regarding the movements of the battery headquarters, so as to avoid more of his staff crowding on the battery commander than he required at each stage of his reconnaissance.

The chief interest however was reserved for the sections dealing with the employment of artillery in the field. Here the changes were more far-reaching still, the most important of them being :—

The reappearance of the artillery reserve.
The disappearance of the artillery duel.
The appearance of "temporary groupings".

In the manuals based upon Manchurian experience it was recognized that in the early stage of an attack fire should not be opened with more guns than were required to accomplish the task in hand, but the implications of this departure from hitherto accepted principle were not fully worked out. In the manual of 1912, however, under the guise of "Economy of Force", this new principle was fully considered, and it was shown how it was particularly suitable to the employment of artillery, owing to the mobility of that arm until subjected to loss, its power of delivering effective fire while remaining concealed, and of regulating the intensity of its fire in accordance with the tactical importance of the objective. The methods by which these objects were to be obtained were by bringing batteries into action in concealed positions where they could remain "in observation" until required; by keeping batteries limbered up in "positions of readiness" whence they could be moved as required; or by keeping batteries actually "in reserve" if their withdrawal from observation or readiness would cause delay. Thus, under French influence, there came a return to Napoleonic practice. When the great Emperor said that it was with the artillery of his Guard that he won the greater part of his victories, he was alluding to the way in which he kept it in reserve until he had selected the point for his decisive attack, when it galloped in to close range and "opened for the infantry an actual breach in the opposing ranks". The

198 THE FIELD ARMY ARTILLERY.

CHAPTER VIII.
The Regulations of 1912.

idea of this reserve artillery had lingered on after the true spirit of its use had been lost, until the war of 1866 against Austria showed the Germans that the increase of range obtained with rifled guns allowed of concentration of fire from guns already in action, while their slow rate of fire rendered it necessary that as many guns as possible should be brought into action from the earliest moment. The campaign of 1870 was the first example of the new method in its perfection. All the world wondered—and then imitated—and for a generation there appeared in our manuals that well-known sentence :—

"The first principle of the employment of artillery is that from the earliest possible moment a number of guns superior to that of the enemy should be brought into action".

What then was the reason for going back to Napoleon and his reserve artillery when the very name "reserve" in connection with his arm was anathema to every orthodox gunner? The answer is not hard to find. Technical progress was once again responsible for the modification of tactical methods—but the principles were unchanged.

As with the artillery reserve, so with the artillery duel, the manual of 1912 carried to a logical conclusion, under French influence, the changes foreshadowed in those inspired by Manchurian experience. The primary object being to assist the infantry to close with the enemy, the artillery fire must be distributed according to requirements on all objectives from which effective fire was being brought to bear on the attacking infantry: the fight with the opposing artillery must be definitely confined to subduing the fire of those batteries which were impeding the advance of the infantry—an artillery engagement must no longer be entered into for its own sake.

It is when we come to consider the third of the three great changes in methods of employment introduced by the manual of 1912, that we are met by a new departure rather than the development of an established practice. This new feature was the formation of "temporary groups"

THE FRENCH INFLUENCE. 199

of artillery and infantry whenever the country necessitated the employment of a division on more than one tactical operation, either in attack or defence, and the appointment of a commander to each group. To this officer the commander of the artillery allotted to the group had to report, so there was left no room for doubt as to the responsibility of the artillery commander; and it was further enjoined that if he were unable himself to accompany the infantry commander it would be advisable to detail an officer with signallers to do so. Here at last was something definite as to the means of securing co-operation.

These "temporary groupings" were, after all, but a logical result of the demand for some practical application of the principle of co-operation. The key-note had been struck by the 1912 edition of the *Field Service Regulations* which laid it down quite definitely that the object of artillery fire was to help the infantry, and that artillery commanders must, therefore, keep touch with the infantry commanders so that the fire of their batteries might be directed against the targets which, for the time being, were the most important from the infantry point of view. The question at once arose—would it be possible for the artillery from their original positions to keep this close touch with the infantry?

The genesis of the "Forward Observing Officer" has been described in the last chapter: the manual of 1912 took the matter a stage further by recognizing the frequent necessity for the establishment of "an advanced observation line" by a divisional artillery commander. But the relations between such observation line and the officer sent by the artillery commander of a temporary group to keep up communication with the infantry were not clear, and the objections with which the idea had been met when first mooted were by no means silenced. Generals were still nervous as to forward observers interfering in the tactical distribution of the fire by short-circuiting infantry brigadiers: artillery officers were alarmed at the prospect of further inroads upon the *personnel* of batteries. The position to be taken up by

CHAPTER VIII.
The Regulations of 1912.

such observers was hotly debated, and the general trend of opinion was that an officer right up with the firing line would not only find his communications a matter of great difficulty, but that his outlook would be far too limited for his information to be of much value even if he could get it back. It seemed therefore that the guns would have to be moved forward if they were to keep their touch with the infantry. But one of the so-called "Lessons from Manchuria" which was strenuously maintained before the accounts of that war had been fully digested, was that any movement of artillery by daylight was impossible. With fuller knowledge the vast difference between the moving of artillery already in action in the open, and the bringing forward to a new position of artillery hitherto in covered positions, or held in reserve, was realized. The manual of 1912 accordingly made it clear that for such a movement to be carried out with success, there must be a line of advance either covered from fire, or over which the guns could move deployed and at speed, as well as the possibility of reasonable protection from fire during deployment and up to the moment of opening fire. Where such conditions did not obtain for complete batteries guns must be dribbled forward as might be found practicable. It was only in cases of extreme difficulty that it should be necessary to wait for night.

There still remained, however, the question of the further advance of at least a portion of the artillery in order to give still closer support to the infantry at the crisis of the fight. Here, again, as told in the last chapter, grave doubts had been expressed as to the possibility of such action, and the advisability even of attempting it under modern conditions. The *Field Service Regulations* of 1909 had maintained the old maxim that the principle of the employment of the artillery in the battle was that the greater the difficulties of the infantry "*the closer should be the support of the artillery*", but in the Regulations of 1912 there were substituted the less inspiring words "*the more fully should the fire power of the artillery be developed*".

THE FRENCH INFLUENCE. 201

At the same time the artillery manual had to admit that artillery "as at present equipped" must reach the crest to develop the full effect of its fire against rapid movement from under cover, such as an unexpected counter-attack or the threat of assault, and *Field Service Regulations* made it clear that in such cases there must be no hesitation in occupying direct fire positions. The artillery must be guided by the principle that "to enable the infantry to effect its purpose, the artillery must willingly sacrifice itself". Here again, however, the artillery manual added the crippling caution "To be destroyed without attaining its object, however, does not further the cause".

Another difficult question connected with the close support of an infantry attack was how long to continue the fire over the heads of the assaulting troops. The *Field Service Regulations of 1912* still retained the clause inserted in 1909 and quoted in the last chapter, that the danger from shell bursting short was more than compensated for by the support afforded, and this seemed to have settled the question. But here again the artillery manual of 1912 introduced a note of warning—"The losses that may be inflicted by wild artillery fire at this period may imperil the success of the whole operation. Unless the infantry has complete confidence in the artillery the effect of the covering fire of the latter may be to delay and hamper rather than to facilitate the delivery of the assault". This made the position of an artillery commander very difficult, for the point at issue was whether he should continue his fire until there might be some risk of hitting his own infantry, or should deny them the support of his fire. *Field Service Regulations* said one thing, *Field Artillery Training* said another—it was very unfair on the artillery commanders on whom the responsibility of the decision must rest.

To sum up. The French influence reflected in the Regulations of 1912 had but given a final impetus to the gradual change in the conception of the part which artillery should play in battle, which had been gradually

CHAPTER VIII.
The Regulations of 1912.

202   THE FIELD ARMY ARTILLERY.

CHAPTER VIII.
The Regulations of 1912.

taking shape during the last decade. This change had been dictated by the successive changes in conditions. The range and rapidity of fire of the guns had been greatly increased, smokeless powder allowed them to remain concealed in action, and appliances for indirect laying enabled them to develop effective fire from covered positions against all but rapidly moving targets. The early deployment, the simultaneous advance, the simultaneous opening of fire, the massed batteries, and the artillery duel as a separate act had dropped out, and in their place had come a much closer association with the infantry from the very start of the action. The infantry must compel the enemy to disclose his position by their advance, while the artillery must be prepared to support the infantry with its fire at every stage. And more guns must not be employed than were necessary for the immediate purpose. If a greater volume of fire were required it must be obtained by increasing the rate of fire of those in action rather than by increasing their number. "Economy of Force" had been added to the principles of employment, fire power was kept in hand.

The French influence did not directly affect the howitzers or the heavy artillery, for, in spite of the lessons of Manchuria, the French had refused to have anything to do with them. They held that in the field army there must be but one nature of artillery. Their doctrine[1] was that the artillery must move side by side with the infantry, that its task was not to destroy the obstacles to the advance but to paralyze their defenders. As a concession to those who urged the value of high-angle fire, they had, however, introduced a device known as the "Malindrin Disc"[2] which could be attached to the head of the gun shell in order to increase the curvature of the trajectory. Such was the infatuation for everything French that there were even proposals that these should be adopted for our field guns.

[1] *L'Artillerie de Campagne en Liaison avec les Autres Armes.*—le Colonel H. Langlois.
[2] The question was further complicated by political issues, any discussion of which would be out of place here.

THE FRENCH INFLUENCE. 203

CHAPTER VIII.

The Regulations of 1912.

The interest aroused by the issue of the Regulations of 1912 was quite unprecedented. The daily papers, as well as the military periodicals, opened their columns to careful analyses of the new manuals of the different arms as well as of the *Field Service Regulations*: foreign text-books, and the works of foreign military writers, such as Generals Langlois, Percin, and von Rohne, were translated and studied; the proceedings at foreign practice camps were described; and the subject selected for the annual prize essay of the Institution was a comparison of British, French, and German methods in the employment of artillery in the field, with deductions as to the system best suited to our army in a European War.[1]

The Practice of 1912.

This interest was focussed on the artillery practice camps, for the *Instructions for Practice* had been entirely rewritten, and they introduced two changes of far-reaching effect in the conduct of the practice—the abolition of "classification", and the institution of "tactical practice".

With classification there disappeared the last vestige of the "competitive" which had done so much to arouse the interest of all ranks in the early days of the great gunnery revival of the last century. Its work was done, and its disappearance caused no regrets, particularly when it was found that, contrary to the prognostications of some, it resulted in no falling off in zeal on the part of either officers or men. With its disappearance the commandants were freed from the necessity of considering the effect on classification when arranging schemes for practice, and could devote them entirely to the training of batteries. Henceforth practice ceased to be a test or examination—the light in which it had hitherto always been regarded by all ranks.

---

[1] Special mention may be made of *The study of Tactics from History*, by Brig.-Gen. J. P. DuCane, C.R.A. 3rd Division, which appeared in the Army Review. In these papers some of the well-known incidents of the Franco-German War were examined as regards the action of the troops if armed and organized as in 1912. They provide an admirable illustration of the "doctrine" with which the British Army took the field in 1914.

THE FIELD ARMY ARTILLERY.

CHAPTER VIII.
The Practice of 1912.

It was, however, in the "tactical practice" that the chief interest was aroused, for this not only stirred the feelings of artillery officers, but drew into the picture officers of all ranks in the other arms. What had been done was to divide the practice into two categories—gunnery and tactical—in tardy realization of the impossibility of imparting instruction in both gunnery and tactics at the same time without an inordinate amount of make-believe. Under the new regulations :—

In the gunnery practice the tactical scheme was subordinated to the necessity of providing for an accurate record by a range-party, so as to allow of subsequent analytical criticism of the observations and orders of the battery commander, and of the laying and fuze-setting of the gunners.

In the tactical practice, both battery and brigade, the object was instruction in applying the principles for the employment of artillery fire so as to meet the requirements of the other arms on the battlefield. The scheme was to be drawn up by the general officer commanding the division, and officers of the other arms were to command the imaginary "temporary groupings" of which the artillery was supposed to form part. Recording by range-parties was subordinated to freedom of choice of positions for the guns.

Regimental interest in the first practice under the new Regulations was shown by a reversion to a custom which had prevailed from 1889 to 1895. During that period, when the new gunnery was just coming into being, and everything was tentative, there had been a great gathering at the Institution every autumn to hear, and discuss, a lecture on the "Okehampton Experiences"[1] of the year by a representative of the School of Gunnery. With the establishment of a definite system, and insistence on rigid adherence to it, such meetings lost their *raison d'être* and were discontinued. Now that theories of gunnery and

[1] Okehampton was the headquarters of the School of Gunnery in the summer and much the most important practice camp.

THE FRENCH INFLUENCE.

methods of practice were again in the melting pot, the custom was revived, and once more the theatre of the Institution was crowded with officers eager to hear the views of the School of Gunnery on the year's experience, and to express their own views—freely and at length.[1]

It is not to be supposed that such radical changes as those which had distinguished the Regulations of 1912 were accepted in all quarters without cavil. As has been shown in previous chapters the successive issues of the manual which had followed the South African War—1902, 1904, 1906, 1908—had indicated no lack of readiness to move with the times. Methods had been modified in accordance with technical progress and war experience, but the movement had been gradual. Under the new influence brought into being by the *entente* there had been a definite break with our traditional procedure in the principles of employment, the methods of fire, and the system of practice. English artillerymen relished as little as had their French comrades the prospect of finding themselves placed under an infantry commander, as the system of temporary groupings promised; but the most strenuous opposition was reserved for the tactical practice, since many experienced officers were gravely concerned as to its effect on gunnery training. The discussions that ensued on these, and the other changes, and the modifications that in some cases resulted, will be fully considered in the next chapter: here it need only be said that the essential features of the Regulations of 1912 remained unaltered.

CHAPTER VIII.

The Practice of 1912.

The Doctrine.

---

[1] The first series was inaugurated by Colonel Walford in 1888, and completed by Captain Headlam in 1894. The second series was commenced by Lieut.-General the Hon. F. R. Bingham in 1912, and continued in 1913.

CHAPTER IX.

THE FINAL PHASE.

(1913—1914.)

The Regulations of 1914—Principles of Employment—Positions—Communications—Ammunition Supply—Aviation—Night operations—Gunnery—The Practice Camps—The School of Gunnery—Progressive Training—Field Firing—Manœuvres—Four-gun Batteries—Field Howitzers—Heavy Artillery—Mechanization—Re-armament—Personal Equipment—Mobilization—Final Distribution—Conclusion.

CHAPTER IX.
The Regulations of 1914.

THERE can be little doubt that those responsible for the Regulations of 1912 had allowed their admiration for the French Artillery to carry them too far in some directions. But the manual had been labelled "Provisional", so correction of those features to which justifiable objection was taken presented no difficulty : it is even possible that these had served a useful purpose in shaking the complacency of those who had scorned the idea of the Royal Artillery being beholden to any foreigner. The next year (1913) saw the issue of amendments to *Field Service Regulations* and to *Field Artillery Training* which, while preserving the essential features of those of 1912, cleared up some of the ambiguities, and modified some of the extravagancies. In 1914 *Field Artillery Training* came out in a final edition.

The changes in the Regulations made during the last eighteen months before the Great War are of peculiar value as illustrations of the trend of opinion during the final phase of preparation, and these changes will, therefore, be examined here in some detail. In considering them it must, however, always be borne in mind that at the time there was no war experience to guide opinion as to the effect of the adoption of quick-firing guns. The military literature of all countries was flooded with theories on the

THE FINAL PHASE. 207

subject, and a host of observers watched the manœuvres of the great powers for indications of new developments—tactical and technical. But it was all groping in the dark, a condition hard to realize by a generation brought up in the quick-firing tradition.

There were, it is true, wars in the Balkans in 1912—13, but little attention was paid to their lessons, although some French artillery officers noted that an infantry attack had little hope of success as long as the field artillery of the defence remained intact, and that to break down the fire of entrenched and shielded field guns the long range and powerful shell of heavy artillery were required.[1]

Taking first in our review the employment of artillery in war, suggestive additions were to be noted in the shape of new sections devoted respectively to "Wood and Village Fighting" and to "Co-operation of Aircraft". Otherwise there was little alteration in the principles so fully explained in the last chapter, except as regards the artillery support during the final stages of an infantry attack. The attitude of the regulations of 1912 in respect to this had been generally hesitating, and in some respects contradictory: the matter was now put on a much more satisfactory footing.

For keeping touch with the infantry official recognition had been given to some form of forward observation, but in studiously vague terms, and the general impression given was that the authorities were dubious as to its utility, and a little nervous as to its possible interference with the orthodox chain of command. But the idea caught on, and in some divisions, parties were told off in every brigade, and given light telephone equipment for the purpose. With the experience thus gained the manual of 1914 was able to put the matter on a business-like footing. "Advanced observation posts" took the place of the meaningless "observation line" of 1912, and their

---

[1] *Revue d'Artillerie*—le Général F. G. Herr.

208   THE FIELD ARMY ARTILLERY.

CHAPTER IX.

Principles of employment.

establishment by divisional artillery commanders, or by officers commanding the artillery of temporary groupings, was authorized. The "forward observing officer" had won a place in the artillery hierarchy.

But this was not enough. The conclusion arrived at during the first year's tactical practice was that if artillery support was to be effective the distances over which communication had to be maintained must be as short as possible, and the details of the enemy's entrenchments and of the ground in front of them must be clearly visible. The necessity for pushing some guns to the front—whatever the risk—so as to render this *close* support was accepted, and the clause "to be destroyed without effecting its object does not further the cause" disappeared from the new manual. Even without this deterrent the choice of the psychological moment for such a movement demanded tactical skill as well as resolution, and no guidance was given as to who was responsible for ordering it. And when, once again, batteries were seen galloping into action, there was an outcry from those who saw in it only the creeping in of the spectacular element.

The position of artillery commanders had been still more difficult regarding fire over the heads of the infantry, for here there had been a definite conflict of authority between *Field Service Regulations* and *Field Artillery Training*. This was now set at rest by the omission from the latter of the note of warning quoted in the last chapter, and the insertion in its place of a new paragraph definitely stating that the "danger from a few shell falling short must not be allowed to prevent the artillery from continuing their fire till the last possible moment". Here at last was the clear guidance for which the artillery had been calling.

Positions.

The controversy which had raged so fiercely round the question of "covered" positions was dying a natural death during these last years. While technical progress[1]

---

[1] Especially the "panoramic" sight—No. 7 Dial Sight—which was by this time in general use.

had solved many of the difficulties in the delivery of effective fire from covered positions, the tactical practice had shown that on the battlefield, whether in attack or defence, the guns would have to be contented with the best positions available, their nature depending upon the ground and the tactical situation. Batteries must therefore be trained to make the best use of whatever positions they might have to take up. But unless the tactical situation demanded a position in the open, even a small amount of cover was preferable, since there might be great difficulties in moving from an open position should a change in the tactical situation render a change of position necessary. And so the "half-covered" position was hailed as a heaven-sent solution, although there was nothing new about it except its name. It was true that it did not permit of complete concealment of the flashes, but practice seemed to show how difficult it was to locate guns accurately from their flashes. It was thought, therefore, that there was good hope of the teams being got away without danger, and there was no denying the immense simplification, and consequent rapid development of effective fire, especially against moving targets and fleeting opportunities, which resulted from the battery commander being sufficiently close to the guns to command by voice, and from the section commanders being able to see the ground to be fired on. In order to keep battery commanders as close to their batteries as possible, even in fully covered positions, the use of trees, haystacks, houses, etc., as observing stations was taken up, and No. 3 director introduced so as to permit of laying out lines of fire by compass bearing. But trees and haystacks were rarely forthcoming just where required, so the idea of an "observation ladder" was revived. Batteries were given a free hand, and a large number of "contraptions" of varying degrees of stability dotted the ground at practice camps and manœuvres,[1] and were used, like all new

CHAPTER. IX.

Positions.

---

[1] The Okehampton Scrap-Book of the 90's has some amusing skits on the efforts of those days in the same direction.

CHAPTER IX.
Positions.

toys, irrespective of whether in reality they would have proved nothing but death-traps. The question of an "observation wagon", which would carry signalling and telephone equipment, directors, and the new one-man range-finder, as well as the observation ladder, was taken up; designs were got out; money for provision was taken in the estimates for 1914/15; and instructions for use were included in the 1914 manual. But, alas, the experimental vehicles proved far too elaborate and expensive, and it was decided to investigate again the possibility of attaching a ladder to an ammunition wagon. Meanwhile it was ordered that a wagon limber should be brought up on the flank for use as an observatory, and also as a protection to the battery headquarters. The procedure was never popular, however: it was perhaps forgotten that the time duration of a practice camp series bore little resemblance to the time that a battery would be in action in battle; and that protection would not then be so lightly foregone.

Whatever the nature of the position selected it was obvious that it should be occupied as quickly as possible, and with the least advertisement; and during the last two years a great deal of attention was devoted to simplifying and systematizing the procedure between the receipt by the battery commander of his orders, and the opening of fire by the guns. The power of bringing a battery into action at the place selected seemed to be in danger of becoming a lost art. Time had been when this was one of the attributes of all good artillery officers: however cramped the ground, they could be trusted to place the guns with the utmost precision on the required spot, without delay or confusion. Attempts to get over lack of skill in leadership by permitting "go as you please" methods only led to the multiplication of adventitious aids. Subalterns were to be seen with their belts as full of flags as the banderillero in a bullfight, pegging out the ground for their guns—to the confusion of the drivers.

THE FINAL PHASE. 211

The battery staff was the despair of all. The wild rush of horsemen, slung round with telescopes, directors, range-finders, and so forth, which streamed after the battery commander[1]—anathema to the staff, amazement to observers—was not only unserviceable : it was ridiculous. Battery commanders had been slow to recognize the distinction between the different stages of their reconnaissance, and to arrange that they should only be accompanied by the assistants actually required at each. It was not until the manual of 1914 directed that the staff should remain at the head of the battery until required, and should then be brought up under suitable command, that they were really got into order.

CHAPTER IX.

Positions

It was not only the occupation of positions which was causing anxiety during the last years : the closer touch with the other arms at practice had led to further examination of the way in which the artillery carried out changes of position, especially when these involved retirement. Here common sense and tradition were at variance, for it was obvious that the quicker the guns could get back to a new position, and reopen fire, the better help they would be to their comrades. The old rule that movements in retreat should commence at a walk, and that their subsequent pace should not be unduly hurried, was replaced by the direction that every care should be taken that retirements were carried out in an orderly manner. There was much confusion until the issue of *Field Artillery Training 1914* in which the whole section dealing with the subject was rewritten, and alternative methods in both advance and retirement, for use according to the circumstances, were laid down as a drill.

In spite of the attention paid to the study of ground after the South African War, successive manuals had been studiously vague as to how the reconnaissance of artillery positions was to be carried out. This was perhaps wise in view of the fact that no *personnel* for the purpose

---

[1] The Rabelaisian comparison, generally attributed to the mordant wit of Sir William Knox, will be familiar to many.

CHAPTER IX.
Positions.

were included in either peace or war establishments; but by 1912 an orderly officer and a patrol of three mounted men had been added to the staff of an artillery brigade, and it was possible to be more definite. The manual of that year accordingly laid down the manner in which these officers' patrols might be employed, either under the orders of the divisional artillery commander, or of their brigade commander. It remained for the last *Training Memorandum* before the War to make clear the distinction between the tactical reconnaissance of the target, with the object of selecting the best position from which to engage it, and the technical reconnaissance of the position so chosen, as regards its occupation by the guns.

Communications.

Another duty for which the necessity of providing *personnel* had at last been admitted, was the communication service. Here again it was not until 1914 that the procedure was regularized. The organization provided batteries with signallers for communication within the battery, and with brigade headquarters. Brigades had sufficient for communication with two of their batteries only, on the assumption that communication with the third battery could be carried out verbally or by message, and with the ammunition column by orderly. The worst equipped were divisional artillery headquarters, which were worse off than a brigade or a battery. It was of course true that the newly constituted divisional signal company was nominally available, but its main duty was to keep the divisional commander in communication with his infantry brigades, and it did not lend itself to easy linking up with the artillery. The necessity of making every signaller a despatch rider and a telephonist was recognized, and a special course in telephony for artillery was instituted. While brigade signallers had to be fully qualified, the training of battery signallers was limited to the use of semaphore, telephone, and buzzer. Many regarded this limitation as a regrettable return to the attitude towards signallers adopted by the artillery in

THE FINAL PHASE. 213

the last century, and considered that all artillery signallers should be as fully trained as those of the other arms. The importance attached to the subject of ammunition supply at the time of the formation of the Expeditionary Force, both as regards the organization of the service and the provision of the personnel, has been shown in Chapter VII. The new system was tested in March 1913 in an elaborate ammunition supply exercise at Aldershot, the result of which was seen in the appearance of a whole chapter on the subject in the manual of 1914. The procedure was elaborated; "Rendezvous" and "Refilling Points" made their appearance; and an artillery officer was allotted to each ammunition park to see that the lorries sent up to the various refilling points contained the nature of ammunition required.

After much discussion the actual distribution of the artillery ammunition carried in the field was settled as shown in the following table :—

	Horse (13-pr)	Field (18-pr)	Howitzer (4·5″)	Heavy (60-pr)
Gun Limbers	24	24	12	—
Battery Wagons	152	152	96	80
Brigade[1] Ammunition Columns ...	220	76	48	40
Divisional Ammunition Columns ...	—	126	44	60
Total carried by Fighting Troops ...	396	378	200	180
Divisional Ammunition Park ...	150	150	80	70
Ordnance Depots	454	472	520	250
TOTAL IN FIELD	1000	1000	800	500

The progress that was being made in military aviation was only brought home to soldiers by the manœuvres of 1912. The one or two aeroplanes which had been

CHAPTER IX.

Ammunition supply.

Aviation.

---

[1] Battery ammunition columns in the heavy artillery.

CHAPTER IX.

Aviation.

employed in the manœuvres of 1910 had been regarded by the troops and the spectators alike as interesting curiosities, but had played no practical part in the campaign either strategically or tactically. In 1912 on the contrary the air service exercised no small influence upon the operations. It was plain that the development of the new arm must be of vital interest to the artillery, for the possibility of observation from the air must affect both gunnery and tactics, while the designing of a weapon capable of engaging an aeroplane, and the working out of suitable methods of fire, presented problems in gunnery and gun design of unexampled complexity.

In co-operation with the Royal Flying Corps, there were a series of trials at practice camps in 1912 and 1913 which resulted in the inclusion in the manual of 1914 of entirely new sections containing definite instructions regarding the co-operation of aircraft with artillery. These provided for the location of targets and the observation of fire during a battle, and the steps to be taken to conceal guns in action from observation from the air. But no practical addition was made to the somewhat vague directions for engaging "captive balloons, kites, airships, and aeroplanes" which had appeared in the edition of 1912.

There had been trials of various experimental anti-aircraft equipments in 1911, but these failed to produce anything really suitable, although, as mentioned elsewhere, they served a very useful purpose in bringing to light several novel features in gun design which were applicable to ordinary field guns. Various objections were raised to motor mountings for guns with the field army, while legal disabilities to the use of trailers were discovered. After much discussion, it was decided in July, 1914, that the best solution would be a field carriage drawn by a motor. There had been no practice against targets approximating in the remotest degree to the height and speed of an aeroplane, and the tendency was to accept the difficulty of hitting such a target as insuperable,

THE FINAL PHASE. 215

and to make no attempt to tackle it.[1] No nation had commenced the equipment of its field army artillery with anti-aircraft artillery before the Great War.

The possibility of observation from the air enhanced the value of night operations, and the manual considerably amplified the section dealing with the artillery share in such work. The occupation and entrenching of positions by night became a familiar feature of military exercises and practice camps; and trials were carried out for the reduction of the noise made by the movement of the guns —clatter of hoofs, rattle of harness, rumble of wheels, and so forth. The chief value of artillery by night, however, probably remained, as it had been in Manchuria, in its power of repelling a night attack. For this star shell were developed, and even "tracers" were tried, but in the small shell of field guns the loss of bullet space was serious, and since there was no difficulty in locating the burst of shell, tracing their trajectory seemed a work of supererogation.

As told in the last chapter, many experienced officers were gravely concerned as to the effect on gunnery of the adoption of the French system of practice in 1912. They feared that this would sound the death-knell of the accurate shooting which had been the aim of the Royal Artillery since the revival of interest in gunnery in the 80's. They believed in the truth of Colonel Walford's weighty warning, then given, that the verdict of the Army on the Regiment would be based solely upon the effect of its fire. And it was not only artillerymen who took alarm. Some of the most distinguished generals of the other arms—notably Sir Horace Smith-Dorrien and

CHAPTER IX.

Night Operations.

Gunnery.

---

[1] Mention should, however, be made of an effort in this direction made by the Transvaal Horse Artillery. The target was a large kite, attached by a light string to the end of a wire rope, which latter was drawn along the ground by a limber and team. The limber and rope were concealed by a ridge, and the string was invisible at a distance, so that the kite sailing along had quite the appearance of an aeroplane—but its height was not more than 500 feet, and its pace only 15 miles an hour. As this volume goes to press other claims to the originating of anti-aircraft gunnery are being put forward in the columns of the *Gunner*.

CHAPTER IX.

Gunnery.

Sir Henry Rawlinson, who were in a position to see what was going on on Salisbury Plain[1]—realized that no amount of tactical training could compensate for loss of skill in shooting. "To Hit" still remained the paramount duty of the gunners.

Under the influence of these misgivings there ensued a remarkable renewal of interest in gunnery questions, especially in relation to their application to the tasks with which the artillery would be called upon to deal in battle.

In the first flush of enthusiasm for the new methods the regulations of 1912 had labelled "collective" ranging with time-shrapnel as being the "normal" method, and had relaxed the old rule as to the necessity of verifying the 100 yards bracket. Another year's practice showed that this was a mistake. The manual of 1914 made it clear that there must be no "normal" method: the method adopted must be that best calculated to obtain effective fire with the least possible delay in each case, and the safeguard of the 100 yards bracket must never be omitted.

With greater freedom in methods of ranging came renewed study of the methods of engaging the different objectives to be expected on the battlefield. Of these the most difficult targets were presented by guns of which only the flashes could be seen, and these were much in evidence at practice camps in 1912-13. From the experience gained it appeared that in many cases the most effective course would be the blinding of a battery by the destruction of its observing station, and the keeping of one gun at this task was advocated.

But the problem to which most importance was attached was that of dealing with infantry moving in small bodies over broken ground before reaching their fire position. The distribution of fire over the whole area described in Chapter VII was still the official method, and the targets designed to teach this method (known

---

[1] Then commanding respectively the Southern Command and the 3rd Division.

familiarly as the "jumpers") had bred a race of battery commanders with a skill in snap-shooting which was sometimes startling. But it was a purely artificial exercise adapted to practice camp conditions, and—as a result of a closer study of the effective zones of shrapnel—the method was changed in 1914 to the establishment of a belt of fire through which the enemy must pass.

There was much talk of "zones" and "tasks", and a good deal of confusion between them. A zone was a task, but a task was by no means always a zone, and a zone could be superimposed on a task. The methods of registering zones were systematically tried in 1912-13, and some modifications were introduced in consequence. But the most important point which emerged was the danger of prematurely disclosing the position of the guns, and the consequent necessity of circumspection. It seemed questionable whether registration should ever be undertaken prior to the opening of an action except by direction of the general officer in command.

The "double objective" was another feature of the practice of these last years. "Section control" had been introduced some years before as the result of reflection on the difference between any probable European battlefield and the bare stony wolds of our practice ranges. In the open this decentralization of direction was comparatively simple, but from covered positions it presented great difficulty, and the *Training Memorandum* of 1913 went into much detail as to the methods by which it could best be managed. Finally, the manual of 1914 inserted a warning against its use during the support of an infantry advance, when the control of the fire must be retained in the hands of battery commanders.

These developments in methods of ranging and in application of fire led naturally to investigations into the power of the guns to deliver accurate fire if properly handled. There was, first of all, the loss of muzzle-velocity owing to wear. The possibility of re-graduating range-dials so as to allow for this was considered, and also

218   THE FIELD ARMY ARTILLERY.

CHAPTER IX.
Gunnery.

the possibility of firing a calibrating[1] series from all the guns at each practice camp, and re-allotting them on the result so that each battery might have a level lot. But the idea was not received with any favour, and trials showed that individual guns ranged so closely together that no practical gain was to be expected—any difference was more likely to be due to want of adjustment in sights or range-dials. So attention was directed to the testing of these, and very elaborate new rules regarding the qualification of layers for proficiency pay came out in 1914.

The next step was from the guns to the fuzes.[2] With the new guns had come new fuzes fresh from the factories, and their regularity of burning had astounded officers who had been accustomed to struggling with the vagaries of those previously used. But with the lapse of years this accuracy had begun to wear off, and there was much discussion as to the possibility of introducing a system of "grouping". With fixed ammunition it was, however, impossible to preserve the identity of the "lots" of both the cordite and the fuze, and the date of the cordite must remain the governing factor in the turnover, for on it depended the system of watching its security.

The investigations into the possibility of improving the accuracy of fire led also to the consideration of the possible effect of changes in the barometer and thermometer. At a discussion in the Institution on the practice of 1913, an officer was bold enough to suggest that, having a good gun and a good range-finder, and having trained men to use both accurately, it was a pity to waste it all for want of working out beforehand the corrections necessary for changes of temperature and pressure. But the voice was that of a garrison artilleryman, and the field artillery would have none of it. "Meteor" found no favour with the mounted branch before the War.

More important than these theoretical discussions

---

[1] The subject of calibration is dealt with in Chapter XV.
[2] The steps that were taken to prevent deterioration of the fuze composition are described in Chapter V.

THE FINAL PHASE. 219

regarding accuracy of fire was the attention they drew to its practical effect. Inadequate as the targets at practice camps must always be as representations of actual troops, they were sufficient to show that shooting which was apparently effective, very frequently had results which were not only disappointing, but positively alarming.

With the adoption of French methods the limits of "effective shrapnel" at practice had been increased from 75 yards short at all ranges to from 100 to 200 yards, while, instead of the fire being considered ineffective unless 10% burst on graze, it was laid down that there should be "not more than 10%". So long as shell burst within these limits they gained credits for batteries however innocuous they might be, and there was a growing feeling that we were bursting shrapnel too short. The matter was brought to a head in February 1913 by a lecture at the Institution on "The Conditions necessary to produce Shrapnel Effect"[1] in which Captain H. W. Hill challenged the accepted ideas as to the depth zone of the service shrapnel. He maintained that to obtain the logical bullet density of one bullet to six square feet shell should be burst only about 50 yards short at ranges over 2,000 instead of more than double the distance, and that with 10 or even 15% of grazes, few shell would be ineffective, while the grazes would be very useful in checking the accuracy of the ranging.

This was a very different story from that told in *Field Service Regulations and Field Artillery Training*, and the question was taken up both officially and unofficially, with the result that the editions of 1914 materially modified the views previously expressed. Instead of a battery being able, without sweeping, to cover with its fire a width of one and a half times its own front, as confidently stated in the manual of 1912, all that was claimed in that of 1914 was that it could cover its own front. Its power of

CHAPTER IX.

Gunnery.

---

[1] This lecture may well be compared with the thorough examination of the same question by Major-General Stuart Nicholson in 1879.

CHAPTER IX.

Gunnery.

covering ground by "sweeping" was similarly affected, and in this case the reduction was from four and a half times its front to only three times, while in "searching" the steps were reduced from 150 and 200 yards to 100. These far-reaching changes necessitated important changes in the methods of "distribution of fire", and this section was materially modified in the manual of 1914, the sub-section devoted to "sweeping" being entirely rewritten. The sections dealing with shrapnel shell, with time and percussion fuzes, and with the use of the fuze indicator were also amplified.

In the closer attention thus devoted to the effect of shrapnel fire the question of the "angle of opening" naturally came under discussion, but this has been dealt with in Chapter V.

The Practice Camps.

During the last two years before the War the artillery practice camps came to fill a very prominent position in the training of the army, and the fires of controversy raged fiercely round the system of conducting the practice. The "tactical" practice was in some cases made the predominant feature to such an extent that the gunnery suffered, and there was an outcry among artillery officers at the falling off in the shooting. They contended that the annual allowance[1] of ammunition was intended for the training of the batteries in gunnery, and should be devoted to that purpose, for which it was none too sufficient—the tactical application of fire could be taught without ammunition. Especially distasteful was the absence of range-parties. Many feared that with targets bobbing up

---

[1] The allowance for gun batteries still remained at 600, and might fairly be considered as adequate for battery and brigade practice, but no more. The 480 rounds allowed to howitzer batteries (made up of 300 shrapnel, 100 lyddite, and 80 "practice") was undoubtedly insufficient, especially in view of the large proportion of lyddite, but demands for an increase had to give way to more urgent services. The heavy batteries were still worse off with a total of 200, made up of 100 shrapnel, 10 lyddite, and 90 "practice", and this was reduced to 190 in the last year by exchanging 60 practice for 50 shrapnel. But the increase of the most important projectile from 100 to 150 was considered worth the sacrifice.

THE FINAL PHASE. 221

here, there, and everywhere, and no one to keep a check on their shooting, layers would get careless. There were, many others, however, who saw the value of the wider training. They noted with satisfaction the way it was bringing home to artillery officers that when they came to shooting in earnest they would not have the field to themselves; they rejoiced in the way the interest of the other arms was expanding as they were brought into the picture instead of being herded apart as mere spectators. In January 1914 the annual staff conference became once again the scene of a debate upon artillery training. On the one side it was contended that the tactical practice had in many cases lost all instructional value as far as gunnery was concerned, owing to too large a measure of control having being given to officers of the other arms. On the other side it was urged that if progress was to be made it was essential to persevere, and that under the new system artillery officers would be better instructed in their duties in war, and the other arms would understand the work of the artillery better than they had ever done before. It was admitted that a very fair proportion of artillery officers now thought that the new departure had been a retrograde step so far as the shooting was concerned, and with good excuse in some cases, but it was urged that this need not be so. It was possible to arrange so that in almost every case the series in the tactical practice could be criticised as closely as those in the gunnery practice.

The spirit of the discussion was reflected in the Regulations of 1914, for while they showed no weakening of purpose they considerably modified the more extravagant tendencies of those of 1912. In the gunnery practice it was accentuated that the primary consideration was the use of correct methods, and accuracy of fire. In the tactical practice it was directed that, although the freedom of commanders should be as little interfered with as possible by the presence of range-parties, yet the results of the practice should be recorded whenever possible, for "even

CHAPTER IX.

The Practice Camps.

if principles are correctly applied, fire is of no use unless accurate, and consequently gunnery must not be ignored". It was a timely reminder that tactics need not, and must not, interfere with gunnery.[1]

The orders as to the drawing up of the schemes for tactical practice were also modified. This had been taken out of the hands of the artillery commanders and given, first to divisional commanders, and then to their general staff officers. Neither of these naturally could have the knowledge of the ground, and of the safety conditions, required for drawing up a scheme which would afford both good tactical practice and gunnery instruction. In 1914 it was therefore directed that the scheme should be drawn up by the divisional artillery commander, but that the divisional commander should approve it, and act as director. If a senior officer of another arm were placed in command, he must be made fully acquainted with the lessons which it was intended to teach, and any limitations imposed by safety conditions, before being called upon to issue his orders. It may safely be said that on the whole the new system of practice had proved a real step in advance, although it had required some modification in detail. During the last two or three practice seasons before the War many brigadiers and senior regimental officers of the other arms had been called upon to give orders to artillery brigades and batteries as if they were part of temporary groupings under their command, and had seen the result of their orders in the actual effect on the targets. Junior officers of cavalry and infantry, attached to the artillery, had had to describe to battery commanders the nature of the support they would require from the guns. Many brigade and battery commanders had enjoyed the experience of carrying out practice under orders from cavalry and infantry officers, and had been made to realize more fully

---

[1] Very considerable sums were devoted to the erection of splinter proofs so as to permit the presence of range parties without interfering with the tactical freedom of the practice.

THE FINAL PHASE. 223

than before that their brigades and batteries existed for the support of the other arms, and that choice of positions and targets for the guns would generally depend upon their dispositions and requirements. Above all the new procedure had given rise to much profitable discussion between officers of all ranks and all arms on their respective shares in combined operations—the first step towards mutual co-operation.

No doubt the system demanded sound tactical knowledge, and some experience of the other arms, on the part of divisional artillery commanders. But there seemed no reason to fear that the Regiment would be unable to meet the demand.

The attempt to move the headquarters of the horse and field branch of the School of Gunnery from Shoeburyness on the acquisition of Salisbury Plain had failed, as we have seen. In the winter the whole staff were concentrated at Shoeburyness, where they were engaged in the instruction of a constant succession of courses. Year by year, however, the absurdity of keeping the School of Gunnery for the field army artillery at a place like Shoeburyness became more and more obvious, and in 1911 the agitation for its removal received powerful assistance from the committee which was trying out French methods of fire. In a rider to their report, they stated their opinion that a school of gunnery on an inland range was imperative if the high standard of training and technical knowledge then required from artillery officers was to be maintained. Such a recommendation, coming from such a representative body, and just when so much interest was being taken in artillery training, could not be ignored. A committee was appointed to consider "what buildings, equipment, personnel, and horses would be required if the School of Gunnery, Royal Horse and Royal Field Artillery, were removed from Shoeburyness to Salisbury Plain, and to suggest the most suitable site for the buildings".

Meanwhile there had been considerable changes in the

224 THE FIELD ARMY ARTILLERY.

CHAPTER IX.

The School of Gunnery.

position of the Commandant of the School. With the appointment of divisional artillery commanders, responsible for the practice as for all other departments of the training of their commands, the title of "Commandant" was no longer appropriate, and one of the instructors was raised to the status of "Chief Instructor, Horse and Field" in his place. At the same time the appointment of an Inspector of Horse and Field Artillery deprived him of the presidency of the conference assembled annually to consider the matters brought to notice in the reports from the camps. Finally the circulation of his Annual Report was given up. With the organization of the training generally on a logical system, under the Chief of the General Staff, there was no longer a place for such a publication, and there appeared instead an annual *Memorandum on the Training of the Royal Horse, Royal Field, and Heavy Artillery* issued by the general staff.[1]

If in some ways the school had lost in position by these changes, it was on the eve of others which would more than compensate for what had been lost. In 1912 the headquarters moved to Larkhill instead of Okehampton for the summer; in 1913 the staff was increased so as to allow of an instructor being sent to each camp;[2] and in 1914 the Chief Instructor was relieved of special responsibility for any one camp, and assigned the duty of supervising and co-ordinating the gunnery instruction at all. Above all the removal of the school from Shoeburyness was approved. The second corner-stone of what was to become the great "School of Artillery" had been well and truly laid.

Progressive Training.

The system of Progressive Training initiated in 1908 had been steadily developed in successive manuals until that of 1912 put the coping stone upon the edifice in the training of the divisional artillery as a unit. But in the

---

[1] At first the title contained the note "Prepared by the Chief Instructor, Horse and Field Artillery, School of Gunnery". But this soon dropped out.

[2] Including the new one—*Ad Fines*, (Redesdale)—opened in 1912.

THE FINAL PHASE. 225

artillery there were peculiar difficulties in carrying out this system owing to the fact that the practice camps opened at the same time as the period of collective training, of which the practice should be the culmination. Attempts were made to arrange furlough so as to allow of sections being struck off duty for section training during the individual training season, and many officers and men sacrificed their leave ungrudgingly; but it was found not to be a practical proposition owing to so many other demands, and especially to the shortage of men—to be referred to later. The physical training experts and the medical authorities insisted that three months uninterrupted gymnastics were essential for recruits, if they were to be fit to perform the duties of soldiers without harm to themselves. The artillery were equally positive that grooming horses, and serving guns, would give them all the physical training they required, while it was essential for their military training that they should attend practice with their batteries. For the cavalryman or infantryman musketry was an individual exercise through which he could be put at any time, but an artilleryman who missed practice with his battery was deprived for a year of the most important part of his training. After somewhat acrimonious discussion a compromise was arrived at. The barriers between the different training periods were relaxed, and the Record Office was instructed to take into account the dates in which batteries were due for practice when posting recruits to them.

The carrying out wherever it was practicable of "elementary" at a period antecedent to the rest of the practice put the practice generally in its proper place as a portion only of the course of progressive training instead of a thing apart. It afforded brigade and battery commanders the opportunity of correcting faults before proceeding to service practice, and generally accentuated the fact that this part of the practice was definitely intended for elementary training. Batteries quartered within reach of ranges carried this out with great success, and a

Chapter IX.

Progressive Training.

226 THE FIELD ARMY ARTILLERY.

CHAPTER IX.

Progressive Training.

general search for ground in the vicinity of artillery stations was instituted.

The old complaint that lieut.-colonels did not fully realize their responsibilities regarding the training of their brigades was still heard, though less frequently. They had been definitely charged with the signalling, range-taking, and reconnaissance training, but their essential function was the training of their battery commanders. In this the model ranges just coming into use proved of inestimable value.

War games and regimental tours had never been very popular in the Regiment; and the long delay in giving brigade-majors to divisional artillery had undoubtedly had an unfortunate effect in this respect, as well as in others. The "staff officers" allowed instead had neither the status,[1] nor the training required to enable them to take the part they should have done in such activities. Owing no doubt to some extent to the above causes it could not be denied that the system of progressive training had made slower headway in the artillery than in the other arms In the last year before the War there was, however, a noticeable improvement, and the Inspector-General was able to report that the exercises on the ground without troops no longer fell below the standard obtaining in the cavalry and infantry.

Field-firing.

In spite of all efforts to make the tactical practice realistic, it had to be admitted that at practice camps it was impossible to place before the eyes of artillery commanders the distribution of the other arms on the battlefield; while at manœuvres it was hard to ensure their paying due attention to gunnery considerations. Field-firing alone called upon artillery commanders both for appreciation of the tactical situation and for fire effect. And yet, as mentioned in Chapter VII, the authorities at home were reluctant to undertake it on anything ap-

---

[1] They were forbidden to wear staff "tabs"

THE FINAL PHASE. 227

proaching the scale on which it had been carried out in India. The question was, however, taken up again and safety precautions overhauled, preparatory to divisional field-firing by the 3rd Division in 1912. But the infantry were not allowed to advance under the artillery fire, so the exercise lost much of its value, although no doubt the infantry learnt something of what artillery fire meant. The general view of the artillery was that unless a special grant of ammunition was given for them such exercises could not be carried out generally without seriously affecting the artillery training.

The last two years before the War saw the most ambitious army manœuvres ever carried out at Home. In 1912 Sir Douglas Haig and Sir James Grierson, each with an army corps and a cavalry division, were opposed in East Anglia; in 1913 Sir John French, with four divisions and a cavalry division, a larger force under one command than had ever before been seen in England, conducted an exercise against a skeleton force in position about Weedon. The King was present, and as he cantered over the Northamptonshire pastures, with his Royal Standard borne on a lance behind, one was carried back in imagination to the tragedy of Naseby Field, only a dozen miles away, where last that standard had been so borne. Imagination was stirred too by the presence of the deputation from the French Army, conspicuous in the place of honour at the King's right hand during the final conference.

As regards the part played by the artillery, mention must first be made of two notable developments in war organization which made their first public appearance at these manœuvres. In 1912 each side included as "Army Troops" a siege company armed with 6″ howitzers. In 1913 a "Major-General, R.A." took his place at general headquarters, and a brigade-major in each divisional artillery. Little progress had, however, been made in overcoming the great obstacle to the proper appreciation of the work of the artillery in combined training, viz:

CHAPTER IX.

Field-firing

Manœuvres.

CHAPTER IX.

Manœuvres.

the difficulty of adequately representing the strength of artillery units, and the effect of their fire.

In the 1909 manœuvres batteries had turned out with four guns and only two wagons, in direct violation of the quick-firing principle that wagon and gun were inseparable. For the 1912 manœuvres this criticism was met by the adoption of a strength of three guns and three wagons, but it led to the occupation of impossible positions, besides conveying a false impression of the size of divisional artillery to commanders and staff officers. It was all a question of horses, and it was decided to place all the batteries belonging to the Expeditionary Force on a uniform peace establishment of 70, instead of having some on a "higher" establishment of 85, and the majority on a ridiculously inadequate one of 55.

The technical difficulty of finding a suitable smokeless blank, explained in Chapter V, reacted tactically upon both artillery and infantry. The use of "smoky" cartridges discouraged the search for concealment on the part of the artillery, and also denied them any practice in locating the hostile guns. The use of "smokeless" led to the infantry showing even less regard than before to artillery fire. It was a vicious circle, and various devices were tried for indicating artillery fire—heliographs with red glasses, coloured screens, signal rounds—but the giving of due consideration to its effect by the umpires remained an insoluble problem.

In spite of such difficulties the published report on the final manœuvres showed plainly that the field army artillery had been rapidly assimilating the new "doctrine". The preliminary reconnaissances were good, guns were deployed on a sufficiently wide front, the approaches were well concealed, and the advantage of acting by surprise was fully recognized. Above all the co-operation between the artillery and the infantry was generally excellent.

Four-gun Batteries.

Ever since the re-armament, there had been an uneasy feeling that our battery organization was not that best

THE FINAL PHASE. 229

suited to the new weapons. With the rise of French influence the question had been brought into prominence, but the elaborate experiments carried out on Salisbury Plain in 1911 had failed to show the expected superiority of the smaller unit. For some reason, or combination of reasons, the officers commanding the experimental four-gun batteries were not able to get from them such a considerable increase of fire power as had been expected. The opinion persisted however that six quick-firing guns were too many for one man to handle so as to obtain the fullest advantage from their special characteristics, and the matter was officially discussed at the General Staff Conference of 1913, and many unofficial suggestions were put forward in the *Proceedings* and elsewhere. Among these may be mentioned the use of half-batteries as fire-units, while retaining the six-gun organization, eight-gun batteries divided into two four-gun "troops", and twelve-gun batteries divided into three such fire-units, But none of these ingenious suggestions for obtaining four-gun batteries without prohibitive increase in cost met with any general acceptance. If we were to adopt the four-gun organization we must pay the price either in reduction of number of guns, as the French had done, or in increased cost. Public opinion was not prepared to accept either alternative.

With the increase in the number of howitzer batteries, described in Chapter VI, their place in the divisional artillery organization naturally came under discussion. It was pointed out that in an attack by a division their fire would probably be wanted at several places, and not at one only, and that it would therefore be better if the howitzer batteries were distributed among the gun brigades instead of being concentrated in a brigade by themselves. This would avoid the necessity of splitting up the howitzer brigade, which was so often inevitable, especially since the introduction of temporary groupings; and would have the further advantage of making all field artillery brigades identical. From the point of view of

230   THE FIELD ARMY ARTILLERY.

CHAPTER IX.

Field Howitzers.

training it would get rid of the tendency to specialize which still clung to the howitzer brigades, and was responsible for the slowness so generally complained of in their work. Opinion was, however, by no means unanimous. It was held by some that the above arguments did not apply to forces larger than a division on a European battlefield, although they might be true for a division fighting alone in close country. But the chief objection was that the proposed mixed brigades would involve the reduction of one gun battery in a division,[1] and it was on the shrapnel of the guns that reliance was placed to deal with moving targets, such as batteries coming into action, and to force the enemy's infantry to keep wide spaces between their lines.

Heavy Artillery.

The difficulties with which the heavy artillery had had to contend have been frequently referred to in previous chapters. As late as 1912 they always practised alone, under the supervision of their own brigade commanders, and they were forbidden by regulation to move out of a walk, or to come into action front. No wonder that there were complaints of the slowness of the proceedings, and in 1913 it was decided that each heavy brigade should practice at the same time as a field artillery brigade, under the direction of the divisional artillery commander.[2] The result was the disappearance of the above restrictions of pace and method in the manual of 1914.

It was wonderful that they had reached any proficiency with their miserable permanent establishment of horses. Up to 1911 the batteries of the 2nd Brigade had only a dozen horses each, and the increase in 1911 was only to a score—a poor provision when it is remembered that all

---

[1] The proposal was for four brigades, each of two gun and one howitzer battery. The idea of four batteries in a brigade does not seem to have occurred to anyone at that time.

[2] The batteries belonging to divisions in Ireland could not unfortunately be sent to their divisions for training or practice, but the divisional artillery commanders came over to see them shoot in 1914, and it was arranged that the heavy brigade commander should attend the divisional artillery training in Ireland.

THE FINAL PHASE. 231

the gunners were interchangeable with drivers, and so had to be taught to ride. With the move of the brigade to Woolwich it had been the intention that the establishment should be raised to the same as the 1st Brigade, viz : 33 per battery, but the extra horses were cut out of the estimates 1914/15. Such, however, was the importance attached by the military authorities to the batteries having a nucleus of trained teams that they decided to provide the horses required at the expense of the field artillery—a striking testimony to the value attributed to the heavy artillery on the eve of the war.

CHAPTER IX.
Heavy Artillery.

The direct use of mechanical transport for heavy artillery, that is for drawing the guns, had been envisaged since the South African War, but as long as steam was the motive power, no progress was possible, for the noise and smoke precluded the use of steam tractors for taking the guns actually into action. If horses were necessary for this, to have tractors for use on the road would be to repeat the story of the Indian heavy batteries with their elephants and their "bails". Moreover trials with the 60-prs. in 1910, at Aldershot, on the march to Trawsfynydd, and during the army manœuvres, found the chain track tractor lagging behind the horses on the road, and showing no superiority across country. For the time being the subject was dropped, except for the fitting of engine-draught connections to 60-pr., 4·7″, 5″ and 6″ guns and 6″ howitzer equipments so as to make it possible to use mechanical transport with these at any time if required.[1]

Mechanization.

In another direction, however, the progress of mechanical transport affected the artillery very closely. Its advantages for the ammunition supply service had long been recognized by artillery officers, both as shortening road space and preserving for the batteries the dwindling supply of suitable draught horses. Its employment was one of the special features of the army manœuvres of 1912 and 1913, and, as described in Chapter VI, the decision to

---

[1] Some Territorial Horse Artillery carried out interesting experiments with motor cars drawing gun and limber.

232   THE FIELD ARMY ARTILLERY.

CHAPTER IX.

Re-armament.

mechanize a portion of the ammunition columns had far-reaching effects on the mobilization arrangements of the field artillery.

In the last chapter it was told how the French influence, coming just when the first enthusiasm for the 13 and 18-prs. was wearing off, caused a general feeling of dissatisfaction with the armament of the horse and field artillery. The trials in 1911 of various designs of anti-aircraft guns—notably the Deport[1] with its "split-trail"—increased this dissatisfaction by bringing to notice many novel and attractive features which were applicable to ordinary field guns. In the ten years that had elapsed since the 13 and 18-prs. had been designed phenomenal progress had been made in the science of gun design, and suggestions for "bringing them up to date" poured in. The most important of the defects charged against the service equipments may be summed up as:—

Slowness of loading,
Side-slip,
Unsteadiness.

The *slowness of loading* was due to the adoption of the "swinging-block" type of mechanism, which required a very high standard of efficiency in the drill to obtain real rapidity in the service of the gun. The *side-slip* was due to the adoption of "pivot-traverse", for whenever use was made of the traversing gear on the carriage, the gun recoiled at an angle to the system. But change to a "sliding-wedge" mechanism, or to "axle-traverse", would necessitate serious structural alterations which were out of the question. The position as regards *unsteadiness* was rather different. In the 13-pr. especially, relaying was necessary after every round, and this it was maintained rendered it unworthy of the title of "Q.F." It was recalled that in the original trials one of the equipments had been fitted with a hydro-pneumatic buffer, and that this had

---

[1] Adopted by the Italian Artillery. It gave 45° elevation, 60° traverse.

THE FINAL PHASE.

shown itself steadier than the others. Trials were carried out, both at Shoeburyness and on Salisbury Plain, with an 18-pr. so fitted, which showed very noticeably improved steadiness and smoothness of run-out, but the buffer was very expensive, and time alone could prove its power of withstanding the wear and tear of war and the climatic vicissitudes of the British Empire. Reports of weak recuperator springs, however, strengthened the hands of the advocates of the hydro-pneumatic system, and further trials in 1913-14 of a design for converting the 18-pr. to this system were so successful, that approval of the change could be given in the early months of the war.

It was generally accepted that re-armament could not be much longer delayed, and the general consensus of informed opinion was that further tinkering with the existing equipments was therefore to be deprecated. Experience showed that such tinkering was always expensive and rarely satisfactory, and it was felt that the money would be better devoted to the trials that would be required before a new design could be decided upon. The formulating of "conditions" for such a design was the first step, and these were issued in October 1913. They are of great interest, for they reveal, better than any description, what were the views of the authorities, on the very eve of the War, as to the requirements of a field artillery equipment. A fairly complete précis will be found in Appendix D.

Shrapnel shell was the only projectile called for. It had been definitely decided that it should be considered the chief projectile for field artillery, and that all efforts should be directed to producing the most effective shell of this nature. If it were eventually required to introduce high-explosive this must be entirely subservient to the shrapnel.

Turning from the main features of gun, carriage, and ammunition to what came to be known as "adjuncts", a reference to Chapter V will show how the number of these mechanical aids had been growing. So much had this

CHAPTER IX.

Re-armament.

234 THE FIELD ARMY ARTILLERY.

CHAPTER IX.

Re-armament.

been the case th in 1914 there had to be brought out a separate "Handbook of Artillery Instruments" which included only those instruments which were used by no other arm. Such a book was certainly needed, but were the instruments? That is a question which it will be for the historian of the work of the Regiment in the War to answer. Certain it is that the demand from regimental officers was insistent, and that every effort was made to satisfy the demand. At the same time the danger of over-reliance on such mechanical aids was recognized, and attention was drawn to the necessity of officers accustoming themselves to extemporizing methods in view of the possible loss and damage of instruments on service.

About one requirement, however, there could be no doubt, and that was the need of a better range-finder. The struggle to find one which combined accuracy and serviceability had been a long one, but at last, in 1913, a "one-man" instrument was approved. It was a vast addition to the efficiency of batteries.

Personal Equipment.

It was not only the re-armament of the batteries which was attracting attention in these last years: the armament of the individual was once again the subject of controversy. The adoption of the rifle as the personal weapon of all horse and field artillerymen as a result of South African experience had been met with general approval at the time, but, as the memories of the veldt faded, the glitter of the swords was recalled with regret. For King Edward's coronation swords had been re-issued "on loan", and before that of King George an Army Order restored their swords to the horse artillery,[1] and it was directed that guards in review order should be armed with them instead of rifles.

At the same time the claims of war were not overlooked. The training of the cavalry division, and the establishment

---

[1] An amusing result was a complaint as to the belt spoiling the set of the jacket!

THE FINAL PHASE. 235

of the horse artillery practice camp, brought the combined work of guns and cavalry under close scrutiny, and it was noticed that the 36[1] rifles in a battery were only sufficient for the 2nd echelon and the baggage guard, leaving the firing battery defenceless. A committee under Lieut.-General Sir J. M. Grierson was assembled in 1911 to consider the matter. They had no difficulty in deciding that neither swords nor revolvers were suitable, but opinion was divided as to the respective merits of the rifle and the lighter and less cumbersome automatic pistol, which it was thought would be equally effective up to 300 yards. Eventually the committee recommended the adoption of the automatic pistol, with the proviso that, pending the discovery of a suitable pattern, rifles should be carried, since it was "imperatively necessary that every man should be at once armed with a personal weapon". For some reason, however, the rifles were withdrawn, and revolvers issued instead, in spite of the fact that regimental opinion was strongly opposed to being left dependent on revolvers even as a temporary expedient. And the justice of their anxiety was fully proved when trouble came at the Curragh in 1914, for the horse artillery brigade were dependent on the field artillery, who were fortunately in the same barracks, for protection, and an escort of the other arms would have been necessary if they had had to be moved by road or rail.

The question of the personal weapon for field, mountain, heavy, and siege artillerymen was discussed at the Staff Conference of 1913. Opinion was unanimous as to all men with the wagon lines and ammunition columns being armed, but there was still some doubt as to this being extended to those with the guns, and also as to whether the weapon should be rifle or automatic pistol. It was proposed to take advantage of the forthcoming

CHAPTER IX.

Personal Equipment.

---

[1] The number had been reduced from 48 in ignorance, apparently, of the fact that 48 had been adopted because war had shown that a half-company of 50 was a sufficient escort for a battery by train.

CHAPTER IX.

Personal Equipment.

mobilization of the artillery of the 2nd Division to test the alternative scales suggested—but nothing came of it.

The armament of the native Indian personnel of the mountain battery in Egypt was also embarrassing the authorities. "Swords, drummers" and "swords, mountain artillery" were competitors, until a genius suggested the combination of the blade of the first with the scabbard of the second, and this duly appeared in the equipment lists. But unfortunately the drummers' sword had a straight Roman blade, while the mountain artillery scabbard was curved in scimitar fashion. There was much correspondence with India and Egypt before both swords and scabbards of the mountain artillery pattern could be issued.

Mobilization.

In Chapter VI the measures taken to put the mobilization of the field army artillery on a business-like footing have been described in some detail, and it only remains to mention here the modifications introduced during the last years before they had to be put in force.

The return to three-years' service in 1909 was very unpopular, although the total number to be enlisted on these terms was only that required to maintain five thousand serving rank and file out of a total establishment of the Royal Field Artillery at home of over thirteen thousand. This limitation was, however, often forgotten, and no doubt the presence of the three-years' men involved many difficulties in the training, especially in the provision of non-commissioned-officers and specialists. The fact that they were debarred from earning proficiency pay,[1] and so were without the incentive to individual effort which had been the object of its introduction, accentuated this disadvantage. A far more serious effect of the change in the

---

[1] The adoption of "Proficiency Pay" in 1906, in substitution for the "Service Pay" introduced after the South African War, had practically abolished the last vestige of the system of individual prizes for "Skill-at-Arms" which had come in with the first practice camps in the 70's of the last century. For Class I a high standard of individual proficiency in what might be called specialists' duties was demanded : Class II was given for general proficiency in the duties of the rank held : but men were not eligible for either unless serving on a more than three years engagement.

THE FINAL PHASE. 237

terms of service was the serious shortage of men in the field artillery due to the abnormal outflow to the reserve produced by it. The effect of this shortage on the training has already been alluded to: in the last winter before the War it rose from just under a thousand in November to over sixteen hundred in March, some brigades being as much as a hundred under establishment. Many of the three-years' men would have been glad to extend their service, and there was a very natural demand that this should be allowed, but the authorities were adamant in their refusal, unless an exchange could be arranged with a six-years' man, on account of its effect in depleting the reserve. The shortage was only a temporary inconvenience, the strength of the reserve was an essential for mobilization.

CHAPTER IX.

Mobilization.

There was a marked increase in the attention paid to mobilization arrangements by divisional artillery commanders and higher authorities. Practice mobilizations of a battery in each brigade were carried out, and a trial was made of the time taken to issue and assemble the harness of a divisional ammunition column—which brought to light the practical importance of such apparently trifling matters as the marking of harness.

In 1913 the title "Reserve Brigade" was substituted for that of "Training Brigade" to bring them into line with the similar formations in the other arms; their strength was reduced from three 4-gun batteries to two 6-gun; and in the next year the process of bringing the depôts and reserve brigades together was completed. But service in the reserve brigades was very unpopular with officers. They felt that they were cut off from association with other troops, and could obtain little knowledge of field work, and the transfer of senior subalterns from batteries was naturally resented. There were obvious objections to the service batteries getting the juniors, but it was decided that there were greater objections to sending young officers to the reserve brigades.

In the last year before the war the withdrawal of a

Final Distribution.

CHAPTER IX.

Final Distribution.

large part of the artillery from South Africa allowed of a general re-distribution of batteries. The principle on which this rearrangement was based was that of reducing as far as possible the number of unallotted and training batteries, and concentrating the personnel available in the batteries of the Expeditionary Force. At the same time, in deference to the sentiment of the Regiment, special steps were taken to avoid the relegation of batteries with distinguished records to reserve brigades, where they would be debarred from any chance of further service, and to select for reduction those most recently raised.

The proportion of horse artillery was unquestionably too large now that it was only required for work with mounted troops, but some of the surplus batteries were saved to act in the same capacity as reserve brigades, thus diminishing the number for reduction to three—Z, A/A, and B/B. In the field artillery, in order to preserve the continuity of existence of the older batteries, a nucleus of all ranks was moved, as representing the battery, to its new station, and by this means the reduction of Nos. 40, 47, and 60 was evaded, and Nos. 148, 149, and 150 disappeared in their stead.

The final distribution is shown in Appendix E.

Conclusion.

The issue, in the spring of 1914, of a new edition of *Field Artillery Training* cleared up all matters which had been left in doubt by the Regulations of 1912, and enabled the Field Army Artillery to commence their last season's training with a clear conception of what would be expected of them in the war that was approaching. There came with it a noticeable return to the insistence upon adherence to "the book" which had characterized the training before the South African War. The reaction which had followed that war had spent its force, and the value of uniformity of method had once again become evident. And this applied also to dress, turn-out, and drill. After making due allowance for the order forbidding the polishing of leather and the burnishing of steel, except for ceremonial parades, the turn-out of many batteries had certainly come to be

THE FINAL PHASE.

lacking in finish, when judged by the standard which had formerly prevailed in the Regiment. The importance attached to such matters by the Japanese, even during active operations in Manchuria, strengthened the hands of those who realized the value of smartness as an incentive to discipline, and resented the free and easy habits acquired on the veldt. Presiding at a lecture on the lessons of the practice in 1913, the Inspector[1] of Royal Horse and Royal Field Artillery took occasion to speak out strongly on the subject. "Now that we have got excellent manuals in the Field Service Regulations and in Field Artillery Training, let us try to stamp out the light regard some of us appear to hold for Regulations. We go aside from the Regulations in our dress, in our turn-out, and in that of our batteries, and we have gone aside to an unlimited extent in our practice. . . . . We have been wrong there, and I would like to say now 'Let us adhere to the regulations: let us work on a uniform system, so that anyone can step in at any moment and command another man's battery'."

In this last chapter an endeavour has been made to indicate the final stages in the organization, armament, and training of the Field Army Artillery; and to put on record the subjects which were then agitating military opinion as regards the part the artillery should play in battle. In such matters, however, a contemporary account has a special value, and extracts from a report by one of the divisional artillery commanders of the Expeditionary Force, signed upon "the first day of mobilization", have therefore been added in Appendix F. The opinions expressed would probably not have found universal acceptance at the time—they are but those of an individual. But the position held by the writer, and the date on which he recorded his views, give the document a special value as affording a direct insight into the state of affairs in the Regiment at the most fateful moment of its existence.

Chapter IX.

Conclusion

---

[1] Brigadier-General (later General Lord) Horne, G.C.B., Colonel-Commandant, R.H.A., Master-Gunner, d. 1929.

PART III.
THE SIEGE ARTILLERY.

CHAPTER X.

THE SOUTH AFRICAN INFLUENCE.

(1902—1904.)

The Field Army Trend—Re-organization—Re-armament.

THE arrangements made for the despatch of the siege train under Colonel Perrott[1] to South Africa, and the various measures taken in connection with the organization and training of the siege artillery during the "war-years" (1899—1902) have been dealt with in Part 1. Here the story is taken up from the resumption by Colonel Perrott of his post of Commandant Lydd, and Chief Instructor Siege, in 1902. He lost no time in formulating his war experience, and next year submitted a revised drill for siege artillery, in which its nomenclature and methods were assimilated to those of heavy batteries. His tenure of the appointment was, however, just expiring, and his successor, Colonel Hickman,[2] was horrified to find that the siege artillery were contemplating the abolition of platforms, and "were being taught to use the 6″ as a field howitzer". Ten years before, while an instructor at Shoeburyness, he had rendered great services to that branch by evolving the method of plotting observations which was the foundation of the system of "exact" observation. Now as Chief Instructor he insisted that, even if siege companies must learn something of heavy battery methods, they should

---

[1] Major-General Sir T. Perrott, K.C.B., d. 1919.
[2] Major-General H. P. Hickman, C.B., d. 1930.

244   THE SIEGE ARTILLERY.

CHAPTER X.

The Field Army Trend.

first be fully trained in all the niceties of the siege system, so as to develop scientific gunnery among the officers, and habits of accuracy and precision in all ranks.

The controversy thus raised bade fair to rival that between the advocates of guns and howitzers which had divided siege artillerymen in the 80's, but the influence exerted by recent memories of experience on the veldt was too strong to be resisted for long. There, the 6″ howitzers had proved too heavy for work with columns in the field; and so, when Colonel Inglefield[1] succeeded to the chief instructorship in 1905 he resumed the trials without platforms. Such a procedure had never been even alluded to in any manual, but the accuracy obtained showed conclusively the possibility of dispensing with these cumbrous *impedimenta* when their carriage would interfere with the mobility of the battery. Without the platforms the anchorage buffers and top carriages would be useless and could also be discarded.[2] In order to deal with the sandy soil in India a light platform, only a quarter of the weight of the service pattern, was devised at Rurki, and taken into general use.

Colonel Inglefield's experience in command of a heavy battery in the war had shown him also the poor effect of lyddite against troops in the open or in field entrenchments, and he pressed for the addition of shrapnel to the equipment. Here also experimental practice showed the truth of his contention.

The elaborate system of "exact" observation adopted by the siege artillery in 1895 was far in advance of anything possessed by the field artillery in those days. But the latter had made great progress in appliances for indirect fire during the first years after the South African War, and there were trials with some of these at Lydd. As they stood, the instruments were not good enough for siege

---

[1] Brig.-Genl. N. B. Inglefield, C.B., D.S.O., d. 1912.

[2] The buffer and top carriage were made separate stores, to accompany the platform when required, instead of being components of the carriage. The platform alone weighed 50 cwt.

THE SOUTH AFRICAN INFLUENCE.

artillery, but the trials paved the way for further investigation of field artillery methods.

In this year (1904) another practical step was taken by an order that siege companies should take their own howitzers to practice with them in future, instead of using those belonging to the school.

Of the siege brigade of 1899, only one company remained at home, and in 1901 it was joined by a garrison company converted to siege. But next year, in spite of protests, the one experienced company was relegated to coast defence in pursuance of the policy which had proved so unpopular in both branches since its inception. Two new companies were converted in its place, thus bringing the brigade back to three companies, but they were taken away again almost at once to be made into heavy batteries. The companies that succeeded them were, however, left undisturbed, and the brigade thus constituted remained unaltered during the rest of the period covered by this volume. It had been decided that its strength should be reduced from the four companies of the 1899 organization to three companies as in the original scheme. These companies were each to expand into two batteries, as before, on mobilization, and were then to form two brigades, a medium brigade of four batteries armed with 6″ howitzers, and a heavy brigade of two batteries armed with heavy howitzers. In addition, three batteries of heavy guns on field carriages were to be manned by personnel drawn from the coast artillery. In India there was a similar reduction by the conversion of one of the siege companies into a heavy battery in 1901, and the siege train for the remainder of the period consisted of only two companies, with no provision for expansion. They were armed with a lighter pattern of 6″ howitzers.

The armament authorised for the six siege batteries at home was :—

6″ howitzers—4 batteries = 16, reserve = 4, total 20.
8·5″ do. —2 do. = 8, do. = 2, do. 10.
6″ guns —3 do. = 12, do. = 4, do. 16.

CHAPTER X.
Re-armament

But of this brave array all that were available were the 6″ howitzers. The 8·5″ howitzers were still in the experimental stage, and although there were plenty of 6″ guns, no field carriage had yet been designed for them. There were, it is true, the four 9·45″ howitzers bought from Skoda, as told in Part I, but these were looked upon as "extras—not to be seriously regarded".

Trials were pushed on with the 8·5″ howitzer, but were so unsuccessful as to lead to the conclusion that the provision of a mobile mounting for such a heavy weapon was beyond the scope of practical politics. It was therefore decided to substitute for it a more powerful piece capable of being moved into position by a light field railway, and designs were put in hand.

As regards the 6″ gun, the conclusion come to was that any carriage designed for both travelling and firing would be too heavy even for mechanical traction, and that it would be necessary to divide the gun and carriage into "loads" as in the 9·45″ equipment. Coming into action would take longer than with a field carriage, but once in action the labour of the detachment would be much less. At the same time a railway mounting for the 6″ gun, on the lines of those made in South Africa, was tried, but proved so unsteady when fired at more than 16° to the line that it was decided to give up the idea.

The only real improvement was the enlargement of the chambers of the 6″ howitzers and the provision of "light" projectiles of 100 lb. instead of 120 lb., thus increasing their range from 5,200 to 7,000 yards.

Such was the position when the siege of Port Arthur drew the attention of the world once again to the problems of siege warfare.

CHAPTER XI.

THE MANCHURIAN INFLUENCE.

(1904—1910.)

Port Arthur—Siege Artillery in the Field—The New Practice Camp—Aviation—Night-Firing—Manœuvres and Staff Tours—The New Manual—Coast Artillery Support.

THE Japanese attack on the land front of the Russian naval base of Port Arthur opened in February 1904, but it was not until New Year's Day that the fortress surrendered, after withstanding ten months blockade, five months close siege, and frequent assaults. As the months dragged by, and success eluded the besiegers in spite of the unexampled power of the artillery and the reckless valour of the infantry, there came a general revival of the interest in siege warfare which had been roused by the fate of the French fortresses in 1870-71, but had again fallen out of fashion with the enthusiasm for mobility which had—or so it was thought—banished spadework from the battlefield. The reports of observers, when duly digested, showed plainly enough how the want of previous experience in siege warfare on the part of the Japanese, and their lack of technical skill, had resulted in the needless sacrifice of thousands of lives. It was realized that the capture of a regularly fortified position would still require resort to regular siege methods, and that accuracy of fire from the artillery, and skill in mining from the engineers, would be as necessary as ever, in order to ensure the success of the infantry assault, on which the result must ultimately depend.

CHAPTER XI.

Port Arthur.

The need for renewed training in siege warfare, in which experience with modern appliances was entirely lacking, was forced upon all the military powers. The Germans led off with siege manœuvres at Cologne in 1905, the French came hard on their heels with similar operations at Langres in the following year, and it was decided that we should follow suit in 1907.

Siege Artillery in the Field.

It was not only on what may perhaps be called the more "legitimate" side of their work that the war had its lessons for the siege artillery. In its later stages it had shown the possibility of employing siege artillery in the field on a scale far transcending anything seen in South Africa, both as regards the number and the size of the pieces brought into play. This tendency of the great battles in Manchuria to assume the character of siege warfare was no doubt to some extent due to exceptional circumstances, such as the narrowness of the theatre of operations between the Chinese frontier and the mountainous country, and the lack of roads which tied both sides to movement up and down a line of rail. But the European nations were not slow to recognise the disadvantage, actual or moral, felt by an army which could not reply to an enemy's weapons with those of similar size or characteristics. To guard against such a risk the development of heavy mobile howitzers was everywhere taken up.

The New Practice Camp.

It has been told in Part II how the instruction of heavy batteries was included in the functions of the siege artillery school, and it was due to that connection that the siege artillery succeeded in breaking the bonds of Lydd. For in 1903 and 1904 the staff of the school were sent to conduct the practice of the newly raised heavy brigades, for whom a new range had been found at Rhayader in Wales. In 1905 the "heavies" were transferred to the field artillery practice camps, and disappeared from the purview of the siege school, but one of the siege companies, which had helped in the preparation of the ranges at Rhayader in the previous years, carried out its regular practice there. It was the first time, since the formation

THE MANCHURIAN INFLUENCE. 249

of the siege artillery in 1882, that a company had practised anywhere but at Lydd, and it had far-reaching results. In 1906 the whole of the siege brigade was concentrated at Rhayader for practice, and thenceforward this was carried out at Lydd and Rhayader in alternate years.

CHAPTER XI.

The New Practice Camp.

The first year at the new camp fortunately coincided with the change from "competitive" to "classification", and this loosening of the trammels allowed of attention being devoted to instruction in the various problems which might confront a battery commander on service rather than to the testing of the training which had been given. Targets[1] were made more realistic than had been possible at Lydd; and the problem of representing guns firing smokeless powder, which had puzzled siege artillerymen for a decade, seemed in a fair way to solution by the introduction of cordite "flashes" to be fired from small mortars. It was possible at last to practice long range fire, which was soon seen to be full of difficulties for low velocity howitzers with their high trajectory and long time of flight.

Perhaps the greatest benefit derived from the change of *venue* was the new light it shed upon the problem of observation of fire. In the last volume of this history it has been told how the siege artillery showed the way in both laying and observation of fire, and how the system of "exact" observation was built up in the 90's. Since then the siege artillery had pinned their faith upon that system, which could indeed be trusted to give absolutely accurate results—provided always that one condition was fulfilled. This essential condition was that the target should show a clear and unmistakable mark on which both the observation of fire instruments could be clamped: unless it was fulfilled the result would not only be inaccurate, it

---

[1] Curiously enough the targets do not appear to have ever included "obstacles", although it had been pointed out in successive manuals that little was known of the best way of destroying them by shell fire, and that attempts to do so might probably render wire entanglements more impassable.

250   THE SIEGE ARTILLERY.

CHAPTER XI.
The New Practice Camp.

would be misleading in the highest degree. At Lydd, with conventional targets and artificial observing stations well known to all concerned, there was no difficulty, but on the moors it was quite a different thing. The observers had to find for themselves, somewhere in the heather, observing stations from which they could see the target and each other without giving away the position of the guns; and they had to recognise from such stations the same point in the indefinite target presented by an actual earthwork. No wonder that there was a demand for methods more suited to such circumstances.

As regards the practice generally, the expense of the ammunition was the chief bar to progress. A round for the 6˙6″ R.M.L. howitzer had cost half-a-guinea, for the 6″ B.L. it was a case of a couple of pounds. Cheap "practice" shell—common iron, filled with powder to represent lyddite, and with pitch and powder to represent shrapnel—were introduced, and occasional grants of obsolete ammunition for instructional and brigade practice, helped things out. Advantage was taken of the arrangement by which the siege artillery practised in alternate years at Lydd and Rhayader to devote special attention to the methods in which instruction could best be given on the respective ranges. At Rhayader—visual observation, selecttion of observing stations, and such methods as might be required when serving with a field army. At Lydd—concealed targets with instrumental observation, and generally all cases in which extreme accuracy was the first essential, as would be required in a regular siege.

Full advantage was taken of the fact that the ground at Rhayader allowed of the actual construction of cover of all sorts. The artillery were responsible for the protection of their guns, and it was impressed on all that, in siege artillery, digging came only second in importance to shooting. Special attention was given to the adaptation of the design of batteries to the conditions of ground and surroundings, not forgetting the possibility of balloon observation by the enemy, as to which the officers of the

THE MANCHURIAN INFLUENCE. 251

Balloon Section were able to give most valuable assistance. This question of air observation was indeed of the utmost importance for siege artillery, for it might well happen that the enemy's guns were so well concealed that not even their flashes could be observed from any attainable position on the ground. The possibility of observing fire from a balloon had been first tested with the heavy brigade at Rhayader in 1903, and was further investigated by the siege artillery at Lydd in the following year. It was then decided to send an officer from each siege company for a three months course in ballooning, and additional interest was given to the first concentration of the siege brigade at Rhayader in 1906 by the presence of the balloon section in camp. The officers who had been through the course were employed to observe for their batteries, and the advantage of having for this duty a trained artilleryman, who knew exactly what information was required, was soon apparent. The introduction of kites, with their greater steadiness in rough weather, still further emphasized the value of aerial observation. It had definitely taken its place alongside "instrumental" and "visual" as one of the service methods.

Moreover, it was not forgotten that the enemy might be equally aware of its uses, and that it behoved the siege artillery to consider how they should deal with such inconvenient attentions. A system of ranging on a balloon was worked out, and appeared in 1909 as an addendum to the manual. A short-range howitzer like the 6″ was a poor weapon for the purpose, but the observation of fire instruments were invaluable, and the 60 prs. of the heavy batteries had brought down balloons at 6,000 yards or more.

In one respect Rhayader was distinctly inferior to Lydd—under the terms of the lease no night-firing was allowed there.[1] During the alternate years at Lydd every

CHAPTER XI.

Aviation.

Night-Firing

---

[1] Except in 1910 when special arrangements were made, and very valuable experience over undulating ground was gained.

252 THE SIEGE ARTILLERY.

CHAPTER XI.

Night-Firing.

opportunity was taken, therefore, to practice such firing with the aid of star shell[1] and searchlights, and also to test the vulnerability of searchlights to artillery fire. It was found that with instrumental observation there was no difficulty at all in bringing effective fire to bear by night upon any target on which the observers had been able to clamp their instruments by day, nor upon searchlights or guns represented by flashes. For picking up scattered targets, such as working parties, at anything over two thousand yards the star shell were more useful than searchlights.

The real difficulty about night-firing was the inadequacy of the means provided for lighting the batteries. The service bulls-eye lanterns[2] gave a poor light at the best, and went out every time a gun was fired. After some years of trials a candle lamp, on the lines of a bicycle lamp, was approved, and proved satisfactory for work in the battery. For plotting something better was required, and an electric lamp was under trial in 1914.

Manœuvres and Staff Tours.

To return now to the siege manœuvres referred to on the first page of this chapter. The Chatham forts, although of an obsolete type, presented many features in common with the Russian works which had for so long defied all the efforts of the Japanese, and it was considered that the close attack of one or more of these would yield the most valuable lessons. To commence the exercise at this stage would, however, have robbed it of much of its instructional value, and it was therefore decided to study the preliminary operations, from the driving in of the infantry of the defence to the opening of fire by the siege batteries, through the medium of a staff tour. This took place in the early summer of 1907, and provided opportunities for the discussion of various questions of great importance to the siege artillery. These included the use of the field army artillery in such operations, the relations

---

[1] Introduced for 6″ howitzers in 1909.
[2] The bulls-eye lanterns were passed on to the coast artillery.

THE MANCHURIAN INFLUENCE.

between its command and that of the siege train, and the organization of the latter—besides the more technical matters connected with the siting of the batteries, the selection of observing stations, the arrangements for the control of the fire, the relief of detachments, and the supply of ammunition and stores.

For the manœuvres proper, which followed in July and August, the troops employed were a brigade of infantry, four companies of garrison artillery (three coast, one siege), and fortress engineers with searchlight and balloon detachments. The artillery dug their own batteries, and would have armed them, but unfortunately the guns with which this was to have been done did not arrive in time. Owing also to lack of troops and to the restrictions of government ground, it was not possible to deal with the artillery of the defence. Consequently the training of the artillery was confined to the design and construction of the types of batteries which would be required in exposed positions where the rival claims of cover and concealment had to be considered. Here, as was only to be expected, the siege company showed the value of its practice at Rhayader.

The manœuvres had undoubtedly proved rather disappointing for the artillery companies which had taken part in them, but they had done a great deal to enforce the necessity for studying siege warfare. From 1907 onwards siege staff tours were held annually in the neighbourhoods of Shoeburyness, Lydd, and Rhayader. They formed a very important feature in the training of the siege brigade as well as of the gunnery staff course, and served also a useful purpose in bringing together the general staff at the War Office and the instructional staff of the School of Gunnery.

The change of practice ground from the flat and restricted ranges on Romney Marsh to the wide rolling moorland of the Welsh March amply confirmed the wisdom of the recommendations made by Colonels Perrott and Inglefield in their endeavours to bring the training of the siege

CHAPTER XI.

Manœuvres and Staff Tours.

The New Manual.

254   THE SIEGE ARTILLERY.

CHAPTER XI.

The New Manual.

artillery more into preparation for a field army rôle. In 1905 they were embodied in a "provisional" manual, to be given permanent form—with some modifications and additions—next year under the title of *Garrison Artillery Training, Vol. II.*[1] This was a great advance upon *Siege Artillery Training 1900*, for in it the lessons of a great siege and of great battles were superimposed upon the experiences of the veldt.

The manual of 1900 had laid it down that, even when using visual observation, the battery commander should only observe for himself when the target was permanently visible from the firing point—otherwise he must send out two observers, and occupy himself with combining the results sent in by them. The manual of 1906 directed him to observe for himself whenever it was possible for him to do so without prejudice to the efficient command of his battery, and pointed out that the use of a telephone or signallers would allow of his being at some distance from it. But it took some years to overcome the reluctance of battery commanders to leave their guns.

It must not be thought, however, that there was any discouragement of the more accurate method when circumstances required it. The effect of the monster howitzers at Port Arthur would have been far more sensational even than it was if their fire had been directed with greater precision. The Japanese had no observation of fire instruments, and in many cases a practicable breach had not been made for the assaulting troops. When ranges were long and observation difficult instrumental observation undoubtedly gave the best results—provided always that the one essential condition for its use was fulfilled.

The new manual commenced with a definite statement of the organization in peace and how it was to be expanded for war;[2] and drew a distinction between a great siege in

---

[1] The reason for the change of title will be found below.

[2] Companies were given the straightforward title of "Siege" instead of having only the cryptic initials "S.T." affixed to their number.

THE MANCHURIAN INFLUENCE. 255

which the siege artillery would be reinforced from the coast artillery, and minor siege operations in which the siege artillery might be employed with the field army—all of which had been discreetly omitted from the Manual of 1900. The objects of siege artillery fire were extended from mere destruction of material with lyddite to the infliction of casualties on men with shrapnel "as it is the *personnel* that has to be overcome before the position, whatever it may be, can be captured".

The importance of control of fire by the "brigade commander"—his first mention under that title—was insisted upon, and some rather vague instructions given as to how it should be exercised. In the work of the battery it was admitted for the first time that the carriage of platforms would often be out of the question, and that the siege companies must therefore learn to shoot without. It devoted considerable space to explaining the difficulties of ranging on rough and undulating ground—the puzzles of the "angle of sight", of "false crests", of the disappearance of ranging rounds smothered in bogs or lost in ravines, and the management of time fuzes—in short all the problems with which the field artillery had been struggling for a generation, but which had come fresh to the siege artillery with their move to a natural range.

The hard and fast distinction between "exact" and "ordinary" observation—or, as they were now termed, "instrumental" and "visual"—was relaxed, and the use of the field artillery indirect laying stores whenever the circumstances of the case rendered them more suitable was authorized.[1]

In addition to the necessity for training in siege warfare, much had been learnt from the experiences of the Japanese at Port Arthur as regards the size and composition of the siege train required for the attack of a

CHAPTER XI.
The New Manual.

Coast Artillery Support.

---

[1] During the next few years improved patterns of these instruments were approved for siege and heavy artillery—No. 2 Director, Marks II & IV Field Plotters, No. 4 Dial Sights. Prismatic binoculars were introduced in 1909.

CHAPTER XI.

Coast Artillery Support.

modern fortress. In addition to the artillery of a field army of three divisions, reinforced by a large number of field guns, they had employed a siege train of rather more than 150 heavy guns and howitzers. A similar figure had been accepted and worked to in the siege manœuvres at home and on the continent, and it agreed with the typical siege train of Peninsular experience, while that maintained in England at the close of the smooth-bore period numbered over a hundred pieces. Thus at the beginning, middle, and end of a century, both theory and practice pointed to somewhere between a hundred and a hundred and fifty pieces being required for the vigorous conduct of a siege. But our siege companies, even when doubled on mobilization, could only man a couple of dozen.

It was not only a question of numbers, but of size. If the Japanese at Port Arthur had followed precedent in regard to the former, they had made a marked departure from it in regard to the latter. Howitzers of 28 cm. (11″) taken out of their coast defences had been dragged by whole battalions to their concrete platforms. The effort had been immense, but it had been well repaid, for it was the fire of these great weapons which had blown the top off 203-metre hill, and brought about the fall of the fortress. We had got nothing to compare with them except the 9˙45″, for all efforts to design a heavy siege howitzer had so far ended in disappointment.

It was obvious that if we were ever to undertake a serious siege we should have to depend largely upon the coast artillery for *personnel*—as indeed we had always done—and now it was suggested that we should do so for *matériel* also—as had the Japanese. The advocates of such a course argued that we should scarcely undertake important siege operations overseas until we had secured the command of the sea, and that then we could safely take the guns, as well as the men, from our coast defences. Moreover it would save further expenditure on efforts to obtain a heavy siege howitzer.

The last argument, at any rate, was one which was

THE MANCHURIAN INFLUENCE.

sure of a sympathetic hearing, and so, in the summer of 1906, the order went forth that the coast artillery was to be prepared to support the siege artillery both with men and guns; the title of the new manual was changed from *Siege Artillery Training* to *Garrison Artillery Training, Vol. II;* and all action on the design of a heavy siege howitzer was suspended.

But the days in which garrison artillerymen were equally capable of fighting a siege or a coast battery were gone by. Guns, mountings, appliances, and, more important still, methods had drifted far apart. If the coast artillery were to undertake siege work in war they must be trained for it in peace. Courses of instruction for them were accordingly instituted at Lydd, and later on extended from a fortnight to three weeks, with a more advanced course for gunnery instructors added. But the subject was quite new to most of those attending, and no great success was achieved by the courses until the issue of siege howitzers to coast artillery stations for preliminary training was sanctioned in 1909.

The trial of a mobile mounting for 6″ guns was pushed on, and the question of adapting 10″ R.M.L. guns on high-angle mountings—of which fifty or so were available—was taken up. Meanwhile the third siege company, destined to expand into the heavy brigade, was given the four 9·45″ to play with. On the return of these howitzers from China, each siege company had fired a hundred rounds with them, but they had not been regarded seriously. When, however, they were used for the annual practice of a company, their many defects were made manifest. Minor modifications were attended to, but nothing could be done to get over the fact that the mounting did not admit of any lower elevation than 42°. In consequence the trajectory was enormously high, putting really accurate fire out of the question. Moreover the change from ballistite to cordite had reduced the range by more than a thousand yards. It was a sorry business.

CHAPTER XI.

Coast Artillery Support.

CHAPTER XII.

"FORTRESS WARFARE".

(1910—1914.)

Field Service Regulations—Aviation—The Mobility of Siege Companies—The Army Manœuvres—The *Matériel*—The Personnel.

CHAPTER XII.
Field Service Regulations

Combined Training 1905 had said not a word about siege artillery or its work; it was outside the interests of the army. Port Arthur had changed all that, and the Chatham manœuvres had shown how urgent was the need for guidance. The early issue of a "Manual of Fortress Warfare" was promised, and although this promise was never literally fulfilled, the *Field Service Regulations*, which superseded *Combined Training* in 1909, devoted a whole chapter to "Siege Operations". In this the general principles to be observed in the attack and defence of fortresses were enunciated, and the relative spheres of action of the different arms defined, while for the duties of the technical branches of the service reference was made to *Garrison Artillery Training, Vol. II*, and *Military Engineering, Part II*, of which new editions followed in 1910 and 1911.

The most important new matter was the portion devoted to the higher organization of siege artillery. In the manuals of 1900 and 1906 everything above the battery had been left studiously vague; these generalities now gave place to definite directions. For the first time the position, responsibility, and duty of a siege artillery commander, and those of brigade commanders, were defined, and the chains of artillery command and communications clearly indicated.

In the work of the battery many field artillery methods made their appearance—the "clock-face" for pointing out the target, the "aiming-point" for obtaining the line of fire, "time-shrapnel ranging", etc. From the heavy batteries was borrowed the use of an "observation officer", and portable telephones were added to the equipment for communication with an observing station, which had hitherto been limited to the "vibrator transmitter" or buzzer.

The only form of aircraft in use when the manual of 1906 was published was the balloon: in the new manual "kites and any other aerial vessels" were legislated for, and the method of ranging upon a balloon or kite elaborated. Dirigibles were, however, already in existence, and dealing with them would be a much more difficult matter. The siege artillery request for one to be sent to their camp had been ignored, but at Christmas 1912, owing to a question in the House, a siege company was despatched in great haste to defend the naval magazines at Chattenden against a possible attack by them, and a method of fire against such targets had to be evolved on the spur of the moment. The lesson was taken to heart, and next year the presence of a flight of aeroplanes from the newly created Royal Flying Corps was the great feature of the siege artillery camp. It was the first experiment in observation of fire from such craft, and many difficulties were found in identifying targets and keeping them in view at the critical moment. The work was also found to be very severe on the pilot, and, generally speaking, only very partial success was achieved.

Throughout the period covered by this volume the trend of the siege artillery towards a closer connection with the field army had been continually gathering strength. Everything possible had been done to make the practice at Rhayader a real preparation for the work which might be expected of them in the field. At their home stations

THE SIEGE ARTILLERY.

CHAPTER XII.

The Mobility of Siege Companies.

companies were called upon to take full advantage of the varieties of ground in the neighbourhood for instruction in the selection of battery positions and observing stations. But they were given little assistance in moving guns or men. During the first few years after the South African War each company had had a "steam sapper",[1] but when these were withdrawn nothing was provided in their place. Efforts to obtain sanction for the hire of horses, or for their loan from the Army Service Corps, were unavailing until the prospect of the siege artillery taking part in army manœuvres in 1911 awoke the authorities to the necessity for giving them some training as mobile units. Teams hired from contractors enabled the companies to get some experience in coming into action, and in 1912 the classification practice included the reconnaissance and occupation of positions, for which the teams available were reinforced by the cobs of the range party in order to horse the battery headquarters and one section of howitzers.

In India the siege companies were much better off. During the drill season they were provided with bullocks, and were thus able to go to practice and manœuvres as really mobile units. They were also issued with 15-pr. guns for field training on heavy battery lines, and this was not found to result in any falling off in their siege work. At manœuvres and field-firing this latter was practically tested by the attack, in co-operation with the infantry, of actual works constructed by the sappers and miners.

The Army Manœuvres.

At home the work of the siege artillery was all veiled behind the purdah of the Welsh mountains. Siege artillerymen had done all that was in their power to prepare themselves for work with the field army : the time had come to familiarize generals and staffs with this addition to its

---

[1] A steam-sapper was a form of traction-engine, too cumbersome for general use on ordinary roads, and quite unsuited for taking guns into action. In this latter respect they bore a striking resemblance to the elephants of the "Bail Batteries" in India described in Volume I.

"FORTRESS WARFARE". 261

strength. With the army manœuvres of 1912[1] the opportunity came, and two out of the three companies took the field in the famous fight between Sir Douglas Haig and Sir James Grierson in East Anglia—one on each side as "Army Troops". On such an occasion it would scarcely have been seemly to have the teams led by the contractor's stablemen, with corduroys tied below the knee and billycock hats, as had been the custom when horses were hired for drill, so the companies were offered A.S.C. drivers. They rightly preferred to depend upon their own men, and with the help of neighbouring mounted units managed to get them sufficiently instructed in riding, driving, and the care of horses and harness to make a creditable appearance.

The experience was abundantly justified. Next year at practice the methods of fire and the executive orders for fighting a siege battery were brought into conformity with those of the other mobile branches; the system of communication with the observing station by a double chain of signallers was adopted; and No. 2 director superseded the observation of fire instruments with great advantage as regards weight and portability.[2] In 1914 a Mark II of greater stability and accuracy than Mark I, but still capable of being carried on a saddle, was approved for medium siege batteries.

Such was the state of the training at the end of the pre-war period, it remains to show the position as regards the *personnel* and *matériel*.

As regards the *matériel* this was very serious. It was known that Germany had included a brigade of four batteries of 15 cm. (5·9″) howitzers in each army corps, and had adopted a 21 cm. (8·2″) howitzer for the siege artillery—primarily intended for work with the field army. It was known also that Krupp had got out a design of

CHAPTER XII.

The Army Manœuvres.

The Matériel.

---

[1] It had been intended to hold manœuvres in 1911, but these had to be abandoned on account of the drought.
[2] Each of the two observation of fire instruments weighed 90 lbs., its stand 70 lbs.: the director with its stand weighed under 50 lbs.

T

262   THE SIEGE ARTILLERY.

CHAPTER XII.

The Matériel.

28 cm. (11″) howitzer which could be fired off the ground without a platform. Fortunately further reflection had shown that the decision to depend for a heavy siege howitzer upon the utilization of high-angle guns taken out of coast defences was hardly a wise one. From the first suggestion of the employment of these ponderous pieces the Chief Instructor Siege[1] had protested vigorously. They were, in the first place, not adapted for cordite, and the idea of using guns firing powder charges in modern war was fantastic. For work with the field army in the attack of the land front of a defended port, or in the defence of a captured harbour, a mobile piece would be wanted, and not one needing a concrete platform,[2] which would require time to set. Even for a formal siege, our experience in the Peninsula and Crimea, that of the Germans in France, and of the Japanese at Port Arthur, all showed the incalculable benefit to the defence of any delay in the collection of a siege train by the attackers.

The design of a heavy mobile howitzer was accordingly taken up again, and the conditions for such an equipment communicated to the armament firms.[3] The principal feature of the 9·45″ was retained in the division into "loads" on separate transporting carriages, to be drawn *en train* by a traction engine. In this case the loads were:—

>   The howitzer,
>   The bed,
>   The carriage and cradle.

The trial mounting was received in 1913, and during the winter it was put through its travelling and firing trials at Woolwich and Shoeburyness. In July 1914 it was sent to Rhayader for final trial by a siege company, and in

---

[1] Colonel (now Major-General Sir Stanley) von Donop, K.C.B., K.C.M.G., Colonel-Commandant.

[2] In 1914 the Royal Engineers had discovered a very quick-setting concrete for the platforms of the 10″ guns which were still nominally included in the siege train.

[3] The chief conditions were—calibre 9″ to 9·2″, projectile not less than 290 lbs., range not less than 10,000 yards.

"FORTRESS WARFARE".

Chapter XII.

The Matériel.

view of the famous part it was to play it may be recorded here that the report of the officer commanding[1] the company was only signed on the day before war was declared. He concluded with the following prophetic words:—"This equipment is a vast improvement on any other in use in the siege artillery, and is worth taking with an army". Sir Stanley von Donop, now Master-General of the Ordnance, lost no time in ordering sixteen more.

Before leaving the subject of siege artillery *matériel* it may be mentioned that the question of introducing a trench mortar was not overlooked. These had been improvised by the Japanese at Port Arthur, a specimen was obtained, and trials took place at home and in India. But the weight of opinion was against the introduction of an extra weapon, and it was decided in 1912 that no further action need be taken in the matter.

The Personnel.

To turn now to the position as regards the *personnel*. The supply of drafts by companies at home was a burning question throughout the Royal Garrison Artillery during the whole period covered by this volume. The siege companies were, however, much better off than the coast, since their annual turnover was generally only about 20 or 25 instead of 50 per cent. The following are the figures for the brigade in three years taken at random:—

Strength	Changes
600	106
573	143
527	119

As regards officers, the situation was unfortunately not so good, for a rule limiting their service in siege artillery to three years caused a considerable exodus in the years immediately preceding the war.

The most difficult problem was that presented by the training of the specialists, on whom the efficiency of a company so greatly depended. Each half-company con-

---

[1] Major (now Brigadier-General) G. B. Mackenzie, c.b., c.m.g., d.s.o.

CHAPTER XII.

The Personnel.

tained in peace the full number required for the fighting of the battery into which it expanded in war, so that out of a peace establishment of 582 in the brigade, the specialists numbered no less than 384. The training of so large a number became a heavy burden on the officers when field artillery methods were superimposed on those of the siege artillery, and the "tests for specialists" increased year by year in number and complexity. Layers had to show their proficiency with dial as well as cross-bar sights; telephonists had to use and test portable telephones as well as vibrator transmitters, and to signal with flag, lamp or helio; observers had to understand all the uses of observation of fire instruments and their slide-rules, as well as those of directors and field plotters. It is perhaps not to be wondered at if some questioned whether the retention of the old system of instrumental observation was justified in view of the enormous expenditure of time and energy which it entailed.

The years that had elapsed since the South African War had brought little but disappointment as regards improvement of *matériel*, but, in spite of such discouragement, the efficiency of the *personnel* had risen year by year. The appointment as brigade commanders of officers who had had experience in command of siege companies, the widening of the training, the new practice camp, the association with the field army in the manœuvres, all had played their part. And there had been no check to progress through the reversion of companies to coast defence. The siege brigade stood in 1914 as it had been reformed in 1902, and its three companies expanded according to plan into the six siege batteries which crossed the Channel in September. They took with them, it is true, but the same weapons with which their predecessors had sailed for Cape Town—but "Mother"[1] was ready.

---

[1] *Official History of the War—Military Operations—France and Belgium.* Vol. II, 1914.

PART IV.

THE COAST ARTILLERY.

CHAPTER XIII.

THE ARMAMENT.

The War-years—Technical Progress—Gun Construction—Breech Mechanisms — Mountings — Shields — Sights — Ammunition — High-Angle-Fire Guns—Anti-Aircraft Guns.

THE South African War neither had, nor obviously could have, any such direct lessons for the coast artillery as it had brought to the other branches. And yet its influence was far-reaching, for it brought to the nation a realization of the general hostility abroad, and of the weakness of our coast defences.

By an unparalleled display of sea-power we were able to defy this hostility during the war-years. But the German Naval Law of 1900 had for its avowed object a challenge to British supremacy at sea, and foreign naval manœuvres showed plainly enough that attacks upon defended ports were looked upon as feasible. The first thing to be done was to look to their defences, and fortunately the coast artillery—more far-seeing than the other branches—had already decided upon the armament required. It will be convenient, therefore, to give here some description of these new weapons before relating the developments in organization and training which followed.

The first to reach the service was the 12-pr. Q.F. adopted in the last years of the XIXth century as told in the preceding volume. It was soon followed by the 6" B.L. Mark VII and the 9·2" B.L. Mark X—weapons which were destined to remain the backbone of coast defence not only throughout the period covered by this volume, but practically unchanged until the time of writing. For some

CHAPTER. XIII.

The War-Years.

THE COAST ARTILLERY.

CHAPTER XIII.

The War-Years.

years, however, they were few and far between. Coast defences can rarely keep pace with naval armaments, and a greater war than that between Britain and Boer was to provide its warning before the rearmament of our coast batteries was tackled in earnest: at the turn of the century their condition was no exception to the above general principle. The manual of 1899 legislated for a heterogenous collection of muzzle and breech-loaders, quick-firers and smooth-bores—[1] 12·5″, 12″, 11″, 10″, 9·2,″, 9″, 8″, 7″, 6″, 5″, 4·7″, 4″—80-prs., 64-prs., 40-prs., 32-prs., 12-prs., 6-prs., 3-prs.—mounted upon every variety of carriage and slide—"common standing", "casemate", "dwarf", "small-port", "central-pivot", "barbette", "pedestal", "Moncrieff", "disappearing". The great 100-ton guns still took their part in annual practice at Malta and Gibraltar, although the famous turret with its 80-ton guns had disappeared from Dover pier. Among such antiquated armament as the majority of these the appearance of the new types—if only as specimens—was a great encouragement to the coast artillery, for it was proof positive that they were at last to be furnished with weapons worthy of their skill.

Technical Progress.

And it was a great stimulus to interest in technical matters. A feature of the period is the constant flow of suggestions for improvements in every detail of the equipments. That inventive talent should be shown by artillery officers was no new experience: its spread, not only to assistant instructors and armament artificers, but also to the rank and file of companies, was remarkable.[2] And almost as surprising was the change in attitude of the experts, who showed themselves sympathetic towards the amateurs, and ready to assist with the resources at their

---

[1] For most of these there were several marks, differing widely in their most important features. There were, for instance, seven such marks of the 9·2″ in use.

[2] It was only in 1901 that the provision for illiterate gunners dictating their answers in the gunnery examination dropped out of the regulations.

THE ARMAMENT. 269

command, in perfecting the details of such designs as showed promise. Change of heart was apparent too in the readiness of the authorities to admit that every detail of an equipment might not be equally suitable to all stations, and to allow some discretion in the adaptation of patterns to local requirements.[1]

It is suggestive that the vast majority of the proposals received were based on tactical requirements. The demand for rapidity and accuracy of fire led to larger scales on sights and elevating gear, the placing of dials and firing gear in the most convenient positions for the numbers using them, the addition of "clickers" for work in the dark, and so forth. Time and again suggestions are based upon the plea "to facilitate the service of the gun", or "for the greater convenience of the layer".

At the same time it must be confessed that the increased complexity of the equipments and the insistence on accurate adjustment of the various gears, led in some cases to a tendency to leave such work to inspectors of ordnance machinery and armament artificers. Steps were taken to impress upon regimental officers their responsibility in such matters, and to provide them with the means of carrying out their duty.

These inspectors of ordnance machinery and artificers had formerly belonged to the Royal Artillery, but just before the end of the XIXth Century they had been absorbed by the newly formed Army Ordnance Department and Corps. Their loss had been much regretted at the time, and their return to the Regiment was recommended by the Owen Committee—but nothing came of it.

Owing to the demands of the Navy for more powerful weapons the whole question of gun construction was being

CHAPTER. XIII.

Technical Progress.

Gun Construction.

---

[1] This attention to local conditions occasionally produced unexpected results. Yard-scale-drums had to be engraved to suit the prevailing temperatures of the stations, and these were therefore classified as having standard temperatures of 80°, 70°, or 60°. This did not, however, at all suit some of those in the first category, which were setting up as health resorts, and indignant protests were received against such an aspersion upon their climate.

CHAPTER XIII.

Gun Construction.

actively investigated during the closing years of the XIXth Century. The effect of various alloys—carbon, nickel, chromium—on the steel was explored, and nickel-steel was very generally adopted for all parts except the jacket. Wire construction, introduced in 1890, and at first applied only to the breech portion, was gradually extended until it covered the tube from breech to muzzle. The length of the guns was also greatly increased, the early marks of the 6″ and 9·2″ having a length of 25 and 26 calibres, while Mark VII of the former and Mark X of the latter had risen to 45 and 46 calibres respectively.

These long wired guns, however, developed a distinct tendency to "droop" until a way was found of providing longitudinal strength in the exterior parts by various devices in building up—breech rings and bushes, stepped shoulders, cannelured rings, shrunk and screwed collars, etc. In order to facilitate repair "Inner A Tubes" extending the whole length of the bore were introduced. They were tapered and forced into position, and thus differed from the "Liners" which were merely a mechanical fit, and so contributed nothing to the strength of the construction.

For upwards of half a century all English guns had been rifled with an increasing twist. But the increased length of bore and higher velocity rendered the continual re-engraving of the driving band due to the change of pitch undesirable, and at the same time the adoption of "M.D." cordite, with its slighter erosive effect, rendered the reduction in the inclination of the grooves at the commencement unnecessary. A reversion to the "uniform" twist was therefore decided upon in 1904, and about the same time a return from the "hook section" grooves introduced with the first B.L. guns to the "plain section" of the later R.M.L.—further modified by rounding off the corners a few years later. With these changes in the rifling came many alterations in the driving bands. A gas-check had been added with the introduction of cordite, which, in addition to sealing the rush of gas in a worn gun,

THE ARMAMENT. 271

prevented over-ramming.[1] Various modifications in the extent and depth of serrations followed, until finally the "Hump" band was adopted for the 9·2″.

CHAPTER. XIII.

The use of metal cartridge cases in quick-firing guns had rendered an obturator unnecessary, and had thus made possible single-motion breech mechanisms.[2] But with the increase in the size of the quick-firers from 12-pr. to 4·7″, and then 6″, and the demand for higher ballistics, involving heavier charges, a reaction set in. In addition to the objections of weight and cost, the use of metallic cartridge cases precluded an enlarged chamber, and therefore, with the large charges now called for, necessitated cartridges of unmanageable length. At the same time the invention of the "Welin" stepped breech screw made it possible to use a de Bange obturator on a single-motion mechanism. Thus came about the type of B.L. gun exemplified by the 6″ VII, which were able to hold their own—and more—in rapidity of fire with Q.F. guns of the same calibre.

Breech Mechanisms.

Single-motion mechanisms obviously called for a quicker firing arrangement than the old locks, and a new pattern for both electrical and percussion firing, on the lines of the strikers of the quick-firing guns, became the normal type. But some serious accidents showed that percussion tubes might be set off if the breech was slammed, while there were constant complaints of missfires with the electric tubes. Rather than suffer the delays caused by the missfires, with their paralysing effect on the training, some high authorities even advocated the banishment of electricity from the gun-floor altogether. After some years of con-

---

[1] "Augmenting strips" were used for this purpose with the previous pattern of band, and "Augmenting rings" with 9·2″ and gas-check bands.

[2] With the cylindrical breech screw four motions were required to unseat the obturator, unlock the screw, withdraw it, and swing it clear; and in heavy guns some form of gearing was necessary. In the Q.F. guns (except 3 and 6-prs.) the breech screw was partly conical, thus allowing of its being inserted and turned by one continuous motion of a lever.

272   THE COAST ARTILLERY.

Chapter XIII.

Breech Mechanisms.

troversy, however, the system of making time allowances for misfires at class firing was abolished, and the results proved that by careful drill and preparation for action missfires could be almost entirely eliminated.

At the same time there were continuous efforts to obtain a more reliable gear. A Mark III "pistol grip" which enabled the tube or primer and the circuit generally to be tested immediately before firing, and a liberal allowance of expendable cable in place of the armoured cable (which had been difficult to repair and too valuable to throw away) did much to improve affairs, and electric firing remained the normal method, with percussion in reserve, should the electric fail.

Mountings.

Up to almost the end of the XIXth century the design of mountings for the fixed armament had shown no change in principle since "garrison standing carriages" had been superseded by those on "traversing platforms" in the Crimean period. Wood had given place to iron, and there had, of course, been many improvements in detail, especially in the control of the recoil, but the gun and carriage still ran back up a sloping slide, and ran up again by their own weight. In 1894, however, a new vista was opened by the appointment of Colonel Sir George Clarke[1] as Superintendent of the Royal Carriage Department. He saw that the weak spot—tactically—of the coast artillery was their slowness of fire, and he set himself to overcome the technical obstacles to a quickening up. The result was soon seen in the "pedestal" mounting for the 12-pr. Q.F. illustrated in the last volume, the principle of which was further developed in the heavier quick-firers—4·7″ and 6″—which were coming into the service in the last years of the century. But by the irony of fate the very excellence of these mountings led to the restoration of breech-loaders to favour. For it became evident that the virtues of the heavier quick-

---

[1] Colonel the Lord Sydenham of Combe, G.C.S.I., G.C.M.G., G.C.I.E., G.B.E., F.R.S. d. 1933.

THE ARMAMENT. 273

firers were due, not to the brass cartridges from which they derived their title, but to their single-motion breech mechanisms and their superb mountings—both of which could be applied equally well to guns firing bare charges. This extension of the principle of "axial recoil" to the medium and heavy mountings of the fixed armament of coast artillery was the great achievement of the period under review, and its first examples—the Mark II "C.P." mounting of the 6″ B.L. Mark VII and the Mark V "Barbette" mounting of the 9·2″ B.L. Mark X—still hold the field. Some account of their principal features is therefore called for here.

The general features of both were the same. The gun was carried in a cradle through which it recoiled axially, checked by a hydraulic buffer, and returned to the firing position by recuperator springs. The cradle was mounted by trunnions upon a carriage which revolved upon a pivot. The pivot fitted into a pedestal sunk in a pit. Stability, essential to accuracy, was ensured by the massive pedestal embedded in a concrete emplacement. Continuous laying, essential to rapidity, was made possible by attaching the sights, elevating and traversing gears to the non-recoiling portion of the mounting. Ease of service, allowing of reduction of *personnel*, was provided for by the use of ball-bearings, perfect balance, and the placing of hand-wheels, etc., in the most convenient positions for those working the various gears.

In the 9·2″ mounting there were some differences owing to the great size and weight. In the recuperator, for instance, compressed air[1] took the place of springs, owing to difficulties in the manufacture of springs of the size required. And there was hydraulic loading gear, in which the energy generated by the recoil was utilized to work hoists which lifted the round, first to a trolley on the shell-pit shield, and then from the trolly to the loading tray.

---

[1] The only previous use was in disappearing and high-angle mountings.

CHAPTER XIII.

Mountings.

The ever-increasing demand for smartness in the service of heavy guns, which was such a feature of the period, necessitated many modifications. Equalisation of pressure in the accumulators had to be speeded up. Automatic flaps to cover the opening in the shell-pit shield through which the loading hoist emerged were no sooner added than the men slipped upon them, and when they were covered with lead to stop this they wouldn't fold back. Then the lever controlling the rear-hoist had to be made fool-proof to prevent dropping the shell into the pit. There was scarcely a year from 1904 to 1914 which did not bring some modification of the gear—if it were only with the object of minimising the intolerable din made by the shield doors and trolley wheels.

Shields.

Protection for guns and gunners from the enemy's fire had in the past been obtained from the work, the guns firing through ports in casemates, or embrasures in high earthern parapets. With the introduction of the modern type of mounting which we have been considering the duty of protection was transferred from the work to the mounting which was provided with shields. A curved vertical shield attached to the front of the mounting covered the numbers working at the gun, while a circular horizontal pit-shield sufficiently thick to keep out shell splinters protected those working below, and the hoists and gear. There was, however, considerable discussion as to the value of shields, for a light shield besides increasing the size of the target would act as a screen for bursting shell which might otherwise have passed harmlessly by. To keep out anything more than light shell and splinters they must be very heavy, and for this reason it was decided not to provide any for the 7·5″ guns supplied to India.

Sights.

With the new mountings there came revolutionary changes in the sighting arrangements. The tangent and fore-sights, carried on the gun itself, had, like the carriages, been unchanged in principle since the smooth-bore days. Their transfer to the mounting allowed of the application of entirely new principles. The rocking-bar sight took the place of the old tangent and fore-sights, and since the movements of the target were confined to the surface of the sea, and the height of the guns above this, and their position on the map were accurately known, they could be layed both for elevation and direction by mechanical means, and under certain conditons by sights which found their own elevation for range. The new mountings were thus furnished with :—

Rocking-bar and automatic sights for direct laying.[1]

Elevation-indicators and traversing-arcs for indirect laying.

The "*Rocking-Bar*" or "*Bar and Drum*" sights were on the same general lines as those already described when speaking of the rearmament of the field artillery in Chapter V, and require no further description here.

The "*Automatic*" sights, which, as told in the last volume, were just emerging from the chrysalis stage at the turn of the century, assumed great importance during the period we are now considering. Their essential feature was a mechanism which united the motions of the gun and sight in such a way that the act of directing the sight on to the target gave the gun the correct elevation for the range. They thus had the great advantage of rendering every gun its own range-finder, and so eliminated many of the delays and errors which arose in taking ranges, transmitting them to the guns, and setting them upon the sights. On the other hand they suffered from the disadvantages inherent in all instruments depending upon the depression principle,[2] which did much to curtail their usefulness. This was due to the fact that a comparatively small movement of the sight-bar governed a large movement of the gun, so that any error in the laying was multiplied, and at a rapidly increasing ratio, as the range

---

[1] Usually one on each side. Combined sights were tried but proved unsatisfactory.

[2] See chapter XVI.

276 THE COAST ARTILLERY.

CHAPTER XIII.
Sights.

lengthened. They required also absolute accuracy in the axis of the pivot, so that central-pivot and barbette mountings had to be fitted with means for re-levelling, or with correctional gear, and in the lighter natures with counterweights to counteract the effect of men stepping on or off the platform.

Tide-levers provided a means of compensating for alterations in height above sea-level, caused by the rise and fall of the tide, by tilting the cam slightly to the front or rear. Variations in the shooting were provided for by *error-of-the-day drums*. Clickers were a later addition, to allow of corrections being put on in the dark. Attractive as the idea was, it drifted on for years without any definite conclusion being reached. There were those who objected on the score of accuracy, since the value of the "click" could only be correct at one range; and those who maintained that anything of the sort was unnecessary, since the ranges in night-firing were so short, and the periods of fire so brief, that no corrections were required. Eventually a Mark II auto-sight was introduced in 1912-13 for 6″ and below, the principal feature of which was the addition of a mechanism giving "audible and sensible" clicks corresponding to the divisions on the scale. But discussion as to the right value of the click was still going on in 1914.

For indirect laying the coast artillery had the great advantage of being able to employ simple mechanical appliances for giving both elevation and direction. These consisted of *elevation-indicators*[1] and *traversing-arcs*. The former were in the form of circular plates, graduated in yards, carried on a horizontal shaft which was revolved by an arc attached to the cradle. By this means quadrant elevation could be given to the gun without the use of the sights. The traversing-arcs in combination with a pointer on the carriage allowed of the gun being directed horizon-

---

[1] It may perhaps be noted here that the Mark I elevation-indicator introduced in 1900 with the 6″ mounting described above has only been superseded by Mark II in 1932.

THE ARMAMENT. 277

tally to any point of the compass. The graduations ran counter-clockwise so that when the pointer was at zero the gun was pointing due north, and when at 270° due east, and were termed "trainings" to distinguish them from "bearings".

Before leaving the subjects of sights mention must be made of a complication peculiar to the coast artillery, namely the special graduations necessitated by the variety of charges and projectiles. Yard-scale-drums had to be provided with different range strips for the full charges used in war, the $\frac{3}{4}$ and $\frac{1}{2}$ charges used at practice, also for the sub-calibre guns and aiming rifles. Similarly the yard-scale plates of the elevation-indicators were issued plain and graduated locally for each charge. For auto-sights separate cams had to be provided for each charge, and those for sub-calibre guns and aiming rifles required special adjusting levers in addition. Finally the adoption of four-calibre-radius heads for 9·2″ projectiles brought another yard-scale ring, plate, and cam.

Great as was the increase in the power of the guns, and the facility of working them, brought about by the improvements we have been considering, the progress in ammunition kept pace with it.

Modified Cordite (M.D. and M.D.T.) approved for the service in 1902, contained a considerably smaller proportion of nitro-glycerine than cordite Mark I, and thanks to its introduction, and various changes in the making up of cartridges, especially in the igniters, the reduction in erosion due to the lower temperature more than doubled the life of the rifling. Allusion has already been made to its effect in bringing about a change in the system of rifling, and a reaction against the use of metallic cartridge cases.

Turning now to *projectiles*, it may in the first place be noted that *case shot* had dropped out;[1] that powder-filled *common* had given place to *lyddite;* and that *shrapnel*

CHAPTER. XIII.

Sights.

Ammunition.

---

[1] Except in a few cases for anti-torpedo-craft defence, chapter XV.

CHAPTER XIII.

Ammunition.

were now confined to the equipment of guns which could be brought to bear in defence of the land fronts of fortresses. The real task of coast artillery projectiles was the attack of armour, and this had become a very much more arduous one with the introduction of hardened steel,[1] with which most modern warships were armoured by the beginning of the XXth century. The power of resistance of these plates, and the action on them of projectiles of various types, were little understood during the first decade at any rate. But there could be no doubt that they were immensely stronger than the armour previously in use, and that the old-fashioned projectiles were incapable of dealing with them. To compete with the new armour there was introduced between 1903 and 1905 a new type of *armour-piercing shell*, to take the place both of the A.P. shot and the old pattern A.P. shell. The new projectiles were of greatly improved material,[2] but their special feature was the "cap" of iron or soft steel fixed over the point, with the object of helping it to get through the hard surface unbroken.

When penetration, even with capped shell, was beyond the power of the gun it was thought that the "smashing" effect of heavy shell might be useful, and with this idea a *common-pointed* shell was introduced for heavy naval guns. It differed from the original "C.P." in having a specially hardened point for the attack of armour, and it had a much larger capacity for the bursting charge than the new armour-piercing shell. Later a "cap" was added to it also, but both were confined to naval service until the last years before the Great War.

However heavily armoured a vessel might be, there must be a very large area which could only be lightly protected and was very vulnerable to shell fire. For the

---

[1] "Harveyed", "Krupp Cemented" (K.C.), and "Krupp Non-Cemented" (K.N.C.).

[2] An alloy containing, in addition to carbon, chromium combined with one or more of the following elements—nickel, manganese, tungsten, molybdenum.

THE ARMAMENT. 279

attack of these portions a steel high explosive shell—*common lyddite*—took the place of the old powder-filled common shell.

The possibility of using high-explosive bursting charges for guns—as distinct from howitzers—had not been accepted by the Royal Artillery until the very end of the XIXth century, and for some years after the introduction of the new armour-piercing and common-pointed shell described above they remained powder-filled, although the common-lyddite were in general use. It was thought that a high-explosive bursting charge could not be carried through armour, and there was also apprehension of the hardened points causing spontaneous cracks. With the adoption of caps the first objection was removed, but a metal container for the charge was insisted upon, although this entailed a removable base.

With light shells the difficulty was in the opposite direction—it was found almost impossible to obtain any certainty of detonation. In consequence the only projectiles in the service for the 12-prs. during the greater part of the period were the old pattern powder-filled shell. It was only in the last few years that a satisfactory pattern of fuze for lyddite was evolved.

The final development in the designs of projectiles which need be mentioned here was the adoption of a four-calibre-radius head for the 9·2″ in 1911. This important departure from previous practice was only made after extended trials had shown unmistakably its superiority in range over the two-calibre-radius. But the new projectiles necessitated alterations in the lifts and loading arrangements generally, involving a further series of trials, so that it was not until 1913 that approval could be given for the modifications to Mark V mounting to enable the new shell to be used.

Pointed shell of course demanded base fuzes, and obviously these could not be of the same simple nature as the direct-action fuzes used with nose-fuzed shell. Their design, like that of graze fuzes, had to include arrange-

CHAPTER. XIII.
Ammunition.

CHAPTER XIII.

Ammunition.

ments to guard against jars in handling, rebound action in the bore, and creeping and boring in flight. Additional difficulties were that safety pins could not be employed, and that the fuze was exposed to the full force of the powder gas. For capped shell a new fuze, "Bronze, Large, No. 15" was approved in 1905. The "Fuze, Base, Large No. 11" and "Medium No. 12" for heavy and medium guns respectively, which had been introduced in 1895, were continued for uncapped shell. In 1909 new patterns of Nos. 11, 12 and 15, entirely different in design from the previous marks, were introduced, and finally in 1911 "Bronze, Large, No. 16" for capped shell when filled lyddite.

With the nose-fuzed shell "lyddite common" the fuzes used were "Direct Action, Impact"—No. 13 with 6″ and above, No. 18 with 4·7″ and below.

Before closing this account of the chief developments of coast artillery armament during the period 1899—1914 mention must be made of some special features.

High-Angle-Fire Guns.

"High-angle" or "High-angle-fire" guns had been introduced in the 90's to meet the threat of bombardment from ranges at which the side armour of the attacking ships would be proof against direct fire. In such cases it was thought that the attack of their decks would prevent them anchoring. The muzzle-loading guns originally provided for the purpose could not fire cordite however, and with the improvement in naval armament their range was insufficient. Early in the XXth century, therefore, the utilization of the earlier marks of 9·2″ B.L. was taken up. The conditions laid down were that they should be capable of fire at all ranges between 6,000 and 15,000 with an angle of descent of not less than 30°. Eventually Marks IV and VI were fitted with continuous motion breech mechanisms, and given mountings admitting of elevation up to 45°, the special feature of which was the use of hydraulic power to return the gun into the firing position, to elevate and depress, and to carry the projectile from the emplacement floor into the breech of the gun.

THE ARMAMENT.

Chapter XIII.

Anti-Aircraft Guns.[1]

In 1912 the protection of localities against attack from the air became urgent. The design of 4″ and 3″ equipments for the purpose was taken up by the Admiralty and War Office respectively, and the use of the existing pompoms was decided upon as a temporary measure. Twenty of these were accordingly adapted for the purpose, half on their field carriages, modified to allow of 75° elevation and 50° traverse, half on 3-pr. pedestals giving 80° elevation and all-round traverse.

In 1914 the new 3″ 20-cwt. on high-angle mounting was approved. It was a reversion to the wedge or sliding block system which had dropped out with the 3 and 6-prs., but with a novel feature in its semi-automatic action. The mounting gave 90° elevation and all-round traverse.

Tracer shell had meanwhile been introduced for 6″ and below, and the various adjuncts were not neglected. Sights, predictors, range-finders, sensitive fuzes to act on fabric, and the explosives required for igniting gas, all were made the subject of investigation.

---

[1] See chapter IX as regards anti-aircraft guns for the field army.

CHAPTER XIV.

THE SOUTH AFRICAN INFLUENCE.

(1902—1904.)

Organization — Practice — The Centenary Cup — Anti-Torpedo-Craft Defence—India.

CHAPTER XIV.
Organization.

THROUGHOUT the various re-organizations which followed each other in such rapid succession during the closing years of the XIXth century the organization of the garrison artillery remained in three Divisions—Eastern, Southern, and Western—although there were changes in the allotment of companies to the respective divisions. The South African War showed, however, that an organization under which certain stations at home and abroad were reserved for each division was not only inconvenient as regards reliefs, but also unworkable when it came to mobilization. An so a special army order in November 1901 abolished the divisions and numbered the companies in one series from 1 to 105. Unfortunately instead of following the example of the field artillery and adopting the principle of seniority the numbering was according to position on the roster for service abroad.[1]

---

[1] In 1912 it was suggested that the companies should be re-numbered in order of seniority, and that they should revert to the title of battery. Originally in *companies* the title of *battery* was adopted in 1859, but changed back to company in the garrison artillery in 1891, with the idea of avoiding confusion between the units and the works they manned. The individual opinions of all lt.-colonels and company commanders on the two proposals were called for in 1914, and the great majority were in favour of both. But it was too late.

THE SOUTH AFRICAN INFLUENCE. 283

For administrative purposes the companies were divided into six groups, affiliated to the existing depôts, and the administrative duties hitherto performed by the officers commanding Royal Artillery in the Divisions were transferred to the lt.-colonels commanding Militia and Volunteer Artillery in the Districts in which the depôts were situated.

CHAPTER. XIV.

Organization.

Far more important to the coast artillery than this purely regimental reorganization was the famous "Army Corps Scheme", which also came into force on the 1st January 1902, for it recognized "Fortresses and Defended Ports"[1] for the first time as separate organizations, in addition to, and side by side with, the field army. The scheme did not go far enough in this direction, for all correspondence from the fortresses had still to go through the army corps, and the staff of these had neither the local nor the technical knowledge required for dealing with questions of coast defence; but it showed plainly the change of opinion regarding the importance of coast defence which had been brought about by the hostility abroad.

At the same time an Inspector-General of Royal Garrison Artillery was appointed. This was a special creation, for the Inspector-Generalship of the Royal Artillery had been abolished in 1889, and the new Inspectorate of all arms had not yet been heard of. The garrison artillery was thus alone in possessing an Inspector, and Major-General F. G. Slade,[2] the officer selected, realized that at this period his functions went far beyond the usual duties of such an office. His position at headquarters enabled him to insist upon due attention being paid to the important place of coast artillery in the scheme of Imperial

---

[1] FORTRESSES—Harwich, Thames and Medway, Dover, Portsmouth, Plymouth, Portland, Milford Haven, Cork Harbour.
DEFENDED PORTS—Aberdeen, Tay, Forth, Tyne, Wear, Tees, Humber, Newhaven, Falmouth, Scilly Isles, Bristol, Cardiff, Swansea, Mersey, Clyde, Dublin, Belfast, Cork Harbour, Lough Swilly, Berehaven.

[2] Lieut.-General F. G. Slade, C.B. d. 1910.

284 THE COAST ARTILLERY.

CHAPTER XIV.
Organization.

Defence. In his overseas tours he was able to impress upon governors, naval commanders-in-chief, and civil authorities—as well as upon general officers—the possibility of attack, and the necessity for organizing the means of defence. His visits did much also to reassure coast artillerymen in distant garrisons where, under the influence of climate and isolation, they were apt to fancy themselves forgotten.

Practice.

Naval tactics had not greatly altered since the 90's. It was still generally held that, in the event of a fleet undertaking a direct attack upon a defended port, the ships would endeavour to run in as close as possible in order to overwhelm the forts with the volume of fire from their secondary armament. It followed that the task of the heavy guns of the coast artillery was to stop the attacking vessels at such a range that their secondary armament would be ineffective. Ships steaming directly towards the defences would cover the distance between 14,000 yards—the extreme range of the 9·2″—to 2,000 yards in less than half-an-hour. To disable them in that time would require rapidity, as well as accuracy, of fire.

The first to see the full implication of this was Major-General J. F. Owen, when commanding the Royal Artillery at Malta. He realized that the element of time must be given more prominence in the practice, and in 1899[1] he proposed that "hits per minute" should be the criterion of excellence. As may be imagined such a revolutionary change was not received with enthusiasm in all quarters. There came warnings that this speeding-up would engender the idea that ranging could be neglected, and would end in "reckless gunnery". Auto-sights, which had been expected to solve all difficulties of ranging,

---

[1] "High-speed" targets were introduced in 1901 to take the place of all towing targets except "Record". A set consisted of a "Portsmouth Pilot" to support the tow-rope, followed by a "Hong-Kong" modified to show a spray, and behind that again a "Portsmouth Pilot". The height of the imaginary ship represented by the target was assumed to be 15 feet, except for the anti-torpedo guns for which it was 4 feet.

THE SOUTH AFRICAN INFLUENCE. 285

had, like the position-finder, only brought many new problems. There were two schools of thought as to whether heavy and medium guns provided with these sights should be fought, like other guns of the primary armament, by battery commanders, or whether each gun should be allowed to fire independently. And there was a very general tendency to use them at ranges entirely unsuitable to the height at which the guns were mounted. But their use had drawn attention to the importance of accurate laying, and the training of the layers was taken up seriously, additional tests added to qualification, and elaborate diagrams introduced with the object of recording the value of each individual.

"Station" and "regimental" practice had been added in the last century—the former to test the equipment, the latter to familiarise all ranks with the various natures of guns and mountings—and in 1902 their combination for the training of fire commands was sanctioned. For such training the use of aiming-rifles was found invaluable, for they enabled forts from which practice with service ammunition was impossible to take part, thus exercising the chain of command and the communications. Introduced with the ordinary rifle calibre ($\cdot 303''$) for 12-prs., they had proved invaluable in the quick-firing courses at Shoeburyness, and their use was soon extended. Their calibre grew to $\cdot 45''$ and then to $1''$, with which observation of fire was found to be quite possible up to a thousand yards.

It was, however, the "competitive" which still dominated the practice, although voices were already being raised in denunciation of the way in which the education of all ranks was subordinated to preparation for this contest. Many lieut.-colonels and majors in particular resented the way in which the competitive denied them their only opportunity of training their units in the main object of their existence. The elaborate rules for calculating the figure of merit, and the artificial method of "estimating" hits, came in also for much criticism. No serious improve-

Chapter XIV.

Practice

The Centenary Cup.

ment was, however, possible so long as the "Centenary Cup" was shot for.

This cup had been presented to the Regiment by Major-General F. T. Lloyd, c.b.—then D.A.G., R.A.—in 1895 to commemorate the centenary of the appointment of the first holder of that office. It was to be a challenge cup for good shooting, to be awarded in alternate years to the best shooting battery of field or company of garrison artillery. But in 1901 the field artillery had given up competitive practice, so that for the next four years it had been confined to the companies of garrison artillery.

It had undoubtedly done much to stimulate interest in shooting in all ranks, but, as the years passed, the spirit of emulation had risen to such a pass that the year's work of a company had practically come to have but one end and aim—the performance of a single group for "the cup". By the end of 1905 it was plain that the conditions of practice could no longer be assimilated sufficiently to make the competition a fair one without sacrificing the training for war. It was decided that the competition must cease, and in accordance with the wishes of the donor, the Centenary Cup was handed over to the School of Gunnery, as the most fitting resting place for such a trophy. The presentation was made with due formality in June 1907, but to the regret of all General Lloyd's health prevented his being present.

During the years in which it had been shot for the Cup had been won by the following batteries and companies:—

Royal Horse and Royal Field Artillery—52/R.F.A., D/R.H.A., 81/R.F.A., 95/R.F.A.

Royal Garrison Artillery—1/Southern, 31/Southern, 40/Southern, 27/R.G.A., 13/R.G.A., 13/R.G.A., 49/R.G.A.

Whatever opinions there might be as to the probability of an enemy's fleet attempting such a deliberate attack upon any of our coast defences as we have been considering so long as we held the command of the sea, it

THE SOUTH AFRICAN INFLUENCE. 287

was accepted that no possible naval superiority could ensure immunity from raids by torpedo-craft. To meet this danger the coast artillery had pinned their faith upon the light quick-firer, and at the end of the century special courses for these had been instituted at Shoeburyness as described in the previous volume.

CHAPTER. XIV.

Anti-Torpedo-Craft Defence.

It soon became evident that there were two great problems to be solved—how the fire should be distributed, and how far it could be controlled. The object was plain and simple—to make every vessel the target of a continuous well-directed fire from the moment it appeared in the illuminated area until it was sunk or disabled. But the best method of attaining this object was hard to determine, although many ingenious systems were suggested, and keenly debated. What was plain was that every preparation must be made in advance—an alarm circuit from a forward look-out to the guns, the guns loaded, tide-levers periodically adjusted, and so forth. The provision of reliefs for the detachments, so that men might be kept on the guns, was the stumbling block. There was no doubt as to the advisability of providing such reliefs, but the men could not be found without an increase to the artillery garrisons, which was at the time out of the question. As a compromise "Special Service Sections" were formed of Volunteer artillerymen who agreed to serve for a month in specified coast defences in case of emergency. It was also accepted that when hostilities became imminent the detachments of the light-quick-firers must be quartered in the work, with a look-out on every gun, who could open fire at once on any vessel appearing in the illuminated area.

In India, thanks to the insistence of Lord Roberts, the armament of the coast defences had for a time been actually ahead of that at home. He was equally solicitous regarding the adequacy of the artillery garrisons, but here the difficulties were much more than financial. Garrison artillerymen were required for heavy and siege batteries, and for "inland defences", as well as for coast batteries,

India.

288   THE COAST ARTILLERY.

CHAPTER XIV.
India.

and now a new demand was coming for men to man the guns of the "frontier defences" which had been commenced in the 90's to meet the Russian menace. There were proposals to turn the Bombay "Marine Battalion" into gunners; to raise an Eurasian Militia Artillery; and to increase the European Volunteer Artillery, of which very efficient corps existed in the principal defended ports. The objections to an increase of native artillery were great, but so serious did Lord Roberts consider the shortage of garrison artillery in India that he was prepared to advocate it. Eventually, however, the situation was relieved by a large increase of Lascars, a class who, since the time of the Company's Army, had been attached to the artillery to assist in the lesser duties connected with the service of the guns, and had proved useful and reliable. The discussions regarding a remedy for the shortage of coast artillerymen had had one good result in bringing together, to a degree rarely attained elsewhere, all those interested in questions of defence—the Navy, the Royal Indian Marine,[1] the Army, the Civil Authorities, and the Mercantile Community.

---

[1] Now the Royal Indian Navy.

CHAPTER XV.

THE MANCHURIAN INFLUENCE.

(1904-1910.)

Port Arthur—Naval Developments—The Esher Committee—The Wood Committee—The Slade Committee—The Owen Committee—Rearmament — Practice — Calibration — Range-finding — Communications — Anti-Torpedo-Craft Defence — Night Firing — Electric Lights—The School of Gunnery—Defence Exercises—The Bacon Committee—The Examination Service—India—The Manuals.

THE influence of the South African War on the coast artillery was only indirect: that of the war between Japan and Russia in 1904-5 affected the coast artillery even more directly than the other branches of the Regiment. For it furnished the first example since Sevastopol of the attack and defence—by land and sea, by fleet and army—of a great fortress and naval base. During half a century all had been theory, here at last were facts. And no time was lost by the War Office in investigating their application to the circumstances of the British Empire. While war was still raging in the East the Esher Committee was presenting its recommendations for the reconstitution of the War Office, and a whole string of lesser committees were soon investigating the organization, the armament, and the training of the coast artillery :—

The "Wood" Committee on the Promotion of Officers.
The "Slade"   ,,   ,,   ,, Maintenance of Overseas Garrisons.
The "Owen"   ,,   ,,   ,, Armament.
The "Stopford" ,,   ,,   ,, School of Gunnery.
The "Bacon"   ,,   ,,   ,, Instruction in Naval Matters.

Before examining the work of these committees it will, however, be well to glance at the momentous developments

CHAPTER XV.

Naval Developments.

in naval affairs which were about to change the whole position for the coast artillery.

In 1905 Sir John Fisher[1] was appointed First Sea Lord; the "Dreadnought" was laid down; and all mine defences were removed from defended ports. In 1906 Germany brought in a new Navy Bill, and our naval strength was concentrated in home waters. The world-wide disposition of the British fleet was disappearing, and the scattered outposts of the Empire became liable to attacks of longer duration than heretofore. The question for the coast artillery was what form these attacks would take.

The Japanese Navy, after a very brief experience of engaging the shore batteries at Port Arthur, had taken good care not again to come within range of their guns. It seemed certain that, with the prospect of having to fight a relieving fleet, no Admiral would risk anything that would affect the value of his ships at sea. Such direct attacks on coast batteries as were considered in the last chapter need no longer be anticipated. But the new type of war-ship imposed on all nations by the Dreadnought had made bombardment possible without appreciable loss of power or risk of damage. For the number of heavy guns carried was three times as many as before, and so a fleet could spare a thousand rounds for the destruction of a dockyard without appreciably depleting the magazines or shortening the individual lives of the guns. Moreover the increased range of the guns would in many cases render it possible to carry out such bombardment from water on which the land batteries could not bear. There might be cases where the volume of mercantile shipping in a port, or the national importance of local industry, would make it worth while to send in a cruiser. And the probability of raids by torpedo-craft, of which so much has already been said, had become a certainty. Moreover the ideas held as to the radius of action of such craft would have to be greatly enlarged, and their arrival might

---

[1] Admiral of the Fleet the Lord Fisher of Kilverstone, G.C.B., O.M., G.C.V.O., LL.D., d. 1920.

THE MANCHURIAN INFLUENCE. 291

be expected before any declaration of war. Port Arthur had provided also an object-lesson in the sinking of larger vessels laden with stones and cement to block a channel: such ventures by "blockers" must be anticipated and provided against, and also the employment of vessels of considerable size as "boom-smashers" where booms formed part of the defence.[1]

The strength of our coast defences would have to be increased, but if due regard was to be paid to economy their strength must be limited in accordance with the nature and scale of the attack to which they might reasonably be liable. It was established that this was a matter on which the Admiralty would provide the War Office with the necessary information regarding all defended ports.

Among the many important reforms due to the Esher committee, there was one which affected the coast artillery very closely. For half-a-century this branch had suffered under the dual control in matters of defence which had existed since the abolition of the Board of Ordnance. In the War Office reconstitution adopted on the recommendation of the committee all questions of coast defence—except the policy of defending particular ports, and the strength of attack to be guarded against—were allotted to the Master-General of the Ordnance, whose department was divided into directorates of Artillery and Fortification to enable him to deal with such matters.

To the recommendations of the Esher Committee was further due the creation of a regular Inspectorate, into

CHAPTER XV.

Naval Developments.

The Esher Committee. (1904).

---

[1] On the 5th February 1904, Japan broke off negotiations with Russia. Port Arthur was six hundred miles from the nearest Japanese port, but on the night of the 8th the Russian Fleet, lying unaware in the outer roads, was attacked by destroyers, and several of the most powerful ships placed *hors-de-combat*—a determining factor in the whole course of the war. Next day the Japanese battle-ships bombarded the port from behind the Liao-Yang Promontory, firing five rounds from each of their 12″ guns at a range of about 13,000 yards, with the cruisers observing from a station at right angles to the line of fire.

Three attempts were made to block the entrance of the harbour, in which 17 ships, of sizes varying between two and three thousand tons, were lost.

v

292   THE COAST ARTILLERY.

Chapter XV.

The Esher Committee. (1904).

which the existing Inspector-General R.G.A. was absorbed, gaining thereby a better definition of his duties, and the support of the Inspector-General of the Forces. And in the reorganization of the commands and staff in the United Kingdom in 1905 the defect in the original Army Corps Scheme was put right, by making coast defence commanders responsible to the Army Council directly, instead of through "commands", in matters of defences, armament, works, communications, and arrangements for communicating with the navy and for regulating traffic into harbours. During the next couple of years the duties of coast defence commanders were further enlarged until, according to the size of their commands, they stood in the same relation to a commander-in-chief as the general officer commanding a division or brigade.[1]

With the appointment of artillery officers as coast defence commanders there had come the abolition of the post of "officer commanding Royal Artillery". No time was lost, however, in representing the impossibility of a coast defence commander being responsible also for the discipline and interior economy of a large number of artillery units.[2] Moreover in the absence of the coast defence commander the next senior officer would rarely be an artilleryman, and it would then be necessary to call in the senior artillery lieut.-colonel, thus dislocating the chain of artillery command. The justice of the plea was admitted, and in 1906 colonels were appointed to command the artillery in the principal fortresses.

The Wood Committee. (1905).

In the slowness—nothing less than stagnation—of promotion at this period the officers of the Royal Garrison Artillery had a real grievance. This stagnation was due to various causes entirely unconnected with the separation, but the dissatisfaction of garrison artillery

---

[1] The title was changed to "Commander of Coast Defences" in 1911.

[2] At Portsmouth (including Portland) there were six lt.-colonel's commands, eleven companies, a depôt, a district establishment between three and four hundred strong, and a school of gunnery.

officers was naturally increased by the phenomenal run of promotion which their brother officers of the mounted branch were enjoying owing to the expansion of the horse and field artillery in the South African War. This could not have been foreseen when the separation was being arranged, but it was none the less irritating on that account. The possibility of "accelerated promotion" was investigated by a committee under Field-Marshal Sir Evelyn Wood, but was found to present great practical difficulties in the case of such corps as the Royal Artillery and Royal Engineers. With their large number of officers, scattered throughout the Empire, serving under numerous commanders whose standards of efficiency must inevitably vary, it would be impossible to secure a fair comparison between the claims of individuals, and the idea of "accelerated promotion" as a relief to the situation was abandoned.

CHAPTER XV.
The Wood Committee. (1905).

With the "other ranks" the service was a favourite one, attracting a sufficient number of recruits of the high physical standard required. The non-commissioned officers and men were a magnificent body—as big as the Guards, and perhaps broader chested—well disciplined and keen at their work. But the disproportion between the home and foreign establishments seriously affected the efficiency of the companies at home. Even if the companies were up to establishment their available strength began to drop after the beginning of September, when the draft season commenced. What with the time spent at sea, furlough for men going abroad, leave for men home again, and men posted pending discharge, hardly enough men remained with the companies during the winter to carry on the duties and keep the armament in order. Yet surprise attacks were to be expected before mobilization had brought the reservists backs to the ranks. With half the trained officers and men gone abroad[1] the "precautionary period" pro-

The Slade Committee. (1904).

---

[1] During a year taken at random 54% of the officers in home companies were changed: in one two-company station all the officers were changed.

mised to be a somewhat precarious one. There was real anxiety as to the power of the coast artillery to defend the home ports, and the Secretary of State admitted in 1904 that the garrison artillery was one of the most pressing and difficult questions with which he had to deal. In December of that year a committee was assembled under the presidency of General Slade "to enquire into the state of the Royal Garrison Artillery with a view to reducing the continual drain on the home companies, and still keeping those abroad up to an efficient strength".

The committee found that, although the total strength had been largely increased, the proportion between the numbers at home and abroad still remained at one to one and a half—8,650 to 12,670. They recommended in the first place a change in the terms of enlistment from three years colour service and nine years reserve, to nine years colour and three years reserve. This was obviously better suited to the requirements of the coast artillery, who were not likely to require large reserves, but did want trained soldiers even before mobilization, and the change was made at once. It did not affect the proportion between the home and foreign establishment, but it did put the home companies into a better position to meet the strain of supplying drafts.

The next step in the committee's plan was the localization of companies. It had been accepted since the turn of the century that the establishment of companies abroad should be based upon the armament they had to man, and could not therefore, be uniform; but this did not provide any cure for the loss of local knowledge whenever companies changed stations. There were bitter complaints from coast defence commanders of the way in which the efficiency of the defence was periodically impaired when this occurred, with insistence upon the value for coast artillerymen of a thorough acquaintance with the armament and general surroundings such as tides, channels, and currents, extent of illuminated areas, position of examination anchorage, and condition of the

THE MANCHURIAN INFLUENCE. 295

atmosphere both by day and night. The committee went to the root of the matter, and recommended the radical measure of localization of companies, with reliefs by individuals as in fortress companies of the Royal Engineers. The fortress establishment could then be dealt with as a whole by the War Office, and the establishment of companies fixed by the fortress commander to suit the fire and battery commands, the whole of the district establishment being absorbed into the companies according to local requirements, thus setting at rest the vexed question of the specialists. The scheme was approved and brought into force by an Army Order in January 1906.

But no sooner was the organization of the coast artillery thus based upon the requirements of fortresses than a drastic revision of those requirements became necessary. In spite of the vast increase in the power of battleships and cruisers, and in the size of the torpedo-craft and other vessels with which the coast artillery might have to deal, its armament had remained stationary. An interdepartmental committee was assembled to report on what additions or alterations were required to the existing authorized fixed defences of the defended ports at home,[1] and to the anti-torpedo-craft defences of commercial ports, in the light shed on naval tactics by the Russo-Japanese War, the changes in the strategical situation, and the fact that the coast artillery was about to be deprived of the assistance of mine-fields.

The committee was a strong one. Its members included two officers from the Admiralty in addition to representatives of the Royal Garrison Artillery and Royal Engineers: its President, General Sir John Owen,[2] had first been brought to notice by his discovery of the true cause of the "Thunderer" explosion; he had gained a

CHAPTER. XV.

The Slade Committee. (1904).

The Owen Committee. (1906-7).

---

[1] In the following year the task of the Committee was extended to defended ports abroad, and H.M.S. *Terrible* was placed at their disposal by the Admiralty.

[2] General Sir John F. Owen, K.C.B., Colonel Commandant. d. 1924, aged 85.

brevet in command of a Gatling battery at Ulundi; and then, after two appointments in Australia, had been, in succession, Commandant of the School of Instruction in the Isle of Wight, General Officer Commanding the Royal Artillery at Malta, and President of the Ordnance Committee. In these important posts he had done perhaps more than any other officer in promoting the efficiency of the coast artillery.

The committee found, in the first place, that in nearly all cases the defences had been designed to meet the close-range attack of vessels trying to force an entrance, rather than the very long-range bombardment now to be anticipated, and that, in consequence, the disposition of the guns gave quite an excessive volume of fire over some areas, and an insufficient one over others.

In the second place they found that the size and heterogeneous nature of the armament was quite beyond what was required for meeting the scale of attack to be provided against, and recommended a reduction in the number and nature of guns to the minimum required by the Admiralty scale, on the assumption that they would be of the most modern type and complete with all accessories.

Taking into account the thickness of the side armour of warships, and the effective penetration of the various projectiles in the service, the committee came to the conclusion that, in the unlikely event of battle-ships exposing themselves to the fire of shore batteries, the capped armour-piercing shell of the 9·2″ B.L. Mark X would inflict an amount of damage sufficient to put them at a serious disadvantage in a subsequent naval action, while against armoured cruisers capped common-pointed would be all that would be required.[1] To maintain an armament of heavier guns than the 9·2″ would therefore be extravagant.

Against unarmoured ships rapidity of fire and shell power were what would be required, and for dealing with

---

[1] The capped shell (both armour-piercing & common-pointed) had not yet been approved for the land service, but were confined to the Navy.

them the committee recommended that reliance should be placed on the 6″ B.L. Mark VII.

The large number of Q.F. guns of medium nature (6″ and 4·7″) which had been mounted to deal with the secondary armament of battle-ships had lost their *raison d'être* with the disappearance of any probability of such attack. Their withdrawal was, therefore, recommended except in cases where they were required for other purposes. These might include meeting the attempts of unarmoured ships against collections of mercantile shipping, the new threat of "blockers" and "boom-smashers", and also use against torpedo-craft instead of 12-prs. when the space only admitted of a few guns and the range was considerable.

For anti-torpedo-craft defence generally the Committee considered that the increase in the size of destroyers had rendered the 6-prs. useless, and recommended their withdrawal: the 12-prs. should be retained for the present, although in view of the increase in the size of destroyers it seemed probable that they would have to give place to guns of greater power in the near future. There were still some cases (such as Garrison Point Fort at Sheerness) where heavy muzzle-loading guns were retained for this purpose. They were provided with special case shot, containing $3\frac{1}{2}$-lb. steel balls, and were kept layed on "running past" points, and fired as the attackers reached these by the group commander in an observing station. There were many advocates of their retention, but the committee would have none of them.

Working on these lines the committee prepared detailed tables of the armament required for each port, which showed vast reductions in the number of works and in the number and nature of guns. Their recommendations were naturally welcomed by the authorities, since they promised economy, not only in *matériel*, but also in the still more important matter of *personnel*. There were protests of course from coast defence commanders who objected to having any of their teeth drawn, and some revision of details had to be made. But the policy of

298 THE COAST ARTILLERY.

CHAPTER XV.

The Owen Committee. (1906-7).

doing away with obsolete and redundant armament, whilst bringing that retained up to date, was so obviously sound that it could not but meet with general approval. As a high authority wrote at the time—"The best way of resisting the applications of local authorities who mistake the cackle of their bourg for the murmur of the world, is to cling like grim death to the recommendations of the Owen Committee".

Re-armament.

In 1904 the last smooth-bores in the defences[1] had been restricted to saluting purposes, and during the following year the remaining R.B.L. and R.M.L. guns were declared obsolete. As a result of the Owen Committee most of the earlier marks of B.L. followed them into retirement, so that by the end of the first decade of the XXth century the coast artillery armament throughout the Empire was standardized in the 9·2" B.L.[2] Mark X on Mark V barbette mounting, the 6" B.L. Mark VII on Mark II central-pivot mounting, and the 12-pr. Q.F.

Such far-reaching changes naturally took some years to carry out, and there were, as was inevitable, some vexatious interruptions. No sooner had two 9·2" and four 6" of the latest pattern been installed at St. Lucia than it was decided to withdraw the garrison from the island. The disastrous Jamaica earthquake of 1907 came in another category. The batteries at Port Royal mounting two 9·2", two 6", and four 12-prs. subsided, their shells were buried, the electric lights submerged, the barracks rendered unsafe for occupation. The officers and men of the companies did valuable work in salving property in Kingston, but they lost much of their own. Then the discovery of certain defects in lyddite shells necessitated the return to England of all those of a certain make and date. It was not until 1912 that this depletion of the authorized "equipment" of ammunition had been sufficiently overcome for the authorities to consider any

---

[1] These were 32-prs. converted to breech-loaders for ditch defence.
[2] In India the 7·5".

THE MANCHURIAN INFLUENCE. 299

expenditure at practice. Moreover, with the rise in the rate of fire due to improved guns and mountings, the scale of equipment ammunition had been increased to 200 rounds per gun for all natures above 6″, 500 per gun for 6″ and 4·7″, and 800 for 12-prs.

CHAPTER XV.

Re-armament.

At the same time there were changes in the proportion of the different natures of projectiles due to the alterations of naval tactics, and of ideas as to how attacks should be dealt with by coast batteries. The 12-pr. and 4·7″ had nothing but lyddite[1]. The 6″ were at first supplied with 40% lyddite and 60% armour-piercing shell, but in accordance with the recommendations of the Owen Committee, this was changed to 70% lyddite and 30% armour-piercing, or 100% lyddite when mounted only for action against blockers and boom-smashers. The tendency was the same with the 9·2″. Originally 40% and 60% like the 6″, this was altered to 50/50 in defences exposed to battle-ship attack, and to 90% lyddite and 10% armour-piercing where required to meet a cruiser attack only.

The effect of these changes on the training must now be considered.

In 1906 competition between companies ceased to be a part of the annual practice, classification taking its place. But the change was more nominal than actual, for the competition still continued, although now against "Bogey". Standards were laid down for each work and group, and the ratio between the standard and that gained by the company gave the "figure of merit" of the company, according to which it was classified 1st, 2nd, or 3rd. The classification on the same scale of companies practising at different stations under different conditions and supervision naturally entailed the issue of elaborate regulations covering every detail of the practice, and complicated calculations before the result could be ascertained.

Practice.

A step towards bringing the practice into closer

---

[1] As soon as a satisfactory pattern for the 12-pr. had been arrived at.—See Chapter XIII.

CHAPTER XV.
Practice.

relations with service conditions was, however, taken in 1907 by the institution of "Battle Practice". As its name implied the main point to be aimed at in this part of the practice was to render it as nearly as possible a rehearsal for what would obtain in time of war; and as the results did not count towards the classification it was particularly enjoined that many of the conditions necessary for class-firing might be disregarded.

Next year the battle practice was expanded to include schemes designed to test the endurance of the *personnel* and *matériel* in sustained fire, the concentration of fire required to stop a blocker or a boom-smasher, and the distribution necessary to prevent any one of several attackers getting through the defences. Attention was thus directed to the control of fire, the tactics of coast defence, and the principles governing the allotment of armament, which had been so long obscured by the interest monopolized by class firing. And to further this object coast defence commanders were empowered to recommend an addition to, or reduction from, the figure of merit of a company on account of its performance in battle practice.

Throughout this period the training of the coast artillery was much hampered by the inferior ammunition provided. Cordite had been approved for the service in 1891, but well on into the XXth century the coast artillery were condemned to carry on their training with black powder charges, although these introduced many conditions totally different from anything which could occur in war. An official circular in 1904 blandly informed them that the stock of powder was too large to admit of the entire discontinuance of its use—but relented to the extent of allowing a proportion of cordite charges.

It was the same story with the projectiles. New natures were adopted for the service, but the coast artillery were given no opportunity of seeing how they behaved in use.

In spite of these drawbacks there could be no doubt that the general standard of shooting was not only higher

THE MANCHURIAN INFLUENCE. 301

than before, but more uniform, and that this was largely due to the revolution in gunnery which was being brought about by the new process of calibration. Ever since the renaissance of gunnery in the 80's the foundation of the whole structure of practice had been the "bracket system", which depended upon the accurate observation of single rounds. But at the increased ranges at which the heavy guns would now fight it would often be difficult to see whether rounds were "over" or "short", while at the shorter ranges of the lighter natures the number of shell would make it equally impossible to distinguish individual rounds. The use of flank observers was taken up, and where the coast-line lent itself to their employment, and there were satisfactory means of transmission, it worked well. But its use was only possible in special cases, and so offered no general solution to the problem of what was to be done when observation—on which the whole system of ranges depended—failed. Some bold spirits began to ask why ranging should be necessary if guns, sights, and range-finders were accurate, and range-tables reliable?

The Navy were the first to take up the subject officially, for the great effect produced by one or two specific hits during the naval engagements in the Russo-Japanese War had impressed upon them the paramount importance of getting in the first blow. But it is to the Regiment that the credit of finding the means is due. Captain Dreyer,[1] had studied the subject after the South African War, struck by the statement of Admiral Sir Hedworth Lambton that the naval gunners at Ladysmith found the range to distant targets altering during the course of the day. This statement was derided in the Press, but Captain Dreyer realized that it was possibly correct. He therefore calculated what the effect at the stated range of a change in the temperature of the air, etc. between dawn and noon would be, and found that it accounted for what the sailors had noticed. He tabulated all the variants which could

CHAPTER XV.

Calibration.

---

[1] Major-General J. T. Dreyer, C.B., D.S.O.

CHAPTER XV.
Calibration.

affect the range, viz., air-density, wind, travel of target during the time of flight, speed of firing ship (for Navy only), charge temperature, and muzzle velocity of gun. Not only had the initial correction to be evaluated in order to hit with the opening rounds, but this correction had to be changed continuously as the range altered with the course and speed of the firing ship or target. A mechanical solution was the only one, and Captain Dreyer designed a *Range Correction Calculator* which was adopted by both services.

Account had also to be taken of the fact that owing to wear and other causes guns do not range alike under similar conditions. Captain Dreyer found that if the difference in shooting between a gun and its range table could be found at one range under normal conditions, it could be calculated for all other ranges. By this means all guns could be made to shoot in agreement with their range tables. In 1904 he invented a sight which could be set to compensate automatically for the divergence in muzzle velocity of a gun from the standard velocity of its range table. Guns fitted with these sights could be made to shoot alike at all ranges, and they were adopted for universal use by the Admiralty. For use in coast defences a range-dial with muzzle velocity compensating gear was adopted. It was, of course, necessary on any particular day to make additional allowances for variations from normal conditions.

"Calibration"—as the process came to be called—was officially adopted by the Navy in 1905, and its investigation was commenced by the Royal Artillery in the following year, and steadily continued. There was no difficulty in this as far as the lighter natures were concerned, for they habitually fired full charges at practice, and this could be arranged for the 6″ also. But it was a very different matter with the all-important 9·2″ owing to the expense involved. After much discussion special full-charge series were sanctioned for two of these guns in 1908, but after that, in spite of the protests of the School of Gunnery, it was insisted that all ammunition for cali-

THE MANCHURIAN INFLUENCE. 303

bration must be taken out of the allowance for practice. From 1909 onwards it was accordingly included in the objects for which the practice ammunition was allotted.

CHAPTER XV.

Calibration

The Navy claimed that the efficiency of their guns had been more than doubled since the introduction of calibration, and the experience of the coast artillery at stations[1] where it was carefully carried out confirmed this estimate. There were, however, not wanting those who mistrusted the movement in fear that it would lead to the neglect of observation of fire; who scoffed at those who imagined that hitting the target could be ensured by calculations based on inaccurate and always changing data; and poked fun at "batteries bristling with thermometers, barometers, and anemometers". It was the story of the position-finder over again.

In 1910 a Committee under Major-General R. A. Montgomery[2] considered the whole question in the light of the experience gained by both services. They had no doubt as to the value of calibration in obtaining earlier hits, and in increasing the percentage of hits to rounds, and especially in the number of hits per gun per minute. They were confident that such improvement would prevail in war, provided the calibration had been carried out with service projectiles and full charges; and they recommended that this should be made a part of annual practice, and that revised instructions for ranging should be issued.

The matter was of such importance that it was referred to high authority,[3] and the recommendations of the Committee were approved—provided no extra expense was involved.

---

[1] Notably in the Isle of Wight where Colonel F. M. Close had devoted his great scientific gifts to the subject. d. 1919.

[2] Major-General R. A. Montgomery, C.B., C.V.O., Colonel-Commandant. d. 1931.

[3] One of these (not a gunner) caused some amusement by committing himself to the statement "give me one ranging round and I would let them have all their scientific calculations on varying data and defeat them".

CHAPTER XV.

Range-Finding.

At the time of the introduction of the bracket system of ranging it had been accepted that "gun-range" would never be the same as the actual range, and that the gun-range must therefore be always found by actual shooting, however accurately the actual range might be found by the range-finder. Calibration modified this considerably, for its essence was that, provided variations from normal conditions were accurately known, guns could be made to shoot to the true range. Thus the whole system of modern gunnery rested upon the accuracy with which the range was given by the range-finder. And yet the service instruments were still those introduced in the 80's. The depression range-finder had gone through the stages of Mark II and II* to Mark III, and had become a larger and sturdier instrument in the process, ranging to 12,000 instead of 8,000 yards. It was also permanently set up, and so more reliable. Similarly the position-finder[1] had gone from "A" to "J-III" and "K-III", bringing its range up to 20,000 yards, but had been shorn of its predicting attributes. In neither depression range-finder nor position-finder had there, however, been any alteration embodying a new principle.

There was no doubt an attractive simplicity about the depression principle, and it had the great advantage of being equally accurate in all directions. · But inherent in it were disadvantages. It was requisite that the coast should afford a sufficiently high site, and that the level of the water to be shot over should be known, and yet there were many ports throughout the Empire where the first of these conditions could not be fulfilled, and many where it was difficult to ensure the second.[2] And in all cases its accuracy depended upon the observer's estimate of the position of the water-line. If this were badly defined

---

[1] In 1905 it was ordered that position-finders should in future be included in the category of range-finders.

[2] Notably in Bombay Harbour and the Hugli and Rangoon Rivers.

owing to refraction, rough sea, or high speed, the results would be irregular. In order to get over the absence of high ground a horizontal-base position-finder was designed, and some of the early instruments were issued before the turn of the century. The first service pattern—"G"— came into the service in 1903. But modifications followed quickly, and although it was brought up to 20,000 yards it was always a disappointment. It depended upon two observers directing their instruments upon exactly the same point, which had been found such a difficulty with the field and siege instruments. And if the targets of the coast artillery were usually better defined than those in the field, the observers were much further apart. Its arc, moreover, was very limited, and its effective base, on which the accuracy depended, might bear only a small proportion to the actual. The horizontal position-finder could therefore only be looked upon as a substitute for the depression instrument when the site did not provide the necessary height for the latter—it did not compensate for the other disadvantages of the depression system.

Comparing the two depression instruments the position-finder had undoubted advantages over the range-finder, being on a larger scale, more solidly constructed, and with a more powerful telescope. Its range and training dials were also actuated mechanically, thus avoiding delay and eliminating human error. Its chief asset was, however, that it gave the range and training from the gun, and so need not be set up in the immediate vicinity of the battery, but might be installed in some concealed position out of the smoke and dust. Hence there ensued a demand for position-finders for all heavy guns, and it was accepted that all 9·2″ of new type should be fought by them. Towards the close of the first decade they were being provided in large numbers, and a great feature of that period was the activity in their installation.

The importance of reliable means of communication had been realized before the close of the XIXth century, and the telephone definitely adopted as the standard

CHAPTER XV.

Range-Finding

Communications.

306 THE COAST ARTILLERY.

CHAPTER XV.
Communications.

method for comparatively long distances, as between fire commanders and battery commanders. Lines solely for the artillery chain of command were laid, an improved pattern of instrument was adopted, and much attention was given to the selection of operators with clear enunciation, and to their practical training. Orders from a battery commander to his gun group commanders were still sent by megaphones or speaking-tubes, while for passing ranges dependence had to be placed upon that fruitful source of error the "clock-face dial". There was no doubt that something better must be devised, and early in the century mechanical and electric dials for passing ranges, and order dials for use within battery commands, were under trial. By the end of the first decade it could fairly be said that these were the normal installation.

With the increased attention given to fire control after the introduction of battle practice "fire command drills", in which all communication *personnel* were practised in their duties, were instituted.

Anti-Torpedo-Craft Defence.

So far reference has only been made to the practice of the primary armament, but that of the light quick-firers was recognized as of equal, or even greater importance. The disaster which befell the Russian fleet at Port Arthur confirmed the foresight of Colonel Barron[1] in instituting the Q.F. courses at Shoeburyness. The coast artillery pursued the study and practice of anti-torpedo-craft defence with the determination that they would not fail in this part of their duty. From a study of the average results attained by the Shoeburyness courses it might be taken that a target 18′ × 4′ should be hit a couple of times while crossing an illuminated area of 60 degrees at 25 knots. It might perhaps be accepted that one gun could keep out one vessel, but an enemy would certainly not attack singly, and if one got through it might do incalculable mischief. The control and distribution of fire still presented the problem indicated in the last chapter, but it was in

---

[1] Major-General Sir Harry Barron, K.C.M.G., C.V.O. d. 1921.

THE MANCHURIAN INFLUENCE. 307

a fair way to solution by the end of the first decade of the century. Moreover it was no longer only the light quick-firers that were concerned in the anti-torpedo-craft defence. The "blocker" and the "boom-smasher" had made their appearance as inevitable adjuncts to a raid by torpedo-craft, and the light quick-firers were no match for these. Fortunately there were available the 4·7″ and 6″ guns which had been provided, as we have seen, for other purposes, and the Q.F. courses were extended in 1907 to include these, their targets running in from 2,000 to 1,200 yards at 15 knots.

CHAPTER XV.

Anti-Torpedo-Craft Defence.

Night practice was at first confined to Shoeburyness, where alone, it was thought, it could be carried out with safety. But if it were impossible—or seemed so—to carry out actual practice by night elsewhere, there was no reason why "night mannings" should not be included in the training, and the Isle of Wight showed the way in making this a regular part of the course of practice at the School of Instruction there. And with the general realization that night practice was the only practice which fulfilled service conditions, came the determination to carry it out with the guns which would be used in war, and under as far as possible the conditions of an actual raid. The great fortresses found out that with a certain amount of local arrangement, and with the help of the Navy to keep the course,[1] it was possible to carry out such practice from the defence works. Portsmouth led off in 1903, followed in 1904 by Portland, Malta, and Esquimault, in 1905 by Plymouth, and so on at other stations where it had hitherto been considered impossible. There were, of course, places where with the best will in the world it could not be carried out. At many of these, however, it was possible to make such safety arrangements as to allow of 1″ aiming rifles being used in conjunction with the electric lights. Where even this was impossible an annual allowance of 30 rounds of blank for light quick-

Night-Firing.

---

[1] By means of a cordon of destroyers round the illuminated area.

Chapter XV.

Night-Firing.

firers was approved. The manual of 1905 insisted upon all works being periodically manned at night, and the Admiralty approved the use of naval craft twice a year to represent an attack.

The night-firing brought to notice many practical matters not previously thought of. The ammunition must be at hand, and after trying "ready racks" as used in the Navy, and other contrivances, the trollies mentioned in chapter XIII were adopted. Then the fired cartridges gave trouble for they were apt to damage the men or to dent themselves, so screens to protect the detachments, and nets to catch the cases, were added. The blinding effect of the cordite flash was a serious matter, and goggles were not a success, so canvas screen to protect the layers were introduced for the 6″. Electric gear for the illumination of the sights was introduced, but found unnecessary, and many devices were tried for the error-of-day drums, until the decision that all quick-firer batteries should be electrically lighted appeared to obviate the need—the "clicker" had not yet appeared.

It was at last accepted that 9·2″ and 6″ guns must be provided with two detachments if required to be fought by night as well as by day. For the 4·7″ and 12-prs. a provision of reliefs was considered sufficient.

Electric Lights.

The use of 6″, and even of 9·2″ guns, in cases where it was necessary to stop blockers and boom-smashers quickly, and the regular addition of 6″ and 4·7″ guns to the anti-torpedo-craft defence, brought the question of the siting and control of the electric lights to the front. In order that the fire of such guns might be fully developed the Owen Committee recommended in many cases the installation of "fighting lights" under artillery control, i.e. as adjuncts to the guns to the same extent as the range-finders. This was a direct *volte-face* from the pronouncement of the manual of 1905 that "artillery fire will be assisted by fixed beams only—search lights may sometimes be employed for discovering the movements of an enemy's ships, but only under very exceptional circum-

THE MANCHURIAN INFLUENCE. 309

stances for following and fighting them by artillery fire". It re-opened the old controversy between the artillery and the engineers.

The question was fully considered in 1907, and it was then definitely laid down that the control of the lights was in the hands of the Royal Garrison Artillery, the fixed lights being under the fortress commander, the fighting lights under battery commanders, and steps were taken to place the operators either in, or adjacent to, the battery commander's post. The actual handing over of the lights to the artillery was considered, but Lord Kitchener's Committee of 1911 on the organization and training of the Royal Engineers could not agree to this.

Perhaps, however, the most important of the results of this spread of night-firing was the far-reaching effect it was found to have in making officers and men quick-witted, ready of resource, and willing to accept responsibility.

One of the most important steps in the "renaissance" of coast artillery in the last century had been the establishment by the School of Gunnery of "Branch" Schools, first in the Isle of Wight in 1888, and then at Plymouth, Sheerness, etc. The coast artillery responded with alacrity to the opportunity at last afforded them of working out the problems connected with their work under conditions more closely approaching those of service than were attainable at Shoeburyness. But as they gained experience and confidence, coast artillerymen began to wonder whether the time had not come to dispense with leading strings. A committee[1] under General Owen, assembled at the turn of the century to consider the whole subject of Garrison Artillery Instruction and Training, had recommended that officers commanding Royal Artillery should be made responsible for all instruction, and, as a corollary, that the local schools of instruction should be placed under them.

CHAPTER XV.
Electric Lights.

The School of Gunnery.

[1] Not to be confused with the more famous "Owen Committee" on coast artillery armament referred to above.

CHAPTER XV.
The School of Gunnery.

Sir Evelyn Wood's appointment in 1901 to the Southern Command, in which all the great coast fortresses were situated, gave impetus to the movement, for (as with the field artillery when at Aldershot) he insisted on the principle that training was a function of command, and confessed himself "horrified" at finding companies carrying out their annual practice under the auspices of these schools, instead of from their own batteries under their own lieut.-colonels.

In 1904 the question was considered by a committee under the Director of Military Training[1] which was investigating various matters connected with the School of Gunnery, and especially a proposal that it should be moved from Shoeburyness to the Isle of Wight. Their recommendations were definitely in favour of the decentralization of instruction, and accordingly the local schools ceased to be branches of the School of Gunnery, but became part of coast defence commands.

The carrying out of such a change necessarily involved much discussion and some readjustments, so that it was found advisable in 1908 to issue a circular letter concerning the functions of the School of Gunnery and its relations with the instructional staffs in commands. In this circular it was explained that it was the duty of the commandant to supervise the gunnery instruction of the various commands at home, and that he was authorised to visit them for this purpose, but that in this there was no idea of undermining the responsibility of coast defence commanders for the efficiency of the garrison artillery under their command—the visits of the commandant School of Gunnery were intended to enable them to exercise their authority more efficiently. It was, however, still to be the duty of the commandant to review the practice reports of all regular garrison artillery units throughout the Empire.

---

[1] Major-General Hon. Sir F. W. Stopford, K.C.M.G., C.B. See also Chapter XXII for the further recommendations of this Committee on the organization of the establishment at Shoeburyness.

THE MANCHURIAN INFLUENCE. 311

This last provision affected regimental officers very closely, for the School of Gunnery insisted upon the practice being conducted in exact accordance with elaborate instructions from which no deviation was allowed without the previous sanction of the commandant, who was authorised to inflict penalties at his discretion whether recommended by coast defence commanders or not. Such centralization necessarily required detailed reports, and it is not too much to say that their compilation entailed a real strain upon company officers. It certainly caused very general dissatisfaction, which was by no means allayed by the custom of recording in the Annual Report of the School of Gunnery caustic comments on the way in which the practice of each company was conducted.

In the duties of the new Inspectorate formed in accordance with the recommendations of the Esher Committee it was especially provided that the Inspector of Royal Garrison Artillery should be consulted by general officers commanding when arranging manœuvres in conjunction with the navy, so that he might be present if practicable. For his inspections the works were manned by day and night, and as far as possible by the troops who would man them in war, warning telegrams were despatched, the steps ordered for the precautionary period were put in force, and whenever possible night attacks either by the navy or by local vessels were arranged.

In addition to major questions connected with the armament these exercises brought to light many minor matters affecting the efficiency of its working—the strain of prolonged periods of tension on all ranks, especially on look-out men peering into the dark; the want of any provision for the occupation of batteries for any length of time, with facilities for sleeping, washing, and feeding. Order and turn-out suffered until proper arrangements were made for accommodation, and working dress regularized according to climate.

The most important matter connected with these exercises was the share the Navy took in them. The

CHAPTER XV.

The School of Gunnery.

Defence Exercises.

The Bacon Committee (1904-6).

THE COAST ARTILLERY.

CHAPTER XV.
The Bacon Committee (1904-6).

Hartington Commission of 1899 had commented strongly upon the want of a proper understanding between the Naval and Military Services, but all that came of it was a general authority for gunnery specialists to attend each others' practice. The *raison d'être* of the coast artillery was the protection of naval vessels and stores, and of mercantile shipping, and they asked in return that the sea service should give them opportunities for gaining practical experience in what would be required of them in case they had to meet the attack of a hostile fleet. It had long been felt by the artillery that this co-operation was essential to a right appreciation of many of the problems of coast defence, but naval manœuvres at home were somewhat discouraging to the artillery, who manned their guns night after night waiting for attacks which never materialized. More cordial relations between the two services were now being established, and in this the great Mediterranean fortresses had given an invaluable lead. There had been similar cases elsewhere, but these were sporadic, due to the personality of commanders: there was still no real working co-operation between the services. The matter was taken up by the Admiralty and the War Office and a joint committee under Captain R. H. S. Bacon[1] appointed in 1904 to consider how best to give increased instruction in naval matters to the garrison artillery in order to ensure more thorough co-operation in war. In view of the fact that a period of sea-service for artillery officers was ruled out of court, they recommended interchange of visits by the staffs of the respective schools, the attendance of representatives of the other service at their courses, the presence of gunnery specialists at each other's practice, and of naval officers in batteries and artillery officers on board ship during combined exercises. At all naval ports joint committees should also be formed to discuss matters of local importance and make officers of the two services personally known to each other.

[1] Admiral Sir Reginald H. S. Bacon, K.C.B., K.C.V.O., D.S.O.

THE MANCHURIAN INFLUENCE. 313

There resulted a real advance towards mutual understanding. The naval war courses were attended by military officers, and naval officers were included in the gunnery staff course. At fortress mobilizations a naval officer was attached to the staff of the coast defence commander, and artillery officers were embarked on attacking flotillas.

Distinct progress during the first decade of the century can also be recorded in the very important matter of the admission of vessels into defended ports in time of war. In order to provide for the safe entry of friendly vessels, and to prevent a hostile vessel entering in the guise of a friend, an "Examination Service" had been elaborated, and the manual of 1905 enjoined on all garrison artillery officers the duty of making themselves thoroughly acquainted with the regulations for the port at which they were stationed. But there were great difficulties in arranging for the necessary rehearsals. The provision of the *personnel*, especially the large number of signallers required, was a strain upon the companies; then a special vessel and special stores were required; the harbour-master had to be brought in as "examining officer", and funds obtained for his fee, and for the hire of the "examination steamer". In India an Act had to be amended so as to secure the representation of the local military authority on the Port Trust. New rules, drawn up by a joint Admiralty and War Office conference in 1907, and revised after discussion at the staff conference, were issued in 1909 and cleared up many doubtful points. But it was not until the issue of the confidential manual on *Fighting the Fixed Armament* with its clear and definite instructions that the working of the service was got into anything like a satisfactory state. The examination service was probably the most difficult task the coast artillery had to tackle, and the responsibility for the recognition and entry of H.M. Ships by day and night, and for the recognition and entry of neutral war-ships and of friendly merchant vessels was a heavy one.

CHAPTER XV.

The Bacon Committee (1904-6).

The Examination Service.

314   THE COAST ARTILLERY.

CHAPTER XV.

India.

As related in Chapter VI the office of Inspector-General of Artillery in India was abolished in 1907, and an Inspector of Coast Defences and of Royal Garrison Artillery appointed. The services of such an officer were urgently required for there was no school of gunnery in India, and the general officers commanding at the defended ports were not specially selected coast defence commanders as at home. The Inspector supplied the directing hand, acting as chief umpire at practice, or assisting the general officer commanding when the latter took this duty himself. He was also the adviser of the commander-in-chief on technical questions connected with coast defence.

In deciding upon the standard to be adopted to govern the scale of fixed defences, it had been accepted that the employment of battle-ships or armoured cruisers in Indian waters was a contingency so remote that it could be disregarded. The object of the defences was to deter raiding cruisers from closing to positions from which they would be able to deliver a fire which would cause serious damage with a limited expenditure of ammunition. The Indian Government decided to strike out a line of its own by adopting a 7·5″ gun instead of the 9·2″ for their primary armament. At home this gun was confined to the naval service: it was a fifty calibre wire gun, with Welin-screw breech mechanism, but on the pure couple system, in which bevel-gear gave a direct gain in power over the earlier skew-gear. The mounting was on the same lines as the 9·2″ barbette Mark V, but without hydraulic arrangements for lifting the projectiles to the breech. Right up to the last years before the Great War, however, the defences of some of the most important ports still depended upon obsolete 10″ and 6″ guns on hydro-pneumatic (disappearing) mountings.

The Manuals.

The *Garrison Artillery Training* in use at the beginning of the XXth century had only been published in 1899, but the new armament coming into the service soon rendered it out of date, and its revision was undertaken before it had been more than a couple of years in use. The custom of

THE MANCHURIAN INFLUENCE. 315

including the gun-drills of all natures in the training manual caused constant delays as changes in equipment were introduced, and eventually it was decided to transfer all these to the handbooks of the guns, and to make Vol. II the siege artillery manual instead of leaving that branch with a book of its own. It was not, however, until 1905 that the first-fruits of this arrangement appeared in the shape of *Garrison Artillery Training, Vol. I, Coast Defence*, and by that time the Russo-Japanese War was in full progress. There had not, however, been time to digest its lessons, and so the manual was really out-of-date when it appeared.[1]

During the next five years the influence of the war was affecting every department of coast artillery work as has been told in this chapter, but it was not until 1910 that the results were summed up in a new edition of the manual. It showed throughout the effects of this period of progress, but omitted all mention of the principles of coast defence as part of the war policy of the Empire, and of the forms which naval attack might take, to both of which the previous edition had devoted considerable attention. Nor was any reference made to the gunnery changes which calibration was bringing about. Such omissions may have been due to a reluctance to publish to the world the results of so much careful study and experiment, but these were matters on which the coast artillery were impatient for official guidance, and for some years they had been put off with veiled allusions to confidential instructions which might be expected. How the pronouncement was made will be told in the next chapter.

CHAPTER XV.

The Manuals.

---

[1] It did not even mention blockers or boomsmashers.

CHAPTER XVI.

"Fighting the Fixed Armament".

(1911—1914.)

Coast Artillery in Imperial Defence—The Batteries—The Guns—The Gunnery—Range-finding—Observation of Fire—The Annual Practice—Instructional Apparatus—Command and Organization—Progressive Training—Co-operation with the Navy—Co-operation with the Field Army—The Block in Promotion—Conclusion.

Chapter XVI.

Coast Artillery in Imperial Defence.

In the last chapter mention was made of the demand of the coast artillery for enlightenment on various important aspects of their work which found no place in *Garrison Artillery Training 1910*. In 1911 the long-looked-for light was given by the issue of a confidential manual on *The Organization and Fighting of the Fixed Armament of a Coast Fortress or Defended Port*—generally known as "F.F.A."[1]

Readers of this and of the preceding volume will remember how time and again during the period covered by this history controversy flared up regarding the value of fixed defences. On the one side the "Blue Water School", who pinned their faith on the doctrine of the "Fleet in Being", and grudged every penny spent on land defences—on the other those who would have every port bristling with guns regardless of what they cost or where the men to man them were to come from. Thus the extremists forced into controversy what should have been a matter of mutual interest. For coast fortresses and

---

[1] G.A.T. 1910 was brought into line with the new manual by the issue of a series of amendments, followed by a new edition which came out only six weeks before the declaration of war in 1914. In this chapter the whole are considered together as showing the final stage in the evolution of coast defence before the War.

FIGHTING THE FIXED ARMAMENT.   317

defended ports, coaling stations and harbours of refuge, existed solely for the protection of shipping, naval or mercantile, and of the docks, repair shops, and stores which enabled ships to keep the sea.

The confidential manual gave at last a definite statement of the accepted doctrine. The maintenance of sea supremacy was assumed as the basis of Imperial Defence, with the Navy following its traditional rôle of seeking the ships of the enemy wherever they were to be found. It was admitted that this policy of active defence might result in the enemy obtaining temporary command of those waters which were outside the action of our main fleets. Fixed defences were therefore necessary to free the Navy from the duty of protecting naval bases and coaling stations; to secure harbours whose position was of strategic value; and to protect commercial ports so that trade might be disturbed as little as possible. They were not designed to provide permanent protection against prolonged operations.

The respective rôles of the navy and of fixed defences in the scheme of Imperial Defence were thus definitely established. At last the coast artillery had been officially assured of the purpose for which they existed. They had, however, little definite knowledge of the force of the attack to which they might be subjected, obvious as it was that the Dreadnoughts and super-Dreadnoughts were far more formidable antagonists than their defences had been designed to withstand.

In 1912 and 1913 artillery officers were given the opportunity of witnessing some special naval practices at targets representing a shore battery and a dockyard, and what they saw convinced them that due weight had not been given to the developments of naval range-finding and fire-control in recent years. The volume and accuracy of the fire necessitated a reconsideration of the protection afforded to *personnel* and *matériel* in the existing works.

For some years there had been growing uneasiness as to how the modern open batteries were to be fought under

CHAPTER XVI.

Coast Artillery in Imperial Defence

The Batteries.

318 THE COAST ARTILLERY.

CHAPTER XVI.

The Batteries.

fire, and there had been some reversion of opinion in favour of the use of "Case III", in which the whole of the laying could be done under cover. This method had been originally intended for guns in casemates, and it had lost popularity owing to the unpractical nature of the "predicted" firing. It now came into its own again (with all reference to predicting deleted[1]) as a practical means of fighting guns when laying over the sights was no longer possible. This fitted in well with the growing conviction that a battery commander must be given a post from which he could observe the fire of his guns, clear of the haze and dust caused by their discharge, and of the smoke and debris of the enemy's shells. Nearly all 9·2″ batteries had been provided with position-finders, and their cells might well be adapted to serve also as command posts.

It was not, however, only attack from the sea that had to be thought of, the threat from the air could no longer be neglected. Bomb-proof cover for the fixed armament was out of the question, but the possibility of making the defences less conspicuous from the air was taken up, and many suggestions considered—ranging from overhead screens to the encouragement of the growth of weeds on concrete. There was no doubt that until some efficient anti-aircraft weapons[2] had been evolved, coast defences were, as a contemporary writer put it, "in the position of birds on the ground relying on protective colouring to save them from the hawk in the air". The other novelty of these last years—the submarine—scarcely affected the coast artillery, for if submerged it was out of their reach, if on the surface an easy prey.

The Guns.

The continuous development of the Dreadnought type

---

[1] Except for high-angle-fire guns, for which it was retained.

[2] Pending the introduction of a regular anti-aircraft gun, it was decided to make use of pom-poms for the protection of fixed defences, and a score of those, discarded by the field army, were adapted for the purpose as described in chapter XIII. The manual of 1914 contained the first mention of "guns specially designed for the attack of aircraft", but said little about their use except in warning against the dangers of "certain projectiles fitted with tracers".

FIGHTING THE FIXED ARMAMENT. 319

of battle ships and cruisers naturally led the coast artillery to demand an all-round increase of power in their guns as well as of protection for them. When introduced the 9·2″ had been more or less a match for the war-ships of the time, but modern ships now mounted 13·5″ and 14″ guns, and their armour was far stronger and more widely distributed than that of their predecessors. The coast artillery saw themselves condemned (to quote a contemporary again) to "shooting all day without putting a gun out of action, or letting in a drop of water"—incapable of keeping bombarding vessels at a distance, or of preventing them running in to a range at which they could overwhelm the batteries with the violence of their fire.

At one time much had been expected of high-angle-fire guns to prevent bombardment, but they had rather dropped out of account owing to the poor effect of the Japanese 11″ howitzers on the Russian ships in Port Arthur. It was held by many that the much more rapid service of the direct-fire guns would be just as effective as a deterrent to anchoring, while their employment would avoid the many objections to the addition to the armament of guns of a special nature requiring extra men and material. There was somewhat heated debate on the subject, in which the rival protagonists were the Inspectors of the Royal Garrison Artillery and of the Royal Engineers, but eventually the possibility of bombardment from areas which could not be touched by direct-fire guns gained the day for the high-angle-fire guns, and a certain number of the earlier marks of 9·2″ were converted to the purpose.

It was not only the capital ships that had to be considered. At the beginning of the century the 6″ Mark VII had been capable of dealing with any cruisers which might attempt to raid a harbour of refuge : it was so no longer. Nor could it even be depended upon to stop the merchantmen that might be used as blockers and boom-smashers. The secondary armament, like the primary, was no longer up to its work.

And it was the same story with the light quick-firers.

CHAPTER XVI.

The Guns.

320 THE COAST ARTILLERY.

CHAPTER XVI.
The Guns.

Torpedo-craft had been growing fast, and extensive trials in 1909 had shown that the 12-pr. could not be relied upon to stop a modern destroyer quickly enough—a knock-out blow was what was wanted.

To put it shortly: the Navy had leaped ahead while the coast artillery had stood still. If the balance was to be restored 12″ guns must take the place of the 9·2″ in the primary armament, and the latter that of the 6″ in the secondary, the 6″ in turn being relegated to the anti-torpedo-craft defence as a supplement to the light quick-firers, in which category the 12-pr. should give place to a heavier gun. Such at any rate was the view held by a considerable body of coast artillerymen. But the authorities were adamant. It was made quite plain that there was no hope of anything heavier than the 9·2″ for the attack of armoured vessels, and that for dealing with unarmoured vessels, blockers and boom-smashers, the 6″ Mark VII must be made the best of. It was only in the case of the anti-torpedo-craft defence that the demands found a sympathetic response. Here a 4″ was introduced to replace and supplement the 12-pr. and it was decided also to utilise the 6″ and 4·7″ Q.F. which had been originally installed as an answer to the secondary armament of pre-Dreadnought battleships. The manual of 1910 legislated for the inclusion of medium guns in the anti-torpedo-craft defence, and for their being fought in the same manner as the light quick-firers.

The Gunnery.

There was, however, another side to the question. If naval gunnery had made vast strides, so had that of the coast artillery, and they still enjoyed the inherent advantages of guns on land.

The auto-sights,[1] introduced at the turn of the century, had gone through the usual stages from adulation to disillusionment during the first decade, and in 1912 their use and value were subjected to a solemn inquisition. The sight had, of course, the limitations common to all instru-

---

[1] Mark II was approved for 6″, and below, in 1912-13. Its chief feature was the addition of a "clicker" as described in Chapter XIII.

FIGHTING THE FIXED ARMAMENT. 321

ments which depended upon the depression principle, and some disadvantages peculiar to itself, such as the rapid increase with the range of any error due to laying, but it undoubtedly afforded the best means of bringing an accurate fire upon a rapidly moving target at short ranges at night. The instructions regarding the effective limits of auto-sights in the manuals had, however, been unduly optimistic, and these were stiffened up, and ordered to be painted on the gun emplacements. As we have seen "Calibration" had been accepted in principle, but no official guidance had been given as to its application in practice, and much diversity of method had consequently prevailed. With fully calibrated guns, tested sights and range-finders, adjusted charges, and calculated corrections,[1] adherence to the bracket system of "ranging" could but result in unnecessary delay in getting to fire effect. The confidential manual now told how ranging was to be carried out under the new conditions, and "deliberate" disappeared from the method of fire. Unfortunately financial considerations forbade the calibrating of 9·2″ guns with service ammunition until mobilization was ordered. It was a risky decision considering what a lengthy process calibration must be, if it were to be reliable, and how dependent it was upon the weather.

The importance of accurate range-finding for calibrated guns was fully realized, and nothing was left undone to get the best out of the instruments in the service. Every captain and lieutenant had to pass a practical examination in their use, tests[1] and adjustments, and lieut.-colonels were held responsible for the efficiency of all the instruments in their commands. But such measures could not get over the defects inherent in their design, and as a result of the trials of a "one-man" range-finder for field artillery on Salisbury Plain in 1909, Zeiss and Barr & Stroud were invited to submit instruments on this

CHAPTER XVI.

The Gunnery.

Range-finding.

---

[1] The tests were being continually elaborated, and the assistance of mechanical appliances in calculating corrections, &c., was freely given in the shape of special slide-rules &c.

322 THE COAST ARTILLERY.

CHAPTER XVI.

Range-finding.

principle with a 9-ft. base for trial by the coast artillery.[1] All through 1910-11-12 there were very extensive trials of these in comparison with the various service instruments, both at the home ports and in India, resulting in a recommendation that some form of self-contained instrument should be procured, provided that sufficient accuracy could be obtained.[2] This condition necessitated a longer base, and trials were going on when the War came. For coast artillery they had the enormous advantages over those on the depression principle that they did not require a high site, need not be layed on the water-line, and were not affected by the height of the tide. Against these must be put the serious disadvantages that they could only take the range from their own position and not from that of the guns, so that Case III could not be used with them; and that continuous range-finding on a moving target, if possible at all, was only so for short periods, thus necessitating the frequent relief of the range-taker.

As long as all shooting was by day, and the ranging was on the bracket system, the tide gauges "of simple make" provided locally in accordance with the directions in the manual[3] had been found sufficient. With the general adoption of auto-sights came a demand for something better, and calibration necessitated tackling the problem in earnest. During the last four years before the war exhaustive trials were carried out with much more ambitious contrivances, designed to record in the battery the actual state of the tide in the fighting area of the guns, but it was not until June, 1914, that a pattern could be recommended for adoption.

Observation of Fire.

However carefully calibrated the guns might be, and however accurate the range-finding, it must not be sup-

---

[1] A very few Barr & Stroud range-finders had been in use by the coast artillery for some years at places where the horizontal form of position-finder could not be installed.

[2] The error not to exceed one per cent up to 16,000 yards.

[3] *Garrison Artillery Training*, Vol. I, 1905.

FIGHTING THE FIXED ARMAMENT. 323

posed that correct observation of the fire had lost its importance. Ranging instead of being a separate process precedent to fire for effect was now continuous throughout the series, and a battery commander had to watch the target closely if he was to keep his mean point of impact in its right place in spite of alterations of course and speed.

CHAPTER XVI.
Observation of Fire.

It was the duty of fire commanders to do everything in their power to facilitate this observation by arranging a scheme of distribution of fire which would enable battery commanders to identify the rounds from their guns. But with the steady increase in ranges it became plain that battery commanders must be provided with a suitable telescope, and trials were carried out at home and in the Mediterranean with the service "garrison and fortress lookout" telescopes, with those of the Mark II depression range-finder, and with Zeiss "stereoscopic". The latter, though costly, were undoubtedly the best, and it was decided to issue one to each 9·2″ battery in the first place, and to extend this issue to 6″ batteries as funds became available, commencing with those on low sites where observation was particularly difficult. An alternative suggestion to develop flank observation was ruled out when it was found that the necessary communications would cost even more than the Zeiss telescopes.

The compromise described in the last chapter, in accordance with which the commandant at Shoeburyness was still charged with the review of all company practice reports, was obviously incompatible with the principles of training laid down in the *Training and Manœuvre Regulations*. The whole question was submitted for consideration to two committees. The first, under Major-General Sir A. J. Murray,[1] the Director of Military Training, were of opinion that too much dependence was still placed on technical experts, and that there was no reason to make

The Annual Practice.

---

[1] General Sir A. J. Murray, G.C.B., G.C.M.G., C.V.O., D.S.O.

CHAPTER XVI.
The Annual Practice.

an exception in the case of the garrison artillery to the general rule that responsibility for the training of officers, non-commissioned officers and men, should lie with the commanding officer. On the basis thus established a regimental committee under Major-General Hickman[1] scrutinized the *Instructions for Practice*. They found that whatever defects there might be in the system were largely due to the tendency to accentuate the testing use of the practice at the expense of its training function. The attempt to arrive at a comparison of companies in all parts of the Empire had led to over-centralized and inelastic regulations, which cramped the initiative of coast defence commanders, discouraged the introduction of service conditions, and necessitated a complicated system of umpiring and marking which had fostered the idea that the school of gunnery could over-ride the authority of coast defence commanders. In the opinion of the committee the above had all tended to discourage coast defence commanders from taking such active and personal part in the training and practice of the coast artillery as was desirable, while the recently ordered employment of chief instructors from the schools as chief umpires at practice had further tended to the supplanting by gunnery experts of the commanding officers who were responsible for the training of the units and the fighting of the defences.

The detailed recommendations of the committee for changes in the system of practice, in order to give effect to their findings, could not be accepted in their entirety, but the *Instructions for Practice* of 1914 showed their inspiration throughout. Classification was retained in deference to the views of a large majority of commanding officers, especially among the seniors, who looked upon it as a useful stimulus to interest in the shooting, but suggestive changes were made in the nomenclature given to the various portions of the practice, and in the object assigned to each.

---

[1] Major-General H. P. Hickman, C.B. d. 1930.

FIGHTING THE FIXED ARMAMENT.

Company practice, which in 1913 had been "chiefly for testing the general training and efficiency of a company with all natures of guns", became in 1914 *battery* practice, to be regarded firstly as a means of affording training in fighting the guns the company would man on mobilization, and only secondly as a test of the company's training. And in the *fortress* practice, by which title the *battle* practice was now to be known, the essential object was stated to be training for war, and not the securing of records or the facilitation of marking.

All service practice had to be carried out at towed or other moving targets, but the targets were poor things compared with those used by the Navy. At Malta in 1909 General Penton[1] had been permitted by the commander-in-chief of the Mediterranean Fleet to carry out battle practice against a naval battle practice target, and its great merit in leaving no one in doubt whether a shot had been a hit or miss had been fully appreciated. The school of gunnery took up the question of improving the service targets; the conference of chief instructors laid down the conditions to be fulfilled; and in 1913 the War Office issued a circular giving particulars of "High Speed" and "Long Range" targets, and instructions for towing them with winding appliances. The latter had first been brought into use with the quick-firing courses at Shoeburyness, and its extension to the vessels used for towing targets was of enormous benefit. Fitted to an 8-knot vessel it allowed of a mean speed of 19-knots, working up to 22-knots. Moreover it allowed of an oblique course being followed. With the ordinary tow-rope of 300 yards considerations of safety necessitated the course of the target being almost directly at right angles to the line of fire, so that little or no instruction was given in dealing with changes of range and direction. With a thousand yards of steel tow-rope the use of targets moving towards the guns at acute angles was found to be practicable. A

---

[1] Major-General A. P. Penton, C.B., C.V.O. d. 1920.

326   THE COAST ARTILLERY.

Chapter XVI.

The Annual Practice.

further advance towards realism was made in the last year before the War by the direction that the targets used should each represent a conspicuous portion of the supposed ship—bow, barbette, and so forth. But, at the best, separate frameworks connected only by a cable were a poor representation of an actual vessel. Battery commanders called upon to range their guns upon the imaginary line connecting the targets could—and did—complain of being set a problem bearing no resemblance to anything with which they would be confronted when engaging an enemy. To meet a demand for something that could be seen up to 15,000 yards special "Travis"[1] targets were introduced—but it was only certain War Department vessels that could tow them.

Instructional Apparatus.

It was not only in improved targets for practice that the closer touch which had been established with the naval gunnery school opened the eyes of the school of gunnery to what might be done in the way of contrivances to assist in the training. Whale Island was infinitely better equipped than Shoeburyness could ever hope to be, but much could be done to suit the needs—and the means —of the land service.

Among the most useful of these instructional apparatus was the *loading-teacher*. The speeding up of the rate of fire had shown the necessity for constant practice in the physical exercise of handling the ammunition, and in the actual art of loading. Various devices in the way of drill shell proved unsatisfactory for one reason or another until the "Apparatus practising loading", modelled on the naval pattern, was introduced about 1908. It proved invaluable in rendering the work absolutely mechanical even at the fastest rate, but unfortunately it was only allowed for 6″ and under: the cost of similar apparatus for the 9·2″ as in use at Whale Island was considered prohibitive for soldiers.

Laying-teachers, were also introduced—primarily as a

---

[1] Mr. H. Travis, Superintending Engineer and Constructor of Shipping at Woolwich Dockyard.

means of training layers with auto-sights, but their use was soon extended to rocking-bar sights, and to exercises in passing ranges and corrections. Combined with aiming-rifles they led to a remarkable advance in the realistic training of all ranks from gun-group-commanders downwards.

CHAPTER XVI.
Instructional Apparatus.

The value of *aiming-rifles* for training purposes (mentioned in Chapter XIV) soon led to their use being extended from the testing of layers to the training of a battery. The smaller natures were particularly valuable in drill-sheds[1] when companies were quartered at some distance from their guns, and for such situations as that of the "inland companies" in India. The larger (one-inch), with which fire could be observed over water up to 1,000 yards, by night as well as by day, were much used to economise ammunition in the elementary practice, and also in night mannings where safety conditions precluded the use of service ammunition.

The next step was the *sub-calibre* gun, and here the light quick-firers, which had become obsolete for fighting purposes, found a new sphere of usefulness. The 3-pr. was first adopted, fitted into the bore of the 6″ Mark VII, and this was followed by mounting a 6-pr. on the top of the 9·2″[2]. The value of sub-calibre guns, especially for the training of fire commands, was at once apparent, and the coast artillery was soon demanding that one should be made part of the equipment of every medium and heavy gun. In view of the rise in cost of ammunition it is hard to see how the training of the coast artillery could have been carried on without their aiming-rifles and sub-calibre guns, for there was no increase in the money-grant for practice ammunition. Every sort of projectile was pressed into the service of economy—practice shot, old

---

[1] The utility of drill-sheds had been greatly increased by the mounting in them of guns of the latest pattern taken from the "Approved Armament Reserve". In 1914 designs were got out for air-rifles for use in them, so as to reduce the dust and noise of the ordinary aiming-rifles.

[2] Dubbed "Excalibur" by its designer, Captain Dreyer

328 THE COAST ARTILLERY.

CHAPTER XVI.
Instructional Apparatus.

Palliser shot, old common shell—although there were complaints that even when fitted with augmenting strips daylight could be seen all round them in the bore. The necessity for economy in cost of ammunition contributed to the popularity of the "practice batteries" established in the last century, chiefly with the object of getting clear ranges. Armed with more or less obsolete guns they allowed of battery practice at a comparatively small cost. But during the later years opinion was hardening against too free a provision of such facilities, for where they existed there was a tendency to overlook the value of companies shooting from the guns which they would use in war, and over the water on which an enemy's ships would appear, and to neglect the study of the local conditions by which an attack would be influenced.

Command and Organization.

Fighting the Fixed Armament brought in no great change in the artillery organization of coast fortresses except as regards the position of the general, or other, officer commanding the Royal Artillery. His position had always been somewhat anomalous, and all that previous manuals had been able to say regarding his duties was that he would be "employed on the staff of the fortress commander" (1905), or "act as technical adviser in artillery matters" (1910). Naturally enough, therefore, advantage was taken of the reorganization of coast defence commands to do away with the appointment. This aroused a justifiable outcry, as told in the last chapter, and "F.F.A." now laid down quite definitely that the whole of the artillery in a fortress should be under the command of an artillery officer. Amendments to G.A.T. defining his duties followed. In addition to advising the fortress commander on technical artillery matters, he was in war to command the section containing the most important portion of the fixed armament.

The most difficult and important duty of fire commanders was the identification of attacking ships. When this had been done, and communicated to battery commanders, it was the duty of the latter to attack those

FIGHTING THE FIXED ARMAMENT

allotted to them in such a manner as to inflict as early as possible such damage as would place the vessels at a disadvantage in a subsequent naval engagement. How to do so depended upon the strength and distribution of their armour, but a battery commander absorbed in the direction of his fire would have little leisure for the consideration of such a problem. It was obvious that everything possible should be done to simplify the tasks of both fire and battery commanders, and with this object in view a joint naval and military conference divided the ships of the world's navies into five classes, lettered A.B.C.D.E. Diagrams were then prepared showing the distribution of the armour of the value of 6" K.C.[1] and above in each class, so that all a fire commander had to do was to send to his battery commanders the letters showing the classification of the ships allotted to them. The battery commanders, knowing the maximum range at which the armour shown in the diagram could be penetrated, had their tasks immensely simplified in deciding whether to attack the armoured or unarmoured portion, and whether to use armour-piercing or lyddite shell.

In the organization of anti-torpedo-craft defence much had been learnt during the first decade, but no definite system had been decided upon. In the last few years before the War all matters in doubt were, however, satisfactorily cleared up. The necessity for relief detachments was at last accepted, and the manning detail increased to allow of two "watches", each strong enough to open and maintain an effective fire. Gun-floor shelters were provided for the watch on duty in which the men could rest comfortably, smoke and read, but not sleep. It was definitely laid down that in an attack layers must work independently, and in order to assist them a setter "for line" was added to the detachments.

In accordance with the decision regarding the electric lights mentioned in the last chapter, the duties of fire

CHAPTER XVI.
Command and Organization.

---

[1] "Krupp's Cemented"—see chapter XIII.

CHAPTER XVI.

Command and Organization.

commanders were expanded to include the tactical employment of the observation lights in the front line and those of the illuminated area, while the commanders of medium batteries were made responsible for the control of the fighting lights serving their guns.

The danger of a hostile vessel slipping past the advanced look-outs undetected was met by making the commanders of medium batteries "personally responsible" if they allowed a vessel to enter their area without engaging her; while in the case of the light quick-firers the gun look-outs had definite orders to open fire on any vessel that appeared in the illuminated area. Fire commanders were responsible for the issue of early and clear information as to any friendly vessels permitted to enter the waters, and how they were to be identified.

Thus before the War an excellent organization for the artillery garrisons of coast fortresses had been worked out, and laid down in regulations. But for its practical working it depended upon the artillery garrisons being present and efficient. Assistance could no longer be looked for from the auxiliary artillery for the artillery of the Territorial Force would not be available before mobilization. The coast artillery must be prepared to face the danger unaided, and in the Agadir Crisis of 1911 —when there was no precautionary period, but only one of apprehension—the artillery of fortresses on the East coast had been hastily reinforced from other stations. If the need had come after the commencement of the trooping season the position would have been very different, for, as shown in the last chapter, companies would then in all probability have been considerably below their established strength[1], with men constantly arriving and departing, and the regular manning tables practically useless. The cause of the trouble was still the same as before—the disparity between the home

---

[1] For two-thirds of the year the important fortress of Portsmouth was, on an average, 180 short of the number of men required to man its guns.

FIGHTING THE FIXED ARMAMENT 331

and foreign establishments.[1] The overseas garrisons must be kept up to their establishment, for the Navy would certainly not hamper their action by escorting transports to these outposts of the Empire. The question was whether their establishments included a sufficient allowance for the inevitable casualties due to climate. In 1910 an increase of 10% had been sanctioned for the more unhealthy stations, but this had been found insufficient in some cases, although in others the moving of the companies to the hills had done much to reduce the sick list. The length of service in foreign stations was also taken up, but the variety in the conditions presented great difficulties, and the grouping of stations in order to reduce the time wasted at sea proved unworkable in practice.

CHAPTER XVI.

Command and Organization.

During the last few years before the War grave doubts regarding the adequacy of the garrisons both of our home ports and overseas possessions were being freely expressed in Parliament and in the press. The whole system of coast defence was brought under scrutiny, and hopes were held out that it would be found possible, in the case of the more important fortresses at home at any rate, to make arrangements which would ensure adequate personnel being available at all seasons of the year. Meanwhile it was ordered that defence exercises should be held in winter as well as in summer so as to gain experience in carrying out the various defence measures with the personnel actually present.

In the last chapter mention was made of the institution of fortress "mobilizations" as the culminating stage in the collective training of the artillery. Here there was an obvious misuse of the term "mobilization", and an amendment to the manual made it clear that what had been intended were merely artillery exercises, although the co-operation of the navy and the engineers was always sought. In these exercises officers were generally so

Progressive Training.

---

[1] The actual figures were now—home establishment 384 officers, and 7994 other ranks, foreign establishment 452 and 9721.

CHAPTER XVI.

Progressive Training.

absorbed in their technical duties that the tactical points of the situation were apt to escape their attention. With the object of instilling into their minds the importance of visualising the tactical problems of harbour defence the various exercises which had been combined in the previous artillery mobilizations and defence exercises were rearranged as follows :—

Manning Exercises—Monthly,[1] by day and by night, and on the manning tables both of the precautionary period and of war.

Communication Exercises—Monthly, in which all the communications within, and as many as possible outside, the chain of artillery command were practised at high pressure.

Mobilizations—Annually, usually coinciding with fortress mobilizations, and as a rule in conjunction with one of the defence exercises.

In addition to the above artillery exercises there were the *Defence Exercises* properly so called, which were combined exercises carried out by the naval and military authorities with the object of testing the arrangements for the entry of H.M. Ships, the examination service, and the efficiency of the shore defence against attacks by ships or torpedo-craft or by landing parties.

Co-operation with the Navy.

The coast artilleryman could not help contrasting the little help he got in preparing himself for his part in the defence with the constant practice enjoyed by the field army artillery. At field days and manœuvres they were constantly called upon to work in co-operation with the other arms, and to engage with blank ammunition such objects as would be presented to them on the battlefield, while at practice their targets bore an indefinitely closer resemblance to the reality than anything the coast artillery ever shot at. How were the latter to visualise a naval attack if they never saw one?

In the last chapter a good deal was said of the steps

---

[1] Fortnightly if possible.

FIGHTING THE FIXED ARMAMENT 333

taken to ensure a better knowledge of each other between the two services whose work was so closely allied. Much had indeed been effected. The general accord between the Navy and the coast artillery was excellent, and the former were always ready with assistance as far as torpedo-craft were concerned. But it was almost unheard-of for them to stage a regular attack upon the shore batteries—in home waters at any rate. This was unfortunate, not only in connection with the training of the coast artillery, but even more so as regards the general conduct of the defence, for such exercises as had taken place had shown vividly the danger of the existing system of divided command. At many ports the submarines and torpedo-craft for local defence still worked absolutely independently of the military forces, with the inevitable consequence of such regrettable incidents as their being fired upon by the anti-torpedo-craft guns when returning from reconnaissance. Although the respective responsibilities of the arms and services had been established, there was no regulation dealing with their combined action. There was nothing for coast defence corresponding with *Field Service Regulations* for the field army. A manual on *Coast Fortress Defence* had indeed been promised, but had never materialized.

It was not only with the Navy that the coast artillery must keep in touch. There could be no doubt that in the case of a great war there would come a call for help from the siege artillery, and probably also from the field army artillery, and if their assistance was to be of value the officers of the coast artillery must have some knowledge of field warfare. Since their separation from the mounted branch they had made an enormous advance in professional efficiency, and, as the flames of controversy died down, it came to be very generally admitted that this improvement was not only since the separation, but in a great measure due to it. The fear that the garrison artillery would prove unpopular with those joining the Regiment had proved groundless. The scientific interest

CHAPTER XVI.

Co-operation with the Navy.

Co-operation with the Field Army.

334   THE COAST ARTILLERY.

Chapter XVI.

Co-operation with the Field Army.

of the work; the extra pay and the many appointments open to garrison artillerymen had brought home to young men—and to their parents—the substantial advantages offered by a career in the dismounted branch.

But, as the years passed on, it began to be noticed that the horizon of coast artillery officers was becoming limited to the highly technical duties of their own branch, and that they were tending to lose touch with the army at large. The matter was taken up: coast artillery officers were attached to field batteries; staff rides were arranged at fortresses for the study of the work of field troops. In spite, however, of these palliatives the drift away from the rest of the army continued to cause misgivings. So much was this the case that the question of re-amalgamating the branches, which had been raised during the discussions which preceded the organization of the Expeditionary Force, was considered again in 1911-12-13. It was decided not to proceed with the proposal, but to appoint a small committee under General Sclater[1] to devise other means of securing the closer association of coast artillery officers with the field army. Their report recommended various measures by which junior officers would obtain a practical knowledge of the working of mobile artillery, and more senior officers that of other arms of the service—but it did not come up for consideration until July, 1914. The lesson was to be given in a rougher school.

The Block in Promotion.

The subject, however, which was causing the greatest uneasiness both to the authorities at Headquarters and to regimental officers, was the absolute block in promotion in the Royal Garrison Artillery. As told in the last chapter, the possibility of relieving the situation by the system of "accelerated promotion" was investigated by a committee under Sir Evelyn Wood in 1905, but found inapplicable to the artillery. Since then nothing had been done, and

---

[1] General Sir Henry C. Sclater, G.C.B., G.B.E., Colonel-Commandant. d. 1923.

FIGHTING THE FIXED ARMAMENT

the reduction of companies had made matters worse. In 1909 the seniors in the ranks of major and captain had 28 and 20 years service respectively, there had been only one regular step among the subalterns in two years, and the first two hundred on the list of lieutenants had all been commissioned in the same year. The prospect for those who had received direct commissions during the South African War was a hopeless one. The press took the matter up, and *Truth* told the sad plight of regimental officers of all ranks from colonel to subaltern in a delightful parody of "I have a song to sing, oh!". To save the scandal of the compulsory retirement of a number of well-known officers of proved efficiency, the age limit for majors was raised from 48 to 50.

This was, however, but a temporary expedient which left the root of the trouble untouched. Fortunately for the garrison artillery they found at this time a representative in the House of Commons who could speak feelingly from personal experience of their wrongs. Mr. Arthur Lee[1] bombarded the Secretary of State for War with questions, and refused to be put off by assurances that all would be right in time. But it took him nearly two years before he succeeded in obtaining an official admission that there was "a certain hardship" in the case of subalterns having to wait 15 or 16 years for promotion; and another eighteen months went by before the Army Order[2] appeared granting "special facilities for retirement and special rates of retired pay to a limited number of officers of Royal Garrison Artillery commissioned in 1900".

To close on such a pessimistic note would, however, leave a very false impression. Although still suffering from the various drawbacks mentioned in this chapter, the coast artillery was a very different service in the second decade to what it had been at the beginning of the XXth century. With its separation from the mounted branch

CHAPTER XVI.

The Block in Promotion.

Conclusion.

---

[1] Captain & Brevet Major R.A. (retired) now Viscount Lee of Fareham, G.C.B., G.C.S.I.
[2] Army Order 183 of May 1913.

CHAPTER XVI.
Conclusion.

it had ceased to be the dumping ground described in the preceding volume of this History. The importance of its share in the Scheme of Imperial Defence had been fully acknowledged, and its rôle definitely assigned. Much had also been done towards providing it with the means for fulfilling that rôle with credit.

Both organization and training had reached a high standard, and the enthusiasm displayed by all ranks at practice was enormous.

The general feeling of coast artillerymen was one of confidence with regard to their power of dealing with attacks by armoured vessels, and of optimism as regards raids by torpedo-craft, and it is not unreasonable to assume that this estimate of their efficiency was shared by our enemies. Certain it is that the practice of the coast batteries, both by day and night, could be watched by anyone interested, and it may well be that the reports which found their way abroad proved the decisive factor in deterring Germany from attempting those raids on the East Coast ports which had been predicted as her opening move.

CHAPTER XVII.

THE LAND FRONTS.

(1902—1914.)

Land Attacks—The Movable Armament—Training with Mobile Guns—India—Conclusion.

NOTE.

DURING the period covered by this volume the collection of more or less mobile guns and howitzers provided in all coast defences for use against land attacks was known under various official designations. At first "Movable Armament", then "Armament for General Defence", and finally "Armament for the Protection of Land Fronts". Abroad it remained "Movable Armament" throughout, and, in common parlance, this was the general use at home and abroad. It will, therefore, be followed here.

In order to avoid interrupting the narrative when dealing with the primary task of coast artillery—the defence of harbours against ships—nothing has been said, so far, regarding their landward defence. Little attention had indeed been paid by the coast artillery to this side of their duty, in spite of the reminder which the ramparts crowning the heights behind many of their stations might have afforded.[1] The concentration of energy on practice with the fixed armament which distinguished the renaissance of the 90's, had naturally tended to obscure

CHAPTER XVII.

Land Attacks.

---

[1] Notably at Portsmouth and Plymouth—erected in accordance with the recommendations of the Royal Commission of 1860 on the Defence of the Dockyards and Naval Stations. See Vol. I.

CHAPTER XVII.

Land Attacks.

the claim of the movable armament to attention: no training manual deigned to devote any space to its use. When, however, the general hostility during the South African War directed attention to the safety of our overseas possessions, history was ransacked for examples of attacks on such places, and its lesson was found to be plain—the land front was the Achilles Heel. Port Arthur confirmed the teaching of history; and if such a lengthy operation as a regular siege need scarcely be anticipated so long as the British Navy held command of the sea, many of our ports were not as adequately defended on the land side as Port Arthur had been. In their case a brusquer attack might well succeed before succour could come, and armies on the continental scale could easily spare a few thousand infantry and artillery for such an enterprise. With modern steamers and facilities for landing they could be easily transported, and put on shore at some spot out of reach of the coast batteries, from whence a rapid advance might be made on the land front of the fortress.

Quite distinct from such regular attacks on the land fronts by military forces of some considerable strength were raids by naval landing parties upon the coast defences. Boat attacks with the object of spiking the guns of shore batteries had been a commonplace of naval warfare a century before, and foreign naval manœuvres showed unmistakably that a return to such enterprises was contemplated. Modern defences, strong as they might be against the fire of big guns, offered a tempting bait to such a raid. Their position was often isolated; the batteries had usually open gorges, protected only by an iron fence which left their interior without shelter from rifle fire; their command posts, position-finding cells, electric light emplacements, and engine rooms were all at the mercy of half-a-dozen resolute men, and the destruction of any of these might paralyze the guns at a critical moment. The possibility of damage by treachery before the declaration of war was also agitating many coast artillerymen, who saw such out-buildings erected on sites

THE LAND FRONTS. 339

which did not give space even for a wire entanglement round them, and, to make things almost too easy, a description of their contents painted upon their flimsy wooden doors.

During the first decade of the century the mass of obsolete guns[1] forming the movable armament were replaced with more modern weapons. But unfortunately the consideration of defence against land attacks was not included in the purview of the Owen committee, and the new armament, although an immense improvement upon its predecessor, had grave defects. The number of natures was bewildering[2], and many of them were quite unsuitable for use in the country for which they were provided. The 4·7″ guns and 6″ howitzers were far too heavy to move off roads;[3] the 15-pr. and 5″ field guns and howitzers were equally immobile in the jungle surrounding many tropical stations; the demand was all for mountain equipments. What few 2·95″, 2·75″, 12½-prs. and 10-prs. were available were issued, but the number was inconsiderable.

A further drawback to the efficiency of the movable armament was the regulation by which all transport had to be provided locally. In practice this generally meant borrowing mules or bullocks from the Army Service Corps in peace, and trusting to being able to hire or purchase on mobilization—with the certainty that neither drivers nor teams would know anything of their duties.

The new movable armament was put into the hands of the coast artillery just when the experiences of the South African War had drawn the attention of the garrison artillery to the opportunities offered to their branch by the use of mobile guns in the field. *Heavy*

CHAPTER XVII.
Land Attacks.

The Movable Armament.

Training with Mobile Guns.

---

[1] 20 and 40 prs. R.B.L., 9, 13, 16, 25 and 40 prs. R.M.L.

[2] As an extreme case mention may be made of the company in Egypt which had six 2·95″ mountain guns, four 5″ on travelling carriages, and two 15-prs., with in addition at Khartum, a 6″ howitzer, four 5″ guns, and four 15-prs.

[3] "To get two 4·7″ into their appointed positions takes a battalion of native infantry two to four days".

Y

Training with Mobile Guns.

Artillery Training which appeared in 1904, was the first training manual to devote any attention to movable armament, and when the heavy artillery were absorbed by the field army, the siege artillery took the movable armament under their wing, and devoted Part II of their new manual to the rules for its employment. The title of the annual report of the school of gunnery on siege artillery was changed to "siege artillery and movable armament", and for the first time the *Instructions for Practice* legislated for the practice of companies allotted to movable armament. The interest of the coast artillery in this branch of their training was definitely roused, and in 1908 two companies at Malta gave the movement further impetus by carrying out their class-firing with their mobile guns. The movement spread widely, especially overseas where the danger of a land attack was so apparent. The *Instructions for Practice* tried to cope with the difficulties of class-firing for companies allotted partly to fixed and partly to movable armament on mobilization, and introduced tests for the specialists of those allotted to the latter. Regular practice camps were established with targets ranging from representations of the boats of a landing party to the guns and infantry of a force attacking the land defences. With the help of the navy defence exercises were extended to include both landings by considerable military forces and naval raids.

Following the general drift towards field methods which had absorbed the heavy batteries in the field army, the field artillery training manual of 1912 was adopted for movable armament. Shrapnel fire with its complexities of angle of sight and length of fuze presented at first, as might be expected, considerable difficulties to those accustomed to shooting over water. *Garrison Artillery Training* was insistent, however, that all coast defence companies should be put in turn through a systematic course of gun and battery drill with movable armament so as to be available to take their part in the defence of the land fronts.

THE LAND FRONTS. 341

The position in India was peculiar in that there were regular frontier defences and also inland forts.[1] The frontier defences had been armed with 4″ and 5″ B.L. guns and 6″ B.L. howitzers by the beginning of the century, but the inland forts were still practising with 40-pr. R.M.L. guns and 6·3″ R.M.L. howitzers up to the end of the first decade. The inland companies were organized in a separate "group" from the coast defence companies, and companies remained throughout their tour of service in India in whichever group they had been allotted on arrival. Endeavours were made to give all the inland companies some training with the guns in the frontier defences, and also some knowledge of siege work, and of that of heavy batteries in the field, but there were great difficulties in providing the transport necessary for work in the field, and much grumbling in the companies at the many varieties of drill in which they had to make themselves efficient.

The first step towards the reorganization of the seaward defences on a logical basis had been the acceptance of the Admiralty decision as to the scale of attack for which each defended port must be prepared. The landward defence suffered from the want of any such definite instructions as to the strength of attack which might be anticipated. The allotment of the movable armament showed no sign of having been based on any principle, and in consequence there was no general understanding of the respective rôles of the various natures of guns and howitzers—a want which was accentuated by the effect of the separation from the mounted branch. By the end of the first decade of the XXth century there were few officers left in coast artillery with any knowledge of field work. The visits of the Inspector-General of the Overseas Forces, and of the Inspectors of Royal Garrison Artillery and of Royal Engineers, contributed greatly to an under-

CHAPTER XVII.

India.

Conclusion

---

[1] The frontier defences were Quetta, Rawalpindi, and Attock, the inland forts Ferozepore, Delhi, Agra, and Allahabad. See Vol. I pp. 287.

CHAPTER XVII.
Conclusion.

standing of the dangers of land attack by the authorities civil, naval, and military of our isolated ports; and much was done to prepare the artillery allotted to the movable armament for their task if such an attempt should be made. The vulnerability of the fixed armament—the batteries and all their accessories—to a naval raid, and their responsibility for the defence was brought home to the infantry. At home combined operations with the navy in 1912 opened the eyes of the authorities to the danger, and a committee was assembled under Brigadier-General H. H. Wilson[1] to consider the matter. They found that in many cases the possibility of a surprise attack on land had not received sufficient attention, and recommended various protective measures. Another committee under General Sclater took the matter further with regard to the artillery, and advised that training and practice with the mobile guns of the movable armament should be part of the annual training of all officers of coast artillery—the movable armament must no longer be looked upon as a "not very important though pleasing relaxation from the tedium of coast defence work". The Inspector-General took up the task of bringing the whole practice of land front defence into accord with the principles of defence in *Field Service Regulations*. At last all were awake to the folly of spending millions on magnificent works, splendidly armed against a seawards attack, and leaving them at the mercy of a few battalions landed outside their field of fire, or a boat-load of bluejackets.

[1] Field-Marshal Sir Henry Wilson, Bart., G.C.B., D.S.O., Col. Comdt., Rifle Brigade. Died 1922.

PART V.

THE AUXILIARY ARTILLERY.

NOTE.

Parts V and VI deal with the whole period from 1860 to 1914 covered by the two volumes of this History, and not only with that between the years 1899 and 1914 to which the rest of this volume is confined.

CHAPTER XVIII.

THE LOCAL CORPS, THE MILITIA, AND THE VOLUNTEERS.

The Auxiliary Artillery—The Local Corps—The Militia—The Field Brigade—The Volunteers—The Position Batteries—The School of Gunnery—The National Artillery Association.

To give anything like a complete account of the origin and development of the many corps which may be included under the title of "Auxiliary" Artillery would be far beyond the scope of this work. But no History of the Royal Artillery during the period between the Indian Mutiny and the Great War would be complete without some notice of their services. Scattered throughout the Empire, these corps exhibited every variety of constitution. Some were on a Regular, some on a Militia, and some on a Volunteer basis. Some were administered by the War Office, some by the Colonial Office, and some by the Local Governments. In their ranks were to be found every class, from the highly educated young Europeans of the professional classes, to whom the ranks of the artillery volunteers at some of the defended ports were restricted, to the pure negroes of the West Indies. But whatever their differences of class, or creed, or colour, or conditions of service, they were all artillery, and gradually, as the shadow of war crept closer, so also were drawn the bonds uniting them with the Royal Regiment of Artillery.

The difficulties under which the garrison artillery laboured, owing to the undue proportion serving abroad, have been frequently alluded to in this and the preceding volume. To supply the increased garrisons required at certain overseas stations without adding to this disadvantage, dependence was placed more and more upon

346 THE AUXILIARY ARTILLERY.

CHAPTER XVIII.
The Local Corps.

local artillery corps, which may be grouped in different categories. Of these the Royal Malta Artillery is entitled to the first mention. During the struggle with the French for the possession of the Island in the first years of the XIXth century a Regiment of Maltese Infantry was raised to assist in the siege of Valetta, and in the year 1861 this regiment was converted into an artillery corps, styled at first the Royal Malta Fencible Artillery, and taking its present title in 1889. Although enlisted only for local service a detachment of 100 volunteers from the Regiment took part in the expedition to Egypt in 1882, and were engaged in the defence of Alexandria; in 1900 two companies were raised for service out of Malta, and one of them served in Egypt until the garrison was reduced in 1905. The strength of the Regiment varied at different periods, rising at one time to nearly a thousand, but in 1914 it stood at 22 officers and 417 non-commissioned officers and men, organized in three batteries.

In another category come corps composed of regular soldiers of various native races officered from the Royal Artillery, and thus on a footing analogous to that of Indian mountain batteries.

The most important of these were the Hong Kong-Singapore and Ceylon-Mauritius Battalions[1] formed in 1891. The *personnel* were drawn from the fighting races of India—Punjabi Mahomedans and Sikhs—and they proved steady, painstaking gunners, and good layers, always well conducted and well turned out. It would have been better, perhaps, if an attempt had been made to get closer to Indian practice rather than to adopt methods which tended "to produce bogus British soldiers instead of good Sepoys". No language qualification was required of the officers, and although subalterns had to pass in Urdu during their three years appointment,

---

[1] The Ceylon-Mauritius Battalion was merged in the Hong Kong-Singapore Battalion a few years later, the latter supplying one company for service in Mauritius.

LOCAL CORPS, MILITIA, & VOLUNTEERS. 347

they could rarely acquire any real familiarity with the language of their men, so that a smattering of English was apt to prove a better road to advancement than more soldierly qualities. Indian experience would have shown also the danger of entrusting the administration of native troops to British non-commissioned officers, and the necessity for expert assistance in recruiting if abuses were to be avoided. But in spite of such initial errors the battalions proved a most valuable addition to the strength of the coast artillery at the stations at which they were quartered.[1]

On the West Coast of Africa various corps had been raised during the early days by the Niger Company and the different Protectorates, and these usually included some gunners for the defence of the forts along the coast. In the 50's, for instance, the "Gold Coast Artillery" figured for a few years in the Army List, though its existence was brief and stormy. With the formation of the West African Frontier Force in 1897 things were regularized, and a battery of artillery officered from the Royal Artillery was eventually included in each of the four battalions. In three of the batteries the guns were the 75$^{m/m}$ afterwards brought into the service as "2·95″ Q.F." entitled locally the "millimetre guns"; the fourth battery still had the old 7-prs. There were local companies of the Royal Artillery at Jamaica and St. Lucia, and in 1903 these, together with a company of Hausas at Sierra Leone,[2] were formed into a West Indian Battalion, R.G.A.

In quite a different category again come the local artillery corps maintained in the Channel Islands and the various colonies and dependencies on a militia or volunteer basis. These were governed by local ordinances and were

CHAPTER XVIII.

The Local Corps.

---

[1] They were sometimes called upon for unusual duties. One Governor proposed to form a "Governor's Escort" out of them, and gave the rank of Duffadar to the Jemadar, little recking of the effect upon the authorized establishment.

[2] Not to be confused with the regular company of the R.G.A. quartered at Sierra Leone of which a portion of the *personnel* remained at home.

348 THE AUXILIARY ARTILLERY.

CHAPTER XVIII.

The Local Corps.

under the civil authorities except when called out—a divided authority which sometimes caused difficulties. In some corps membership was restricted to pure Europeans of good social standing, in others the majority were of mixed descent, in other again they were pure natives. As might be expected in view of this variety in their composition, the corps varied enormously in efficiency, but they were as a rule good at their drill, and in the tropical stations the natives had special value for many duties. There is no doubt that taking them all in all they formed a useful supplement to the artillery garrisons, and when Queen Victoria's Jubilees, and the Coronations of King Edward and King George, brought representative detachments to England they were made welcome by their comrades of the Royal Artillery. In *Notes by Various Hands 1902-3* (published by the Institution) is to be found an admirable photograph of a group taken at Shoeburyness, entitled "The Artillery of the British Empire", in which are to be seen—all in full dress—three representatives of each branch of the Regiment—Horse, Field, Mountain, and Garrison—and of the following Local Corps—Bermuda, Ceylon, Hong Kong, Jamaica, Malta, Mauritius, St. Lucia, Sierra Leone, and Singapore.

The Militia.

At home the Auxiliary Artillery consisted of two entirely distinct branches—the Militia Artillery and the Volunteer Artillery. Their conditions of service were very different, and they drew upon different classes of the community for both officers and men.

Originally a compulsory levy, dating back many centuries, the "Old Constitutional Force", had become for all practical purposes a voluntary force a few years before the commencement of the period covered by this history.[1] In 1871 Mr. Cardwell transferred the control from the Lord-Lieutenants of countries to the War Office, and the Militia Act of 1875 further consolidated the position of the force.

---

[1] By an Act of 1852..

LOCAL CORPS, MILITIA, & VOLUNTEERS. 349

It consisted of 32 county Regiments, organized on the same lines as infantry battalions, and the first step towards associating them with the Regiment was the appointment of Lieut.-Colonels R.A. as inspecting officers of Auxiliary Artillery. The artillery reorganization of 1882 went a good deal further. Under the provision of this far-reaching measure the garrison artillery was organized in eleven Territorial Divisions. These Territorial Divisions were each to be "composed of one brigade of the present artillery, and of regiments of Artillery Militia, which latter will now become part of the Royal Artillery, and form the junior brigades of the division occupying the territorial district to which they belong".[1]

CHAPTER XVIII.

The Militia.

Unfortunately the distribution of these Militia Regiments by no means fitted in with defence requirements. Twelve of them were Irish, considerably more than were wanted for coast defence in that country, while the regiments belonging to the southern counties in England and Wales were insufficient for the defended ports and fortresses which studded the coast from Harwich to Milford Haven. *Garrison Artillery Drill 1892*—the first to devote any real consideration to coast defence—recognized these difficulties, but postponed any action until mobilization had been actually ordered. It was not until 1895 that the necessity of previous training in the works to be manned in war was enjoined, and regiments came every third year for their annual training to the fortress to which they were allotted on mobilization.[2] During the South African War they were embodied at their war stations, and then it was brought home to all what difficultes could arise owing to peculiarities of pronunciation—especially over the telephone which was fast becoming the general means of communication in coast artillery. A primary condition for an auxiliary coast artilleryman was

---

[1] General Order 72 of 1882. The "Territorial Divisions" referred to have no connection with those of the Territorial Force.

[2] The training in these years was extended from four to six weeks.

350 THE AUXILIARY ARTILLERY.

CHAPTER XVIII.

The Militia.

The Field Brigade.

The Volunteers.

that he should live near enough to the gun he was to fight to be able to attend frequently for training. And so, when the great organization of 1907 came, it was decided to rely upon the Volunteers for this branch, and to utilize the Militia as a supplement to the R.F.A.—to the regret of many of their comrades in the R.G.A.

The whole of the 32 regiments of militia artillery were garrison artillery, but in the South African War four companies were sent out either with heavy battery equipment or to take over from the Navy the guns they had put into the field. The idea of forming militia field batteries for home defence was also raised, and eventually it was decided to try the experiment of raising a brigade of Royal Field Artillery (Militia) in Lancashire. Its composition was exceptional in that, when first raised, the brigade and battery commanders, the adjutant, and one-third of the non-commissioned officers and men, were regular artillerymen, and that the period of annual training was twice as long as that of the ordinary militia. The brigade came to Salisbury Plain for training every year from 1902 to 1907 and reached a very satisfactory standard of efficiency; its ranks were always full; and it cost much less than a regular brigade. But with the formation of the Territorial Force there was no place for it in the organization, and in 1908 it dropped out.

It was under the threat of invasion by Napoleon I that the original Volunteer Force sprung into existence in the first years of the XIXth century: it was a similar apprehension which brought about a revival of that movement when Napoleon III declared war on Austria in 1859.[1] The period covered by this History therefore coincides with the life of the Volunteer Force as we know it. Although never incorporated in the Royal Artillery the corps were placed under the lieut.-colonels R.A. already referred to in connection with the Militia, and in 1889 they were apportioned

---

[1] For an interesting discussion on the subject see the debate in the House of Lords on the 11th February, 1897.

LOCAL CORPS, MILITIA, & VOLUNTEERS. 351

to the three divisions into which the garrison artillery was then divided. Their permanent staff had for many years past been drawn to a great extent from the Royal Artillery, and by this time their adjutants were all regulars.

When the artillery volunteers came into being they were given some batteries of 18-pr. and 32-pr. smooth-bore guns. These were mounted on the old "garrison standing carriages"[1] placed on rough wooden platforms let into the ground. They were usually on the coast so as to be able to practice out to sea, but were sometimes on moorlands where a range of 1,200 yards could be found. In either case they were left in position year in and year out, entirely unprotected from the weather, and the preliminary to practice consisted in searching the bore for old caps and boots and such-like which had found a resting place there during the year. With the adoption of rifled guns in the 60's some found their way into the hands of the Volunteers, but it was another five years before the smooth-bores dropped out, and the 64-prs. took their place. These two—the 40-pr. R.B.L. and the 64-pr. R.M.L.—remained the standby of the Volunteers until the end of the century, although some corps, which could train in a fortress, were privileged to use the heavier R.M.L. guns—7″, 9″ and 10″—which were coming into the coast defences in the 80's.

The great difficulty in connection with the training of the Volunteers was, as in the case of the Militia, that the corps were distributed all over the country quite irrespective of the position of the fortresses they were required to defend. And this difficulty was accentuated by the fact that they only went into camp for a week (of which only three days were compulsory) and so could not go, as the Militia did, to a fortress if it was at any distance. In spite of these difficulties many defence schemes provided for works being manned entirely by volunteers on mobilization except for a small number of regulars as telephonists,

CHAPTER XVIII.

The Volunteers.

---

[1] *The History of the Royal Artillery (Crimean Period)*—Colonel J. R. J. Jocelyn, p. 35.

352 THE AUXILIARY ARTILLERY.

Chapter XVIII.

The Volunteers.

storemen, etc. And as the lessons of South Africa were realized, "Special Service Sections" were formed in Volunteer Corps in the neighbourhood of coast defences to assist the regular coast artillery in manning the anti-torpedo-craft defence during the dangerous days before mobilization brought in the regular reservists. Finally, the movable armament of home fortresses was renamed the "land front armament" and handed over to the Volunteers.[1] There is no doubt that the Volunteers were excellent material for making coast artillerymen. It was just the sort of work an intelligent mechanic could pick up at odd hours without spending a continuous period away from his work, as was required in the Militia, and so, when the great reorganization came, it was decided to rely entirely upon the Volunteers as auxiliary to the coast artillery.

The Position Batteries.

As stated above, the smooth-bore guns handed over to the Volunteer Artillery comprised some 18-prs. These were the guns "of position" which had played such a famous part at Inkerman, and there was naturally a tendency in some corps to form position batteries, accentuated by the issue of Armstrong 20-prs. and 40-prs. as the re-armament of the regular artillery was completed. But except in the Honourable Artillery Company, and one or two other corps, there was no real attempt to form mobile batteries until the 80's. The attention then directed to schemes of home defence showed the possibility of making use of such guns, and steps were taken to improve the organization and armament of the Position Batteries. The 40-prs., drawn by two heavy-draught horses, tandem fashion, led by their carters in smock frocks, with the Nos. 1 marching at their head with drawn swords, were a popular feature of Volunteer field days. Batteries were required to turn out horsed four times a

---

[1] Batteries which were allotted to the defence of the land fronts of coast fortresses as "Auxiliary Units" received a miscellaneous armament including 4·7″, 12-pr. B.L., 13-pr. R.M.L., guns, and 5″ and 6″ B.L. howitzers.

LOCAL CORPS, MILITIA, & VOLUNTEERS. 353

year, for which they received a grant of £100. A few smooth-bore field guns—6 and 9-prs.—had been issued in the early days, and as the rifled field guns, discarded by the field artillery on the re-introduction of breech-loaders, found their way into the hands of the volunteers, some corps took to hiring light-draught horses, and turning out with four-horse teams. By the end of the XIXth century there were in existence about eighty position batteries, thirty of which had 40-prs. and the remainder 16-prs., and it was proposed to send a considerable number to South Africa. But there were two fatal objections to the project—the high rate of pay of the men, and the short range of their guns. Under the influence of the war steps were, however, taken to improve the armament and to provide greater facilities for training. On the 12th February, 1900, the Secretary of State announced in the House that it was proposed to "give Volunteer Position Batteries 4·7″ guns, which have done such excellent service in South Africa, and which are apparently regarded as the most efficient guns of that description which we can find". It was an unfortunate statement, for the defects of the 4·7″ guns for use in the field—however excellent for their own purpose—were well known to all artillerymen. But those mystic syllables "four-point-seven" had captivated the popular imagination, and the money was voted for the re-armament of the volunteers *with the nature of the guns specified.* There was no possibility of evading such a vote, manufacture was pushed on, stimulated by constant questions in the House, thirty batteries were to be provided in 1902, thirty more in 1903. And all the time a real heavy battery gun—the 60-pr.—was being evolved for the Regulars, which the Volunteers might have had if it had not been for that unfortunate specification in the vote.

The question of volunteer field (as opposed to position) batteries had also come to the front. In the same speech in which he announced his intentions regarding the re-armament of the heavy batteries the Secretary of State

CHAPTER XVIII.

The Position Batteries.

z

354   THE AUXILIARY ARTILLERY.

CHAPTER XVIII.

The Position Batteries.

proposed to give the light batteries "15-prs. of the latest type". But there was great doubt as to the value of volunteer field batteries, and this found expression in the House. In March, 1901, the Secretary of State assured the House that Lord Roberts was willing to make a great step in advance, and to agree that with certain training he would rely, from the experience of the South African War, on Volunteer batteries in the proportion of one-third in each of the last three Army Corps.[1]

Lydd had been established as the siege artillery branch of the School of Gunnery, and also as the School of Instruction for position batteries. The ranges were not at all suitable for the practice of such batteries, but they were better than firing out to sea, and many corps carried out their practice there. And this had the further advantage that officers and specialists who could spare the time could come to Lydd for a week's instruction before the arrival of their batteries.

Gradually the 40-prs. and 16-prs. were replaced by the 4·7" and 15-prs., and, what was perhaps of more importance, indirect laying stores were provided, so that modern gunnery methods could really be practised. But some corps had the disadvantage of being composed partly of coast defence and partly of position batteries, and one adjutant could not look after the training of both. The force had grown up haphazard and was ripe for reorganization.

The School of Gunnery.

Previous to 1870 the only facilities offered to officers of the Auxiliary Artillery for professional study were through attendance at the Department of Artillery Studies at Woolwich, and their work there seems to have been conducted in a somewhat desultory fashion. In 1870 a special "School of Instruction for Reserve Forces" was established, and twenty gunners, at 3d. a day, were told off daily to be drilled with, and by, those under instruction. On great occasions as many as fifty were obtained for

---

[1] See the "Army Corps Scheme" in Chapter II.

LOCAL CORPS, MILITIA, & VOLUNTEERS.

battalion drill. The school does not appear to have lasted very long, being superseded by the Royal Military Repository, which, in addition to its duties as a branch of the School of Gunnery was "intended to train the Militia and Volunteer Artillery".[1] There were courses for officers in the new "Fire Discipline" of a battery, and to qualify for "P.S."; for regular non-commissioned officers to qualify for appointment to the permanent staff; re-drilling courses for the permanent staff, and so forth. But at Woolwich there was no possibility of practical instruction, and the closing of the Repository in 1900 brought no regrets to the Auxiliary Artillery.

The courses were transferred to the branch schools,[2] a certain number of corps being allotted to each, but the staffs were fully occupied, and the schools were insufficiently equipped, so there were difficulties at first, especially as the local C.R.A.'s. held that the first charge on the schools should be for the benefit of the regular companies. When Militia Regiments trained at fortresses the schools assisted them, and when it became necessary to call on local volunteers to man some of the quick-firing guns volunteer detachments were allowed to attend the "Q.F. Courses" at Shoeburyness.

Ready as the School of Gunnery were to afford all assistance in their power to the auxiliary artillery, due acknowledgment must be made of the valuable services rendered to Volunteer Artillery by the National Artillery Association. Very early in the existence of the Volunteer Artillery the need was felt of some organization for the advancement of the science and practice of artillery, and the Association was formed in 1863, with, as its main object, "to increase the efficiency and foster a keen spirit of rivalry in the Volunteer Artillery by means of competitions". Originally started as a private association,

Chapter XVIII.

The School of Gunnery.

The National Artillery Association.

---

[1] Royal Artillery Standing Orders.
[2] The School at Leith was instituted in 1898 primarily for the Militia and Volunteers. Lydd dealt with position batteries and those allotted to the Land Front Armament.

356 THE AUXILIARY ARTILLERY.

CHAPTER XVIII.

The National Artillery Association.

it was soon found that the outside assistance received was inadequate, and application for government aid had to be made. This took the form of a capitation grant for all taking part in the final competitions at Shoeburyness, which soon aroused very general interest, as is shown by the life-like picture of the scene published by the *Illustrated London News* in 1867.[1]

These competitions included various repository exercises as well as the actual shooting. For the first year this was with smooth-bore guns, and at ranges of only 1,200 yards, but as the armament improved the conditions were changed so as to keep pace, and the ranges were gradually increased until they had reached 2,000 yards by the end of the century. But plugged shell or shot at a nine foot square target remained the chief interest. After the break caused by the South African War came breech-loading guns, and towed targets, with ranges to 3,000 yards.

The competitions for position artillery only commenced in 1889, and they included putting the harness together, saddling up, and trotting into action—the teams being provided by the School of Gunnery. Until the South African War the guns used were 40-pr. R.B.L. and 16-pr. R.M.L., after it 4·7" Q.F. and 15-prs. B.L.; dummies took the place of the square targets; and ranges were increased to 3,500.

Queen Victoria and King Edward were both Patrons of the Association, as is King George, and all have presented valuable prizes for annual competition, as has the Prince of Wales.

---

[1] Republished, by permission, in the *Gunner* of March, 1931.

CHAPTER XIX.

THE SPECIAL RESERVE AND THE TERRITORIAL FORCE.

The Act of 1907—The Special Reserve—The Territorial Force—The Field Batteries—The Heavy Batteries—The Coast Defence Companies—The School of Gunnery—The National Artillery Association

IN 1906 Mr. Haldane became Secretary of State for War, and set about the great reorganization of the military forces with which his name will ever be associated. An essential feature of his scheme was its dependence upon the Auxiliary Forces, and on the 2nd August, 1907, the "Territorial and Reserve Forces Act" received the Royal Assent. It transferred the Militia into a section of the Army Reserve as an integral part of the first line, and brought into being, under the title of Territorial Force, a second line army for home defence, to be formed from the Yeomanry and Volunteers. In this chapter the result of these changes will be shown as far as it affected the artillery.

The part destined for the Militia in Mr. Haldane's scheme was to supplement the Regular Army both in the Expeditionary Force and for Coast Defence. In all past mobilizations the formation of the necessary ammunition columns without sacrificing batteries had been a problem for which no solution had been found. Mr. Haldane decided that the militia artillery, although all garrison artillery, should be used for this purpose.

After conference with representatives, selected at a large meeting of officers of the Militia Artillery, a

358   THE AUXILIARY ARTILLERY.

CHAPTER XIX.

The Special Reserve.

scheme for carrying this project into effect was agreed upon. Under it the Regiments of Militia Artillery were to retain their territorial designations, their bands, and local associations, but as Royal Field Artillery instead of Royal Garrison Artillery. On mobilization they were to furnish the whole of the brigade and divisional ammunition columns for the Expeditionary Force under their own officers. For training they were to be affiliated to regular training brigades, and to use their guns, horses, etc.

The scheme was considered by a committee of artillery officers under Major-General L. W. Parsons, who came to the conclusion that men trained on a militia basis might be depended upon for divisional ammunition columns but not for replacing casualties in the fighting line. With this modification the scheme was accepted, and an Army Order of December, 1907, converted the Royal Garrison Artillery (Militia) into "Royal Field Reserve Artillery", under which title the various Militia Artillery Regiments appeared in the Army List. But garrison artillerymen cannot be changed into field artillerymen by a stroke of the pen, and the experiment was not a success. The story has been told in some detail in Chapter VI when dealing with the mobilization of the field army artillery, and it is, therefore, only necessary to say here that the attempt had to be abandoned, at least in its original form. The *personnel* of the militia artillery were absorbed into the regular army as "Special Reservists", and the Regiments were disbanded. The field officers, not being required under the new organization, were given commissions in the Reserve of Officers, the captains and subalterns placed on the supplementary list of the Royal Field Reserve Artillery.

Two Regiments escaped this fate, the Antrim and the Cork, for owing to the fact that there were no Volunteers in Ireland, they were required to supplement the regular garrison artillery in the defended ports—Lough Swilly, Belfast, Queenstown, and Berehaven. Instead, therefore, of being converted into field artillery they became "Royal

SPECIAL RESERVE & TERRITORIAL FORCES. 359

Garrison Reserve Artillery", and preserved their identity as units, even when this was changed into "Royal Garrison Artillery (Special Reserve)".

In March, 1908, Special Army Orders dealt with the establishment and organization of the Territorial Force to be formed out of the Yeomanry and Volunteers, and on the 1st April of that year it came officially into being. It was to consist of 14 Mounted Brigades and 14 Divisions, with Army Troops and Troops for Defended Ports, and the organization throughout was modelled upon that of the regular army. The requirements in artillery were, therefore :—

- 14 Horse Batteries, each with a Mounted Brigade Ammunition Column.
- 14 Divisional Artilleries, each consisting of three gun[1] and one howitzer brigade, R.F.A., one heavy battery R.G.A., and a divisional ammunition column.
- 6 Heavy Batteries
  96[2] Garrison Companies } for Defended Ports, formed in "groups" under County names.

There was little doubt but that, with proper organization and facilities for training, the Volunteers could make efficient heavy batteries and coast defence companies: field—and, above all, horse, batteries—were a very different thing, and in these they had had little experience.[3] It was not too much to say that on this the value of the Territorial Force really turned.

The consensus of opinion among the officers of the Regiment since the Franco-German War had always been that field artillery could not be efficient unless under continuous training. When there was talk of forming

CHAPTER XIX.

The Territorial Force.

The Field Batteries.

---

[1] In one division a mountain brigade took the place of one of the field gun brigades.
[2] Reduced to 76 before 1914.
[3] The two horse batteries of the Honourable Artillery Company were in quite an exceptional position in this respect.

CHAPTER XIX.

The Field Batteries.

volunteer field batteries for home defence in the 80's Lord Roberts had been so much alarmed by the rumours that reached India that he had written home to protest. When the idea was mooted again during the South African War years Lord Roberts accepted the necessity for the "Army Corps Scheme", but the Regimental opposition was too strong, and the experiment of raising a brigade of militia field artillery was tried instead. It is true that some of the Volunteer "Position" Batteries had been armed with field guns, but only a very few corps made any pretence at true field artillery mobility—the great majority were what had now come to be called "Heavy Batteries", and belonged to the garrison artillery.

The new batteries had indeed a hard task, and the opponents of the whole idea of a Territorial Force concentrated their attack very unfairly upon them, contrasting especially the results of their amateur efforts at practice with the more finished performances of the regulars—a comparison which there was no material for making in the case of the other arms.

They were given good guns—15-pr. Q.F. (the famous "Ehrhardts") for the horse artillery, 15-pr. B.L.C. and 5″ howitzers for the field artillery.[1] These were, of course, the discarded weapons of the regular batteries, but they had been brought up to date as far as possible. The horses were not so satisfactory. Thanks in large measure to the ungrudging assistance of the regulars, the initial difficulties due to complete ignorance of horse management were soon got over, but the inadequacy of the allowance for horse-hire, and the consequent indifference of the teams with which many batteries had to go to camp, was a great drawback. In some counties the Associations helped batteries to purchase a small nucleus which proved of great value for training. Ground was another difficulty, for in very few places was space available for both manœuvre and practice, and so, since the first essential for a gunner was ability to shoot, many batteries had to

---

[1] See Chapter V.

go to Lydd and Shoeburyness where no manœuvre was possible. The need was, however, recognized, and in 1911 a large amount of additional ground was made available on Salisbury Plain, while the following year saw the opening of the new range at "Ad Fines" (Redesdale) on the Cheviots. The situation was relieved in the meantime by the adoption of biennial practice, which gave opportunities also for the territorial artillery to join their infantry in camp on alternate years, and get some combined training.

The real difficulty was the officers. The acquirement of the tactical insight required for the placing of guns, and the technical skill for the direction of their fire, was no easy task, especially under the circumstances mentioned. In some cases regular officers had to be put in to command brigades, but in a few years a new generation of territorial officers, thoroughly imbued with the field artillery spirit, were making their influence felt. There were attachments to regular batteries, summer attendance at regular practice camps, winter courses at the School of Gunnery, and, in the very last year before the War at divisional headquarters. The progress made far exceeded the expectation of even the most optimistic, and astounded the sceptics. The general consensus of regimental opinion came round to believe that, with some months continuous training, the Territorial R.H.A. and R.F.A. might be fit to take the field against a continental army.

An interesting experiment in the organization of the Territorial Force was the substitution of a mountain artillery brigade for one of the field brigades in the Highland Division. The fluctuation of opinion regarding the value of mountain artillery for warfare generally and not only in the hills has been recounted in Part II, and this latest development drew attention to the subject once more.

The service proved popular, and drew men of good stamp, but they were very much scattered on the main-

362 THE AUXILIARY ARTILLERY.

Chapter XIX.

The Field Batteries.

land and islands of Argyll, Bute, Ross and Cromarty, which was a great difficulty in the non-training period. Their armament consisted of the 10-pr. B.L., but the ponies, though of a sturdy type, were unaccustomed to pack. There was a demand for shafts to be fitted as an alternative.

The Heavy Batteries.

It will have been noticed that the organization of the Territorial Force included two categories of "heavy" batteries (as the "position" batteries were now called) viz: those for the divisional artillery of the field army and those for the garrisons of defended ports.

The former did not fare so well as the field batteries. They were armed with 4·7″ guns, and the provision of suitable horses and their driving presented peculiar problems, so that there were considerable misgivings as to their power to compete with the difficulties of movement and shooting in the closely intersected country in which they were most likely to be called upon to fight. They were hampered also by the old "Ammunition & Store Wagons, Royal Artillery" with which they were equipped in lieu of ammunition wagons.

The batteries allotted to the land fronts of fortresses were not in such a bad way, for they were only required to possess sufficient mobility to occupy selected positions previously prepared. But the want of land ranges was sorely felt, and many had to fall back on the pernicious old practice of firing over the sea.

Some of these batteries were armed with 6″ howitzers, and they came in for the echoes of the controversy which stirred the siege artillery regarding the line of training to be adopted. It was not until 1913 that it was definitely decided that in their case it should be on "field" rather than "siege" lines, that they should therefore practice at Trawsfynydd rather than Rhayader, and that their observation of fire instruments should be withdrawn.

The Coast Defence Companies.

As in the case of the Militia and Volunteers, the scheme for the utilization of the Territorial Artillery in coast defence provided for their allotment to all the coast

SPECIAL RESERVE & TERRITORIAL FORCES. 363

fortresses and defended ports in the numbers required to bring the strength of artillery garrisons—including the regular companies and their reservists—up to war establishment. In preference, however, to mixing them with the regulars, the policy adopted was to allot territorial units to particular forts or groups of guns, so as to give them a proprietary interest.

Chapter XIX.

The Coast Defence Companies.

Like their comrades of the field and heavy batteries the coast artillerymen had many difficulties to contend with. Their 15[1] days in camp was all too short a time in which to learn how to fight a modern fort, even if they could have come fully prepared to make the most of the time. But the miserable equipment of their drill halls and peace stations made it impossible. Without coast guns, or any apparatus for teaching, they could not even learn their gun-drill. No wonder that the keen spirits were disheartened, and that the strength of companies fell off. This was a warning not to be neglected, and provision was made for the gradual issue of loading and laying teachers, and of guns which could at least serve as stands for them. The end of the first decade saw a turning of the tide.

The steps taken to provide the field artillery with adequate practice ranges have been already mentioned. Lydd legislated for "Heavy Artillery and Land Front Armament", and this included the two Irish Militia Regiments[2] which had been saved. The heavy artillery included the 14 batteries belonging to the territorial divisions and the 6 for defended ports. For the coast defence companies Shoeburyness took up the direction of the practice, and devoted a special section of the annual report of the School of Gunnery to its consideration. The *Instructions for Practice* gave space to the conduct of the company practice and to the competition for badges for

The School of Gunnery.

---

[1] The legal minimum was 8 days and some left then without seeing a shot fired.
[2] The Antrim and the Cork. They came over to Lydd for their practice in most years.

CHAPTER XIX.

The School of Gunnery.

skill-at-arms; class badges were introduced restricted to one company in each corps; and in the last year before the War, the Territorial companies were promoted to taking their share in fortress practice. A general improvement set in, for the officers were intelligent if inexperienced, and the men, of the skilled artisan class, made capital garrison gunners. The records of the practice during the last two years showed a marked gain in efficiency.

The National Artillery Association.

Except for a break during the South African War the meetings of the National Artillery Association had been held at Shoeburyness for very nearly half a century, and their annual visit was looked forward to by the regulars, who did their best to assist the volunteers. But in the year which saw their conversion into territorials the association decided, though with much reluctance, that they must follow the example of the regulars, and make a move to better ranges. In this year also the whole position of the National Artillery Association was examined, and the conditions for the various competitions brought up to date.

The competing batteries were to be selected by the officers commanding the Royal Artillery of divisions or districts; the field batteries were to compete at Okehampton with four guns and wagons fully horsed; coast defence companies at the Isle of Wight with two 6″ Mark VII.

But the cost of keeping the range at Okehampton open, and providing horses for the competing batteries, led to the decentralization of the competition. From 1912 it was confined to batteries attending the authorized practice camps, and the award was based upon the report of the umpires which covered the whole of the work done in camp.

At the same time coast artillery competition was confined to companies practising at the Isle of Wight, where the company in each unit obtaining the highest figure of merit was entitled to compete, and 4·7″ or 12-pr. Q.F. were allowed as an alternative to the 6″ Mark VII.

In conclusion the official verdict upon the work of the Association may be quoted :—

"The Army Council feel that it was to a large extent due to the activities of the National Artillery Association that the artillery of the Territorial Army were during the late war able so promptly and so efficiently to answer the calls made upon the corps".

PART VI.

THE REGIMENTAL INSTITUTIONS.

NOTE.

Parts V and VI deal with the whole period from 1860 to 1914 covered by the two volumes of this History, and not only with that between the years 1899 and 1914 to which the rest of this volume is confined.

CHAPTER XX.

THE DEPARTMENT AND THE ESTABLISHMENT.

THE REMOUNT DEPARTMENT.
The Regimental System—The Army Department—The Expeditionary Force—The Remounts.

THE RIDING ESTABLISHMENT.
The Riding House—Reduction—Revival.

THE REMOUNT DEPARTMENT.

UNTIL the year 1887 the troop horses for the army were purchased regimentally, those of the cavalry regiments by their commanding officers and those of the artillery by an artillery officer appointed for the purpose.[1] The first holder of this appointment to figure in the Army List as "Inspector and Purchaser of Horses, Royal Artillery", was Colonel F. G. Ravenhill, who was appointed in 1882 with the rank of Colonel-on-the-Staff. He was almost immediately faced with the task of finding the couple of thousand horses required to mobilize the artillery for the Egyptian Expedition owing to the failure of the dealers who had hitherto been entrusted with the supply of remounts to produce such a number. Colonel Ravenhill undertook it himself, going round the fairs and buying direct from the breeders—a system which he followed throughout his tenure of the appointment.

The Egyptian Campaign was followed by the usual series of Committees, and among these was one, under the Presidency of Lieut.-General Sir Frederick Fitz-Wygram, which inquired into the horse requirements for a

CHAPTER XX.

The Regimental system.

---

[1] Those for batteries in Ireland were brought by the officer commanding Royal Artillery in that country.

370 THE REGIMENTAL INSTITUTIONS.

Chapter XX.

The Regimental system.

The Army Department.

general mobilization. Colonel Ravenhill was a member, and in 1886 he was sent to Canada to ascertain the possibility of obtaining horses suitable for the service there. It was the first attempt to investigate in advance sources of supply outside the United Kingdom, and the 80 specimens of Canadian horses he sent home brought a host of distinguished visitors—from the Duke of Cambridge to Mr. Tattersall—to the Remount Stables at Woolwich.

Colonel Ravenhill fully realized the danger of the system—or rather want of system—that prevailed, with so many independent buyers in peace and no arrangements for war, and he succeeded, in the face of all the opposition due to regimental jealousy, in getting the service put upon a businesslike footing by the establishment of an Army Remount Department. This was brought into being by a General Order in 1887, with Colonel Ravenhill at its head with the title of Inspector-General and the temporary rank of Major-General. He was charged with the purchase of all horses for the army (except the Household Cavalry), and the setting-up of a system of registering a reserve, and by 1889 the Secretary of State was able to inform the House of Commons that the scheme had been successfully launched, and to pay a well-deserved tribute to the able and energetic action of General Ravenhill.

Under the Inspector-General were Inspectors for Cavalry and Artillery, the first representative of the Regiment in the new organization being Colonel S. P. Lines. He was succeeded in 1889 by Colonel B. L. Tollner, who started buying in Ireland, and soon depended almost entirely upon that country for his horses. His phenomenal soundness of judgment, especially of the gun-horse, was universally acknowledged.

One more change was to take place before the Great War, and that more a change in men than in methods, for Colonel H. M. Ferrar, who succeeded Colonel Tollner in 1910, had been intimately associated with the work of the Department as Staff Captain since 1893, so that there was no change of system.

THE DEPARTMENT & THE ESTABLISHMENT.

The unprecedented demand for horses during the South African War had proved conclusively the value of the system of registration inaugurated by the Army Remount Department. This was further developed in connection with the formation of the Expeditionary Force. With the help of the Board of Agriculture, of Chief Constables, and Masters of Hounds, Remount Officers were able to arrive at an approximate estimate of the horse population, and in 1908 the position was put before the public at a meeting in the United Service Institution.[1] In the discussion which followed, in which the heads of many of the big firms engaged in the business—such as Mr. Tilley—took part, the most disquieting feature was the decline in the number of foals dropped annually. At the same time the experience of the Manchurian War showed that the requirements of the artillery for ammunition columns must rise. The position was thus especially serious for the field army artillery, and Mr. Haldane set to work to get the necessary amendments made to the Army Act, so that a thorough census of the horses in the country could be enforced. This took place in 1912 and disclosed the fact that the number of "light-vanners" in the country was only 28,000 while the requirements of the artillery on mobilization were 18,000. This was the class that the artillery wanted, for they would only be doing their everyday work when put into a gun team. Not only was the margin far too small, but these were just the horses that were being displaced by the movement towards motors, so that their numbers might be expected to decrease. The situation was serious, and the steps taken to meet it are of some importance in regimental history. In the first place two heavy horses were substituted for four light-draught in the general service wagons throughout at the "trains" of the Expeditionary Force : this set free 6,000 "trotting-vanners" for the artillery—and inciden-

CHAPTER XX.

The Expeditionary Force.

---

[1] *The National Horse Supply and Our Military Requirements* by Colonel (later Brigadier-General) E. J. Granet, R.A., Asst. Director of Remounts, d. 1918.

372 THE REGIMENTAL INSTITUTIONS.

CHAPTER XX.

The Expeditionary Force.

tally saved men and road-space and forage. Then a section of the "Army Horse Reserve" (into which the "Registered Horses" had now developed) was set aside for the artillery, and subsidized to £4 a year. The strength of this section was fixed at 10,000, and it not only ensured batteries being filled up with horses of the right stamp, it was also an inducement to the big firms to retain their "vanners".[1]

One special cause of anxiety came to light, however, in the years immediately before the Great War, and that was the large proportion of horses of 16 years and upwards in the ranks. This was due to the addition of 55 batteries a dozen years before, and presented an awkward problem. To cast them ruthlessly in accordance with the letter of the law would flood the batteries with remounts, particularly undesirable in the case of those on the lower establishment who could not avoid putting them into work while still immature. The casting authorities were therefore called upon to exercise some discretion in the matter, while keeping no horse not fit for at least a month's service in the field.

The Remounts.

The Royal Horse Artillery had been magnificently mounted from the first, but the Field Batteries had only been given the permanent status of mounted units in the 60's, and even then their mobility had been severely restricted until after the Franco-German War. It is not therefore surprising that the quality of the remounts served out to them was very different from that of those reserved for the horse artillery. In India it had been much the same. In the early days the field batteries had ordinarily had only bullocks, and at the time of the Mutiny some still retained these, and were designated "No. — Bullock Field Battery" to distinguish them. Remounts for the Horse Artillery, and for the "Horse

[1] *The Horse Mobilization of the Army*—a lecture delivered at the Royal Artillery Institution by Lt.-Colonel G. F. MacMunn, D.S.O., R.F.A., Deputy-Assistant Director of Remounts, now Lieut.-General Sir George MacMunn, K.C.B., K.C.S.I., D.S.O., Colonel-Commandant.

Field Batteries" were obtained by the expensive stud system in Bengal, while in Madras and Bombay Arabs and Persians were imported. With the amalgamation of the Indian Artilleries with the Royal Artillery in the 60's the bullocks disappeared, and imported Australians, first introduced under the East India Company, gradually superseded all other sources of supply for artillery purposes.[1] The result was that up to the end of the XIXth century the field batteries in India were much better horsed than the generality of those at home. Towards the close of the century a great improvement began to be apparent at home, and throughout the period between the South African War and 1914 it would be hard to beat the class of remounts which were issued to field as well as horse batteries. The flat-sided, hairy-heeled, coarse and common brutes had disappeared from the field artillery, while in both horse and field, owing to the experience gained on many a weary trek, the 16-hand "leader" type had given place to compacter animals 15·2 and under, well-bred and active, but strong and fitted to withstand the stress of war. The Field Army Artillery were never better horsed than when they crossed the Channel, and the same claim may justly be made for the batteries of the Indian Divisions which followed them to France.

Nothing has been said so far of the heavy batteries, but these had been permanent units in India since the Mutiny, and had been called into being at home after the South African War. In India, however, they had depended upon elephants and bullocks until 1901, when horses came with the re-armament with breach-loading guns. At home they had always depended upon heavy horses, but had gone through many vicissitudes before they got them to their liking, as told in Part II of this Volume.

CHAPTER XX.

The Remounts.

---

[1] While in command of A/A during its first tour of service in India, Major F. G. Ravenhill succeeded in getting this famous troop horsed with chestnuts as at home. At Lord Mayo's famous Durbar for the Amir Shere Ali in 1868 they attracted general attention. (Blackwood, January 1870).

374   THE REGIMENTAL INSTITUTIONS.

CHAPTER XX.

The Remounts.

In conclusion a word may be said as to how the remounts fared in the hands of the Regiment. In spite of the multiplication of other calls the reputation of the Royal Artillery for horse-mastership was fully maintained. However hard the work, or trying the weather, a tribute to the condition of the artillery horses was rarely absent from a Manœuvre Report.

THE RIDING ESTABLISHMENT.

The Riding House.

The formation of a "Riding House Establishment" had been taken in hand by the Board of Ordnance at the beginning of the XIXth century. Commencing with a modest establishment of 20 "Riders" selected from the Drivers Corps, it became the "Riding-House Troop" of Royal Horse Artillery in 1808, and its establishment was gradually raised until it had reached 48 men and 40 horses by the time the Regiment came under the Commander-in-Chief. In 1860 when this history commences, it had risen to 116 with 90 horses under a 2nd Captain with two Riding-Masters. Two years later this was almost doubled, and thenceforward up to nearly the end of the century the number of horses never dropped below the hundred. In 1873 the "Captain Superintendent" became a "Major Superintendent", while in 1884 the Superintendent had become a Lieut.-Colonel with a Major under him as Commandant. These were the palmy days of the Establishment, when appointment to the "Riding Troop" was most eagerly sought, and conferred an undoubted *cachet*. It was during this period—in 1882—that a Military Tournament was first held in London. It was started at the Agricultural Hall, and became at once a popular success, although it was designed entirely for the promotion of skill-at-arms, and so presented few of the spectacular events which are the features of the present entertainment. For its inspiration, and its management during the early years, the Life Guards and the Riding Troop (then commanded by Lieut.-Colonel the Hon. A. Stewart) were

THE DEPARTMENT & THE ESTABLISHMENT.

practically responsible. In the first year a subaltern of the Troop[1] was best "Man-at-Arms" (mounted); and for many years Captain Dann,[2] the senior riding master, was Steward of the Arena and as such a popular character in London. The non-commissioned officers and men of the Troop carried out the whole of the duties in the Arena, and any whose memories go back to those days will remember the smartness of their appearance—always in dress jackets.

CHAPTER XX.

The Riding House.

A less prosperous era was to follow, for in 1897 the Riding Establishment was transferred to the Field Artillery, and its strength reduced to scarcely more than half what it had been. The lieut.-colonel and major both disappeared, the captain lost his title of Superintendent,[3] and all ranks were mulcted of their horse artillery pay as well as of their jackets! It is possible that even more ruthless measures might have been taken had it not been for the existence of the Academy. Riding had been introduced there as part of the course in 1830, and it was found that the War Office were "responsible to parents that every cadet is given, so far as is humanly possible, absolute equality of instruction, in order to give him an equal chance with others in the competition for R.E. and R.F.A. on obtaining either of which his career in life may depend". The War Office were therefore bound to maintain the Riding Establishment at a sufficient strength to enable the instruction of the cadets to be carried out.

Reduction.

The XXth century brought a considerable revival of interest in military equitation. It was decided that the training in this, as in all other branches, must be the duty of battery officers, instead of being left in the hands of riding-masters, too often appointed rather as a reward for good service in the past than for skill in horsemanship. In 1901 the Riding Establishment was remodelled on the

---
[1] Now Major-General Sir Richard Bannatine-Allason, K.C.B., C.M.G., Colonel-Commandant, R.H.A.
[2] Captain & Riding-Master George Dann, d. 1909.
[3] This title was also borne by the Superintendent of the branch of the School of Gunnery at the Royal Military Repository.

CHAPTER XX.
Reduction.

lines of the Cavalry School, its strength was raised, and its duties were defined as the training of officers and non-commissioned-officers as equitation instructors. In 1903 its status as horse artillery was restored, but it did not receive its independence, being combined with the Depôt R.H.A.

Revival.

There ensued a period of great activity in which the eyes of all interested in military equitation were turned towards Woolwich, where Major J. F. N. Birch[1] had initiated a series of experiments in instructional methods with a view of ascertaining the quickest way of teaching a man to ride—a matter of growing importance when gunnery was every year claiming more and more of an artilleryman's time. Methods of riding instruction and horse breaking were investigated on scientific lines, and the principles thus arrived at incorporated in *Cavalry Training*. It is not too much to say that the whole system of teaching riding throughout the Army was revolutionized by the Woolwich experiments.

Naturally enough all artillery officers could not be "good military horsemen and instructors in riding and in addition able to direct the training of remounts" (as the manual said they should be) without themselves undergoing a regular training. But unfortunately the Riding Establishment was not equipped for the instruction of all artillery officers in the way the Cavalry School was, although in 1910 it regained its independence from the Depôt, and the title of "Superintendent", which had been in abeyance since 1897, was revived. Additions to the strength were considered year after year, but always postponed in favour of more pressing demands, although something was done by the loan of remounts. Eventually the whole subject of equitation in the horse and field artillery was referred to a Committee under the presidency

---

[1] *Modern Riding with Notes on Horse Training* by Major Noel Birch, R.H.A., now General Sir Noel Birch, G.B.E., K.C.B., K.C.M.G., Colonel Commandant, R.H.A.

of Brig.-General G. F. Milne.[1] While accepting the general concensus of opinion that the riding had improved since the instruction had passed into the hands of battery officers, they were of opinion that modern developments in artillery demanded a higher standard of horsemanship than was formerly the case, and that the existing standard was not as high as it should be owing to the lack of a uniform system of training regimental officers in instruction. They recommended :—

That the Riding Establishment should be constituted a School of Equitation under the Director of Military Training like all other schools of instruction, divided into two portions, only sufficient establishment for the instruction of the cadets being left at Woolwich, the remainder moved to some place where there was open country in the vicinity.

That at least one officer in each brigade should go through a course at the school annually, and that this course should be a qualification for appointment as adjutant; that refresher courses for riding-masters and roughriders should be instituted; and that a riding-master should be attached to the staff of the divisional artillery since the duties of battery officers were now too varied to allow of their carrying out the whole training of recruits and remounts.

But these recommendations were not made until May, 1914.

---

[1] Field-Marshal the Lord Milne, G.C.B., G.C.M.G., D.S.O., Colonel-Commandant, Master-Gunner.

CHAPTER XXI.

THE INSTITUTION AND THE COLLEGE.

THE ROYAL ARTILLERY INSTITUTION.
The Institution in the 60's—Expansion—The Prize Medals—The "Proceedings".

THE ARTILLERY COLLEGE.
The Department of Artillery Studies—The Artillery College—The "Young Officers"—The Advanced Class—The Firemasters' Course.

THE ROYAL ARTILLERY INSTITUTION.

CHAPTER XXI.

The Institution in the 60's.

AN account of the founding and early life of the Institution is given in the *History of the Royal Artillery (Crimean Period)*, by Colonel J. R. J. Jocelyn, and, in greater detail, by the same author in articles of much interest entitled *Two Regimental Institutions* which appeared in the *Proceedings* in 1904 and 1905[1]. It only remains therefore to take up the story at the commencement of the period with which this history deals. In 1860, then, we find the Institution housed in the fine building which it still occupies. But at that time, and for more than a quarter of a century afterwards, it had to share the use of the building with what was then termed the "Department of Artillery Studies".

The Institution was still almost entirely occupied with educational functions, and other services mainly for the benefit of officers quartered at Woolwich—as had been the intention of its founders. But the expansion of regimental interests due to the amalgamation of the Indian Artilleries, the development of Aldershot, and the growth of the great

---

[1] Vols. XXXI and XXXII.

THE INSTITUTION & THE COLLEGE. 379

fortresses on the coast, all tended to reduce the relative importance of Woolwich as compared with that of the Regiment at large. Here was the parting of the ways, and the Committee fortunately chose service to officers, wherever they might be stationed, as their future policy.

In 1870 an attempt was made to get some of the activities of the Department of Artillery Studies transferred to the Observatory,[1] but without avail. Not until 1888 did the Institution secure undivided possession of the edifice which had been built for its use thirty-five years before.

The departure of the Department made available sorely-needed accommodation for displaying the many objects of interest which the Institution possessed, and so enabled the Committee to transform what had been little better than a store into a Museum worthy of the Regiment. A modest Library already existed, but in 1911 it was decided to transfer to the Institution the Regimental Library which was at that time under charge of the Mess, and which contained a very large number of books, some of ancient date and great historical interest.[2] In order to find place for the books, and room for the better display of the objects of Military and Regimental Interest, the Natural History collection was largely reduced, the Laboratory was dismantled, and the Workshop done away with.

Successive Secretaries introduced helpful innovations, and special mention made be made of Captain H. W. L. Hime,[3] who took up the appointment in 1880 and held it for seven years. In previous years he had contributed many brilliant articles to the *Proceedings*, and he developed the services of the Institution to officers not at Woolwich

CHAPTER XXI.

The Institution in the 60's.

Expansion.

---

[1] The Observatory had proved useful as a home for the Institution in its early years, but had now become something of a white elephant. Talk of selling it to the Government in 1866 led to nothing. A telescope was however installed in 1872 in some justification of its title.

[2] The removal was still in process when the period covered by this Volume closed with the Declaration of War in 1914.

[3] Lieut.-Colonel H. W. L. Hime, d. 1929.

380 THE REGIMENTAL INSTITUTIONS.

CHAPTER XXI.
Expansion.

in ways unknown before, thus greatly increasing the general popularity of the establishment, and its professional value. Classes were established at out-stations: liberal allowances were given to teachers of foreign languages:[1] a regimental agency was created; and encouragement was given to contributors to the *Proceedings* in the shape of grants. When the South African War came on the Institution laid itself out to help in every possible way. Many were the enquiries from officers ordered to the front as to outfit, equipment, handbooks, and so forth. When brigades were rearmed with howitzers on the eve of sailing, lectures were arranged on these novel weapons, and notes on their gunnery and tactics printed and put on board.

The Prize Medals.

The Institution have been fortunate in receiving no less than three separate Memorial Medals for periodical presentation—the Duncan, the Lefroy, and the Walford.

The first of these is in memory of Captain Francis Duncan, the author of the first "History of the Royal Artillery". A Gold and a Silver Medal are offered each year as rewards to the winners in a Prize Essay Competition.

The Lefroy Gold Medal, given by Lady Lefroy in memory of her husband to the most distinguished student in each Advanced Class at the Artillery College, was placed at the disposal of the Institution by Lady Lefroy when the College ceased to be a Regimental Institution in 1899. It is given biennially to an officer who has made distinguished contributions towards the scientific study and application of artillery.

After the death of Colonel N. L. Walford in 1901 a memorial fund was raised which provides a Silver Medal and an honorarium of ten guineas biennially. In view of

---

[1] Certain War Office officials found two artillery officers at the Staff College studying Russian, which was not included in their list of subjects. It was explained to them that the class was supported by the Institution, with the result that the War Office undertook the charge in future.

THE INSTITUTION & THE COLLEGE.

the facts that original work was already rewarded by the Duncan and Lefroy Medals, and that Colonel Walford's name would ever be associated with his brilliant translation of Prince Kraft's Letters[1] which had done so much towards the gunnery renaissance of the last century, it was decided to award this Medal to the writer of the best translation or précis from a foreign language on an artillery subject.

The first volume of the *Proceedings* was issued just before the commencement of the period chronicled here. It contained all the papers contributed between 1848 and 1857, and was followed by a second volume covering the period 1857—1861. From that date up to 1885 a new volume was issued every two or three years. With the installation of a more efficient printing press it became possible to convert the casual publication of numbers into a regular monthly issue, and since 1885 each volume has comprised twelve such monthly numbers.

In 1924 the completion of the fiftieth volume was marked by the issue of a Special Number, the key-note of which was "Reminiscence". In this and the preceding volume of the "History of the Royal Artillery from the Indian Mutiny to the Great War" there have been frequent references to the valuable services rendered by the Institution to the Regiment, but it would be impossible to find better evidence of the way in which its activities touched Regimental life than in the table of contents of that Jubilee Number. Although its date is a decade beyond the period covered by this volume the list is printed here, for the papers are mostly concerned with the life of the period to which this volume belongs, and the names of the contributors were household words throughout it :—

CHAPTER XXI.

The Prize Medals.

The "Proceedings".[1]

Foreword	General Lord Horne.
The Proceedings	Lieut.-Col. H. W. L. Hime.
The Regiment	Lieut.-Colonel J. H. Leslie.
The Rock	Major-General J. C. Dalton.

[1] In 1905 the name was changed to *The Journal of the Royal Artillery*.

382   THE REGIMENTAL INSTITUTIONS.

CHAPTER XXI.

The "Proceedings".

Reminiscences of 40 Years of Peace & War	Major-General R. Bannatine-Allason.
Artillery Equipments used in the Field	Major-General Sir Stanley von Donop.
The Royal Military Academy	Major-General Sir W. Gillman.
Soldiering in India	Major-General G. F. MacMunn.
The War Commemoration Fund	Brig.-General F. T. Ravenhill.
Fox-Hunting	Brig.-General J. E. C. Livingstone-Learmonth and Captain Gilbert Holiday.
Coaching	Major-General G. H. A. White.
Indian Sport	Major-General A. E. Wardrop.
Theatricals at Woolwich	Colonel J. R. J. Joycelyn.

THE ARTILLERY COLLEGE.

The Department of Artillery Studies.

The conclusion of the Crimean War found public opinion somewhat exercised as regards the professional education of officers of the army. The creation of a Council of Military Education in 1857 had followed the Report of Special Commissioners appointed to consider the "Best mode of Reorganizing the System of Training Officers for the Scientific Corps". The Department of Artillery Studies at Woolwich, which had been created in 1850 with the object of supervising the studies of young officers on first joining the Regiment, and had suffered the usual vicissitudes of educational establishments in war time, was revived in 1858 with wider functions. The Director was instructed to assist officers of all ranks in their professional qualifications; to arrange classes in chemistry, photography, drawing, French and German; to be fully acquainted with the processes in the manufacturing departments; to arrange and conduct the annual Military Tours on the continent; and to direct the

THE INSTITUTION & THE COLLEGE. 383

studies of young officers on joining. In 1862 Lieut.-Colonel J. H. Lefroy, Major C. F. Young, and Major C. H. Owen[1] were called upon by the War Office to submit some "Observations on the present state of the higher instruction of the Royal Artillery", with the result that a Regimental Order of the 2nd October 1863 established the Advanced Class in the Department. Not contented, however, with all this, the House of Commons in 1868 appointed a Royal Commission to inquire into the subject. Their Report extended to 1,200 foolscap pages, and so a Committee of Royal Artillery officers had to be called together in order to work out the regimental arrangements for carrying it into effect. The President of this Committee was General Warde,[2] commanding at Woolwich, and their report is of special interest because it was written while the Franco-German War was in progress, and so shows the reaction of regimental opinion to the great part being then played by the Prussian Artillery. So impressed were the Committee with the importance of a thorough professional education for artillery officers that they based their scheme on making "a current of knowledge flow from some fountain head throughout the whole extent of the British Artillery"; and this fountain-head was to be the Department of Artillery Studies at Woolwich.

CHAPTER XXI.

The Department of Artillery Studies.

It cannot be claimed for the Department that it ever filled the place suggested for it in this grandiose scheme, but the twenty years that remained to it as a regimental institution were fruitful of much good work, especially after its change of name to "Artillery College" in 1885, and move to a home of its own in the Red Barracks in 1888. In addition to the main courses for officers—the "Young Officers", the "Advanced Class", and the "Firemasters"—the "Long Course" of the School of Gunnery came for three months every year, and there were constant

---

[1] Respectively, Secretary of the Ordnance Committee, Director of Artillery Studies, and Professor of Artillery at the Academy.

[2] Major-General Sir Edward C. Warde, K.C.B. d. 1884.

384 THE REGIMENTAL INSTITUTIONS.

CHAPTER XXI.

The Department of Artillery Studies.

The Artillery College.

The "Young Officers".

short courses on elecrticity, steam, hydraulics and kindred subjects. In the early days when Staff College students and officers of Militia and Volunteer Artillery attended at Woolwich in a somewhat desultory manner the Department arranged for their instruction, and when examinations for promotion were instituted in the artillery in 1860 it was the duty of the Director to carry them out.

From its first establishment the Department had been housed in the same building as the Institution, and there it remained, although as years passed the expansion of the activities of both establishments rendered such close quarters increasingly irksome. But with the transfer to the Department of the work hitherto carried out by the Instructors belonging to the Arsenal, and the change of name to "Artillery College" in 1885, it became imperative that it should find a home for itself, and in 1888 a move was made to its present abode in the Red Barracks. The Director at that time was Colonel C. B. Brackenbury,[1] who was succeeded in 1890 by Colonel C. Chenevix Trench,[2] and under his rule much progress was made during the next eight years in both practical and theorétical work, and more especially in their combination, due to the association of the workshops in the Arsenal and Dockyard with the class-rooms in the College. But on the 1st January 1899 its name was changed to the "Ordnance" College, its courses were thrown open to the army generally, and it ceased to be a Regimental Institution.

Shortly before the commencement of the period under review the practice of sending young officers to Woolwich on first appointment had been abandoned on the recommendation of the Commissioners of 1857, who thought they would be better employed in obtaining practical field instruction with a battery. In 1868, in consequence of the shortening of the time at the Academy it was revived, but the way it was conducted led to very general dissatis-

---

[1] Colonel C. B. Brackenbury. d. 1918.
[2] Colonel C. Chenevix Trench. d. 1933.

THE INSTITUTION & THE COLLEGE. 385

faction. The young officers were nobody's children, or perhaps it would be more correct to say that they had too many masters. In the mornings they were under the captains of the batteries to which they were attached, or were sent to the Repository or the Riding Establishment for drill; in the afternoons they were supposed to attend at the Department of Artillery Studies for lectures, but the Director had no control, and battery commanders were apt to detail them for parades just at the time they were expected in the lecture room.

CHAPTER XXI.

The "Young Officers".

The opinions regarding the right treatment of young officers on first appointment recorded by Sir Edward Warde's Committee of 1870-71 are of great interest, for they give the views of all the best known gunners of that day on a subject of perennial interest, on which regimental opinion has always been sharply divided.

There were those who considered that young officers should join at Woolwich as being the Headquarters of the Regiment, and those who thought that it was the worst place in the world for both their morals and their manners. There were those who held that the only place for the young officer was in the saddle, and those who would have him spend laborious days in the lecture room and the workshop. One distinguished officer considered that the greatest importance attached to the acquisition of a proper tone in the conduct of military correspondence, and recommended a study of the office letter books. Another, even more distinguished, in the hope of avoiding the reproach of "the British artillery being the most unscientific in Europe", insisted that young officers should be called upon for no regimental duties, so that their whole time might be free for mathematics.

As for tactics some declared roundly that this was a matter for staff officers only—"the Regimental Officer has little use for tactics". Others held very different views. Among thoughtful soldiers, and not least in the artillery, the fate of Austria in 1866 had inspired grave misgivings, and the weak spot in our training had not escaped the

BB

386 THE REGIMENTAL INSTITUTIONS.

CHAPTER XXI.

The "Young Officers".

eyes of certain brilliant young officers whose evidence before the committee is of special value owing to its having been given before any rumours of the approaching Franco-Prussian War had arisen in Europe. Captain Henry Brackenbury spoke of the failure of the Prussian Artillery to render proper support to the infantry on many occasions in 1866 owing to want of tactical knowledge on the part of their officers, and argued that technical training alone was not sufficient to fit an artillery officer for his work in war. Lieutenant H. W. L. Hime was even more incisive. Summing up a scathing indictment of the instruction then given to young officers, he concluded "In a word they have received no instruction worth speaking of in practical artillery—they have received a long and careful education in artillery, but it was in technical and theoretical artillery, not in practical or tactical artillery". Or, as another said, "The great fault of his education hitherto has been that he was taught to manufacture guns, and to drill gunners on a parade ground, but learned hardly anything of the art of war".[1]

The committee reported, that though fully alive to the temptations and peculiarities of Woolwich, they were satisfied that on the whole it was most to the advantage of the service, and of the young officers themselves—as it certainly was to that of the Woolwich Mess—that they should join there. They insisted, however, that they should be entirely under the Director of Artillery Studies, who should be responsible for their conduct and discipline as well as for their instruction. After six months at Woolwich they were to go for three months to Aldershot, and then for three months to Shoeburyness. Aldershot soon dropped out, but otherwise there was little change, until 1888. In that year it was decided to assimilate the

---

[1] Even Staff College officers had been given such technical instruction on their visits to Woolwich. The Warde Committee drew attention to the fairly obvious fact that "it is the use of artillery in the field, not the details of its construction, which is needed for staff officers".

THE INSTITUTION & THE COLLEGE.

system of instruction in the artillery to that of the other arms of the service, the Young Officers' Course was abandoned, and their instruction was placed upon the shoulders of lieut.-colonels. In actual working, however, under the conditions of service in the artillery, this proved impracticable, and a two-months course on first appointment was reverted to—but this time at Shoeburyness only, as will be told in the next chapter.

The Memorandum of 1862 which led to the formation of the Advanced Class has already been alluded to. This urged the expediency of forming within the Regiment a body of officers possessing mathematical and mechanical science sufficient to grapple with the questions arising out of the recent improvements in the science of artillery. The Regimental Order of October 1863 was the result, and the first examination for admission took place in March 1864.[1] The Class did not, however, prove as successful as had been anticipated, although some of the most distinguished scientists passed through its ranks.[2] The inducements held out seemed scarcely worth the ordeal of two years study and seclusion from regimental life, particularly as there was a suspicion that the authorities held the view that an officer could not be a practical artilleryman if he was a scientific one, and that regimental prospects would therefore be impaired by going through the course.[3] So serious was the scarcity of candidates that a Regimental Order had to be issued in 1868 promising that in all first appointments to special employments of a scientific character preference should be given to those who had passed the Advanced Class with credit. And so with varying fortunes the class went on, never entirely fulfilling the

CHAPTER XXI.

The "Young Officers".

The Advanced Class.

---

[1] It may be noted that there was a qualifying examination in French for the reason that gunnery had then to be studied in that language.

[2] Among these may be specially mentioned Major P. A. MacMahon and Major H. C. L. Holden who both received the Fellowship of the Royal Society.

[3] A similar idea regarding the Staff College certainly prevailed in the Regiment right up to the end of the century.

high hopes of its founders, even when it changed its name to "Senior Class Artillery College", until eventually it ceased to be confined to artillery officers.

For many years prior to the period considered here artillery officers had been posted to foreign stations to conduct the proof of guns and powder, with the old title of "Firemaster". In 1870 these appointments were extended and confirmed under the title of "Inspectors of Warlike Stores", and it was their duty to examine and test all technical stores in charge of the Ordnance as well as those of the artillery. A one-year qualifying course was instituted in the Department of Artillery Studies, and was known in general parlance by the old name. Although there were complaints in the early years that officers who had passed the Staff College were given preference over those who had passed the Firemasters Course, the latter proved generally more popular than its more scientific rival the Advanced Class. In 1898 both were abolished with the transformation of the Artillery College into the Ordnance College.

CHAPTER XXII.

THE REPOSITORY AND THE SCHOOL.

The Royal Military Repository—Shoeburyness—The Courses—The Long Course—The Young Officers' Course—The Short Courses—The Colonial Course—The Annual Reports.

THROUGHOUT this, and the preceding volume, there have been frequent references to the great part played by the School of Gunnery in the training of the various branches of the Regiment. It remains only to give here some account of its formation and organization, and of its work in connection with the instruction of officers and non-commissioned officers individually.

The first school of gunnery was that in the Royal Military Repository[1] at Woolwich, which was founded by Sir William Congreve (the elder) in 1778. From the beginning the instruction specialized in the embarkation, disembarkation, moving, mounting and dismounting of guns. "To this also", so wrote Colonel Congreve,

"is added the construction of military bridges, and in short everything that can occur in the most difficult service, and which does not fall within the regular field or garrison practice of artillery; cases of difficulty which previous to the formation of this establishment seldom came within the observance of the officer or soldier until in actual service he was called upon to overcome them, and could not therefore be prepared with the best and readiest means".

---
[1] "The Royal Military Repository" by Major H. B. Stanford.—*Proceedings*, XXVII.

390   THE REGIMENTAL INSTITUTIONS.

CHAPTER XXII.

The Royal Military Repository.

Shoeburyness.

With the establishment of the School of Gunnery at Shoeburyness the Repository became a subsidiary school, the headquarters of instruction in siege work, and many still living can remember seeing practice on the Common with smooth-bore mortars which were retained in the siege train long after the introduction of rifled guns. It appears to have been abolished in the early 70's,[1] and thenceforward the instruction was principally confined to the exercises to which the Repository had given its name, and to the shifts and expedients so graphically described by its founder. Courses of instruction for Militia and Volunteer Artillery were also held there as told in Part V.

The adoption of rifled guns in place of smooth-bores called for the creation of a school of gunnery with adequate ranges for practice and experiment. Lieut.-Colonel J. H. Lefroy, the Secretary of the Ordnance Committee, prepared a paper urging its necessity, and the first entry in the War Office Registry under the heading "S of G" is dated 5th January 1858 and reads "Establishment of a School recommended". His suggestions were accepted, and the School was established at Shoeburyness by a General Order dated the 1st of April 1859. It consisted of two separate departments—the instructional and the experimental—with a Commandant who was also Superintendent of Experiments, having under him a Chief Instructor and an Assistant Superintendent of Experiments. The establishment was small at first, but there was rapid development in both *personnel* and *matériel* to keep pace with the progress in artillery science.

The Repository and the School of Gunnery had been excluded from the purview of the Council of Military Education referred to in the last chapter as being of a purely regimental character. The Royal Commission of 1868 was bound by no such considerations, but ready as

---

[1] In Vol. I an earlier date was given, but the above has been verified by officers who were at the R.M.A. in the 70's and remember seeing the practice.

THE REPOSITORY AND THE SCHOOL. 391

they were to criticize every other branch of military education, they had nothing but blessings to bestow on the School, and their final recommendation is worthy of record in regimental history :—

> "The connection of the School of Gunnery at Shoeburyness with the later instruction of officers of the artillery is so important that our report would be incomplete without some reference to it. We have satisfied ourselves of the thoroughly useful character of the training afforded at this school. . . . . . Each year upwards of twenty officers, besides non-commissioned officers, are sent out fully trained as instructors of artillery. Batteries of the Royal Artillery, and squads of non-commissioned officers are also continually passing under a course of instruction for longer or shorter periods. . . . . We are of opinion that the utility of the establishment might be still further extended both by increasing the number of officers annually under instruction, and by making a short course at the school a regular part of the system of instruction for all young officers of artillery on first entering the service".

The extensive ranges over the sands at Shoeburyness proved of incalculable value both for instruction and experiment during the early years of rifled guns, and the school was able to fulfil the objects of its existence with the success to which the Royal Commission had borne witness. But under the influence of the Franco-German War the field artillery insisted on land ranges. Okehampton was established in 1875, and others followed—each under a commandant independent of the School of Gunnery. It was not until 1891 that a Horse and Field branch of the school was formed under a Commandant who moved to Okehampton in the summer but returned to Shoeburyness in the winter.

With the siege artillery events followed an almost identical course, a practice camp being established at Lydd

392   THE REGIMENTAL INSTITUTIONS.

CHAPTER XXII.
Shoeburyness.

in 1882, with the Superintendent from the Repository as Commandant during the practice season. It was not long before the coast artillery likewise found Shoeburyness inadequate for their needs, and in 1888 a Regimental Order announced "the formation of a camp at Golden Hill, Isle of Wight, for instruction in the defence of a Coast Fortress and Channel in connection with position-finders". The establishment of the practice camps at Okehampton, Lydd, and Golden Hill are landmarks in the progress of the School of Gunnery during the XIXth century.

With the first year of the XXth century a new influence came into play, that of the South African War. The Horse and Field Branch of the School were given the chance of moving bag and baggage from Shoeburyness to Netheravon, but let it slip.[1] The Siege, wiser in their generation, used the war influence for the development of Lydd. The Repository was closed as a School of Instruction,[2] and its staff transferred bodily to Lydd, which became the siege artillery branch of the School of Gunnery. But as a range it was far from ideal, and the inclusion of heavy artillery training in the functions of the school necessitated a practice ground more suited to their requirements. This was found at Rhayader in 1903, and by the time the heavy artillery was transferred to the field army artillery the Russo-Japanese War had shown the need for experience in field work for the siege artillery also. For this Lydd offered no facilities, but Rhayader was well suited, and it became their practice ground in alternate years.

In the meantime some differences of opinion were developing between the School of Gunnery and the Coast Artillery as told in chapter XV. The great advance in

---

[1] Until 1914—when it was approved, but too late to be carried out before the War.

[2] The "Rotunda" in the grounds became a State Museum, administered by the Committee of the R.A. Institution. The grounds were also utilized for various purposes—e.g., for the practical work of position-finding courses at the Ordnance College.

THE REPOSITORY AND THE SCHOOL. 393

efficiency which the coast artillery had made during the last decade of the XIXth century undoubtedly owed much to the labours of the school. But the coast artillery resented being kept in leading strings, and the school was loth to relax its control over the practice of companies, although such control was incompatible with the principles of training as expounded by the general staff. By 1907 the branch schools had been handed over to coast defence commands, and the school at Shoeburyness had become a central school charged with the training of the Gunnery Staff, and such special instruction as that of the Young Officers and the Q.F. Courses. The Commandant still retained certain powers of supervision over the system of instruction in the commands and of review over the practice of companies as told in Chapter XV, but even these were considerably reduced in 1914.

This was not all. One of the matters referred to by the Stopford Committee of 1904 had been the separation of the experimental from the instructional branch at Shoeburyness. With the developments in artillery science it was clearly time to put an end to this illogical arrangement, and in 1905 it was agreed that the separation should take effect from the expiry of the tenure of the present "Commandant and Superintendent of Experiments". The latter portion of the title then passed to the head of the experimental branch, which came directly under the Director of Artillery at the War Office.

The weakest spot for many years was the equipment. In comparison with the naval establishments it was terribly behindhand, not only in the instructional apparatus referred to in Chapter XVI, but in the actual guns used for practice and repository work. Shoeburyness had been provided with the heavy muzzle-loading guns with which the coast defences were armed in the 70's and the 80's,

CHAPTER XXII.

Shoeburyness.

---

[1] A proposal to move the school from Shoeburyness to the Isle of Wight was ruled out of court on account of the expense of lands, buildings, &c.

394   THE REGIMENTAL INSTITUTIONS.

CHAPTER XXII.
Shoeburyness.

but when these gave place to breech-loaders in the defences the School lagged behind.[1] Right on into the XXth century officers and non-commissioned officers under training as instructors had to learn their work with obsolete material, and companies from well-equipped modern works going to the school for the benefit of practice under a school of instruction had to set to work to learn the drill of these antiquated weapons before shooting with them. It was not until well on in the first decade that the progress of coast artillery re-armament allowed of reserve guns and mountings being made available for instructional purposes.

The Courses.

To turn now to the various courses through which the individual instructional work was effected. It cannot be denied that many regimental officers objected to sending their officers and non-commissioned officers to courses—not only from a dislike to losing their services, but also on the principle that training was the business of their commanding officer. On the other hand there can be no doubt that many profited greatly from the experience. In addition to the direct gain in actual instruction received, their time at a central school had an indirect advantage in widening the outlook of both officers and non-commissioned officers. They not only had the opportunity of hearing lectures by experts — naval, military, and civilian—on every aspect of artillery work,[2] but also of exchanging ideas with comrades serving under different conditions. And at Woolwich and Shoeburyness they became aware of quite another side of artillery work, to which they had probably never given a thought—the

---

[1] An exception must be made in regard to the equipment provided for the Q.F. courses.

[2] Among the subjects of such lectures may be mentioned:—Armour and its attack—Torpedo-craft raids—Submarine mines—Electric lights—Commerce Protection—Attack and Defence of Land Fronts—Medium Guns in the Field—Garrison Companies as Heavy Batteries with the Field Army or in a Siege—Mechanical Traction for Heavy Artillery—Balloon Observation—Q.F. Field Guns—Howitzers in the Field—Entrenchments in the Field—Wireless Telegraphy—Proof of Projectiles.

THE REPOSITORY AND THE SCHOOL. 395

manufacture, inspection, and proof of the weapons they were learning to use—and got some idea of the care and ability devoted to the task.

The most important of the courses, the "Long Course", coeval with the School itself, had early gained an Imperial almost an International reputation.[1] There can be few military institutions which passed through those strenuous years between the Indian Mutiny and the Great War with so little change. Originally instituted for the purpose of training officers and non-commissioned officers as instructors, this remained to the end its principal function. And there were surprisingly few alterations in the general arrangements. After approximately three months at Woolwich under the "Director of Artillery Studies", chiefly devoted to the manufacturing departments in the Arsenal, the course proceeded to Shoeburyness for the rest of the year. There "repository exercises" held the field for many years, the erection of the heavy sheers forming the climax of the course. But as the interest in gunnery grew in the 80's more time was devoted to shooting, and there were visits to the newly established practice camps at Okehampton, Lydd, and the Isle of Wight. With the development of the tactics of coast defence in the 90's these visits were extended to the forts guarding the entrances to the Thames and Solent with their accessories of torpedoes, mines, and booms.

The last years of the XIXth century brought a serious set-back. An order that officers coming home from abroad for the course must pay for their own passages to and from England cut off more than half the supply just when the demand for officers with a "g" after their name was

---

[1] It was originally called the "Shoeburyness Gunnery Class", and was the only course acknowledged by the School of Gunnery. The Dominions and Colonies regularly sent officers of their artillery, and on one occasion at least a foreign artillery officer went through the course. The diary of Lieut. (later Major-General) J. B. Richardson during the first Long Course may be seen in the Institution.

396 THE REGIMENTAL INSTITUTIONS.

CHAPTER XXII.

The Long Course.

growing.[1] The Owen Committee of 1899—1900 on Garrison Artillery Instruction took the matter up. This committee, as we have seen, had recommended the transfer of the branch schools from the School of Gunnery to coast defence commands, but with the proviso that Shoeburyness should be retained as the centre of garrison artillery instruction, charged with the training of all officers and non-commissioned officers for the instructional staff. This had always been the principal object of the Long Course, and to accentuate its function, it was renamed the "Gunnery Staff Course" in 1902, and its syllabus extended to include the duties of Inspectors of Range-finding and Position-finding, which were added to the qualifications required of an Instructor in Gunnery. At the same time various improvements were made in the position of the latter, and the obnoxious order about passages was rescinded. In consequence the number of artillery officers attending the course gradually rose again from the mere dozen of 1899 to the score or so which it was calculated was required to meet normal requirements. But in a few years the demands for passages from the most distant corners of the Empire became alarming. It was asked whether the Government was getting value for the expense incurred, and the conclusion arrived at was that when an officer had been sent out on a tour of foreign service he should not be brought home at the public expense for courses which he might attend during his periods of home service. In 1907 a new order restricted the privilege to those who had been successful in competitive examinations such as those for the Staff College, Ordnance College, etc. There remained also the difficulty that officers were not seconded for the course, and that volunteering for it was therefore not encouraged by commanding or company officers.

---

[1] In 1890 the original small "(g)" after an officer's name in the Army List, which marked him as having "passed" the long course, was varied in type to show the grade of qualification gained.

THE REPOSITORY AND THE SCHOOL. 397

The changes in armament and works which were taking place in the coast defences during the early years of the century emphasized the importance of giving as much time as possible during the training of officers and non-commissioned officers for the instructional staff to the service and practice of heavy guns in actual fortresses, and to learning the character and working of all batteries of modern design. In pursuance of this policy the officers of the course were employed as assistant umpires at various coast fortresses during the naval manœuvres, and their time in the Isle of Wight for coast artillery practice was extended to a month, so as to include a whole week in the naval establishments at Portsmouth—seeing the latest types of warships under construction and in commission in the Dockyard, hearing lectures on naval strategy and tactics in the War College, and studying naval instructional methods in the "Excellent" and "Vernon".

The course at Shoeburyness had always included instruction in siege artillery, but the ground and equipment available had become hopelessly out of date before Lydd was established as the siege artillery practice camp. After that the course always went there for a fortnight, and with the development of heavy artillery which followed the South African War further attention was directed to drill and practice with medium guns and howitzers on travelling carriages. The Manchurian War led to the introduction into the syllabus of a siege staff ride, and the working out on the ground of the defence of the land front of Dover defences, as well as a visit to Rhayader in order to see the siege artillery working under very different conditions from anything to be found at Shoeburyness or Lydd.

With the separation of the mounted and dismounted branches of the Regiment there had come a decision to exclude officers and non-commissioned officers of field artillery from the course, and to confine the instruction to purely garrison artillery subjects. This decision was at

CHAPTER XXII.

The Long Course.

CHAPTER XXII.

The Long Course.

variance with the principle on which the course had always been conducted, which was to provide a thorough all-round training in artillery which would serve an officer anywhere: it was resented by the Dominion Governments who had looked to the course to qualify their officers for dealing with artillery in any shape; and in the Imperial Service it ignored the necessity for some knowledge of field artillery in connection with the movable armament which was provided in all fortresses. Some fear of the scientific side of gunnery becoming a lost art in the mounted branch was also entertained, and it was decided to revert to the old system. In 1906, for the first time for several years, the course included field artillery officers, and three weeks were devoted to field artillery work, with, in the following years, visits to the practice camps at Okehampton and Larkhill. There could be no doubt that this admixture of officers of both branches, and the broadening of the basis of instruction, increased the utility and value of the course as a whole, in spite of the fact that instruction in some branches had to be curtailed.

A further extension followed next year when three naval officers joined the course for the coast defence portion (which the field artillery did not attend) and thus gave the garrison artillery in this and succeeding years the opportunity of hearing coast defence discussed from the point of view of the attack.

The Young Officers' Course.

In the last chapter some account has been given of the vicissitudes of the "Young Officers" course until it was decided in 1888 to hand over the completion of their military education to their lieut.-colonels. With the failure of this attempt the course was revived, and a new block of quarters for their accommodation built at Shoeburyness on the site of the old coast-guard barracks. They were completed in 1898, but just when they were ready for occupation there came the re-organization of the garrison artillery, and then the South African War with its demand for officers with the companies, to cause once more the interruption of the young officers' course.

The Owen Committee of 1899—1900 on Garrison Artillery Instruction and Training pointed out, however, that owing to the presence of cadets for other arms at the Academy the military education now given there was of a more general character than formerly, and that the greater part of the technical artillery teaching must therefore be given afterwards. It was therefore decided that they should go to Shoeburyness for three months as young officers. The first of the revived courses took place in 1900, and in 1901 there were five courses to meet the requirements of those who had been at the Academy for a shortened period, and for those who had been through the Militia or received direct commissions. The various expedients resorted to during the South African War to obtain officers necessitated the continuance of these special arrangements to meet their requirements for some years, but by 1905 things were getting into order with two courses of three months each.[1] In this year a new departure was made by sending the courses to Woolwich on the termination of their time at Shoeburyness for a month's practical instruction at the Ordnance College in the complicated mechanisms and electric circuits then coming into the armaments so that they might not have to depend upon their armament artificers.

Time brought the inevitable swing of the pendulum. The feeling grew that after their time at a University or Military College young gentlemen were somewhat satiated with instruction, and it was decided that they were more likely to profit by the course if they had had a year or two with a company first. Companies complained, however, at having to let them go just when they were becoming useful, and coast defence commanders protested that they could learn all that they were taught at Shoeburyness more practically at their stations. The School of Gunnery retorted by pointing out the want of facilities

CHAPTER XXII.

The Young Officers' Course.

---

[1] The officers of the field artillery were only one month at Shoeburyness.

The Young Officers' Course.

for training at the majority of stations, as shown by the very limited knowledge displayed by officers when they came from their companies. In the very last year, however, some slight reduction was made in the length of the time at Shoeburyness by confining it entirely to coast defence work, and cutting out all that could be better learnt with a company. The final decision was that the course should consist of three weeks at the Ordnance College and eight weeks at the School of Gunnery—the wheel had turned full circle.

The Short Courses.

The Long Course and the Young Officers' Course were by no means the only means by which the school made its influence felt throughout the Regiment. Chief of these were the "Short" courses. These had been instituted in the 60's to diffuse as widely as possible a knowledge of the new rifled guns which had just been adopted, and were intended more especially for the benefit of the officers of Indian artilleries about to be absorbed into the Regiment. In subsequent years the principle of short courses was continually extended. There were the regular ones for officers and non-commissioned officers held every winter at Shoeburyness by both the field and the garrison branches of the school. There were also special courses from time to time as occasion called—as for example those for the howitzer brigades before embarkation for South Africa, those for pom-pom sections going to China, and those for heavy batteries when first formed. Then when new gunnery methods were coming in there were courses for battery commanders in which they were given exhibitions of the latest systems of ranging and so forth.

The most notable of the short courses was undoubtedly the "Q.F." course which had been instituted in 1899 as described in Volume I. Throughout this volume, when dealing with the training of the coast artillery, frequent witness has been borne to its value. This met indeed, with general recognition, and the number attending was soon raised from the 80 officers and 300 non-commissioned officers and men of the early years to double that number.

There were special courses for officers and men from the Mediterranean, and from 1904 onwards for the Volunteers —afterwards Territorials. The official objects of the course were threefold—(1) to train officers, non-commissioned officers and men as instructors in anti-torpedo-craft defence; (2) to turn out as large a number of thoroughly trained layers as possible; and (3) to teach shooting by night with anti-torpedo-craft guns. But they did much more than this. They bid fair to solve for coast artillery the problem of raids, and they gave to all branches an object lesson in how rapidity and accuracy of fire could be developed by suitable methods and appliances.[1]

CHAPTER XXII.

The Short Courses.

In the summer there were courses for officers at the practice camps of the field and siege artillery, and with the opening of the school in the Isle of Wight somewhat similar courses were started there so as to afford officers of artillery and engineers an opportunity of seeing the working of coast defences properly equipped. At all these courses officers on leave from abroad were made welcome, and they were, of course, especially valuable for those who had been away from regimental work for any time. But they were by no means confined to them, for in consequence of the very broad hint given by the institution of confidential reports by camp commandants, many majors and captains were to be found attending with the object of improving their powers of observation. There were also frequent courses for auxiliary artillery, but these have been dealt with in Part V.

All the above were for the artillery, but the other arms were not neglected. The allotment of definite camps to army corps did much to increase the popularity of the courses at the field artillery practice camps and the adoption of the divisional organization with its welding together

---

[1] No reference to the Q.F. Courses would be complete without mention of the remarkable work of Quarter-Master-Serjeant (Instructor in Gunnery) W. I. Morris, who was the life and soul of the Courses from 1906 to 1914. He received his commission in the latter year, and died in 1917 while serving with the Inspection Mission in the United States.

402   THE REGIMENTAL INSTITUTIONS.

Chapter XXII.

The Colonial Courses.

of the arms, and the share given to officers of the other arms in the practice, changed their whole character. Those attending were no longer spectators but actors.

Long before the question of loans, attachments, and interchanges between officers of the Regular Army and officers of the Forces of the Overseas Dominions was taken up as a result of Imperial Conferences, the School of Gunnery had thrown open its most important course to officers belonging to the artilleries of the Dominions. Year by year these sent representatives to the Long Course, and many officers of the Royal Artillery will remember the friendships so formed. But this was not all—there was a minor development of the same desire to serve all part of the Empire in the "Colonial" courses. These were for officers desiring to enter the Police or similar services in various colonies, who were instructed in the handling of the weapons with which these forces were armed, such as the 7-pr. of 150 lbs. and Hales war rockets—somewhat prehistoric no doubt, but quite suitable for the purposes for which they were required.

The Annual Report.

Before concluding this short notice of the work of the School of Gunnery a word must be said regarding the Annual Reports. Right through the last twenty years of the XIXth century and the first ten of the XXth, there was no official publication half so widely and attentively read throughout the Regiment. In the 70's these Reports had been but a collection of bald statistics as to the number of companies that practised, the guns they used, and so forth. With the 80's came a remarkable increase in fulness and interest, but it was not until the 90's that they took on their most useful form with the incorporation of the reports of the commandants and chief instructors of the various practice camps and schools of instruction.[1] With their tables of times and results, and accounts of such experiments and trials as might be published, they formed

---

[1] After the establishment of a separate school for Horse and Field Artillery in 1891 their report appeared under a separate cover. In 1909 the Siege report was also separated from the Coast.

THE REPOSITORY AND THE SCHOOL.

not only a very complete record of what had been accomplished, but an invaluable basis for comparison and estimation of progress. Above all they gave the views of leading authorities on the questions of the day—gunnery, drill, equipment—and thus kept the Regiment at large *au courant* with both what was being done and what was contemplated. With units so widely scattered this taking of officers generally into the confidence of the authorities during a period of transition undoubtedly did much to stimulate interest, and so bore an important part in the remarkable progress in gunnery which was the distinguishing characteristic of the period in all branches of the Regiment.

But with the formation of a branch of the staff specially charged with the training of the army such measures ceased to be appropriate. From 1906 only "Extracts" from the Report were published, and in 1910 these gave place to a "Memorandum on Training" issued by the General Staff.

CHAPTER XXII.

The Annual Report.

CHAPTER XXIII.

THE MESS[1] AND THE BANDS.

The Regimental Band—The Bugle Band and The Brass Band—The Horse Artillery Band—The Brigade and Battery Bands—The Mounted Band—The Garrison Artillery Bands—Uniform—Conclusion.

CHAPTER XXIII.

The Regimental Band.

ONE consequence of the Royal Artillery having been administered by the Board of Ordnance rather than the War Office up to the year 1855 had been that the Regimental Band had stood on a totally different footing from others. It had been at least partially paid for out of public funds provided in the annual estimates, and it had therefore been a fully recognized official institution, whereas the ordinary regimental bands were at that time maintained entirely by the officers, and were therefore, strictly speaking, unrecognized. Their existence was, of course, accepted by the authorities, and their procedure was to a certain extent governed by official regulations.

The establishment sanctioned for the Royal Artillery Band in 1855 comprized a bandmaster and 23 non-commissioned officers and musicians, but within a year of the Regiment coming under the control of the Commander-in-Chief considerable changes were made. A band fund was instituted, to which each officer contributed two days pay a year; the establishment was increased to 80; and a new bandmaster was appointed. This was a Mr. James Smyth who had gained a considerable reputation as bandmaster of the 19th Foot at the Chobham Camp before the Crimean

---

[1] In view of the publication of *The Royal Artillery Mess, Woolwich, and its Surroundings* by Lieut.-Colonel A. H. Burne, D.S.O., the account of the Mess has been omitted from this chapter.

THE MESS AND THE BANDS. 405

War. If he could lay no claim to the title of a great musician, he proved a most efficient bandmaster, and under his leadership during the next quarter of a century the Band acquired a high reputation.

Previous to their amalgamation with the Royal Artillery the three Regiments of Indian Artillery had maintained bands in their respective Presidencies. These were however, abolished in the early 60's, and a Regimental Order laid down that from 1st April, 1868, all officers would be called upon for a proportion of the subscription enjoined by the Queen's Regulations for the maintenance of the Regimental Band at Head Quarters at Woolwich.

An important event in the early years of the period chronicled here was the completion of St. George's (Garrison) Church at Woolwich in 1863. There was a great Regimental gathering, headed by the Duke of Cambridge, at its dedication, and the Royal Artillery Band, the Horse Artillery Band, and the Bugle Band, supplied a choir of 150 voices. But the special benefit conferred on the band by the new church was that it permitted the transformation of the old chapel in the barracks into a Royal Artillery Theatre. Thenceforword the band concerts, which had hitherto been given in the Mess, were given in the Theatre.

In 1880 Mr. Smyth retired, and it was decided to throw open the post for competition, the examination of applicants being entrusted to a committee of leading professional musicians. Their choice fell upon Ladislao Zavertal, whose family had come to Glasgow from Italy ten years before. He took over the duties at the beginning of 1882, and under his masterly direction the band speedily attained a standard of excellence such as no military band in England had hitherto approached.

It was frequently commanded to play at the State Banquets at Windsor and Buckingham Palace, and at Marlborough House Balls. In 1897 its establishment was raised to 93, and it took part in the Military Tattoo at Windsor—the first ever held. At the celebration of

CHAPTER XXIII.

The Regimental Band.

406 THE REGIMENTAL INSTITUTIONS.

CHAPTER XXIII.

The Regimental Band.

Queen Victoria's Diamond Jubilee it was selected to play in St. Paul's Cathedral. In 1899 it gave a State Orchestral Concert in St. George's Hall, Windsor, when the Queen signified her appreciation by presenting Cavaliere Zavertal with a gold-mounted baton.

From early in the XIXth century it had been the habit of the Officers at Woolwich to give band concerts in their Mess, and on the conversion of the chapel into a threatre, these had been transferred there. This had the advantage of providing much increased accommodation, and also of making it possible to admit the public. So popular did these concerts become that it was decided to extend them to London, and in 1889 the first series of four orchestral concerts was given there. At first in St. James's Hall, and then in the Queen's Hall, these concerts came in due course to be recognized as one of the musical institutions of the metropolis, and the principle of letting the band be heard by the general public was carried yet further in 1895 when its Sunday afternoon concerts in the Albert Hall were commenced—to draw immense audiences for many years.

An interesting incident in connection with the London concerts may be mentioned here. The phenomenal rise in the orchestral attainments of the band under Zavertal during the closing years of the XIXth century had caused some anxiety lest it might have resulted in some falling off in their powers as a military band. It was decided that the first concert in 1902 should be two parts. In the first half the programme should be for a military band, in the second half for an orchestra. The performance set all anxiety at rest.

In 1903 the Band went to New Zealand to play at the Auckland Exhibition, and made two tours throughout the country.

On the occasion of the Diamond Jubilee Queen Victoria had wished to mark her appreciation by conferring commissions on a few Bandmasters who by their musical ability, length of service, or the excellence of their bands,

THE MESS AND THE BANDS. 407

were considered most worthy of advancement. Mr. Dan Godfrey of the Grenadier Guards had previously received the rank of Hon. Lieutenant, but difficulties were raised as to the extension of the practice, and the matter was dropped for the moment, only, however, to be revived in the following year, with the result that early in 1899 the Bandmasters of the Royal Horse Guards, the Royal Artillery, the Royal Engineers, and the Royal Marines were gazetted as second lieutenants. Everyone naturally assumed that this meant that they were to be officers, but it appeared that they still remained Warrant Officers[1] although "with the honorary rank of second lieutenant". This was not at all what the Queen had intended, and it was a matter in which Her Majesty was personally much interested, so, although the Court was at Cimiez, no time was lost in pressing for the mistake to be rectified. At last, in November, 1899, the substantive rank was granted, the above Bandmasters being gazetted to "the rank of second lieutenant in the Army".

Mr. Zavertal had already received the order of Cavaliere of the Crown of Italy from King Humbert, and in 1901 he received the Victorian Order from King Edward VII. On his retirement[2] in 1907 he was given the honorary rank of Captain in the Royal Artillery, and advanced to Commandatore in his Italian Order. He was also the recipient of many foreign decorations.

Captain Zavertal was succeeded by Mr. E. C. Stretton,[3] the Musical Director of the Royal Naval School of Music, who—as well as Mr. A. J. Stretton, so many years Director of Music at Kneller Hall—had served his apprenticeship in the Royal Artillery Band. The establishment of the Royal Artillery Band had now risen to:—

---

[1] Mr. Smyth had been graded as a staff-serjeant, Mr. Zavertal had received warrant rank—the first bandmaster to do so.

[2] Captain and Mrs. Zavertal are now living at Canderabbia on Lake Como, where they celebrated their "diamond wedding" in 1934.

[3] Major E. C. Stretton, M.V.O.

408 THE REGIMENTAL INSTITUTIONS.

CHAPTER XXIII.
The Regimental Band

1 Bandmaster (W.O.).
1 Band-Serjeant.
4 Serjeants (including one hon. Q.M.S.).
9 Corporals and Bombardiers.
20 Musicians.
58 Gunners.
14 Boys.

———

107

———

In the above account mention has been made of the Royal Artillery Band at Woolwich only. It was the Regimental Band *par excellence*, but it is not to be thought that it was the only Royal Artillery Band. Even at Woolwich there had been others, and some account of these will be given before passing on to those at out stations.

The Bugle Band and the Brass Band.

A corps of "Drummers and Fifers" had come into existence as part of the Royal Artillery so far back as the year 1747, and it had been maintained at Woolwich during the succeeding century. At the time of the Crimean War it used to act as a marching band, relieving the Royal Artillery Band of much regimental duty. But on Sir Fenwick Williams of Kars taking over the command at Woolwich in 1856 he decided to abolish drums and fifes, and to establish instead a Bugle Band. This numbered 24, and proved such a success that it was gradually re-instrumented, and by 1869 was definitely constituted a brass band, its strength increased to 47, and its title changed to the Royal Artillery Brass Band. In 1877, on the formation of the Royal Artillery Mounted Band, the Brass Band was broken up, and some of its personnel transferred to the new unit.

The Horse Artillery Band.

A few years after the creation of the Royal Horse Artillery in 1793 a mounted band had been formed out of trumpeters of the troops quartered at Woolwich. It was equipped with wind instruments at the expense of the officers, and became in due course a very efficient mounted

THE MESS AND THE BANDS. 409

band which always played its part during reviews on the Common. By 1875 it had a strength of 36, but difficulties arose owing to its being expected to play for the field artillery as well as the horse, although it was paid for only by the latter. In 1877 it was decided to form a Royal Artillery Mounted Band, and the horse artillery band shared the fate of the brass band just recorded in the previous paragraph.

The fact of Woolwich being the acknowledged headquarters of the Regiment at the time, had no doubt been helpful in making the maintenance of these bands a practical proposition. It required a somewhat broadminded interpretation of the duties of a depôt to account, for instance, for the horse artillery band. In theory this consisted of the trumpeters of the units in garrison, but as only two batteries were ordinarily quartered there in addition to the depôts it is rather difficult to understand how they were able to turn out on parade a mounted band of 36 musicians. Those who were quartered at Woolwich in the 80's will remember, however, that even in those days the horse artillery depôt were able to produce an excellent bugle band among the boys.

Before leaving the subject of the Woolwich bands mention must be made of the bandmaster of the horse artillery band from 1869 until its dissolution, for, as the author of "England's Artillerymen", Mr. Browne has a special claim upon the gratitude of the Regiment.

In addition to the bands at Woolwich, the adoption of the "Brigade System" in 1859 had led to the formation of unofficial bands at the headquarters of several of the Brigades. The most successful of these were those at Warley and Sheerness, of which the former lasted until 1868, and the latter was maintained—with some vicissitudes—until 1883. They were purely local institutions, under the brigade trumpet-majors.

There have also from time to time been battery and company bands in various units, some of which have reached a sufficient proficiency to obtain engagements for

CHAPTER XXIII.

The Horse Artillery Band.

The Brigade and Battery Bands.

410 THE REGIMENTAL INSTITUTIONS.

The Mounted Band.

local functions. But these have been purely amateur efforts, with no official recognition.

The Royal Artillery Mounted Band at Woolwich was as we have seen, constituted out of the Horse Artillery Band and the Brass Band, and the *personnel* transferred from the former helped in particular to establish it on a sound basis within a short space of time. It numbered 60 performers, and although only 42 of them were mounted, it was the largest mounted band in the service. Under its band-master, Mr. Lawson, it proved an almost immediate success, fulfilling engagements in all parts of the country, always taking part in the Lord Mayor's Show, and taking turns with the Regimental Band to give concerts in the Theatre. But the tide of fashion was turning to Aldershot as the most important station for the mounted branch, and in 1886, it was decided that an artillery mounted band was to be formed there. In pursuance of this design the Royal Artillery Mounted Band at Aldershot was formed in 1886 with Mr. Henry Sims, from the Cavalry depôt at Canterbury, as bandmaster, 28 members of the Woolwich Mounted Band being transferred to Aldershot to form the nucleus. The remainder joined the Regimental Band, and it was ordained that this latter was to provide a mounted section for parade work at Woolwich. In 1897, however, this mounted section was dissolved, and thenceforward the horse and field artillery at Woolwich had to dispense with music on mounted parades.

The Garrison Artillery Bands.

One of the many proposals for popularizing the garrison artillery which had been considered during the period in the 80's when that branch was at a low ebb, had been the establishment of bands at the principal garrison artillery stations. The suggestion had been warmly supported by Lord Harris's Committee in 1887-8, and their formation was frequently discussed during the following decade. Its advocates pointed out that since there were no longer any garrison artillery units at Woolwich, and never had been at Aldershot, the garrison artillery got no benefit from

THE MESS AND THE BANDS. 411

the regimental bands at these stations. Its opponents contended that this was a matter which concerned officers rather than units, since it was the former who paid the piper, and that Woolwich was full of garrison artillery officers holding appointments in the Arsenal and going through courses at the Artillery College. The decision was in favour of the garrison artillery bands, but it had only taken effect at Gibraltar when the outbreak of the South African War diverted attention to graver matters.

CHAPTER XXIII.

The Garrison Artillery Bands.

The formation of a band at Gibraltar was authorized in April, 1899. Its establishment was fixed at a bandmaster, band-serjeant, corporal, and 20 musicians, with the same government allowance (£80) as for cavalry and infantry. The bandmaster came from the infantry, but the Regimental Band found the non-commissioned officers, and also undertook the selection of boys to be sent out for training, and gave a donation for the provision of stringed instruments.

Meanwhile there had come the separation of the mounted and dismounted branches, and no sooner was the South African War over than the provision of bands for the Royal Garrison Artillery was taken up again, and in March, 1903, approval was given for the formation of such bands at the three great fortresses—Portsmouth, Plymouth and Dover.

At first their establishment and government allowance were to be the same as that authorized for Gibraltar, but both were subsequently increased, and although, as at Gibraltar, the bandmasters were transfers from other arms, they had in almost all cases been originally trained at Woolwich.

A further extension of the principle was to Malta where the Band of the Royal Malta Artillery, which had been in existence since the formation of that Corps, became in 1911 the Royal Artillery (Malta) Band. After this change it was controlled by the headquarters, Royal Artillery, in Malta, received grants from the Royal Artillery Band Fund, and the bandmasters had to undergo a course at

412   THE REGIMENTAL INSTITUTIONS.

<small>CHAPTER XXIII.

The Garrison Artillery Bands.</small>

Kneller Hall before appointment. The *personnel*, however, remained entirely Maltese, borne on the establishment of the Royal Malta Artillery.

The Dover Band was transferred to Sheerness in 1913, but otherwise the situation remained as above until the War.

<small>Uniform.</small>

As previously mentioned, a new uniform had been adopted for the Regimental Band in the 50's on coming under the Commander-in-Chief. It differed little from that worn to-day except that the plume was at the side of the busby instead of the front, but in 1879 came the unfortunate change to blue helmets, those served out to the Band being rendered still more repulsive by a plume of scarlet horsehair. More fortunate than the rest of the Regiment, however, the Band got their busbies back again in 1895, and the only subsequent change in uniform was the transfer of the plume to the front.

The Horse Artillery Band, the Bugle Band, and Brass Band wore the ordinary regimental uniform, though with certain unofficial embellishments, but on the formation of the Mounted Band a special uniform was provided, the tunic trimmed with gold braid, and with red collar and cuffs. This was subsequently extended to the out-station bands, with the exception of those in the Mediterranean where special thin serges, trimmed as above, were worn instead of tunics.

<small>Conclusion.</small>

In concluding this brief sketch of the progress of the various bands belonging to the Royal Artillery during the period between the Indian Mutiny and the Great War, attention may perhaps be drawn to the signal service to the art of music in England rendered by these Bands, and especially by the Regimental Band at Woolwich, the oldest permanent band in the country.[1] In maintaining these bands the officers of the Regiment have made a contribution which they may well regard with pride, while the

---

[1] In this whole period there have only been three Bandmasters in the Regimental Band.

THE MESS AND THE BANDS. 413

members of the Band are fully cognisant of their heritage, and zealous to maintain unimpaired the traditions handed down to them. On every Sunday morning throughout the whole period covered by this History the Church Call of the Royal Artillery—"Christchurch Bells"—has been played at Woolwich.

CHAPTER XXIII.

Conclusion.

In 1914 the official designations of the Bands were as follows:—

The "Main Band" at Woolwich, entitled The Royal Artillery Band.

The "Out-Station Bands", viz:—

    The R.A. Mounted Band.
    The R.G.A. Band, Sheerness.
        do.   do.   Portsmouth.
        do.   do.   Plymouth.
        do.   do.   Gibraltar.
    The R.A. (Malta) Band.

APPENDICES.

APPENDIX A.

ARMY ORDER 149, SEPTEMBER 1899.

ROYAL ARTILLERY.—DESIGNATION OF UNITS.—DESCRIPTION OF OFFICERS.—EXCHANGES BETWEEN MOUNTED AND DISMOUNTED BRANCHES.

The following changes in the designation of units and description of officers of the Royal Regiment of Artillery, and in the rules for exchanges of officers between the mounted and dismounted branches, have been approved:—

Designation of Units.

1. Units will be designated as shown in the following examples:—

"A" Battery, Royal Horse Artillery.
1st Battery, Royal Field Artillery.
Riding Establishment, Royal Artillery.
No. 1 Mountain Battery, Royal Garrison Artillery.
No. 1 Company, Eastern Division, Royal Garrison Artillery.
No. 1 Company, Western Division, Royal Garrison Artillery.
No. 1 Company, Southern Division, Royal Garrison Artillery.

Description of Officers.

2. General Officers (except Colonels-Commandant Royal Horse Artillery) and Colonels will be described as belonging to the Royal Artillery.

3. Lieut.-Colonels and Officers below that rank performing regimental duty, will be described as belonging to the Royal Horse Artillery, Royal Field Artillery or Royal Garrison Artillery, according to the branch to which they have been appointed.

4. Lieut.-Colonels and Officers below that rank whilst holding staff, or extra-regimental appointments, will be described as belonging to the Royal Artillery.

Exchanges between Mounted and Dismounted Branches.

5. Subject to the provision of paragraphs 109 to 116 and 124 to 127 of the Queen's Regulations and Orders for the Army, 1899, exchanges will be permitted between officers of the Royal Field Artillery and those of corresponding rank in the Royal Garrison Artillery, provided that the dates of their commissions in their existing rank are within two years of each other, under the following conditions:—

(a) For all Officers for a period of one year from 1st June, 1899, without loss of seniority.

(b) For Majors, Captains, and Subalterns, for a further period of two years from 1st June, 1900, on condition that the senior Officer will take for regimental seniority the date of the commission of the junior Officer with whom he exchanges.

(c) For Second Lieuts. commissioned on and after 1st June, 1899, during the first year of their service without loss of seniority.

(d) Officers of the Royal Garrison Artillery, who have not previously served in the mounted branches, and are desirous of exchanging to the Royal Field Artillery, will forward equitation certificates with their applications.

6. Paragraph 117 of the Queen's Regulations is cancelled.

APPENDIX B.

Terms of Reference
to Special Committee on
Horse and Field Artillery Equipments, 1901.

1. Whether any, and if so, what modification is required in the equipments of Horse and Field Artillery; what is the maximum weight, exclusive of *personnel*, permissible behind the teams in each case; and, subject to this condition of weight behind team, what weight of shell and what range are desirable.

2. Whether a system on which the gun recoils in a cradle, recoil being checked by hydraulic buffers, and the gun returned to position by the action of springs, is permissible or desirable.

3. What nature of projectiles, and in what proportion, Horse and Field Artillery guns and howitzers should carry.

4. Whether the height of wheels should be reduced, in order to lighten equipment.

5. What spare stores, harness, and materials for repair, should be carried with a battery.

6. Whether any change in the pattern of harness is desirable.

7. What vehicles are required to carry the stores (other than ammunition), kits, forage, etc., of a battery.

8. What provision of telescopes and binoculars should be made for brigade-division staffs and for batteries.

9. What should be the composition of ammunition columns and parks in future, and whether parks should be in charge of the Royal Artillery or the Army Ordnance Department.

To report generally upon any improvements which the Committee consider desirable in the equipments of Horse and Field Artillery.

The Committee may call such witnesses as they require to give evidence.

APPENDIX C.

Precis of Conditions
to be fulfilled by Proposed New Equipments.
1901.

Horse Artillery Gun.

1. To be quick-firing with shield, and the total weight behind the team with 40 rounds, not to exceed 28 cwt.
2. To give accurate and effective shrapnel fire up to 6,000 yards, with an elevation of about 16 degrees, and a remaining velocity of 600 f.s.
3. Weight of projectile 12½ lbs.
4. Importance is attached to the above conditions in the following order:—

    (a) Weight behind team.
    (b) Ballistics.
    (c) Rapidity of aimed fire.
    (d) Weight of shell.
    (e) Provision of shield.
    (f) Number of rounds carried.

Gun.

5. If found impossible to fulfil all conditions modifications may be made in (d), (e), and (f), commencing with (f).
6. Breech mechanism of a single or continuous motion type, with extractor, and percussion firing.
7. Calibre optional.

Sighting.

8. Conditions which an ideal sight should fulfil:—

    (a) To remain up in gun during firing.
    (b) To be capable of being re-set with one hand.
    (c) Graduations such that no skill is required in setting.
    (d) Elevation to be capable of being altered without altering the line of sight.

(e) A telescope to be fitted to the tangent sight when required.

9. Reference (c) the open sights are paramount, the telescope an auxiliary.

Carriage.

10. Cradles and buffers not desirable, but will be accepted if found necessary to obtain rapidity of aimed fire.

11. Buffers should not be placed between carriage and spade allowing carriage as a whole to recoil.

12. Designs with air as the running up agent will not be considered.[1]

13. Wheels not to be less than 4' 8" in diameter.

14. Traversing gear only to be provided if jump and recoil are so reduced that gun can be kept on same objective without recourse to handspike.

15. If provided should give 4 degrees on each side.

16. Shield to give adequate protection to man kneeling inside the wheel or sitting on the laying seat.

17. Means for carrying ammunition on the gun carriage not required.

18. Line of sight to be 38 inches above the ground, with a clearance of 18 inches between the carriage and the ground.

19. Travelling brakes required.

Ammunition Wagon and Limber.

20. Weight of wagon not to exceed that of gun and carriage.

21. Some form of tray system of parking and supplying ammunition, but trays not to be made of metal.

22. Wheels the same size as those of carriage.

Stores, etc.

23. In addition to the service stores shown in list, such spare parts as considered necessary, including spare sights, to be provided, and the weight to be included in the total.

---

[1] Subsequently cancelled.

Ammunition.

24. Fixed.

25. Only shrapnel and case shot.

26. 48 rounds case to be carried in battery, 4 rounds on gun carriage or limber, and 4 rounds on wagon or limber.

27. Shrapnel to contain as many bullets (about 41 to lb.) as possible, but none in the head. Base burster. Amount of smoke to be as much as possible without sacrificing a considerable number of bullets.

28. Shells and fuzes to be such that shells can always be issued and carried fuzed.

29. Time and percussion fuze, to act up to the extreme range of the gun.

30. To be damp-proof.

31. To be capable of being set far more rapidly than the service fuze, and so marked as not to require a highly educated man to understand it.

32. No objection under certain conditions to a fuze which, when once set, cannot be re-set at a longer range.

Field Artillery Gun.

The same as for horse artillery with the following exceptions:—

1. Total weight with 15 rounds not to exceed 38 cwt.

2. Weight of projectile not less than 18 lbs.

3. Conditions in order of importance.

   (a) Shell power.
   (b) Ballistics.
   (c) Weight behind team.
   (d) Rapidity of aimed fire.
   (e) Provision of shield.
   (f) Number of rounds carried.

4. The shell power to be judged by the ratio of weight of bullets (41 to lb.) to total weight of shell.

APPENDIX D.

PRECIS OF CONDITIONS
TO BE FULFILLED BY PROPOSED NEW EQUIPMENTS.
1913.

Gun and Carriage.[1]

To be capable of delivering accurate fire at not less than 20 rounds per minute, necessitating absolute steadiness of the carriage during recoil and run-up. Semi-automatic breech mechanism preferred. To give accurate and effective fire up to 8,000 yards with elevation of not more than 23 degrees and remaining velocity of not less than 600 feet seconds. To allow of elevation to 25 degrees, depression to 5 degrees, traverse 45 degrees.

Shield.

To give frontal and overhead protection, and to be proof against the ·276 bullet at 850 yards.

Sighting.[2]

The system to provide the "Independent Line of Sight", or some system giving similar advantages; an open sight compensating for difference of level of wheels; and some form of panorama on the lines of the existing dial sight, but smaller and if possible compensating for difference of level of wheels. Arrangements for laying with clinometer to be provided.

---

[1] A note was added to the effect that it would be considered an advantage if additional elevation, and the necessary adjuncts for use as an anti-aircraft equipment could be provided without sacrificing field artillery advantages. If this was impossible, it might be necessary to provide similar guns on special carriages for anti-aircraft work, such guns to be also capable of taking their place in battery.

[2] A Krupp development of the French *Collimateur* was under trial in six batteries, and the adoption of the *millième* system of graduation was under consideration.

Ammunition.[1]

A shrapnel shell weighing not less than 16lbs. 8oz., but a weight of 18lbs. desirable. A time and percussion fuze to range to 8,000 yards, no safety pins permitted.

Limbers and Wagons.

To carry not less than 24 rounds in the limber, 60 in the wagon body, and the latter to be of the French type, i.e., to be tipped up in action, and to carry a fuze-setter. Wheels to be 4 ft. 8 ins. in diameter.

Springs to be provided if possible, and also in the draught.

Weight.

The total weight including spare parts and service stores to be not more than 24 cwt. on the gun wheels, and 38 cwt. behind the team, 22 cwt. and 36 cwt. respectively preferred.

Special attention to be paid to the provision of springs to lessen wear, and to the necessity of economical repair of wearing parts. Durability and simplicity in use of great importance.

Designs were received in March, 1914, for both 16 and 18-prs., but it was decided that there was no reasonable probability of obtaining the latter without exceeding the weight limits, and attention was therefore concentrated on the $16\frac{1}{2}$-pr.

---

[1] It had been agreed that shrapnel should be considered as the chief projectile, and all efforts directed to producing the most effective shell of this nature. If it were eventually decided to introduce high-explosive this must be entirely subservient to the shrapnel.

APPENDIX E.

Table showing the Distribution of Units in August 1914.

Establishment	Allotment	R.H.A. Gun	R.F.A. Gun	R.F.A. Howitzer	R.G.A. British Mn.	R.G.A. Indian Mn.	R.G.A. Heavy	R.G.A. Siege	R.G.A. Garris'n	R.G.A. Local	Remarks
Home	Expeditionary Force	6	54	18	—	—	6	3	—	—	
	Home Defence	7	15	—	—	—	—	—	—	—	
	Reserve Brigades	—	12	—	—	—	—	—	—	—	
	Coast Defence	—	—	—	—	—	—	—	34	—	
Indian	Field Army	9	33	3	6	8	6	2	—	—	
	Internal Security	2	9	—	2	3*	—	—	8	—	*Not including the Frontier Garrison Arty.
	Coast Defence	—	—	—	—	—	—	—	11	—	
Colonial	...	1	3	—	1	1	—	—	28†	6‡	†Not including the Legation Guard at Peking and the Detachment at Khartum.
Total	Batteries and Companies	25	126	21	9	12	12	5	81	6	‡Hong Kong—Singapore Battalion (5 companies) and Sierra Leone company.
			147					98			
Home	Riding Establishments	1	—	—	—	—	—	—	—	—	
	Depôts	1	6	—	—	—	—	—	4	—	
India	Ammunition Columns	9	11	1	—	—	—	—	—	—	

APPENDIX F.

EXTRACTS FROM THE REPORT ON THE PRACTICE OF THE "X" DIVISIONAL ARTILLERY, BY BRIGADIER-GENERAL "Z."

(k) PROGRESS.

27. Considering the enormous attention paid to gunnery now for what is practically a generation, and the fact that for the last ten years we have had a quick-firing equipment, I cannot think that our progress is what it should have been.

Although it is now rather the fashion to decry our equipment, there can be no doubt that it is a thoroughly serviceable one, while in many important points it is still ahead of that of any other nation; our non-commissioned officers and men are young perhaps, but they are intelligent and keen and respond freely to the great care lavished upon their training by their officers. The officers themselves are of excellent quality—well educated and devoted to their work. I do not believe there is any more efficient body of officers in existence than our battery commanders —highly trained and in the prime of life, they grudge no trouble in the training of themselves and their batteries; while lieut.-colonels are now realizing and rising to their responsibilities.

Why is not the result better? Is it our system of practice that is wrong, or our organization? I believe that in both we have failed to keep pace with the general advance in the conception of what preparation for war should mean.

Organization.

28. As regards organization we still adhere to the 6-gun battery although it is now very generally acknowledged that to get full advantage from quick-firing guns four is the largest fire unit. The length and complexity of the battery commander's orders is a matter of general

remark. It is impossible to believe that the mass of verbiage given in the column "Battery Commander's Orders" in the examples in the Manual can be suitable to a battery of quick-firing guns. . . . What is the reason for these orders? Chiefly that our fire-unit—the battery—is too large for quick-firing guns. In my opinion we shall never get the full benefit of our guns until we adopt the organization suited to them.

Although the brigade organization has at last been definitely adopted, we are still half-hearted about giving brigade commanders their full powers. Recent memoranda on training have invariably drawn attention to the failure of brigade commanders to rise to their responsibilities as regards the training of their commands. But how can they be expected to do so unless the brigade is really recognized as the unit? At practice one, or at most two days, is all that is given to brigade practice, and in Part III of the Practice Report, in which the capacity of a battery commander for fighting his battery is reported upon, the brigade commander is allowed to express no opinion in spite of the clear directions as to the responsibilities of the Commanding Officer in such matters given in paragraph 133 of the King's Regulations. There are many other matters in which the brigade commander's hands would be enormously strengthened if he were entrusted with the same powers as a battalion commander: —e.g. officers, men and horses should be posted to brigades and allotted to batteries by the brigade commander— messes, regimental institutes, etc., should be "brigade", and so forth.

29. Another point in which our organization is defective is in its failure to provide for the combination of gun and howitzer fire in any lower formation than the divisional artillery. In my opinion it will rarely be advantageous to employ the howitzer brigade as a whole, while in all the smaller operations the combination of gun and howitzer fire will be invaluable. But it results from the homogeneous organization of our brigades that

this combination can only be obtained by breaking up a brigade, thus upsetting the organization and throwing the whole machinery out of gear. In my opinion all brigades should contain a howitzer battery. Not only would this ensure the combination of fire, it would also have many ulterior advantages. In the first place the establishment of all field artillery brigades, of all brigade ammunition columns, and of all sections of the divisional ammunition column would be the same—an enormous practical gain. Again, general and staff officers, and officers of the other arms, would have far more opportunity than at present of seeing the combined work of guns and howitzers, for it would be seen whenever a brigade of artillery was used.

At present howitzers get comparatively few opportunities of working with small forces of the other arms, and when they do are apt to be used as guns instead of in their proper rôle. Finally the closer connection of guns and howitzers in the same unit would be good for officers and men of the artillery.

System of Practice.

30. To turn now to the system of practice. What progress has there really been since the period shortly before the South African War, by which time the importance of "gunnery" had become firmly established?

We can of course do some things that could not be done in those days, but is our practice really more warlike? It seems to me that we still fail directly we come to anything approaching service conditions. The contrast between the long delay which ensues when firing shell and the rapidity of our performance with blank, is still a matter of general comment among officers of the other arms who attend our practice camps. On service their comments will be more severe. Artillery officers seem more prone than ever to look upon such matters as obtaining ideal positions for their guns as of more importance than fulfilling their rôle in battle. Is not this due to the way in which the artillery side of the question is placed so very much in the foreground at our practice camps, whereas in real warfare, when working with the other arms, this side has invariably to be subordinated to other considerations? We have even invented a language of the practice camps, and talk about "half-cock" positions, and "cracknel" and "taking on jumpers". I look to the new system under which infantry and cavalry brigadiers will command artillery at practice camps[1]—as they will so often on service—to do much to make our practice a more real preparation for war than it is. Theoretically no doubt we are all agreed that the whole object of our practice should undoubtedly be to fit artillery units to do their work in war. But is it really devoted to this? Is it not rather devoted to teaching officers how to range a battery? With the result that we have become absorbed in the niceties of difficult problems in ranging and a great deal of our practice has become almost a duel between the ranging officer and the range officer. In fact our whole conception of practice has become artificial and we have forgotten that the efficiency of the artillery in war will be judged not by the skill shown in the solution of some difficult problem in ranging but on the efficiency of the support it affords to the infantry in the decisive phases of an action.

The experience of all armies shows how difficult it is to keep the realities of war constantly in mind throughout years of peace training. This is perhaps particularly the case with artillery practice where so much must of necessity be unreal, and we are also still suffering from the traditions of "competitive", which officers and men find it so difficult to eradicate from their minds.

Battery Practice.

32. Thus Battery commanders are inclined to look on the objectives merely as targets, and not as enemy's

---

[1] At brigade practice the brigadier of the affiliated infantry brigade took command. He was accompanied by a senior officer from each of his battalions, and when the scheme included the action of a detachment (such as a battalion and a battery in advanced guard) one of these infantry officers took command of it.

troops capable of hitting back. Excellent instructions as to "the methods of engaging various objectives" are given in Field Artillery Training, but officers are inclined to look upon the operation of ranging more as an academic exercise than as an operation of war. The obtaining of "parallel lines" in particular has become almost a fetish, and is often laboriously pursued quite regardless of the time occupied, or even of whether when obtained it will make the fire a bit more effective against the particular objective engaged. Again many officers seem unable to realize that in war the *number of rounds* used in ranging is practically of no importance compared with the expenditure of ammunition after that process has been completed, while the saving of a few *seconds of time* may make just the difference between success and failure—where failure means defeat and ruin. The tendency is to be penurious in rounds and prodigal in time—and, curiously enough, especially in the case of gun targets where a very small effort of the imagination would show that it is of the utmost importance to subject an enemy's battery to fire for effect at the earliest possible moment.

But perhaps this tendency is most forcibly exemplified in dealing with targets representing advancing infantry. The methods to be employed are clearly laid down in Field Artillery Training both in the Sections on the "Employment of Artillery in war" (159 and 160) and in those dealing with the "Methods of engaging various objectives" (224) but how often are these methods followed in practice? Even without these instructions their own experience at manœuvres should have shown officers the futility of hoping to deal effectively with individual columns or individual rushes. But at practice one still hears the cry of "target up" and sees battery commanders indulging in snap shooting at the few dummies shown. This is a direct result of practice camp conditions. Officers are not thinking of effect against the enemy's troops represented by the target, but of that product of competitive "the effective shell".

Brigade Practice.

33. At brigade practice the same tendency to look at the practice as an academic exercise rather than as a rehearsal for war is shown in the selection of positions which do not allow of the brigade performing the task allotted to it, and in the time required to bring effective fire to bear upon the enemy.

The brigade is the tactical unit and in serious war all practice will be in brigade. Yet, out of the whole course it is rare to see more than one day and 100 rounds, say one-fifth of the time and ammunition, given to brigade practice. Moreover "the brigade day" is usually the last, when ammunition is being used up, and when there is a general air of the serious part of the business being over. The reason that has been given for this for many years past is that in brigade "gunnery falls off". If this is so, surely the right course is to increase the brigade practice so as to teach batteries to shoot in brigade since they will have to do so in war. The old saying of Prince Kraft's about the whole duty of artillery being to hit is often quoted against brigade practice, and even against battery tactical practice, but surely it applies just the other way. We want our batteries to be able to hit when firing under as near an approach to service conditions as we can attain in peace. The first of these is that they should be working in brigade.

And there is the brigade headquarters to be considered as well as the batteries. Does the brigade commander require no practice in fighting his brigade? This may be a comparatively simple task when firing blank; it is only when firing shell that its difficulties are realized. It is then seen how much thought must be devoted to the selection of positions, the allotment of zones and tasks, the indication of objectives and the maintenance of communication, if the brigade is really to be able to bring effective fire to bear when and where it is wanted.

At this year's practice out of the four days gunnery and tactical practice, I gave only the first days gunnery practice to batteries, the remaining three were brigade and

I am convinced that not only the brigades but the batteries as well would now be more efficient if I had given all four days to brigade practice. For after all, what is wanted of batteries in war? Not that the commander, when given the whole ground to himself, may be able to solve some difficult problem; but that, when restricted in ground and time, as he will be in war, the battery may be able to give effective support to the infantry.

34. There is no reason whatever that the "gunnery" of the batteries should fall off in any way in brigade practice if once it is understood that this is as serious a part of the practice as the battery work—and that the "gunnery" will be as carefully scrutinized—with a little arrangement it is quite possible to employ range parties in most cases. But I admit that battery officers may get less practice in ranging than they do at present. No one could be more convinced than I am of the necessity of officers being thoroughly familiar not only with the theory, but with the practice of ranging. It is an essential qualification for battery command. What I object to is the present system under which the training of units for war is sacrificed to this one portion of the work.

School of Gunnery.

35. In my opinion it is the business of the School of Gunnery to teach officers how to range a battery. It is one of the things I believe can be learnt better at a school than with a unit. We have got in the School of Gunnery a body of officers of the highest possible qualifications. During the summer their services are invaluable at the various practice camps—but during the winter their talents seem to me to be to a great extent wasted. In the first place although we have now an excellent land range, the headquarters of the Field Artillery School of Gunnery still move to Shoeburyness—a place admitted to be entirely unsuitable for the purpose when the Field Artillery School of Gunnery was first formed more than twenty years ago. There they are employed during the greater part of the winter in teaching gun drill to courses of non-commissioned officers. This is just one of the

things which in my opinion should not be done at a school. Non-commissioned officers should be taught their work by their own officers in their own batteries. If this were so the whole power of the School of Gunnery could be devoted throughout the winter to teaching officers "ranging" on on the excellent ranges on Salisbury Plain, batteries from Bulford being placed at their disposal as required. The French have followed this system for years, and I see in the last issue of *The Journal of the Royal Artillery* that each officer attending one of these "ranging courses" is to fire 600 rounds. This is perhaps an almost unnecessarily liberal allowance, but the dictum of old Lord Seaton that the best way of learning a soldier's work was "fighting and a d——d lot of it" is certainly applicable to shooting.

CONCLUSION.

36. If all officers were perfectly familiar with the methods of ranging—as they would soon be if the courses I have suggested were adopted—there would be no necessity to devote the practice of their batteries to teaching them this portion of their work. "Elementary" would only be required to accustom young soldiers to the use of service ammunition, and the whole of the rest of the practice could be devoted to teaching units as a whole their work in war. The distinction between "gunnery" and "tactical" practice would disappear, and we should have only "elementary" and "service", the greater part of the latter being naturally carried out by the "tactical unit"—the brigade. And then in all cases when the ground permitted, it would be possible to go a step further, and give time and ammunition to the practice of the divisional artillery as a whole. I am confident that if such a change were made in our system all ranks would respond with eagerness to the new call made upon them, and that good as our brigades and batteries now are, their value as instruments of war would be enormously increased.

(sd) *"Z", Brigadier-General.*

5th August, 1914.

INDEX.

	Page
"A" Tubes—Introduction in gun construction	270
Abbreviations—Use of	iii
Academy, Royal Military :—	
Article by Major-General Sir Webb Gillman in Jubilee Number of *Proceedings*	382
Visits of Colonels-in-Chief	xviii, xx
Cadets at Memorial Service	37
Riding Establishment and instruction of Cadets	375
Changes in Course and Cadets of other arms	384, 399
Accelerated Promotion—Investigation of possibility for R.G.A.	293, 334
Accumulators—Hydraulic gear in mountings	274
Accuracy of Fire :—	
Probability of obtaining direct hits on guns	159
Investigation of regularity of shooting of field guns	217-8
Fear of French system of practice affecting accuracy of fire	215-6
Fear of introduction of time element in Coast Artillery practice affecting accuracy of fire	284
Development of accuracy of fire in the Navy	317
See also "Calibration".	
"Ad Fines"—New practice camp 1912. (now Redesdale)	224, 361
Adjuncts—Multiplication	233-4
Adjusting laths—One-man range-finders	109
Adjutants—Field Artillery brigades	26, 54, 163
Auxiliary Artillery	350-1, 354
Adjutant-General in India—Responsibility for training	147
Admiralty :—	
Relations with War Office and Ordnance Board	86
Responsibility for stating nature and scale of attack to which coast defences are liable	291, 296, 314, 341
Share in design of anti-aircraft equipment	281
Approves use of naval craft to represent attack on coast defences	308
Inter-departmental and joint committees	295-8, 312-3
Advanced Class—	
Formation and progress	383, 387
Change of name to "Senior Class, Artillery College"	388
Aeronautical Society—Discussion of aerial target for anti-aircraft guns	166
Aeroplanes—*see "Aviation."*	
Affiliation—Artillery to infantry brigades	168
Afghan War—Issue of rifles to drivers	57
Africa—Local corps	347
Agadir crisis of 1911—Precautionary measures	xvi, 330
Agra—Indian inland defences	341
Agriculture, Board of—Assistance in estimating horse population	371
Aiming-posts—Indirect laying	105
Aiming-rifles—Development and use in training	285, 307, 327
Aircraft—*see "Aviation."*	
Alarm Circuits—Anti-torpedo-craft defence	287

EE

434 HISTORY OF THE ROYAL ARTILLERY.

Page

Aldershot:—
"The Army Corps" ....ix, 16, 127, 130
Sir Evelyn Wood's command 27, 310
Return of Sir George Marshall from South Africa 41
Sir Redvers Buller's memorandum on artillery training 47
Début of the Heavy Brigade 67
Transfer of Mounted Band from Woolwich 410
Alexandria—Royal Malta Artillery at in 1882 346
Algeciras—The Conference of 1906 and re-armament 80
Allahabad—Indian inland defences 341
Alma, Battle of the—Sir Collingwood Dickson in xxiii
Ambala :—Durbar for the Amir of Afhghanistan 1868 373
       Brigading of mountain batteries 65
America, South—General Poole Vallancy in Expedition xxii
   ,,   North—Mortar fire in Civil War 159
Amir Shere Ali—Durbar at Ambala 1868 373
Ammunition :—
   Field Army Artillery 53, 60, 109-17, 121-2, 138, 220, 313
   Siege   ,,   246, 250, 255
   Coast   ,,   277-80, 299-300, 302-3, 327-8
   Anti-Aircraft ,,   166, 281
   Method of packing 77-9
   Effect of enemy's fire, or of conflagration 90
Ammunition Supply—Battery limbers and wagons   161-2, 177,
                                                                 181, 362
Ammunition Columns and Parks :—
   Investigation of system after South African War 136-9
   Re-organization .... xii, 59, 139-42, 213, 231-2, 358
   The system in India 34-5, 149-50
Andes—Use of Krupp fuzes by Argentine troops 118
Angle of Sight—Instruments for determining 106
Anglia, East—Manœuvres of 1912 .... 227, 261
Ansell, Bombardier—Experiences as battery range-taker 107
Anti-Torpedo-Craft Defence 287, 297, 307, 320, 329-30, 352, 400-01
Antrim Militia—"Royal Garrison Reserve Artillery" 358-9, 363
Application of Fire in the Field 157-9, 163, 195-6, 216-7
Arab Remounts—in Madras and Bombay 373
Argentine—Use of Krupp fuzes 118
Argyll—Mountain Brigade of Territorial Force 362
Armament :—
   Horse and Field Artillery x, xi, 13-17, Chapters IV & V, 148,
                      162, 177-8, 184, 191, 232-3, App. B. C. & D, 425
   Field Howitzers 81-2, 92, 94, 98-9, 102, 124, 179
   Mountain Artillery .... xi, 36, 84, 98, 103, 104, 112-3
   Heavy   ,,   xi, 67, 82-3, 96, 98, 102-3
   Siege   ,,   17-9, 92, 245-6, 156-7, 261-3
   Coast   ,,   Chapter XIII, 295-9, 314, 319-20
   ,,   ,,   Land Fronts 339, 341, 347
   Auxiliary   ,,   104, 351, 353-4, 357, 360, 362
   Anti-Aircraft Artillery 166, 214-5, 281, 218
   Anti-Torpedo-Craft ,,   287, 297, 307, 320
   Dominions xi
   Navy .... xi, 269, 290, 317-20
Armament Artificers 268-9
Armament Firms 12, 73-4, 81-3, 97-8, 118
Armament for General Defence .... ⎱ Designations of ⎰ 337
    ,,   for Protection of Land Fronts⎰ movable armament⎱

INDEX.

	Page
Armour :—	
Introduction of Hardened Steel[1]	278, 319, 329
Method of attack by artillery	319-20
Armour-piercing Projectiles	278, 296, 299
Armstrong—Armament Firm	74, 81, 83
Army—Interest in artillery matters	ix, xiii, 220-3
Army Act—Inclusion of horse census	371
Army Corps :—	
The Scheme of 1902	24-5, 130-1, 133, 283, 292, 354, 360
,, ,, 1905	130-1, 133, 292
Army Council	292, 365
Army Manœuvres	227, 261
Army Ordnance Corps and Departments	90, 269
Army Review—Articles	190, 203
Army Service Corps	260-1, 339
Arnold-Foster, the Rt. Hon. H. O.—Secretary of State	76
Arsenal, Royal—see "Ordnance Factories"	
Artificers	67, 90, 269
Artillerie de Campagne en Liaison avec les Autres Armee.—	
Colonel H. Langlois	202
Artillery College :—	
Change of name and quarters	384, 388
Courses at	387-8
Artillery Equipment used in the Field—Article by Major-General	
Sir Stanley von Donop in Jubilee Number of *Proceedings*	382
Artillery, School of	224
Artillery Studies, Department of	354, 378-9, 382-4
Courses at	384-6, 388, 395
See also "Artillery College".	
Assistant Adjutant-General R.A. :—	
War Office	1, 2, 128
India	146
Assistant Military Secretary R.A.—War Office	1, 2
Attachment of Artillery Officers to the Other Arms	167-8, 251
Attock—Indian frontier defences	341
Augmentation of horse and field artillery	4, 5, 20
,, ,, garrison artillery	5
Augmenting Rings and Strips—Use with driving bands	271
Australian Remounts in India	373
Austro-Prussian War—Lessons	198, 385-6
Automatic Sights	275-6, 284-5, 320-1
AuxiliaryArtillery :—	
Connection with Royal Artillery	24, 287, 345, 349, 351-2
Instruction of Officers	354-5
School of Gunnery	363-4
The Local Corps	345-8
The Militia	348-50, 357-9
The Volunteers	350-4
The Territorial Force	359-63
The National Artillery Association	355-6, 364-5
Aviation :—	
Advent and development of air-craft	xv, 166-7, 195, 214, 251, 259
Use for location of targets and observation of fire	xv, 166-7, 214, 251, 259

---
[1] "Harveyed", "Krupp Cemented" (K.C.), "Krupp Non-Cemented" (K.N.C.).

436 HISTORY OF THE ROYAL ARTILLERY.

Page

Aviation :—(continued).
 Methods of attack by artillery .... xv, 166, 195, 214, 251, 259
 Concealment and protection from 214, 250-1, 281, 318
 Trials at practice camps .... xv, 166, 214-5, 251, 259
 Inclusion of instructions in manuals .... xv, 207, 214
 Anti-Aircraft equipments 166, 214-5, 281, 318
 Precautions against attack by 259
Axial Recoil 17, 94-5, 272-3
Axletrees :—
 Uniformity of pattern of arm 92
 Cranked for field howitzers and mountain guns 102-3
Axletree-seats—Removal from 15-pr. Q.F. and 18-pr. Q.F. equipments 93, 100

Bacon, Admiral Sir Reginald—Committee on Instruction of Garrison Artillery in Naval matters 289, 311-3
Baggage-guards—Arming of 57, 235
"Bail-Batteries"—India 66, 231, 260
Balfour, Rt. Hon. A. J.—Prime Minister 76, 128
Balkan Wars—Lessons 207
Ball-Bearings—Use in mountings 273
Ballistite—Replacement by Cordite in charges 93, 257
Balloons—see "Aviation."
Bally, Major-General J. F.—Committee on Manning 23
Bandoliers—Personal Equipment 58
Bands, Regimental :—
 Official Designations in 1914 413
 Uniform 412
 Service to Music 412
 The Main Band 37, 404-8, 410, 412-13
 The Bugle Band 408
 The Brass Band 408
 The Horse Artillery Band 408-9
 The Mounted Band 410
 The Brigade and Battery Bands 409-10
 Garrison Artillery Bands 37, 410-12
Bannatine-Allason, Major-General Sir Richard 375, 382
Bandmasters 404-7, 409-10
Bar-and-Drum Sights—or Rocking-Bar 95-6, 275
Bar-Indicators—to supersede fuze-dials 124
Barbette mountings 268, 273
Bare charges 110, 271-4
Barracks—Want of accommodation for batteries after South African war 25
Barometer—Effect of changes on shooting 218, 303
Barron, Major-General Sir Harry—Commandant, School of Gunnery 306
Barr & Stroud—Range-finder 108-9, 321-2
Battalion—Title in Artillery 136
Batteries :—
 Titles and precedence 28-30, 66, 282
 Organization in horse & field artillery ... 189-92, 194-5, 228-9, 425-6
 Design and Construction in siege and coast artillery ... 253, 317-8
Battery Commanders 65-6, 148, 163, 226, 425, 428-32
 ,, Headquarters 197, 211

INDEX.

	Page
Battery Leaders	48
,, Officers	375, 425
,, Bands	409-10

Battery Practice :—
  Horse & field artillery 20, 53-4, 163, 177, 189, 428-9
  Heavy artillery 68, 181
  Siege artillery 244-5, 248-9
  Coast artlllery 325

Batteries mentioned individually :—
  R.H.A.—"A", "D", "N", "O", "W", "Y" ... xxii, 28-9, 79, 178, 286, 373
  R.F.A.—1st, 26th, 37th, 52nd, 81st, 92nd, 95th 28, 62, 79, 286
  R.A.—1/Southern, 31/Southern, 40/Southern 286
  R.G.A.—13, 27, 49 286

Battle Practice—Coast artillery 300
"Bearings"—Distinction from "Trainings" 277
Belfast—Irish defended ports 358
Belfield, Lieut.-General Sir Herbert—Judge of Prize Essays 173
Bengal—Stud system for remounts 373
Berehaven—Irish defended port 358
Bermuda—Local Corps 348
Bethell, Brig.-General H. A.—Articles on *Progress in Matériel* in *Proceedings* 89
Biddulph, Lieut.-General Sir Robert—at Memorial Service 37
Bigge, Sir Arthur (Lord Stamfordham) 29
Billets—Inclusion in *Field Artillery Training, 1912* 194
Bingham, Major-General Hon. Sir Francis—Visit to French Artillery practice 187-9
  Lectures on practice at home 1912 & 1913 205

Binoculars :—
  Issue to batteries 49, 50
  Supersession of Galilean by Stereoscopic or Prismatic 50, 107, 255

Bivouacs—Inclusion in *Field Artillery Training, 1912* 194
Blackwood—Article on Durbar for Amir of Afghanistan, 1868 373

Blank Ammunition :—
  Difficulty of obtaining smokeless 111, 228
  Use during night-firing 307-8

Blériot, M—Channel flight in 1909 166
Blewitt, Major-General W. E. 64, 75
Blinding—Of enemy's guns 216
  ,, Effect on detachments of cordite flash 308
Blockers—Introduction and method of attack by artillery xi, 291, 297, 307-8, 319-20
Bloomfield, General Sir John—Master-Gunner xxii
"Blue-Water-School"—Opposition to Fixed Defences ...... ix, 316
Boards—see "Committees"
Boers—Impression made by unorthodox methods 43, 46-7
  Use of heavy guns and howitzers 66, 81
  ,, captured guns 78

Bombardment :—
  Of trenches prior to infantry attack 43
  Of coast defences by Navy 280, 290-1, 319

Bombay—Arabs and Persians as Remounts 373
Boom-smashers—Introduction and method of attack by artillery xi, 291, 297, 307-8, 319-20
Bordon—Construction of Camp 25

438 HISTORY OF THE ROYAL ARTILLERY.

Page

Brackenbury, General Rt. Hon. Sir Henry :—
   Evidence before Warde Committee 386
   Director-General of Ordnance 10, 11 13-9
   The horse and field equipment committee 72-3
Brackenbury, Colonel C. B.—Direcor, Artillery College 384
Bracket-system :—
   Modification of use with quick-firing field guns 160-1
   ,,   ,,   ,,   calibrated coast guns 301, 321-2
Brakes—adoption of "swinging-arm" type 99, 100
Branch Schools—Transfer from School of Gunnery to Coast defence commands 309-10, 393
   Instruction of Auxiliary Artillery 355
Brass Band, The 408
Breech-mechanisms :—
   The "swinging-block" for field guns 97-8, 232
   The "sliding-wedge" for field howitzers 98
   The cylindrical breech screw for heavy artillery guns 98
   The "Welin" screw for coast guns 271
   The "Semi-automatic" for anti-aircraft guns 281
Brigade—Army 133, 176, 222
   ,, —Artillery .... iii, 54, 136
Brigading of batteries .... xi, 21, 26-9, 35, 54, 60, 65, 67-8
                                                                                                                  245, 249, 264
Brigade Commanders ... 54-5, 148, 163, 212, 222-3, 226, 255, 259, 426, 430
   ,,   Organization 229-30, 426-7
   ,,   Practice 54-6, 60, 163, 428, 430-1
   ,,   Bands 409-10
Brigade-Division—Abolition of title 54
Brigade-Major :—
   Divisional Artillery 135, 226-7
   Royal Artillery in India 146
British Empire—see "Empire"
Brodrick, Rt. Hon. St. John (Viscount Midleton)—Secretary of State 24
Browne—Bandmaster Horse Artillery Band, and author of "England's Artillerymen" 409
Bubbles—Adoption of "cats-eye" for spirit levels 109
Buckingham Palace—Inspection of guns by Colonel-in-Chief 79
Buffers :—
   Hydraulic 94-5, 102-4, 244, 272-3
   Hydro-pneumatic 191, 232-3, 273
Bugle Band 408
Bulford—Headquarters of practice camp 50
Bullets—Development in rifle 101
   ,,   ,,   ,,   shrapnel 114
Buller, General Sir Redvers :—
   Memorandum on artillery training 47
   Views on ammunition supply 138
Bullock-draught :—
   Field batteries in India 372-3
   Heavy and siege batteries in India 66, 69, 103, 231, 260
   Movable armament overseas 339
Burls, Mr. E. Grant—Member of Mowatt Committee 11
Burne, Lieut.-Colonel A. H.—Author of *The Royal Artillery Mess, Woolwich, and its surroundings* 159, 404

INDEX. 439

	Page
Bute—Mountain Brigade of Territorial Force	362
Buzzer—or "Vilrato-Transmitter" in siege artillery	259, 264
Cable—Electric for firing gear	272

Cadets, Royal Military Academy :—
    At Memorial Service 37
    Of other arms at Woolwich 399
    Choice of Corps and of Branches 4, 375
Calibration :—
    Investigation by Captain Dreyer 301-2
    Adoption 302-3
    Modification of bracket system of ranging .... xiv, 301, 321
Cams—Auto-sights 277
Cambridge, H. R. H. Duke of—Colonel and Colonel-in-Chief ... xviii
    Visits to Woolwich 370, 405
Campbell-Bannerman, Rt. Hon. Sir Henry—Prime Minster 130
Canada :—
    Grant of Commissions to Royal Military College 6
    Investigation as source of supply of remounts 370
Caps—Use on armour-piercing projectiles 278-9, 296
Cape of Good Hope—General Poole Vallancey in Expedition xxii
"Captain's Cart"—Abolition in batteries 126
Carbines—Personal equipment 56-8
Cardwell, Rt. Hon. E.—Secretary of State 348
Carlist War—General William Wylde in xxii
Carriage-Smiths—Substitution for wheelers 90
Cartridges :—
    Bare charge 98, 110, 271
    Case 6, 110-1, 271, 273, 277
    Fixed 109-10
    Blank 111
    Drill 124-5
"Case III"—Revival of use with position-finders 318, 322
Case-shot—General abolition 111, 114, 277
    "Special" for Anti-torpedo-craft defence 297
Casemates—Protecton afforded 274
Casemate mountings 268
Casting of battery horses 372
Casualties—Special considerations regarding replacement 138
Cavalry :—
    Revival of importance of cavalry action 175
    Horse artillery allotted to cavalry brigades and divisions ... 176-7
    Pom-poms transferred to 85, 177
    Remounts and equitation 370, 376
Census of horses 371
Centenary Cup—Presented by Deputy Adjutant-General R.A. 54, 286
Central-pivot mountings 268, 273
Ceylon—Local Corps 346-8
Chain of Command .... xii, 133-5, 253, 255, 292, 306
 ,, ,, Signallers 46, 261
Chambers of guns—Enlargement of 246, 271
Channel Island—Local Corps 347
Chaplain-General—at Memorial Service 37
Charges of guns—Increase 271
Chatham—Siege manœuvres 252-3
Chattenden—Alarm of attack by aircraft 259

440 HISTORY OF THE ROYAL ARTILLERY.

Page

Chenevix-Trench, Colonel C.—Director Artillery College 384
Chestnut Troop—"A" Battery .... xxii, 28-9, 178, 373
Chief Constables—Assistance in estimating horse population 371
Chief Instructor—see "Instructor in Gunnery."
Chief of Staff in India—Responsibility for training 147
China—Boxer Rebellion 19, 257
Christchurch Bells—Church call of the Royal Artillery 413
Civil authorities and Coast Defence 284, 288, 342
Classification—See "Competitive."
Cleeve, Major-General W. F.—Mountain Artillery Committee ... 84
Clickers—Addition to auto-sights 269, 308, 320
Clinometers—Field army artillery 96-7, 105
Clock-Code—Use for pointing out targets 53, 259
Clock-face Dials—Use for passing ranges 306
Close, Colonel F. M.—Chief Instructor, Isle of Wight 303
Coaching—Article by Major-General G. H. A. White in the
  Jubilee Number of the *Proceedings* 382
Coaling Stations—see "*Coast Defence*".
Coast Artillery and Coast Defence :—
  Position in Imperial Defence ... ix, xiv, 22, 267, 283-4, 289-90,
                                            312, 316-7, 336
  Defence schemes and exercises 22, 284, 311, 331-2
  Batteries and other Works 317-8
  Armament .... Chapter XIII, 295-9, 318-20
  Command and Organization ... xii, xiv, 24, 283, 292, 310-11,
                                            328-31
  The Examination Service 22, 292, 313
  Influence of the Separation of Mounted and Dismounted
    Branches .... xvi, 3, 333-6, 341
  Influence of the excessive proportion serving abroad ... xii,
                                  xiv, xvi, 5, 22-3, 293-4, 330-1 345
    ,,   ,,   South African War .... ix, 22, chapter XIV
    ,,   ,,   Manchurian War .... xi, Chapter XV
    ,,   ,,   Naval developments .... xi, 290-1, 318-20
  Co-operation with the Navy ... xiv, 307-8, 311-3, 316-7, 331-3 397
    ,,   ,,   ,,   Field Army .... xiv, 333-4, 342
    ,,   ,,   ,,   Siege Artillery 21, 253, 256-7
    ,,   ,,   ,,   Auxiliary Artillery 249-52, 362-3
  Relations with the School of Gunnery ... xii, 31-2, 309-11, 323-4
  The Land Fronts .... x, Chapter XVII
  India 146-8, 287-8, 314, 341
      See also "*Anti-torpedo-craft Defence*".
Colenso—Battle 10, 111
Collars, horse—Change from neck to breast 126
Collar-makers 126
College, Artillery 384, 387-8
  ,,   Ordnance 90, 384, 388, 396, 399
  ,,   Staff 130, 171, 380, 384, 387-8
Cologne—Siege manœuvres 248
Colonels, R.A. 1, 24, 133, 176-7, 292, 328
Colonels-Commandant .... xxiii, 37
Colonels-in-Chief .... xviii, xix, xx, 78-9
Colonial Courses at School of Gunnery 402
Colonial Forces 4, 6, 175
Colton, Mr. W. R., A.R.A.—South African Memorial 36
Combined Exercises—Naval and Military ... xiv, 22, 174, 307-8,
                                            311-12, 332-3, 397

INDEX. 441

	Page
Combined Shell—Shrapnel and high-explosive	116
Combined Sights—Automatic and rocking-bar	275
Combined Training	xiv, 170-1, 258

Commands :—
  Army 24
  Divisions and Cavalry Brigades 133, 164, 176, 222
  Coast Defences .... xii, xiv, 24, 283, 292, 295, 310-1, 328-31, 393
  Field Army Artillery :—
    Generally 3, 133, 227
    Of Army Corps 24, 41-2, 56, 133
    Of Divisions ... xii, xv, 131-5, 147, 163-4, 176-7, 212, 239, 425-32
    Brigade 28, 54, 148, 163, 212, 222, 226, 430
    Battery 21, 65-6, 148, 163, 222-3, 425, 428-32
  Siege Artillery :—Of Siege train 253, 258-9
                          Brigade 21, 255, 259, 264
                          Battery 254-5
  Coast Artillery :—Of Fortress 292, 325, 328
                        Fire Command 295, 321, 323, 328-30
                        Battery 295, 318, 323, 325, 329-30

Commandant :—
  School of Gunnery 310-11, 323-4, 393
    ,,   ,, Horse & Field 41, 134, 224-5
    ,,   ,, Siege 243, 392
  Practice Camps 4, 51, 55-6, 59, 135, 163
Commander-in-Chief 314, 325
        See also "*Kitchener*" and "*Roberts.*"
Commercial Ports—Responsibility for defence 317

Commissions :—
  Direct during South African War 5, 7
  Competition for, at Royal Military Academy 4, 375

Commissions, Committees, and Boards :—
  General. Board of Ordnance 10, 291, 404
            War Office Reconstruction ... viii, 128-30, 289, 291-2, 311
            South African War 128
  Organization. Separation of Mounted and Dismounted
                                    Branches 26, 410
                Promotion in R.G.A. 289, 292-3, 334
                Maintenance of Garrisons abroad 289, 293-5
                Four-gun v. six-gun batteries 189, 192, 229
                Mobilization 33, 142, 145-6
                  ,, Horse Requirements 369-70
  Armament. Ordnance Board and Committee and R.A. and R.E.
                Committees .... ii, 32, 73, 80, 85-7, 108, 117
                Reserves of guns and ammunition 11-13
                Field Army Artillery Equipment
                                26, 72-6, 82-6, Apps. B & C
                Coast Artillery Armament 289, 295-8, 308, 339
                Personal Equipment 235
  Training. Of officers for the Scientific Corps, Council of Mili-
             tary Education, Royal Commission, Regimental
             Committee 382-5, 390-1
             School of Gunnery 223-4, 310, 393
             Coast Artillery Practice 323-4
             Defence of Land Fronts 337, 342
             Co-operation 289, 311-3, 334
             Equitation 376-7

442 HISTORY OF THE ROYAL ARTILLERY.

Page

Common Shell :—
   Abolition in Horse & Field Artillery 112
   Retention of powder-filled in Coast Artillery 277-9
   Introduction of "Common-pointed" in Coast Artillery ... 278, 296
Common, Woolwich—Mortar practice on 390
Communications :—
   Field Army Artillery 46, 70, 157, 169, 212
   Siege Artillery 254, 259, 261, 264
   Coast Artillery 305-6, 332, 349
Competitive Practice :—
   Field Army Artillery 53-4, 162, 203
   Siege Artillery 249, 260
   Coast Artillery 285-6, 299, 324, 340
Compressed air—Use instead of springs in recuperators 191, 232-3, 273
Concealment—*see* "*Cover.*" ....
Concentration of Fire 46-7, 198
  ,,   of Guns 47, 157, 202
Concerts—Regimental Bands 405-6, 410
Concrete—Gun Platforms 256, 262
Conditions to be fulfilled by New Equipments ... xi, xvi, App. C & D
Conferences, Imperial .... xi, 129, 180
  ,,   Staff 179, 221, 229, 235
Congreve, Sir William—Founder of the Repository 389
Connaught, H.R.H. the Duke .... xx, 37, 129
Constitutional Force—Term for Militia 348
Continent—Possibility of War 130
Control of Fire 46-7, 61, 157, 253, 255, 287, 300, 306, 317
Control of Electric Lights 309, 330
Controversies :—
   Relative values of cover and effect 44, 156, 208
   The advantages and disadvantages of a "Forward Observing Officer" 169, 199-200
   French methods 189-94, 205, 220-2
   The efficiency of Territorial Field Artillery 359-60
   The Field Army trend in Siege Artillery 243-4
   The place of Fixed Defences in Imperial Defence .... ix, 316-7
   The control of electric lights 309
   The value of high-angle-fire guns 319
   The relative advantages and disadvantages of electric and percussion firing 271-2
Conversion of breech-loading equipments to quick-firing 93-4
Co-operation of Field Artillery with the other arms ix, xiii, 51-2, 65, 167-8, 174, 199-200, 202, 207-8, 214, 222-3, 251, 259, 401-2, 428
  ,,   ,, Siege Artillery with the other arms ix, 244, 247-8, 252-3, 258, 260-1
  ,,   ,, Coast Artillery with the other arms ... xiv, 333-4, 342
  ,,   ,, The Navy with Artillery xiv, 307-8, 311-3, 316-7, 331-3, 397
  ,,   ,, Aircraft with Artillery .... xv, 166-7, 207, 251, 259
Cordite—Difficulties with 110-11, 218
   Adoption of "Modified" (M.D.) 270, 277
   Objections to issue for practice 300
Cork—Militia 358-9, 363
Cork Harbour—Irish defended port (Queenstown) 358

INDEX. 443

	Page
Coronations—Re-issue of swords to Horse Artillery	234
Presence of Representatives of Local Corps	348
Corps Artillery—Command and Organization	21, 24, 41-2, 63
Corrector—Advantages and disadvantages of "Proportional"	123-4
Courses :—	
Artillery College—Advanced or Senior Class	383, 387-8
Firemasters	388
School of Gunnery—Long or Gunnery Staff	31, 37, 313, 395-8
Young Officers and Junior Officers	90, 383-7, 398-400
Short and Colonial	45, 394, 400-2
Quick-firing	285, 287, 306-7, 325, 400-1
Coupling-Block—60-pr. equipment	103
Coventry Ordnance Works—Armament Firm	81-2
Cover—Covered Positions	43-6, 61, 154-6, 208-9, 217
Concealment from the air	214, 250, 318
Crimean War—Veterans of	ii, xxii, xxiii
Organization and equipment of artillery	132, 272
Examples from	27, 66, 170-1, 262, 289, 352
Cromarty—Mountain brigade of Territorial Force	362
Cruisers—Attack by and of	290, 296, 299, 319-20
Curragh—The trouble in 1914	235

Dalton, Major-General J. C.—Asst. Milty. Secretary, R.A.	ii, 1
Article on *The Rock* in the Jubilee Number of the *Proceedings*	381
Dann, Captain and Riding-Master—at Military Tournament	375
Dartmoor—Trials of Equipment on	79
Dawnay, Captain Hon. H.—Author of article on *Artillery and Infantry in the final stages of the Attack* in the *Proceedings*	171
de Bange—Obturator	98, 271
Débouchoir—Fuze-setter used by French artillery	122-3
Defence, Imperial—Conference and Scheme	ix, xiv, 5, 22, 129, 180, 283-4, 289-90, 316-7, 336
See also "Anti-Torpedo-Craft," and "Coast Defence."	
Defended Ports—See Fortresses.	
Delhi—Indian inland defences	341
Denbigh, Earl of—Commanding Hon. Artillery Company	51
Department of Artillery Studies	354, 378, 382-5
Department—Remount	369, 372
"Depot"—Design of field and anti-aircraft equipments	232
Depôts	65, 145-6, 237, 283
Depression range-finders and position-finders	275-6, 304-5, 320-2
Deputy Adjutant-General R.A.—Abolition	viii, 1, 286
Deputy Assistant Adjutant-General R.A.—in India	146
Description of Officers and Designation of Units after "Separation"	2, App. A
Despatch-Riders—Training	43, 212
Destruction and Disablement of Guns	91
Dials—Fuze, Range and Order	99, 123-4, 269, 302, 306
Dial-Sights	96-7, 105
Diamond Hill—Battle	111
Dickson, General Sir Collingwood—Master-Gunner	xxiii
Dinner—Regimental	xviii
Direct Commissions—Grant during South African War	6, 7, 9, 399
Director—Indirect laying	45, 50, 105-6, 155, 209, 261, 264

444 HISTORY OF THE ROYAL ARTILLERY.

	Page
Director of Artillery	129, 291, 393
,, ,, Artillery College	384
,, ,, Fortification	129, 291
,, ,, Military Operations	129
,, ,, Military Training	310, 323-4
,, ,, Remounts	371-2
,, ,, General Staff in India	129
Director-General of Ordnance	10

Dirigibles—See "Aviation."
Disablement and Destruction of Guns 91
Disappearing Mountings 268, 273
Disbandment of batteries 29, 65, 143, 238
Dismounted Branch—Effect of "Separation" 3, 4, 335-6, 341
 Rules for appointments and exchanges ..... 2, App. A
 Stagnation of promotion ..... xvi, 2, 3, 292-3, 334-5
Dispersion of Guns 46-7, 61, 157
Displacement—Importance in indirect laying 155
Distribution of Units in 1900, 1903-4, 1907, 1909, 1913-14
            4, 5, 25, 131, 143-5, 237-8, App. E
Distribution of Fire—In the field 53, 158, 216-7, 220
     In anti-torpedo-craft defence 287
     To facilitate observation of fire 323
District Establishment 7, 23, 295
Division—Army ..... xii, 131, 359
   Artillery 54, 282
Divisional Artillery—Command and organization xii, 133-6, 143-4,
            176, 194-5, 224, 226-7
    Combination of natures 62, 178-9
    Practice 56, 135, 163-4, 176, 432
    Co-operation with the other arms 135, 168
    India 146-7
Dockyard—Woolwich and Artillery College 384
,, Portsmouth and School of Gunnery 397
Doctrine—Changes after the South African War ..... ix, 42-4, 61-3
 ,, ,, ,, ,, Manchursian War 152-4
 ,, ,, under French influence ..... xii, xiii, 194-205
 ,, Final phase 206-8, 238-9
Dominions—Adoption of Imperial Manuals and Armament ... xi, 180
   Relations with School of Gunnery 395, 398, 401
Double-Objective—Development of Section Control 217
Double-Shell—Use in mountain artillery 104, 112
Dover—Siege exercises 397
  Turret on pier 268
  R.G.A. Band 411-2
Drafts—Drain on coast defence companies at home xiv, 182-3,
              293-5, 330-1
Draught—Horse 67-8, 104, 125-6, 182, 230-1, 260-1, 352, 360, 362
   Mule 104-5, 339
   Bullock and Ox 66-69, 103, 231, 260, 339, 372-3
   Elephant 68, 231, 373
   Engine 58, 82-3, 103, 214, 231, 260
   Shaft and Pole 92, 104-5, 125
"Dreadnoughts"—Effect of introduction ..... xi, 290, 317
Dress—Insistence on uniformity 238
Dress-rehearsal—Before South African War ix
Dreyer, Major-General J. T. 301-2, 327
Drill Ammunition 124-5

INDEX. 445

	Page
Drivers—Use of gunners in Heavy and Siege Artillery	68, 261
Driving-Bands—Development of	270-1
Droop—In long wire guns	270
Du Cane, Brig.-General J. P.—Author of *The Study of Tactics from History* in the *Army Review*	203
Duel, Artillery—Change of views regarding	42, 61, 152-3, 198, 207
Duffer's Drift—First efforts at entrenching	165
"Duke's Day" at the Royal Military Academy	xviii
Duncan, Colonel Francis—Author of the *History of the Royal Artillery*	9, 126, 380
Memorial Medal	380
Durbar at Delhi in 1903—Horsing of heavy batteries	68
Dust-caps—Introduction for wheels	99
Dwarf-mountings	268

Eagle Troop—"N" Battery	29
Earthquake in Jamaica	298
Economy of Force—Adoption of Principle	197-8, 202
Education—Officers	382-5, 390-1
Non-commissioned officers and men	23, 268
Edward VII—Coronation	234, 348
Colonel-in-Chief	xvii-xx, 28-9, 58, 67, 78-9
Patron National Artillery Association	356
Egypt—Expeditions	126, 346, 369
Garrison	65, 180, 236
Egyptian Artillery—Armament	104, 118
Ehrhardt Guns	13-7, 72, 89, 93-4, 99, 160
Electric Dials	306
Electric Firing Gear	271-2
Electric Lights	308-9, 330
Elementary Practice	225-6, 327, 432
Elephant Batteries	231, 373
Elevating Gear	99, 273
Elevation-Indicators	275-6
Embarkation and Disembarkation—Inclusion in *Field Artillery Training, 1912*	174, 194
Embodiment of Militia—During South African War	349
Embrasures—Protection afforded	274
Empire, British—European hostility	ix, x, 5, 22, 283, 338
Schemes of Defence	ix, xiv, 22, 180, 283-4, 289-90, 316-7, 336
Employment in the Field :—	
Field Army Changes after the South African War	ix, 42-9, 61-3
Artillery.	
,, after the Manchurian War	125-7
,, under French influence	xii, xiii, 194-203, 205
The Final Phase	206-12, 238-9
Siege Artillery. Changes after the South African War	243-4
,, ,, ,, Manchurian War	248, 250, 253-5, 259-61
Engine-draught	58, 82-3, 103, 214, 231, 260
Engineers, Royal. Commissions	375
The Royal Engineer Committee	87
Comparison of organization	293, 295
Co-operation with artillery	247, 258, 262, 309, 331

446 HISTORY OF THE ROYAL ARTILLERY.

	Page
England, General Poole Vallancey—Master-Gunner	xxii
Entente Cordiále—Influence of xii-xiii, 130, ch. VIII, 206, 215-6, 219-20, 229, 432	
Entrenching—Revival of interest	165-6, 247, 250
Equipments—Tests for experimental	91
Uniformity of pattern	91-2
Necessity for care of modern	89-91
Modification and Conversion	92-4, 233, 360
Interest in progress	89-90
See also "Armament."	
Equipment—Personal	56-8, 234-6
Equitation—Revival of Interest	375-7
Error-of-day Drums	276, 308
Erosion of Rifling—Introduction of modified cordite	277
Esher—Viscount	128
Committee	viii, 128-30, 289, 291-2, 311
Esquimault—Night-firing	307
Essays—Annual Prize at Institution	173, 203
Essen—Visits to Krupp works	81
Establishment, Riding	374-7
Establishment of Units—Home	228, 245, 293-5, 330-1
India	34, 60, 149-50
Eurasian Militia—Proposal to raise in India	288
European Hostility—During South African War	ix, 5, 22, 283, 338
Eustace, Major-General Sir Francis	41
Examination—Officers for Promotion	384
Examination Service—Entry into defended ports	22, 313, 332
"Excalibur"—Nickname for sub-calibre guns	327
Exchange—Officers between branches	2, App. A
Expansion—Siege companies on mobilization	245, 264
Expeditions—*See "Wars"*	
Expeditionary Force. Formation	xii, 62, 128, 130-1, 139-46, 238
Use of non-regular *personnel*	141, 358
Horses for	371-2
Experimental Branch at Shoeburyness	390, 393
Experimental Equipments—Field Army Artillery xvi, 14-5, 72-6, 81-4, 91, 232-3, App. C, D	
Siege Artillery	246, 262-3
Anti-Aircraft	xv, 166, 214, 281
Explosives Act—Interference in Re-armament	78
Ferozepore—Indian inland defences	341
Ferrar, Colonel H. M.—Inspector of Remounts	370
Field Army Artillery—Composition	ix, x, 21, 62
Re-armament	x, xi, xv, 62, Chapter IV & V, App. B, C, D
Re-organization	xi, xii, Chapter VI
Field Artillery—Augmentations and Reduction	4, 5, 20, 238
Use with mounted troops	175
Shortage of men in	237
Mobilization of	139-146, 236-7, 357-8, 369, 372-3
Auxiliary Artillery	350, 353-4, 359-362
"Royal Field Reserve Artillery"	143, 358
Field Artillery Training 21, 42-5, 60-3, 69, 90-1, 152, 161, 165, 169-72, 175, 181, 194, 200-06, 211, 214, 216-20, 238-40	
Field Calls—Revival of use for field artillery	175

INDEX. 447

	Page
Field-Firing	172,174-5, 226-7
Field Glasses—Issue to batteries	49-50
Supercession of Galilean by Stereoscopic and Prismatic	107, 255
Field Parks—Ordnance (India)	149-50
Field Service Regulations xiv, 170, 172, 200-04, 206, 219, 239,	258-9, 333, 342
Fighting Lights—Electric Lights in Coast Defence	308-9, 330
Fighting the Fixed Armament ("F.F.A.") xiv, 313, 315, Chapter XVI	
Figure of Merit—In classification practice	299-300
Financial Secretary—Control of Ordnance Factories	129
Fire—Accuracy	159, 215-8, 247, 269, 284, 317
Application	50-1, 157,-9, 195-6, 216-7
Control	46-7, 61, 253, 255, 287, 300, 306, 317
Discipline	50-1, 60-1, 70, 355
Distribution	53, 158, 216-7, 220, 269, 287, 323
Effect	215, 219-20, 244
Indirect	45-6, 61, 154,-6, 173, 193, 209
Methods	xii, 45, 189-92, 195, 205, 216
Observation 32, 49-50, 70, 115, 165-7, 209-10, 214,	244-5, 249-50, 254-5, 259, 264, 301, 313, 322-3
Rapidity	43, 159-62, 195, 202, 269, 272, 284
Over Infantry	63, 170-2, 201, 208
Naval developments	317
Firemasters—Inspectors of Ordnance Stores	388
Firing Battery—Constitution	162
Firing gear—Percussion or Electric	271-2
Fisher, Admiral of the Fleet, Lord	128, 290
Fitters—Replacement of wheelers in batteries	90
Fitz-Wygram, Lieut.-General Sir Frederick—Remount Committee 369	
Fixed Defences—Place in Scheme of Imperial Defence ix, xiv, 22,	283-4, 289-90, 316-7, 336
Fixed Lights—Electric Lights in Coast Defence	308-9
Flags—Use by infantry to indicate position to supporting artillery 172	
"Fleet-in-Being"—Doctrine of "Blue-Water-School"	316
Fleeting opportunities—Practice in seizing	160,209
Flying Corps—See "Aviation."	
Foreign Naval Manœuvres—Lessons	267, 338
Foreign Office—Influence on re-armament	xi, 72, 80
Foreign Service—Excessive proportion in Coast Artillery xii, xiv,	xvi, 22-3, 293-4, 331
Fore (and Tangent) Sights	95, 274-5
Forge Wagons—Abolition in batteries	126
Fortification—Abolition of Inspector-General and creation of Director 128-9	
Fortresses and Defended Ports—Nature and Scale of Attack to which liable	291, 296, 314, 341
Place in Imperial Defence ... ix, xiv 22, 283-4, 289-90, 316-7, 336	
Place in Army Organization	xii, 24, 283, 292
Command and Organization ... xiv, 292, 295, 310-1, 328-31, 393	
Defence of Land Fronts	x, Chapter XVII
Fortress Practice—Coast Artillery	325
Fortress Warfare—Promised Manual for Siege Operations ... xiii, 258	
Forward Observing Officer	168-9, 199-200, 207-8
Fox-Hunting—Article by Brig.-General J. E. C. Livingstone-Learmonth and Captain Gilbert Holiday in Jubilee Number of the Proceedings	382

448 HISTORY OF THE ROYAL ARTILLERY.

	Page
France. The first quick-firing field guns	14-5
The Influence of the *Entente Cordiale* xii, xiii, 130, Chapter VIII, 206, 215-6, 219-20, 229,	432
Deputation at Army Manœuvres 1913	227
Siege Manœuvres at Langres 1906	248

Franco-German War :—
  German army organization ...24, 131
  German artillery 43, 57, 158, 198, 386
  Demand for land ranges 391
  Siege experiences 247, 262
Frankfort—International Exhibition 1909 166
Frazer, General Sir Augustus—Assemblage of batteries for despatch on overseas expeditions 27
Frederick, Empress—Comments on South African War x
French, Sir John 41, 227-8
Frontier of India :—
  Defences 36, 288, 341
  Use of star shell 116
  Unsuitability of 60-pr. 83
Fuzes :—
  Percussion. Direct-Action 117, 279-80
    Base 279-80
    Graze 117
    High-explosive 116-7, 279
    Anti-Aircraft 166, 281
  Time & Percussion. French and Ring Types 118
    Adoption of Krupp pattern 79, 118-21
    Carriage of Shell fuzed 16, 119-20
    Grouping proposed 218
    Mechanical 121-2
  Time. For Star Shell 122
Fuze-covers 120
Fuze-setters 122-4
Fuze-dials and Fuze-indicators 123-4, 161, 220

Galilean Binoculars 50, 107, 255
Gardiner, General Sir Robert—Master-Gunner xxii
Garrisons—Coast Defence ... xii, xiv, xvi, 5, 22-3, 287-8, 293-5, 311, 330-1, 345-6
Garrison Artillery :—
  Effect of Separation xvi, 3, 333-6, 341
  Inclusion of Mountain and Heavy in Field Army Artillery
    ix, x, 21, 62
  Command and Inspection 253-5, 258-9, 264, 283-4, 292, 311, 314, 319, 321, 323, 328-30, 341
  Stagnation of officers' promotion xvi, 3, 292-3, 334-5
  Popularity of service with other ranks 23, 293-4
  Bands 410-12
  Auxiliary Artillery 345-52, 362-3
  "Royal Garrison Reserve Artillery" 358-9, 363
  See also "Mountain", "Heavy", "Siege", and "Coast Artillery".
Garrison Artillery Training 22, 314-7, 322, 328
Garrison Point Fort—Sheerness 297
Garrison Standing Carriages 268, 272
Gas-checks—Use on projectiles 270-1
Gatling Battery—at Ulandi 296

INDEX. 449

	Page
General Staff:—	
Formation	129-30, 147
Conferences on artillery questions	179, 186-7, 221-2
Training Memoranda	224, 403
George III—Inspections at Woolwich	159
George V:—	
Coronation	234, 348
Colonel-in-Chief	xx, xxi
Army Manœuvres	227
Patron, National Artillery Association	356
Germany:—	
Artillery in Franco-German War	43, 57, 158, 161, 198, 386
Development of heavy and siege artillery	66, 248, 261-2
Naval expansion	xi, 267, 290
Threatening attitude	xvi, 80, 130, 259, 330
Gibraltar—Armament	268
R.G.A. Band	411, 413
Gillman, Maj.-General Sir Webb—Article on *The Royal Military Academy* in Jubilee Number of *Proceedings*	382
Glenbeigh—Irish Practice Camp	52
Glen Imaal— ,, ,,	52-3, 133, 163
Gold Coast—Artillery	347
Gordon, Lieut.-General Sir Alexander H.	179
Graduations on Scales:—	
Method of marking	109
To include variations of charges, projectiles, and local conditions	269, 277
Granet, Brig.-General E. J.—Lecture on *The National Horse Supply and our Military Requirements* at United Service Institution	371
Graticules—Addition to binoculars	107
Great War:—Absence of References	ii
Despatch of Mowatt Reserve guns to France	13
,, ,, "Mother" to France	264
Comparison of equipments with those in South African War	127
Modificaton of equipments during war	93
Grierson, Lieut.-General Sir James	15, 129, 227, 235, 261
Ground—Importance of study	47-9, 211-2
Ground-scouts	48
Groupings—of artillery and infantry	185-6, 198-9, 205
Guards of Honour	37, 58
Guns:—	
General use of term	iii
Provision for new batteries during South African War	ix, 9-11, 15-19, 67
New pattern for field army artillery	xi, 36, 74-6, 82-85, 94-105
Comparison with those used in the South African War	127
Siege	245-6, 257, 261-3
Coast	xvi, 256-7, 262, 267-8, 270-7, 280, 314, 319-20, 339, 341, 347
Anti-Aircraft	166, 214-5, 281, 318
Anti-Torpedo-Craft	287, 297, 307, 320
Auxiliary artillery	104, 351-4, 356, 360, 362
Naval	269, 290, 319-20
S.B.—Smooth-bore	268, 298, 351-3
R.B.L.—Rifled Breech-loading (Armstrong)	268, 298, 339, 351-6
R.M.L.—Rifled Muzzle-loading	84, 103, 268, 298, 339, 341, 351-6

FF

450   HISTORY OF THE ROYAL ARTILLERY.

Guns :—(*Continued*).

B.L.—Breech-loading ... 15, 82-4, 93-4, 96, 100-4, 112, 231, 245-6, 250, 256-7, 267-8, 270-4, 284, 296-9, 308, 314, 319-22, 326-7, 339, 352-4, 356, 360, 362, 364
B.L.C.—Breech-loading converted to Q.F. 93-4, 112, 360
Q.F.—Quick-firing ... 74-6, 82-4, 93-102, 98, 104, 177-8, 231-2, 268, 271-2, 281, 285, 297-9, 307-8, 320, 339, 347, 352-6, 360, 362, 364
A/A.—Anti-Aircraft .... xv, 166, 214, 281, 318
H.A.F.—High-angle-fire ....xvi, 256-7, 262, 273, 280, 319
Pom-poms—37″/″ Automatic .... xv, 84-5, 94, 281, 318, 400
Gun-arcs—Indirect laying 96, 105
Gun-construction—Demand for greater power 269-70
Gun-powder 64, 84, 110, 300
Gunner, *The*—Illustration of National Artillery Association 356
Gunnery, Field :—
 Indirect Fire 45-6, 61, 154-6, 209
 Dispersed Batteries 46-7, 157
 French methods 186-9, 192-5
 Accuracy and effect 158, 205, 215-22
 Night-firing 165
Gunnery, Siege :—
 The Field Army Trend 243-5, 249-50, 254-5, 259
 Night-firing 252
Gunnery, Coast :—
 Quickening up of practice 284
 Calibration .... xiv, 217-8, 301-3, 315, 320-1
 Anti-Torpedo-Craft 287, 306-7
 Night-firing 307-9
Gunnery, Anti-Aircraft 166, 214-5, 251, 259
Gunnery, The School of :—
 The Repository 32, 389-90
 Shoeburyness 390-1
 Decentralization. The Horse & Field School 30-2, 42, 55-6, 59-60, 134-5, 223-4, 391, 431-2
  The Siege Branch ... xi, 32-3, 243-4, 248-50, 262, 392
  The Local Schools 31-2, 309-10, 355, 364, 392-3, 395, 401
 Re-organization of the Central School ... 31-2, 309-11, 323-4, 392-3
 The Courses. "Long" or "Gunnery Staff" 31, 313, 395-8
  "Young officers" and "Junior officers" ... 90, 383-7, 398-400
  "Shore" and "Colonial" 45, 392, 400-02
  "Quick-Firing" 285, 287, 306-7, 325, 400-01
  Auxiliary Artillery 354-5, 363-4
 The Instructors .:........................ 187, 224, 243, 257, 262, 324, 396
 The Equipment 393-4
 The Annual Reports 161, 224, 402-3
 The want of a School in India 59, 60, 147, 314
 The Naval School 312-3, 326, 393, 397-8

Haig, Sir Douglas 145-6, 227, 261
Haking, General Sir Richard—Lecture on Co-operation 173
Haldane, Viscount—Secretary of State ...... xii, 130-1, 142-4, 357, 371
Handbooks—Transfer of gun-drill from Drill Book 315

INDEX. 451

	Page
Hangers—For use with one-man range-finders	109
Harbours of Refuge—For Mercantile Shipping	317
Harris, Lord—Committee on Artillery Organization 1888	26, 410
Harness—Change from neck to breast collar	125-6
Hartington, Lord—Commission of 1899	312
"Harveyed"—Process applied to "hard" armour	278
Hausas—Native soldiers in West African local corps	347
Hay, Maj.-General E. O.—Assistant Adjutant-General R.A.	... 1, 301
Headlam, Maj.-General Sir John—Lecture on "*Okehampton Experiences*" at the Institution	205
Heavy Artillery :—	
Definition of	iii, 66
Use in Crimean War	xxiii, 66, 352
Use by Boers in South African War	66
Raising and development	ix, x, 21, 32, 62, 67-70, 181-3, 230-1
Armament	67, 82-3, 102-3
French and German views	66, 202, 207
Auxiliary Artillery	352-4, 356, 362
Heavy Artillery Training	69, 70, 181, 319, 340
Helder—Expedition of 1799	178
Helio—Use for communication	264
Herr, General F. G.—Lessons of Balkan Wars	207
Hickman, Major-General H. P.—Chief Instructor, Siege	63, 243
High-angle-fire guns :—	
Use to prevent bombardment of coast	273, 280, 318-9
Use as siege howitzers	xvi, 256-7, 262
High-explosive Shell :—	
Poor effect in South African War	63-4 112-14, 244
Difficulty in securing detonation in smaller natures	112, 279
Reluctance to adopt for guns	113, 233, 279, 424, App. D
High-speed Targets—Coast Artillery	284, 325-6
Hime, Lieut.-Colonel H. W. L.—Secretary of the Institution	379, 381, 386
History of the Royal Regiment of Artillery—Captain F. Duncan	9, 126, 380
History of the Royal Artillery (Crimean Period)—Colonel J. R. J. Jocelyn	ii, 351, 378
History of the Royal and Indian Artillery in the Mutiny of 1857	ii
History of the Royal Artillery from the Indian Mutiny to the Great War Vol. I (1860—1899)—Maj.-Generals Sir Charles Callwell and Sir John Headlam	i, vii, 381
Holden, Brigadier-General Sir Capel—Superintendent, Royal Gun Factory	58, 387
Holiday, Captain Gilbert—Article on *Fox Hunting* in Jubilee Number of *Proceedings*	382
Home Defence—Requirements of	5, 144
Home Office—Influence on re-armament	72, 126
Hong Kong-Singapore Battalion	346-8
Honourable Artillery Company	51, 352, 359
Hook Section—Form of rifling	270
Horizontal Base Position-finder	305
Horne, General Lord—Inspector, Horse & Field Artillery	239, 381
Horse Artillery :—	
Decline and Revival	176-8
Augmentation and reduction	5, 238
Re-armament	74-5, 85, 148, 177-8
Personal Equipment	58, 234-5

452 HISTORY OF THE ROYAL ARTILLERY.

Horse Artillery :—(*Continued*).
   Remounts 372
   Band 405, 408-9
   India 148-9
   Auxiliary Artillery 359-60
Horses :—
   Formation of Remount Department 369-70
   Provision for Field Army Artillery 67-8, 126, 182, 228, 230-1,
      360-2, 371-3
   Provision for Siege Artillery 260
   ,, ,, Auxiliary Artillery 67, 352-3, 360, 362
Horse-Mastership 374
Horse-shoes—Carriage 127
Hospital, Royal—Pensioners at Memorial Service 27
Hostility, European—During South African War ix, 5, 22, 283,
      290, 338
Howitzers :—
   Field. Organization 131, 144, 178, 229-30, 426-7
      Armament .... xvi, 81-4, 94, 98-9, 102, 179
      Employment 62-4, 112-3, 159, 179
      Proposed addition to Horse and Mountain Artillery 84, 178
      India 35, 83, 92
   Siege. Armament .... xvi, 17-9, 243-6, 256-7, 262-3
      Utilization of High-angle-fire Guns .... xvi, 256-7, 262
   French and German views 202, 261
   R.M.L. (Rifled Muzzle-loading) 250, 341
   B.L. (Breech-loading) 17-9, 81, 83, 92, 94, 101, 178-9, 231,
      243-6, 256-7, 262-4, 339, 352, 360, 362
   Q.F. (Quick-firing) 82, 84, 98-9, 101-2, 178-9
Hugli, River—Defences of 304
Hump—Pattern of driving band 271
Hyderabad Contingent 2, 34
Hydraulic Power—Use in mountings 273-4, 280
Hydro-Pneumatic Buffers—Use in carriages and mountings 94-5,
      102-4, 191, 232-3, 273

Identification of War-ships 328-9
Illustrated London News.—Views of National Artillery Association 356
Imperial Conferences .... xi, 129, 180
   ,,   Defence .... ix, xiv, 22, 283-4, 289-90, 316-7, 336
   ,,   General Staff 129, 147
Increasing Twist—System of rifling 270
Independent Line of Sight—Adoption of principle 95-6, 99, 275
India, Soldiering In—Article by Major-General G. F. MacMunn
   in Jubilee Number of *Proceedings* 382
Indian Sport—Article by Major-General A. E. Wardrop in Jubilee
   Number of *Proceedings* 382
India :—
   The India Office and re-armament 72, 77, 84
   General Artillery questions 129, 146-8, 405
   Field Army Artillery 33-6, 56-7, 59-60, 83-4, 91-2, 98, 103,
      116, 137, 147-50, 172-5, 227, 372-3
   Siege Artillery 92, 244-5, 260
   Coast Artillery 274, 287-8, 313-4
   Frontier and Inland Defences 83, 287-8, 327, 341

INDEX. 453

	Page
Indirect Fire	45-6, 61, 154-6, 173, 193, 209
Indirect Laying Stores	45-6, 60, 68, 70, 96, 105-6, 155, 202, 244-5, 255, 261, 276-7

Infantry Attacks :—
    Disappearance of the Artillery "Preparation" 42-3, 61, 153
    Change in nature of the Artillery "Support" 153, 167-9, 187, 199-200
    Final stages 63, 170-3, 200-1, 203, 207-9
Influences on Artillery :—
    The Separation of the Mounted and Dismounted Branches ...
    The South African War viii, x, 4-6, 13-8, 20-2, 27-9, 36-7, 293, 335, 398, Chapters III, X, XIV
    The Manchurian War viii, x, xi, 62, 116, 122, 136, 215, 239, 263, 319, 338, 371, 392, Chapters VII, XI, XV
    The *Entente Cordiále* ... xii, xiii, 130, 206, 215-6, 219-20, 432, Chapter VIII
Inglefield, Brig.-General N. B.—Chief Instructor, Siege 244, 253
Inkerman—Battle of .... xxiii, 66, 352
Inspections by Colonels-in-Chief .... xviii, xx, xxi
Inspector-General of the Forces 129, 226, 283, 291-2, 341-2
  „ „ „ Artillery 59, 146, 283, 314
  „ „ „ Fortifications 128
  „ „ „ Communications 139
  „ „ „ Remounts 370
Inspector of Royal Horse & Royal Field Artillery 129, 148, 224, 239
  „ „ Royal Garrison Artillery ... 148, 283-4, 292, 311, 314, 319, 341-2
  „ „ Coast Defences 148, 314
  „ „ Artillery (of armies in India) 146-7
  „ „ Remounts 370
  „ „ Range-finding and Position-finding 396
  „ „ Royal Engineers 319, 341-2
  „ „ Warlike Stores (Firemaster) 388
  „ „ Range-Finding and Position-Finding 396
  „ „ Ordnance Machinery 269
Institution, Royal Artillery :—
    Acknowledgement ii
    Change of Policy and Expansion 378-80
    Proceedings 381-2
    Lectures 22, 173, 204-5, 218-9, 239, 372
    Essays and other Papers in *Proceedings* 61, 171, 173, 190, 203
    Prize Medals 380-1
Institution, Royal United Service :—
    Acknowledgement ii
    Journal and Lectures 180, 371
Instructional Apparatus 326-8
Instructions for Practice :—
    Field Army Artillery 194, 203
    Coast Artillery 324, 340
    Auxiliary Artillery 363-4
Instructor in Gunnery 187, 224, 243, 257, 262, 324, 396
Instruments :—
    Multiplication 233-4
    Graduation 109, 269, 277
    Elaboration of tests and adjustments 109, 218, 321
Interest in Artillery Questions :—
    Army ....xii, 49, 143, 190, 203, 220-3, 247-8
    Public .... ix, 5. 16, 22, 77, 87, 128, 143, 203

454 HISTORY OF THE ROYAL ARTILLERY.

                                                      Page
Invasion—The origin and basis of the Volunteer movement 350
Inventive Talent—Development in all ranks 268-9
Ireland :—
    Command of Artillery 41, 56
    Practice Camps 52, 133, 163
    Militia 349, 358-9, 363
    Remounts 369-70
Isle-of-Wight—School of Instruction 303, 309-10, 364, 392-3, 395, 401

Jamaica :—
    Earthquake in 1907 298
    Local Corps 347-8
Jane, Mr. F. T.—Lectures on Coast Defence 22
Japan :—
    Alliance xi
        See *"Russo-Japanese War."*
Jocelyn, Colonel Julian R. J.—Regimental History ...ii, 351, 378, 382
Journal of the Royal Artillery—Change of title of *Proceedings* ... 381
Jubilees :—
    Queen Victoria 348, 406
    Proceedings 381-2
"Jumpers"—Nickname for appearing and disappearing targets 217, 429
Junior Officers—Course at School of Gunnery 399-400

Kenyon, Major-General L. R.—Articles on *Progress in Matériel* in *Proceedings* 89
Khaki—First painting of guns 100
Kiggell, Colonel L. E.—Remarks on article in *Proceedings* 171
King Edward VII ...... xviii-xx, 348, 356
King George V ...... xx, xxi, 348, 356
Kingston (Jamaica)—Earthquake in 1907 298
Kitchener, Lord 59, 129, 133, 138, 309
Kites—*see "Aviation"*
Knapp, Brig.-General K. K.—Papers on Pack Artillery in *Journal of United Service Institution* 180
Kneller Hall—Connection with Regimental Bands 407, 412
Knox, Major-General Sir William—Command of Royal Artillery in Ireland 41, 56, 211
Kraft, Prince—Letters 57, 381, 430
Krupp—Fuzes 79, 118-9
        Howitzers 63, 81, 261-2
        Anti-aircraft guns 166
        Armour 278

Ladysmith—Naval gunnery 301
Lambton, Admiral Hon. Sir Hedworth 301
Lamps—Pattern for lighting batteries 166, 252
    See also *Electric Lights.*
Lancashire—Field Artillery Militia 350
Land Fronts of Coast Defences :—
    Recognition of importance ...... x, 337-8, 342
    Training 339, 340, 342
    Armament 339, 341

INDEX. 455

	Page
Langlois, Colonel H.—*l'Artillerie de Campagne en Liaison avec les Autres Armes*	202
Langres—Siege manœuvres	248
Language Qualification—Officers of native batteries	9, 347
Lanterns—Pattern for lighting batteries	252
Larkhill—Practice Camp	50, 55, 85, 224, 392, 398, 432
Lascars—Attachment to garrison artillery in India	288
Lawson, Lieut.-General R.—Report on horses supplied to artillery for Egyptian Expedition 1801	126
Layers—Increased attention to training	23, 218, 264, 285, 327
Laying-Cords—Indirect laying	45
Laying-Teachers—Use in battery training	326-7, 363
Lectures—Artillery Institution	22, 173, 204-5, 218-9, 239, 372
United Service Institution	180, 371
School of Gunnery	394
Lee, Viscount—Work for R.G.A. Officers in Parliament	335
Lefroy, General Sir J.	383, 390
Memorial Medal	380
Legal Difficulties:—	
Separation of Mounted and Dismounted Branches	3
Re-armament	77-8
Leith—Branch School	355
Length of guns—Increase	270
Leslie, Lieut.-Colonel J. H.—Article on *The Regiment* in Jubilee Number of *Proceedings*	381
Lettering—of batteries	28
Levée—Presentation of "State" by Master-Gunner	xviii, xix
Level of wheels—Importance in heavy artillery	96
Library—Transfer of Regimental from Mess to Institution	379
Lieut.-Colonels:—	
Responsibility of	54, 226, 321
With Auxiliary Artillery	349-50
"Light-Vanners"—Value as Remounts	371
Lighting of batteries during night-firing	166, 252, 308
Linch-pins—Abolition of	99
Liners—Use in repair of guns	270
Lines of Fire—Indirect laying	155
Lining-planes—Indirect laying	45, 96
Livingstone-Learmonth, Brig.-General J. E. C.—Article on *Fox-Hunting* in Jubilee number of *Proceedings*	382
Lloyd, Major-General F. T.—Presentation of Centenary Cup	286
Loading-Teachers—Use in battery training	326-7, 363
Loading-Trollies	273-4, 308
Local Corps	345-8
Localization—Adoption for Coast Defence Companies	xii, 294-5
Long Course:—	
Origin	395
Development into "Gunnery Staff Course"	383, 395-8
Long-Range Fire:—	
Field Army Artillery	43, 66, 82, 94, 164, 181, 187, 193, 202
Siege Artillery	32, 246, 249, 257
Coast Artillery	290, 296, 301, 319, 323, 325-6
Long-Range Targets	325-6
Long-Recoil—Principle of	15, 17, 94-5
Look-out-men	48, 287
Lord-Lieutenants—Control of Militia	348
Lord Mayor's Show—Attendance of Mounted Band	410

456 HISTORY OF THE ROYAL ARTILLERY.

	Page
Loubet, President—Visit to Aldershot	67
Lough Swilly—Irish Defended Port	358
Lydd—Siege School	32-3, 243-4, 250-2, 257, 391-2, 395
Auxiliary Artillery	354, 361, 363
Lyddite—*See "High-Explosive Shell"*	
Lynes, Colonel S. P.—Inspector of Remounts	370

Machine Guns—Method of attack by artillery	195
Machinery Gunners—Specialists	23
MacMahon, Major P. A.—Fellow of the Royal Society	387
MacMunn, Lieut.-General Sir George	372, 382
Madras—Arabs and Persians as remounts	373
Mailly—French practice camp	187-9
Main Band—Official designation of Regimental Band	413
Majors—Command of Indian Mountain Batteries	65-6
Malindrin Discs—Use in French Artillery	202
Malta—Coast Artillery	268, 284, 296, 307, 340
Royal Malta Artillery	346, 348
R.A. (Malta) Band	411-3
Manning—Tables and Exercises	xvi, 23, 332

Manœuvres :—
   Army ....xv, xvi, 59, 174, 213-4, 227-8
   Siege .... xiii, xvi, 248, 252-3, 260-1
   Naval and Coast Artillery 22, 174, 312, 332-3, 397
   Foreign 185, 190, 248, 338
Manchuria—*See "Russo-Japanese War"*
Manuals :—
   Adoption of Imperial 180
   Army. *Combined Training* .... xiv, 170-1, 258
      Field Service Regulations xiv, 170, 172, 200-3, 206, 219,
                                          239, 258, 333, 342
      Training and Manœuvre Regulations 323
   Field Army *Field Artillery Training* 21, 42-5, 60-3, 69, 90-1,
     Artillery.   152, 161, 165, 169, 171-2, 175, 181, 194, 200-6,
                                        211, 214, 216-20, 238-9
          Instructions for Practice 194, 203
          Heavy Artillery Training 69-70, 181, 339-40
   Siege Artillery. *Siege Artillery Training* 33, 254, 257, 315
                   Garrison Artillery Training, Vol. II 258, 315
                   Military Engineering, Part II 258
                   Fortress Warfare .... xiii, 258
   Coast Artillery. *Garrison Artillery Training* 22, 314-7, 322, 328, 340
                   Fighting the Fixed Armament xiv, 313, 315,
                                                       Chapter XVI
                   Coast Fortress Defence .... xiv, 333
                   Instructions for Practice 324, 340
   Auxiliary Artillery. *Instructions for Practice* 363-4
Manufacturing Departments—*See "Ordnance Factories."*
Map-Reading—Instruction 49
March-Discipline—Inclusion in *Field Artillery Training 1912* 194
Marindin, Captain—One-man range-finder 108
Marine Artillery—Officers from 6
   ,,   Battalion—Proposed conversion to artillery 288
   ,,   Indian (now Royal Indian Navy)—Co-operation in Coast
             Defence 288

INDEX. 457

	Page
Marks of guns—Multiplication	268
Marshall, Major-General Sir George—In Command of Royal Artillery at Aldershot and in South Africa	41
President of Committees	26, 36, 72-3
Mary, Queen ⎫ At Woolwich with King George V	xx
,, Princess ⎭	
Master-General of the Ordnance	10, 81, 129, 263, 291
Master-Gunners	xxii-iii, 37
Masters of Hounds—Assistance in estimating horse population	371
Material for Repair—Reduction of amount carried	127
Mauritius—Local Corps	346, 348
May, Major-General Sir Edward	143
Mayo, Lord—Durbar for the Amir of Afghanistan	373
Mayor, Lord—Attendance of Mounted Band at Show	410
Mechanism—Breech	97-9, 232, 271-2

Mechanization :—
Guns	xiv, 58, 83, 214, 231, 260
Ammunition Supply	xv, 59, 231-2

Medals—Rarity prevous to South African War	viii
Memorial at Institution	380-1
Mediterranean—Fortresses and Naval Co-operation	5, 22, 312, 323, 325
Medium Artillery—Definition	iii
Megaphones—Use in batteries	46, 70, 306
Mekometer—Disadvantages	46, 107-8

Memorial : —
South African War	36-7
Medals at Institution	380-1

Mercantile Community—Part in defence organization	284, 288
Mercantile Shipping—Protection of	290, 297, 312, 317
Mercer, Major-General Sir Frederic—Inspector of Horse and Field Artillery in India	148

Mess, Regimental :—
Visits of Colonels-in-Chief	xviii, xx, xxi
History by Lieut.-Colonel A. H. Burne	159, 404
The Young Officers Course	379, 386

Meteor—Refusal of aid	218
Methuen, F.M. Lord—Opinion regarding ammunition supply	138
Midleton, Lord (Rt. Hon. St. John Broderick)—Secretary of State	24
Militär Wochenblatt—Correspondence on attack of shielded guns	158

Militia : —
The "Old Constitutional Force"	348
Incorporated in Royal Artillery	349
Grant of Regular Commissions	6, 399
Supplement to field artillery	141-3, 349-50, 357-8
Eurasian, for coast defence in India	288

"Millimetre Guns"—Nickname for 2·95" Q.F. in West Africa	104, 347
Milne, Brig.-General G. F.—Equitation Committee	377
Minorca—Sir Robert Gardiner present at capture	xxii
Minefields—Abolition of	295
Missfires—Effect on training	271-2
Mixed Brigades—Gun and howitzer	229-30, 426-7

Mobility :—
Field Army Artillery	74-5
Siege Artillery	246, 259-62
Movable Armament	339
Auxiliary Artillery	352-3, 360-2

	Page
Mobilization :—
   The problem of the Field Artillery .... xii, xv, 139-141
   The Militia solution .... xv, 139-46, 236-7, 350, 357-8
   The Horses 369-371
   India 33-4, 149-50
   The Siege Artillery 245, 264
Model Ranges—Use in training battery commanders 226
Modern Riding with Notes on Horse Training, by Major Noel
   Birch, Superintendent Riding Establishment 376
Moncrieff—Disappearing Mountings 268
Mondragon, General—Design for conversion of 15-prs. 93
Mons—The *pavé* to 79
Montgomery, Major-General R. A.—The Calibration Committee 303
Morocco—Visit of German Emperor 80
Morris, Lieutenant W. J.—Instructor to Q.F. Courses 1906-14 ... 401
Mortars—Practice on Woolwich Common 390
          Use in Civil War in America 159
Mortars, Trench—Decision not to adopt 263
"Mother"—Nickname for 9·2″ Howitzer .... xvi, 264
Mountain Artillery :—
   Effect of Separation and of South African War 2, 64-6
    ,, ,, Manchurian War 179-81
   Augmentation and Reduction 35-6, 65, 180
   Re-armament 36, 84, 102-5
   Personal Equipment 236
   Auxiliary Artillery 361-2
Mounted Bands 409-10
Mounted Branch—Effect of Separation .... 2-4, 35, 397-8, App. A
Mounted Troops—Requirements in Artillery 4, 74, 175
Mountings :—
   Variety of natures in use by coast artillery 268, 272-4, 280, 298
Movable Armament :—
   Revival of interest 337-8
   Armament 339, 341, 352, 362
   Training 339-40, 342
   Auxiliary Artillery 352, 355, 362, 398
Moves :—
   Horse and Field School of Gunnery to Salisbury Plain 30-2,
                                            223-4, 392, 431-2
   Siege Artillery   ,,   ,,   ,,   ,, Lydd 32, 392
   Coast Artillery   ,,   ,,   ,,   ,, Isle of Wight ... 310, 393
   Artillery College to Red Barracks 384
Movement—On the battle-field 153, 168, 200, 209
Movements and Quarterings—Inclusion in *Field Artillery Training
1912* 194
Moving Targets—Difficulty of engaging from covered positions
                                                             196, 209
  ,,   ,,   Coast Artillery 284, 325-6
Mowatt, Sir Francis 11
  ,,   Committee 11-18
Mules—Use in artillery 104-5, 339
Murray, General Sir A. J. 323-4
Musketry—All ranks to be trained 57-8
Mutiny—The Indian ii
Muzzle-loading—See "Guns".

INDEX. 459

	Page
Nairne, Lieut.-General Sir Charles—Inspector-General of Artillery in India	147-8
Napoleon, I and III	46, 197-8, 350
Naseby—Battlefield	227
Natal—Despatch of artillery brigades in 1897 and 1899	26
Handling of artillery during war	42, 51
National Artillery Association	355-6, 364-5
National Horse Supply and our Military Requirements—Lecture by Colonel E. J. Granet at the United Service Institution	371

Navy, Royal :—
    Rôle in Imperial Defence .... ix, 316-7
    Developments in warship design ...... xi, 290-1, 295, 297, 307, 319-20
      ,,   in armour 278, 319, 329
      ,,   in guns and gunnery ... xi, 269-70, 295, 301-3, 317-9
      ,,   in methods of attack xi, 284, 287-91, 296, 306, 308, 319
    Co-operation with Artillery xiv, 22, 86, 295-8, 307-8, 311-3, 316-7, 332-3, 340, 342
    Instructional Establishments 312-3, 326, 397-8
Navy—Royal Indian 288
Navy—Expansion of German .... xi, 267, 290
Netheravon—Offer to School of Gunnery Horse and Field 31, 392
Neutralisation of guns—Methods 196
Newport—Artillery Station 65, 182
New Zealand—Visit of Regimental Band 406
Nicholson, Major-General Stuart—Paper on Shrapnel Fire 219
Niger Company—Local Forces 347
Night Operations :—
    Field Army Artillery 165-6, 215
    Siege Artillery 251-2
    Coast Artillery 269, 276, 307-9, 327
Nitro-glycerine—Change of proportion in cordite 277
Noble, Sir Andrew—Witness before Mowatt Committee 11
Non-commissioned officers and men 20, 23, 225, 268, 293, 348, 425
Norfolk—Volunteer Artillery 2
Northamptonshire—The King at manœuvres 227
Numbering :—
    Batteries and Companies 28, 282
    Fuzes in series 118

Obligatory Garrisons—Indian inland defences 34
Observation of Fire :—
    Field Army Artillery 49-50, 70, 115, 209-10
    Siege Artillery 32, 244-5, 249-55, 264
    Coast Artillery 301, 318, 322-3
    From the air 165-7, 214, 251, 259
Observation Lights—Electric Lights in Coast Defence 330
Observation Officer—Siege Artillery 259
Observing Officer, Forward—Field Army Artillery 168-9, 199-200, 207-8
Observing Stations—Method of attack by artillery 195, 216
Observatory, Woolwich—Use by Institution 379
Obturators—Breech mechanisms 98, 271
O'Callaghan, Major-General Sir Desmond—President, Ordnance Committee .... ii, 80
Officers :—
    Provision and Promotion during South African War ... viii, 5-9, 20

460 HISTORY OF THE ROYAL ARTILLERY.

Officers :—(Continued).
    Effect of separation of Mounted and Dismounted Branches
        xvi, 2-3, 165, 292-3, 334-5, 341, 397-8, App. A
    Education 382-5, 390-4, 398-400
    Examination for Promotion 384
    Limitation of Service in Siege Artillery 263
    Quality in 1914 .... 336, 425
    Auxiliary Artillery 346-7, 350, 354-5, 357-8, 361
Ogive of Projectiles—Increase in radius 116, 119, 277-9
Okehampton :—
    Practice Camp 52-3, 55, 111, 204-5, 209, 364
    Headquarters School of Gunnery, Horse and Field 30-1, 52,
        224, 391-2
Old Kent Road—Effect of granite "setts" on new equipments 79
Omdurman—Battle 62
One-man range-finders 108-9, 210, 234, 321-2
Optics—Discussion in the *Proceedings* 50
Orders—Army .... 24, 29, 46, 282, 335, App. A
    General 349, 370, 390
    Regimental 1, 49, 355, 405
Ordnance—Board of 10, 291, 404
    ,,   Board and Committee .... ii, 32, 73, 80, 85-7, 108, 117
    ,,   College 90, 384, 388, 396, 399
    ,,   Corps and Department 90, 269
    ,,   Depôts in the Field 127
    ,,   Director-General 10
    ,,   Factories 11-3, 73, 81, 129
    ,,   Field Parks (India) 149-50
    ,,   Master-General 10, 81, 129, 263, 291
Organization :—
    Field Army   The Army Corps Scheme of 1902
    Artillery.   24-5, 130-1, 133, 283, 292
        The Army Corps Scheme of 1905 130-1, 133, 354, 360
        The Expeditionary Force 62, 128, 131, 139, 144
        Previous steps in artillery allotment 34, 132
        Brigades .... xi, 26-9, 35, 54, 60-8, 229-30, 426-7
        Batteries 189-92, 194-5, 228-9, 425-6
        Depôts and Training Brigades ... 65, 142-6, 237, 283
    Siege Artillery.   The Siege Brigade 245, 264
        General 253-6, 258-9
    Coast Artillery.   Territorial Divisions 282
        Localization of Companies .... xii, 294-5
        Coast Fortresses .... xiv, 329-31
Oscillating Sights 96
Out-Stations—The Bands 413
Overseas Defences :—
    Threats of attack .... ix, 5, 22, 284, 290, 338
    Garrisons .... xii, xiv, 5, 22-3, 287-8, 293-4, 331, 345-6
    Scale and nature of attack to which liable 291, 296, 314, 341
Owen, General Sir John :—
    In Command of Artillery at Malta 284
    President of Committee on Garrison Artillery Training 31,
        309-10, 396, 399
    President of Committee on Coast Artillery Armament 289,
        295-8, 308, 339
Owen, Major C. H.—One of originators of the Advanced Class ... 383

INDEX.

Oxen—Use for draught in artillery ... 66-7, 69, 103, 231, 260, 339, 372-3

Packing—Ammunition in complete rounds ... 77-9
Paget, Brig.-General W. L. H.—Proposed howitzer for horse artillery ... 178
Panipat—Manœuvres on battlefield ... 59
Parliament :—
    Augmentation of Horse and Field Artillery ... 5
    Officers' education and promotion ... xvi, 335, 383
    Re-armament ... 13, 77
    Horse census ... 370
    Garrisons of coast defences ... 331
Parallelism—Lines of Fire ... 107, 155
Parks—Ammunition ... 139
Parsons, Lieut.-General Sir Lawrence :—
    In Natal ... 42, 48, 51
    On Salisbury Plain ... 49, 51
    In India ... 59-60
    President Committee on Battery Organization ... 189
    ,,   ,,   ,, Militia *Personnel* ... 142
Patrols—Introduction and training ... 47-8, 212
Paterson, Major—Instructions for new Howitzer Brigades ... 63
Pay—Proficiency and Service ... 236
Pedestal Mountings—Coast Artillery ... 268, 273
Peninsular War :—
    Veterans ... xxii
    Artillery Organization ... 132, 256
    Artillery Support at storming of S. Sebastian ... 171
Pensioners—At Memorial Service ... 37
Penton, Major-General A. P.—In command of artillery at Malta ... 325
Percin, General—Inspector-General French Artilleyr ... 185-6, 190, 203
Percussion Firing—Comparison with Electric ... 271-2
Permanent Staff—Auxiliary Artillery ... 351, 355
Perrott, Major-General Sir Thomas :—
    President Heavy Battery Equipment Committee ... 82
    Chief Instructor, Siege ... 243, 253
Persians—Remounts in Madras and Bombay ... 373
Personal Equipment ... 56-8, 234-6
"Persons"—Origin of nickname ... 9
Peshawar—Field-firing ... 175
Philippines—Use of Krupp fuzes by American artillery ... 118
Physical Training—Interference with attendance at practice ... 225
Picardy—Manœuvres ... 185-6, 190
Pieters Hill—Battle ... 171
Pistols—Personal Equipment ... 57, 235
Pistol-Grip—Firing gear ... 272
Plain-Section—Form of rifling ... 270
Platforms—For guns ... 33, 243-4, 255, 262, 272
Plotter, Field—Indirect laying ... 45, 60, 70, 105, 155, 255
Plymouth :—
    Winter quarters Heavy Brigade ... 68, 182
    Branch School ... 309
    Anti-torpedo-craft defence trials ... 22
    Night-firing ... 307
    Land-Front defences ... 337
    R.G.A. Band ... 411, 413

462 HISTORY OF THE ROYAL ARTILLERY.

Page
Pointing-out the target—Study of methods 53, 259
Pole-draught—Adoption 92, 125
Politics—Influence in re-armament 72, 77, 80, 87
Pom-poms :—
    Introduction and final disposal 84-5, 94, 400
    Use as Anti-aircraft guns .... xv, 281, 318
Ports—In Casemates 274
Port Arthur :—
    Lessons of Siege 246-8, 252, 254-6, 258, 262-3, 319, 338
    Naval attacks 290-1, 306
Portland :—
    Garrison 292
    Night-firing 307
Port Royal, Jamaica—Earthquake 298
Portsmouth :—
    Inspection of R.G.A. by Colonel-in-Chief .... xx, 31, 68
    Winter quarters of Heavy Brigade 68, 182
    Garrison of Fortress 292, 330
    Night-Firing 307
    Land-Front defences 337
    R.G.A. Band 411, 413
    Naval Establishments 397
Port Trusts—Share in Examination Service 313
Positions :—
    Choice 44-6, 61, 154-6, 193, 196-202, 208-12, 217
    Occupation and change 196-7, 210-11
Position Artillery—*see Heavy Artillery.*
Position-Finders :—
    Development of 304-5, 318, 392
    Specialists 23
    Qualification for Instructor in Gunnery 396
Practice :—
    Extracts from 1914 Report .... xvii, 239, App. F
    Place in Progressive Training 225
    Field Army. Interest and presence of the other arms xii, xiii,
        Artillery.   51-2, 65, 190, 203-5, 220-1
           Allowance of ammunition 53, 60
           Elementary 225-6, 432
           Competitive 53-4, 162, 203
           Brigade 54-6, 163, 428, 430-1
           Divisional 56, 163-4, 432
           Gunnery 204, 221-2, 427-31
           Tactical 203-5, 221-2, 427-31
           Heavy batteries 68-70, 181-2, 230-1
           Practice Camps 20, 30-1, 49-56, 59-60, 65, 162-4,
                              181, 187, 220-4
             ,,   ,,   French .... xii, xiii, 187-8
           Auxiliary Artillery 351, 356, 361
    Siege Artillery. Allowance of ammunition 250
           Competitive 249, 260
           Practice Camps 31-3, 245, 248-50, 259-60, 264
    Coast Artillery. Allowance of ammunition 300, 327-8
           Company and Battery (including Competition)
                          284-6, 299-300, 323-6
           Fire-Command, Regimental, and Station 285
           Battle and Fortress 300, 325
           Anti-Torpedo-Craft 287, 306-7

INDEX.

Practice :—(*Continued*).
   Coast Artillery. Movable Armament 340
                 Practice Batteries 328
                 Auxiliary Artillery 351, 354, 360-4
Precedence—Brigades, Batteries and Companies 28, 282
Predicted Firing—Position-Finders 318
Predictors—Anti-Aircraft 281
Prematures 113, 115, 121, 279
Preparation of Infantry Attacks—Artillery action 42-3, 61, 153
President Loubet—Visit to Aldershot 67
Primary Armament—Fixed defences 320
Prime Minister 76, 128, 130
Primers—Difficulties with smokeless powder 110-11
Prince of Wales—Presentation of Prize to National Artillery
                                    Association 356
Princess Mary—Visit to Woolwich xx
Prismatic Binoculars 50, 107, 255
Proceedings of Institution :—
   Change of title to *Journal* 381
   Essays, Lectures, and other Papers 22, 61, 171, 173, 190, 203-5,
                            218-9, 239, 372
   The Jubilee number 381-2
Proficiency Pay 236
Progressive Training 224-6, 331-2
Projectiles :—
   Case Shot 111-2, 114, 277, 297
   Shrapnel Shell xv, 64, 112-6, 121, 158-9, 219-20, 230, 233, 244,
                           255, 277-8, 340
   Combined or Universal Shell 116
   Common Shell 103, 112, 277-9
   Common-lyddite 279
   Common-pointed 278, 296
   High-Explosive Shell 63-4, 112-4, 158-9, 233, 244, 277, 279,
                           299, 424
   Armour-piercing Shell 278-9, 296, 299
   Star Shell 116, 215, 252
   Tracer Shell 166, 281, 318
Promotion :—
   Effect of Separation .... xvi, 3, 292-3, 334-5
   ,, ,, Augmentation 7-9
   Examination 384
Propellants :—
   Gun-powder 64, 84, 110, 300
   Ballistite 93, 257
   Cordite 93, 110, 218, 257, 270, 277, 300
Provision :—
   Guns for new batteries 9-11, 13-19
   Officers ,, ,, ,, ... 5-7, 9
Punch—Cartoons during re-armament 77
Punjab :—
   Garrison Battery 35-6
   Recruits for local battalions 346
Purchase—Remounts 369-70

Quadrant Elevation—Employment with fixed armament 276
Quarter-Masters—Addition to Establishment 7

464 HISTORY OF THE ROYAL ARTILLERY.

Page
Quarters—Battery and Brigade 23, 25, 65, 182, 231
Queen Victoria :—
    Jubilees 348, 406
    Patron, National Artillery Association 356
Queen Mary—Visit to Woolwich xx
Queenstown—Irish defended port (Cork Harbour) 358
Quetta :—
    Brigading of mountain batteries 65
    Field-Firing 174-5
    Frontier Defences 341
Quick-Firing Guns :—
    Re-armament of Horse and Field Artillery x, 13-7, 62, 71-82, 87
    Necessity for care of equipment 89, 91
    Acquisition of the "Quick-Firing Spirit" 152, 159-60, 206-7
    Reversion to breech-loading in fixed armament ... 271-3, 297-8, 320
Quick-Firing Courses—School of Gunnery ... 285, 287, 306-7, 325, 401-2

Radius of Action—Torpedo-Craft 287, 290-1
Radius of Ogive—Projectiles 116, 119, 277-9
Raids :—
    Torpedo-Craft 290-1, 336
    Naval landing parties or military forces 338
Railway Clearing House—Interest in re-armament 72, 78
Railway Transport—Inclusion in *Field Artillery Training 1912* ... 194
Rainsford-Hannay, Colonel F.—Sound-ranging 164-5
Range :—
    Increase in Field Army Artillery 43, 66, 82, 94, 164, 181, 183,
        193, 202
    ,, Siege ,, ... 32, 246, 249, 257
    ,, Coast and Naval ,, ... 290, 296, 301, 319, 323, 325-6
Range-Correction-Calculators 302
Range-Dials 99, 269, 302, 306
Range-Indicators 105
Range-Finders :—
    Watkin, Telemeter and Mekometer 46, 107-8
    Depression 304-5
    "One-Man" 108-9, 210, 234, 321-2
    Anti-aircraft 281
Range-Parties 188, 204, 220-2
Range-Takers 23, 226, 321, 396
Ranges, Practice :—
    Field Army Artillery 30-1, 49-56, 59-60, 65, 162-5, 164, 181,
        187, 220-4
    Siege Artillery 32-3, 248-50, 259-60, 264
    Coast Artillery 328, 340-1
    Auxiliary Artillery 351, 354, 356, 361-4
Ranges, Model—Use for instruction 226
Ranging :—
    Methods of Field Artillery 123, 155, 160-1, 179, 187-90, 195, 216
    ,, Coast ,, ... 284-5, 301-4, 321-2
    ,, Anti-Aircraft ,, ... xv, 166, 251, 259
    Teaching by School of Gunnery 428-9, 431-2
Rangoon River—Defences 304
Rapidity of Fire—Realization of value 43, 159-62, 195, 202, 269, 272, 284
Ravenhill, Major-General F. G.—Inspector-General of Remounts
    369-70, 373

INDEX. 465

	Page
Ravenhill, Brigadier-General F. J.—Article on *"The War Commemoration Fund"* in Jubilee Number of *Proceedings*	382

Rawalpindi :—
Brigading of mountain batteries 65
Frontier Defences 341
Rawlinson, Sir Henry—Commanding on Salisbury Plain 216
Rayleigh, Lord—Explosives Committee 86
Ready-Racks—Ammunition for quick-firers 308
Re-armament :—
   Field Army Artillery during first decade xi, 13-7, Chapters IV and V, App. B and C
   Preparations for during second decade ..... xv, 232-4, App. D
   Siege Artillery 17-9, 246, 256, 261-3
   Coast Artillery ... 104, 298-9, 314, 319-20, 351-4, 356, 360, 362, Chapter XIII
Recoil :—
   Field carriages 15, 17, 83, 93-5, 102-4
   Fixed mountings 272-3
Reconnaissance—Increased importance 47-9, 226
Record Office—Posting of recruits 225
Record Targets 325-6
Recruits—Physique and Physical Training 20, 225, 293
Recuperators :—
   Spring 94-5, 233, 273
   Compressed air 191, 232-3, 273
Redan—Assault 171
Red Barracks—Occupation by Artillery College 383
Redesdale—Practice camp *"Ad Fines"* 224, 361
Reduction—Batteries and Companies 29, 65, 143, 238
Refilling Points—Ammunition Supply 213
Re-formation—Reduced Batteries and Companies 29
Refuge, Harbours of—Mercantile Shipping 317
Regiment :—
   Proposal as title for Brigade 136
   The Regiment—Article by Lieut.-Colonel J. H. Leslie in the Jubilee Number of the *Proceedings* 381
Regimental Band 37, 404-8, 411-13
   ,,   Orders 1, 49, 355, 405
   ,,   Practice 285
   ,,   Tours 226, 382
Regulations and Orders—Adherence to 44, 238-9
   See *"Manuals"*, and *"Orders"*.
Reliefs—Gun detachments 253, 287, 308, 329
Reminiscenses of 40 years of Peace and War. Article by Major-General R. Bannatine-Allason in the Jubilee Number of the *Proceedings* 382
Remount Department :—
   Establishment 369-70
   Horse Mobilization 371-2
   Type of Remounts 372-3
Renaissance—Gunnery ..... vii, 301, 309, 337
Rendezvous—Ammunition Supply 213
Re-organization—Field Army Artillery during first decade xi, xii, Chapter VI
   See also *"Organization."*
Repair of guns 270

GG

466   HISTORY OF THE ROYAL ARTILLERY.

Page
Report on Practice 1914 by a Divisional Artillery Commander xvii, 239, App. D
    Serviceability of *matériel* and efficiency of *personnel* 425
    Battery and Brigade Organization 425-7
    System of Practice and School of Gunnery 427-32
    Summary and Conclusion 432
Repository, Royal Military :—
    Establishment 32, 389-90
    Instruction 355, 385, 390
Reserve Artillery—Reappearance in the Field 197-8
Reserves :—
    Matériel 10-13
    Personnel 18, 140-46, 237, 294
    Horses 370-2
    "Royal Field Reserve Artillery" 141-5, 357-8
    "Royal Garrison Reserve Artillery" 358-9, 363
    Special Reserve 142-5, 357-8
Retirement—Special terms to officers R.G.A. .... xvi, 335
Reversion :—
    Heavy batteries to Siege companies 182
    Siege companies to Coast Defence 22, 264
    Fixed armament from Q.F. to B.L. guns 271-3, 297-8
Revolvers—Personal Equipment 57, 235
Revue d'Artillerie—Comments on Balkan wars 207
Revue Militaire—Comments on 18-pr. equipment 76
Rhayader—Practice Camp ... 68-9, 83, 248-51, 253, 259-60, 262, 362, 392
Rheinische Metallwaaren und Machinenfabrik—Makers of Ehrhardt
    guns 15
Riding Establishment :—
    The Riding House 374
    Varying fortunes of the Establishment 374-6
    Plans for School of Equitation 377
Riding-Masters 7, 374-5, 377
Rifles—Personal Equipment 58, 235
Rifled guns—Effect of adoption in place of smooth bores vii, 88-9, 111, 268, 390-1
Rifling—Changes in system 270-1
Roberts, F.M. Earl :—
    In India 146-7, 287-8, 360
    In South Africa 6, 41, 72, 82, 133
    At the War Office 29, 64, 76, 133, 354
    As Master-Gunner .... xxiii, 36-7
Rochfort, Major-General Sir Alexander—Inspector of Horse and
    Field Artillery 129
The Rock—Article by Major-General J. C. Dalton in the Jubilee
    Number of the *Proceedings* 381
Rockets—Instruction of Colonial Courses 401
Rocket Troop—"O" Battery 29
Rocking-Bar Sights 95-6, 275
Romney Marsh—Lydd 253
Rooney, Captain Owen—Invention of "Plotter" 45
Ross, F.M. Sir Hew—Master-Gunner xxii
Ross—Mountain Brigade of Territorial Force 362
Ross—Pattern of Binoculars and Telescopes 107
Roster—Adherence to when numbering and brigading batteries and
    companies 26-9, 282
Rotunda—Museum in the Repository 392

INDEX.

	Page
Royal Society, Fellows of :—	
Brig.-General Sir Capel Holden	387
Major-General Sir J. H. Lefroy	383, 390
Major P. A. MacMahon	387
Sir Andrew Noble	11
Rurkie—Station of Siege Artillery in India	244

Russia :—
  Horse Mountain Batteries 104
  Menace of advance in Central Asia 288
Russo-Japanese War—Lessons ...... viii, x, xi, Chapters VII, XI, XV
  Field Army The rival artilleries 101, 112-3, 151
  Artillery.   The new doctrine 62, 152-4, 197-8
              Co-operation 167
              Night operations 116, 122, 165, 215
              Insistence on maintenance of smartness 239
              Ammunition supply 136, 371
              Horse Artillery, Field Howitzers, Mountain
                                                        Artillery x, 178-80
  Siege Artillery. Port Arthur .... x, 247, 254-6, 262, 319
                    In the Field .... x, xi, 248, 392
                    Trench Mortars 263
  Coast Artillery. Sea Attack .... xi, 290-1, 301
                    Land Attack .... x, 338

Saddles—Abolition of special pattern drivers 126
Safety-pins—Time and Percussion Fuzes 119-20
St. George, General Sir John—Master-Gunner xxii
St. George's Church, Woolwich—Dedication 405
St. James's Park—Master-Gunner xxii
St. Lucia—Defended Port, and Local Corps 298, 347-8
St. Paul's Cathedral—Memorial Service 37
San Sebastian—Artillery support to stormers 171
Schools of Gunnery :—
  The Repository 32, 389-90
  Shoeburyness 32, 306-7, 309-11, 323-4, 390-3
  Horse and Field 30-2, 42, 51-2, 55-6, 59-60, 134-5, 223-4, 391, 431-2
  Siege .... xi, 32-3, 243-4, 248-50, 262, 391-2
  Branch 309-11, 392-3
  Naval 312, 326
Sclater, General Sir Henry 334, 342
Scouts, Ground 48
"Screw-gun"—Nickname for 2·5" R.M.L. 84
Searching—Method of distributing fire 220
Search-lights—Practice at and with 165, 252
Seaton, Lord—Advice on learning work as soldiers 432
Second-Lieutenants—Establishment of 8
Secondary Armament—Change in task 320
Secretary-of-State :—
  Grant of sub-titles to batteries 29
  Move of School of Gunnery to Salisbury Plain 30
  Re-armament 76
  Re-organization 130, 141, 370
  Garrisons of defended ports 294
  Promotion in garrison artillery 335
  Auxiliary Artillery 357, 370

468 HISTORY OF THE ROYAL ARTILLERY.

	Page
Section-Control—Method of Fire	217
Semaphore—Communication in batteries	46, 212
Senior Class, Artillery College—new name for "Advanced Class"	388
Separation of Mounted and Dismounted Branches ... viii, 2-3, App. A	
Effect on Branches .... xvi, 3, 35, 65, 292,-3, 333-6, 397-8, 341	
„ „ School of Gunnery	397-8
„ „ Bands	411
Service—Terms	140-1, 144, 236-7, 294
Service Pay	236
"Setts", granite—Effect on new equipments	79
Sevastopol—The Siege	x, 289

Shaft-draught :—
  Abolition in Field Artillery 92, 125
  Addition in mountain artillery 104-5

Sheerness :—
  Anti-torpedo-craft Defence 297
  Branch School 309
  R.G.A. Band 409, 412-3
  Firing Party at Memorial Service 37

Shields :—
  Field army equipments 95, 97, 100-3, 153
  Method of attack by artillery 116, 158-9, 207
  Fixed armaments 273-4

Shipping Companies—Interest in re-armament 16, 18, 72
Shoeburyness 30-2, 37, 45, 223-4, 243, 253, 306-7, 309-10, 325-6,
                                                386-7, 389-402
Shortage of men—Field Artillery 237

Shrapnel :—
  Field Army Artillery xv, 64, 112, 114-5, 159, 219-20, 230, 233,
                                                              App. D
  Siege Artillery 244, 255
  Coast Artillery 277-8, 340
  Navy 121

Side-slip—Fault of quick-firing field guns 232

Siege Artillery :—
  Conversions of batteries between Mountain, Heavy and Siege
                                            65, 67-8, 70, 182, 245
  Proposed "Siege and Fortress" and "Siege and Position"
                                                    Branches 21-2
  Command and Organization 245, 254-9, 263-4
  Armament 17, 19, 92, 245-6, 256-7, 261-4
  Personal Equipment 235-6
  Siege-warfare .... xiv, 247-8, 258
  Field Army Trend .... ix, x, 21, 33, 243-5, 248, 259-61
  Manœuvres and Staff Tours .... xiii, xvi, 248, 252-3, 260-1
  Practice Camps 32-3, 248-50, 259-60, 264

Siege Artillery Drill 33, 254
Sierra Leone—Defended Port and Local Corps 347-8
Sight—The Independent Line of 95-6

Sights :—
  Anti-aircraft 281
  Automatic 275-6, 284-5, 320-1
  Bar and Drum or Rocking-Bar 95-6, 275
  Dial, Goniometric, or Panorama 96-7, 105
  Oscillating 96
  Tangent and Fore 95, 274
  Telescopic 95-6

INDEX. 469

Sights:—(*Continued*).
   Illumination for night-firing 308
   Testing 218
Signalling—Revival 46, 48, 60, 212, 226, 261, 264
Sikhs—Enlistment in local battalions 346
Silencing of guns—Methods 42, 153
Simpson, Colonel H. C. D.—Lecture on Heavy Artillery 67
Singapore—Local battalion 346, 348
Single guns—Employment 47
Single-motion—Breech-mechanisms 97-8, 271
Skill-at-Arms—Prizes 236, 375
Skoda—Howitzers 17, 19, 246, 256-7
Slade, Lieut.-General F. G.—Inspector of Garrison Artillery 283, 294
Slide-Rules—Use with Observation of Fire Instruments 264
Slowness:—
   Loading 232
   Ranging 61, 155
Small-port mountings—Coast Artillery 268
Small-Wars—Requirements in artillery ..... vii, 1
Smith, Major-General Sir Hubert—Invention of "Plotter" 45
Smith-Dorrien, General Sir Horace 174-5, 215
Smoke-Shell—First suggestion 115
Smokeless Powder:—
   Use in guns 43, 110, 202
   Blank cartridges 111
   Representation in gun targets 249
Smooth-Bores:—
   Replacement by rifled guns vii
   Rapidity of fire 159
   Effectiveness of case-shot 111
Smyth, Mr. James—Bandmaster 1856-1880 404-5
"*Soixante-Quinze*"—French field gun 14-5, 184, 187-8, 190-2
Soldiering in India—Article by Major-General G. F. MacMunn in Jubiless Number of *Proceedings* 382
Sonite—Use for smokeless blank 111
Sound-Ranging—First suggestion 164-5
South African War:—
   Influence ..... viii-x, Chapters I, II, III, X, XIV, 293, 335, 398
   Mobilization 26, 145, 371
   Command and Organization 26-7, 133
   Employment 33, 41-5, 61-7, 171, 179, 244-5
   Ammunition Supply 136-7, 139
   Equipment 12, 18-9, 57-9, 72, 78, 90, 96, 100-01, 107, 111-2, 117-8, 127, 246
   Auxiliary Artillery 349-50, 353-4
   Navy 301
   Royal Commission 128
   Memorial 36-7
Spanish-American War—Lesson of 174
Speaking-Tubes—Use in batteries for communication 306
Specialists—Garrison Artillery 23, 263-4, 295
Special Reserve—Auxiliary Artillery 142-4, 357-8
Specal Service Section—Auxiliary Artillery 287, 352
Splinter-Proofs—On ranges 222
Split-Trail—Feature of "Deport" design of carriage 232
Sport in India—Article by Major-General A. E. Wardrop in the Jubilee Number of the *Proceedings* 382

470 HISTORY OF THE ROYAL ARTILLERY.

Page
Springs—Recuperator 94-5, 233, 273
Staff—Increase in number of artillery officers 129-30
    Increased interest in artillery subjects ...... ix, 179, 221, 229, 235-6
    Artillery 133, 135-6, 147, 163, 226
Staff College 130, 171, 380, 384, 387-8, 396
Staff Tours .... xiii, 252-3
Stamfordham, Lord (Sir Arthur Bigge) 29
Stanford, Major H. B.—Article on *The Royal Military Repository*
    in the *Proceedings* 389
Star Shell—Extension of use 116, 215, 252
"State" of the Regiment—Presentation to Colonel-in-Chief ...xviii, xix
Stationery Office—Controller iii
Stations—Battery and Brigade 23, 25, 65, 182, 231
Station Practice—Coast Artillery 285
Steam Sappers—Siege Artillery 260
Steam Tractors—Heavy Artillery 58, 231
Steel—Improvements in Quality 270
Stereoscopic—Binoculars and Telescopes 50, 323
Stewart, Lieut.-Colonel Hon. A.—Superintendent Riding
    Establishment 374
Stopford, Major-General Hon. Sir F. W.—Director of Military
    Training 127, 393
Strength :—
    Batteries at manœuvres 228
    Garrisons of defended ports xii, xiv, xvi, 5, 22-3, 287-8, 293-5,
    311, 330-1, 345-6
Stretton, Mr. A. J.—Director of Music, Kneller Hall 407
  ,, Major E. C.—Bandmaster 1907-1936 407
Striking Force—Original designation of Expeditionary Force 130
Stud System—Remounts in Bengal 373
Study of Tactics from History—Articles by Brig.-General J. P.
    Du Cane, C.R.A. 3rd Division, in the *Army Review* 203
Sub-calibre guns 277, 327
Sudan—Use of Krupp fuzes by Egyptian artillery 118
Superintendent—Departments, Ordnance Factories 58, 272
    ,,   Experiments 390, 393
    ,,   Repository 32, 392
    ,,   Riding Establishment 374-6
Support of Infantry Attacks—Artillery action ... 63, 153, 167-73,
    196, 199-203, 207-9
Sweeping—Method of distributing fire 219-20
Swords—Personal Equipment 56-8, 235-6
Sword-Bayonets—Personal Equipment 56-7
Sydenham, Lord (Sir George Clarke) 128, 272

Tactics :—
    General Revival of Interest vii
    Study at Practice Camps ... xiii, 26, 30, 50, 177, 188-9 196-7,
    204-5, 209-11, 216-7, 220-2
    Coast Artillery 300, 332
    Naval Changes .... xi, 284, 287, 290, 296, 319
Tangent Sights 95, 274
Targets :—
    Field Army Artillery Practice 49-50, 52-3, 163-4, 217
    Siege Artillery Practice 249

INDEX. 471

Page

Targets :—(*Continued*).
   Coast Artillery Practice 284, 325-6
   Anti-Aircraft Practice 166, 215
Tattersall, Mr.—Inspection of Canadian Remounts 370
Technical Features in Re-armament of Field Army Artillery Chapter V
Technical Developments in Coast Artillery Armament ... Chapter XIII
Technical Vehicles in Battery Transport 126-7
Telemeter—Range-finder 46, 107-8
Telephone—Communications in Batteries 46, 157, 212, 259, 264, 305-6
Telescope—Observation of fire 50, 106-7, 323
Telescopic Sights 95-6
Terrible, H.M.S.—Placed at disposal of Owen Committee 295
Territorial Force :—
   The *Territorial and Reserve Forces Act* 357-8
   Organization 359-363
   Armament 93-4, 360, 362
   School of Gunnery and National Artillery Association 363-5
Territorial Divisions—Garrison Artillery Organizations 282, 349-51
Tests :—
   Experimental Equipments 91, 93
   Instruments 109, 218, 321
   Specialists 264, 321
Thames Defences—Study of 395
Theatre—Regimental 405
Theatricals at Woolwich—Article by Colonel J. R. J. Jocelyn in
   the Jubilee Nnmber of the *Proceedings* 382
Thermometer—Effect of changes on accuracy of fire 218, 303
Thompson, Mr.—Inventor of Mechanical Fuze 122
Thunderer, H.M.S.—Bursting of gun 295
Tibet—Expedition 103
Tide-gauges 322
Tide-levers 276, 287
Tilley, Mr.—Advice on Horse Mobilization 371
Times—Article on re-armament 77
Titles—Batteries and Companies 28-9, 282
Tollner, Colonel B. L.—Inspector of Remounts 370
Torpedo-Craft :—
   Raids 287, 290-1, 336
   Defence 287, 297, 306-8, 320, 329-30, 352, 400-01
Tournament—The Military (now the Royal) 374-5
Tracer-shell—Anti-aircraft 166, 318
Traction-engines }
Tractors   } Heavy and Siege Artillery 58, 231, 260
"Trade"—Proportion of orders to go to 8
Traffic—Regulation in defended ports, See *"Examination Service"*
"Trainings"—Distinction from "Bearings" 277
Training :—
   Field Army   South African Influence ... ix, x, 42, 44-56, 59-61,
     Artillery.   63-70
                 Manchurlan   ,, ...x, 62, 152-93, 163-9, 176-82
                 French   ,, ... xii, xiii, 185-90, 192-205
                 Final Phase .... xv, xvii, 207-12, 216-23
   Siege Artillery.   South African Influence .... ix, x, 33, 243-5
                 Manchurian   ,,   x, xi, 248-50, 252-5, 257
                 Final Phase .... xiii, xiv, xvi, 259-61
   Coast Artillery. South African Influence .... ix, x, 22, 284-7
                 Manchurian   x, xi, 290-1, 299-300, 306-7, 309-15

Training :—(Continued).
    Coast Artillery. Final Phase .... xiv, xvi, 321, 323-6, 331-6
            Movable Armament 339-40
            Field and Siege Methods .... xiv, 257, 333-4
    Auxiliary Artillery 349, 351, 355-6, 360-5, 401
    All Branches. Night-operations ... 165, 215, 251-2, 269, 270, 307-9, 327
            Aviation 166-7, 195, 207, 214-5, 251, 259, 281
Training Brigades 142-6, 237
Training and Manœuvre Regulations 323
Travelling Position—Guns on carriages 102
Traverse—Guns on carriages 95, 232
Traversing-arcs—Fixed Armament 275-7
Traversing-Platforms—Fixed Armament 272
Travis, Mr. H.—Designer of Long-Range Target 326
Trawsfynydd—Practice Camp 52-3, 163, 231, 362
Treachery—Danger to Coast Defences 338-9
Treasury—Influence on re-armament 72
Trench, Colonel C. Chevenix—Director Artillery College ...... ii, 384
Trench-Mortars—Decision not to introduce 263
Trollies—Ammunition Supply 273-4, 308
"Trotting-Vanners"—Value as remounts 371
Truth—Song on promotion in R.G.A. 335
Turner, Colonel A. H. P.—Discover of Ehrhardt guns 15
"Turn-out"—Value of uniformity and smartness 238-9
Turret—80-ton gun on Dover Pier 268
Two Regimental Institutions—Article by Colonel J. R. J. Jocelyn
    in Proceedings 378
Tyler, Major-General T. B.—Inspector-General of Artillery in India   59

Ulundi—Battle 296
Uniform :—
    King Edward VII as Colonel-in-Chief xx
    Band 412
Uniform Twist—System of rifling 270
Uniformity—Value in turn-out, methods, etc. 238-9
United Service Institution :—
    Acknowledgment of assistance ii
    Lectures and Articles in Journal 180, 371
United States :—
    Separation of Field and Coast Artillery 3
    Use of mortar-fire in civil-war 159
    Use of Krupp fuzes in Philippines 118
Universal (or combined) Shell 116
Universities and Colleges—Grant of direct Commissions 6
Unsteadiness—Fault of quick-firing field guns 232-3

"Vanners"—Value as remounts 372
Variety of charges, projectiles, and local conditions in coast ar-
    tillery 269, 277
Vehicles—Abolition of technical in battery transport 126-7
Vereeniging—Treaty .... x, 36
Veterans—Peninsula, Waterloo and Crimea .... xxii, xxiii

INDEX.

	Page
Vibrator-Transmitter—Telephone in Siege Artillery	259, 264
Vickers—Armament Firm	74, 81, 97-8, 118

Victoria, Queen :—
    Jubilees 348, 406
    Patron National Artillery Association 356
Villages—Inclusion of method of attacking in *Field Artillery Training 1912* 195, 207
Volunteers :—
    Grant of Direct Commissions 6
    Origin of movement 350
    Organization 287, 346, 351-4
    Armament 351-3, 355-6
von Donop, Major-General Sir Stanley 262-3
    ,,   Article on *Artillery Equipment used in the Field during the last 25 years* in Jubilee Number of the *Proceedings* 127, 382
von Lobell—Annual Reports 101
von Reichenau } Controversy regarding method of attacking
von Rohne   } shielded guns 158

Wagons—"Artillery", "ammunition and store", "forge" 126
Walcheren—General Sir R. Gardiner in Expedition xxii
Wales, Prince of—Prize to National Artillery Association 356
Walford, Colonel N. L. :—
    Insistence upon *effect* of fire 215
    Memorial Medal 380-1
War Commemoration Fund—Article by Brig.-General F. T. Ravenhill in the Jubilee Number of the *Proceedings* 382
War Experience—Lack in Artillery .... vii, viii
War Games—Place in Progressive Training 226
War Office—ii, viii, ix, 1-19, 20, 27, 35, 72, 76, 128, 281, 289, 291, 312, 375, 380, 393, 404
War Precautions—Examples in Final Stage xvii
War Requirements—Basis of organization, armament, training, etc. xii, 62
War-ships—Development xi, 269-70, 278, 290-1, 295, 297, 307, 319-20, 329
War-years—During South African War vii, viii, ix, Chapters I & II, 41-2, 243, 267-8
Wars and Expeditions :—
    Minorca, Walcheren, The Weser, The Cape, South America xxii
    The Helder 178
    Peninsula .... xxii, 132, 171, 262
    Waterloo .... xxii, 27, 131
    Carlist xxii
    Crimea ... ii, xxii, xxiii, 27, 66, 132, 170, 262, 272, 289, 352, 382
    American, Civil 159
    Austro-Prussian 198, 385-6
    Franco-German 24, 43, 57, 131-2, 198, 203, 262
    Afghan 57
    Egyptian 140, 369
    Zulu 57, 296
    China 19, 40, 257
    South Africa—*See "South African War"*. ....
    Russo-Japanese—*See "Russo-Turkish War"*. ....

Wars and Expeditions :—(Continued).
　Tibet 103
　Balkan 207
　Great War .... ii, 79, 264
Warde, Major-General Sir Edward—President of Committee on Officers' Education 383-5
Wardrop, Major-General A. E.—Article on *Indian Sport* in the Jubilee Number of the *Proceedings* 382
Warley—Brigade Band 409
Waterloo—Battle of .... xxii, 131
Waters, Brig.-General W. H. H.—Military Attaché Berlin 15
Watkin, Colonel H. S.—Inventor of Range-finders, Position-finders, and Clinometers 46, 97, 107
Weedon—Army Manœuvres 1913 227
Welin—Single-motion breech-screw for bare charges 271
Welsh—The March 253, 260
Weser—General Poole Vallancey in Expedition xxii
West Africa—Local Corps 104, 347
Whale Island—Naval Gunnery School 326
Wheels of gun carriages :—
　Changes in pattern 92, 99-100, 105
　Compensation for difference of level 96
Wheelers—Substitution of carriage-smiths 90
White, Major-General G. H. A.—Article on *Coaching* in the Jubilee Number of the *Proceedings* 382
Whitehall—Master-Gunner xxii
Wight, Isle of—School of Instruction 309-10, 364, 392-3, 395
Williams, Major-General Sir W. J. 30, 42, 48
Wilson, Brig.-General H. H.—Committee on Defence of Land Fronts 342
Windham, Mr. George—Member of Mowatt Committee 11
Winding Apparatus—Use for moving targets 325-6
Wire—Use in gun construction 270
Wire Entanglements—Effect of shell fire 249
Wolfe-Murray, Brig.-General Sir James—Article *Do we require Field Artillery?* in *Proceedings* 74
Wolseley, F.M. Viscount—Efforts to get breast-harness 125
Wood—Elimination from equipments 90, 100, 272
Wood, F.M. Sir Evelyn :—
　At Aldershot 27, 54, 310
　Adjutant-General 30, 47
　Southern Command 51, 55, 310
　Committee on Promotion in R.G.A. 293, 334
Wood, Major-General Sir Elliot—Protest against treatment of Major-Generals R.A. and R.E. 133
Wood-Fighting—Inclusion in *Field Artillery Training 1914* 207
Woolwich :—
　Visits by Colonels-in-Chief and Royal Family .... xviii, xx, 58
　Move of 2nd Brigade Heavy Artillery 231
　Auxiliary Artillery 354-5
　See also "*The Regimental Institutions*" .... Part VI
Wylde, General William—Master-Gunner xxii

Yard-scale-drums and plates 269, 277
Yeomanry—Guns for 4, 175
　　　　　Presence at practice camps 51
Young, Major C. F.—One of originators of "Advanced Class" 383

INDEX.

                                  Page

Young Officers' Course :—
    Abandonments and Revivals 384-5, 387, 398-9
    Substitution of "Junior Officers" 399-400

Zavertal, Captain L.—Bandmaster 1880-1907 405-7
Zeiss—Binoculars and Telescopes 50, 107, 323
    One-Man range-finders 108-9, 321-2
Zones—Registration 196, 217
Zulu War :—
    Issue of revolvers 57
    Battle of Ulundi 296